VISUAL dBASE PROGRAMMING

ROBERT L. BUCHANAN

A DIVISION OF COURSE TECHNOLOGY
ONE MAIN STREET, CAMBRIDGE, MA 02142

an International Thomson Publishing company I(T)P

Cambridge • Albany • Bonn • Boston • Cincinnati • London • Madrid • Melbourne • Mexico City
New York • Paris • San Francisco • Singapore • Tokyo • Toronto • Washington

Visual dBASE Programming is published by CTI.

Managing Editor:	Wendy Gordon
Production Manager:	Patty Stephan
Production Services:	Beckwith Bookworks
Cover Designer:	Hannus Design Associates

For more information contact:

Course Technology
One Main Street
Cambridge, MA 02142

International Thomson Publishing Europe
Berkshire House 168-173
High Holborn
London WCIV 7AA
England

Thomas Nelson Australia
102 Dodds Street
South Melbourne, 3205
Victoria, Australia

Nelson Canada
1120 Birchmount Road
Scarborough, Ontario
Canada M1K 5G4

International Thomson Editores
Campos Eliseos 385, Piso 7
Col. Polanco
11560 Mexico D.F. Mexico

International Thomson Publishing GmbH
Kônigswinterer Strasse 418
53227 Bonn
Germany

International Thomson Publishing Asia
211 Henderson Road
#05-10 Henderson Building
Singapore 0315

International Thomson Publishing Japan
Hirakawacho Kyowa Building, 3F
2-2-1 Hirakawacho
Chiyoda-ku, Tokyo 102
Japan

ISBN 0-534-24006-2

Printed in the United States of America

10 9 8 7 6 5 4 3 2 1

To my mother

Contents

CHAPTER TWO

Getting Started with Visual dBASE 20

CHAPTER THREE

Visual dBASE Command Syntax 36

PART TWO

CHAPTER SIX

Efficient Search Techniques 116

PART THREE Object-Oriented Programming with Visual dBASE 141

CHAPTER NINE

Data Entry Windows Design 212

CHAPTER TEN

Using Codeblocks and User-Defined Functions 248

CHAPTER ELEVEN

Multiple Table Views 276

CHAPTER TWELVE

Reporting from Visual dBASE 306

Preface

A complete rewrite of all earlier versions of the language, Visual dBASE is an exciting development environment for the Windows application programmer. It is an object-oriented, event-driven product used to visually develop object-oriented, event-driven Relational Database Management System (RDBMS) applications. Using the Visual dBASE Graphical User Interfaces (GUI) design tools, one can develop an entire application without writing a line of code. However, thorough applications require programming skills beyond the point-and-click visual designs of the nonprogramming user. Fortunately, the unique two-way design tools of Visual dBASE maximize programmer productivity and reduce the amount of hard coding required in earlier versions of the language.

Before the development of Visual dBASE, literally millions of programmers developed applications in DOS versions of dBASE. Its popularity was based primarily on the simplicity of the language syntax and the ease with which an application could be developed. Fortunately, the simplicity of the language continues in the object-oriented extensions of Visual dBASE, and all prior versions of dBASE for DOS are 100 percent upward compatible to the current version. The new programmer can take advantage of the product's ease of use, and experienced dBASE programmers need only add the object extensions to their current knowledge of the language. There is no need to learn an entirely new base language.

WHO THE BOOK IS FOR

The book is for the business student, or any student learning Visual dBASE programming for the first time. It can also be used effectively in a Visual dBASE programming seminar. It assumes the student has completed a fundamentals of data processing course and has PC keyboard dexterity plus experience using the DOS and Windows operating systems. Experience with a microcomputer word processor would also be helpful. No prior programming education or experience is assumed. However, an experienced programmer learning relational database management or object-oriented programming for the first time could also benefit.

EXTENT OF COVERAGE

Visual dBASE has become a very comprehensive language. If all its features and all its alternative programming strategies were included here, this would be an enormous textbook—its contents could not be covered in a semester course or week-long seminar. However, as a thorough programming introduction, this text includes features important to the development of most systems. The student will learn the fundamentals of objects and the corresponding code needed to create and manipulate them. Although it could be used in other classes, it is designed primarily for an introductory course in Visual dBASE object-oriented programming.

LAYOUT OF THE BOOK

The book is divided into three parts: Part One is an introduction to relational database management systems and Visual dBASE. Part Two is an introduction to structured programming. Part Three is a comprehensive introduction to object-oriented programming.

Part One discusses the definition, history, and evolution of relational database management systems. It also discusses how to design to reduce redundancy and the corresponding inconsistency of data in a database. The student also learns how to boot Visual dBASE and how to begin using the Navigator and Command windows. Command syntax, development of expressions, and database creation are also introduced.

In Part Two, the student learns the concepts of structured programming. It is shown here that structured programming is a prerequisite to object-oriented programming and that object-oriented programming does not replace structured programming, but rather enhances it. A major benefit of Visual dBASE is that when methods are programmed within objects, the programmer is using the structured code of eariler versions of dBASE.

Part Three introduces object-oriented programming concepts and terminology. Before using the two-way design tools, the student constructs various objects by entering commands into the Command window. In Chapter 8, the Form Designer is introduced, and its value as a two-way design tool is emphasized. The chapters that follow introduce other design tools such as the Menu Designer, Query Designer, and Report Generator. Modules are added to the Case System to create an application desktop, present a banner (About) screen, provide password entry, present a utilties menu to modify the password, edit and reindex tables, and, finally, print reports using multidimensional views of database developed in the Visual dBASE Query Designer. A method of executing DOS modules from within a windows application before their conversion is also added to the Case System.

LAYOUT OF CHAPTERS

In Part One, the layout of the chapters is self explantory. In Parts Two and Three, the chapters are sturctured as follows:

- **Objectives and topic outline.** The objectives and topic list serve as a chapter guide and present what the student should learn as a result.
- **New commands, functions, and properties.** New commands, functions, and properties associated with the concepts presented in that chapter are introduced. The amount of discussion and examples will vary with the new syntax. Certain commands can be demonstrated adequately when they are introduced, whereas others are listed and briefly discussed before being demonstrated in the Concepts section. When its advanced or otherwise irrelevant options mignt confuse the student, the full syntax of a command is not covered at the point of introduction. In these situations we present only that portion needed to solve the Review Exercises or Case System. Appendixes A and B present the full syntax of all Visual dBASE commands and functions.
- **Concepts.** This section contains relevant information not covered in New Commands, Functions, and Properties. The objective is to enable the student to solve the Review Exercises for that chapter and to develop the Case System on an ongoing basis.
- **Review Exercises and Case System.** Each module of the Case System is developed and tested with in a chapter and then added to the complete system. However, certain chapters lack material that would lend itself to a case module. These chapters contain either review questions or a programming exercise designed as a prerequisite to Case System modules that follow.
- **Chapter Summary.** This is a review of the chapter's learning objectives and a brief recap of the topics covered. It also provides a transition into the next chapter.

HANDS-ON LEARNING ENVIRONMENT

The material has been designed for a student in a computer lab environment. It is assumed the student will enter most commands, functions, or programming concepts into an IBM PC or compatible computer as they are presented. When material does not lend itself to this approach, this fact is noted. However, most of the chapter discussion information, and all of the student Case System, are in a hands-on mode of learning.

THE STUDENT CASE SYSTEM

A logical learning path is outlined here to introduce the new student to Visual dBASE object-oriented concepts. The concepts are then reinforced with an ongoing case study. Techniques are learned by hands-on student programming of a complete system—not through isolated exercises or review of preprogrammed systems.

The book is self-contained in the sense that all information needed to solve the case is either contained in a previous chapter or demonstrated within the current chapter. Database tables are provided by the instructor for the student to use in the Case System solution. For readers not participating in a formal course of instruction using this text, a copy of the database tables, exercise solutions, and Case System solutions files can be obtained from CTI by using the URL **http://coursetools.com.** For more information on student files, see the inside back cover of the book.

SYSTEM REQUIREMENTS

All exercises and the Case System were developed using Visual dBASE, Version 5.5 and tested again using 5.5a. It is recommended that earlier versions of the product be updated prior to using this text. In addition, the following system requirements are listed:

- Hardware requirements:

  Intel 386-based PC or higher

  Windows 3.1, Windows 95, or 100% compatible

  6 MB RAM required, 8 MB recommended

  29 MB free disk space for a complete installation

  11.5 MB free disk space for minimum installation
- Visual dBASE is compatible with Win-OS/2 and Windows 3.1 running under 0S/2 Warp.
- Supported network operating systems (the latest network parameter changes are noted in the Readme.txt file installed with Visual dBASE): Netware 3.11, 3.12, 4.1, Personal Netware, Banyan Vines 5.5, IBM OS/2 LAN Server 4.0, Lantastic 6.0, Microsoft LAN Manager 2.2, Windows for Workgroups 3.11, Windows NT Server 3.5.

- On a single machine, to access the same table concurrently using Sessions or multiple instances of Visual dBASE, the DOS SHARE.EXE utility must be loaded before starting Windows with the command: SHARE/F:4096/L:40. Visual dBASE uses the Windows print software and drivers to send output to the printer.

Acknowledgments

Authoring a textbook would be virtually impossible without the help of many very knowledgeable friends and associates. The most enjoyable part of authoring is acknowledging their help.

A special thank you to Joe Dougherty of Course Technology for moving the manuscript forward so efficiently. And thank you to those members of the Course Technology team who assisted in the production of this book. Many thanks to Jack Beckwith of Beckwith Bookworks for the excellent job of managing the production of the book and to Carol Beckwith for being such a gentle grammarian with this author. Also, my appreciation to Dick Hannus for the excellent cover design.

During the beta tests of dBASE for Windows and then Visual dBASE, Borland's staff and members of Borland's Team B were key to the development of the materials in this text. Borland has historically maintained an open line to authors, as it does with all users of its products.

Finally, to my good friend and associate, Fred Kostenko of Fred Kostenko & Associates, I extend a very sincere thank you. His thorough review of the manuscript, exercises, Case System, and Instructors Guide has been a valuable and essential contribution.

PART ONE

Introduction to Database Management Systems

CHAPTER ONE

TOPICS

Background

Definition of Terms

Database Management System Analogies

- Library analogy
- Desk analogy

Types of File Structures

- Hierarchical model
- Network model
- Relational model
- Nonintegrated file management systems

A Brief History of dBASE

Review Exercises

Chapter Summary

Database Management Systems and Visual dBASE

1

CHAPTER OBJECTIVES

In this chapter, we introduce the basic concepts of database management systems and present an overview of Visual dBASE. We do not want to delve too deeply into the theory of database management systems. However, to use the language effectively, it is important to have an adequate understanding of relational database management system theory and terminology.

After studying this chapter, you should be able to define a relational database management system, explain the basic terminology associated with a relational database management system, and discuss the history and concept of the Visual dBASE programming language.

BACKGROUND

A database management system (DBMS) is software designed to act as an interface between the user and the computer. Its purpose is to build, manipulate, and report from integrated databases. Unlike a simple file management system, a DBMS allows multiple file processing, reduces data redundancy, and increases data integrity. It should contain a language that is friendly and interactive while translating the user's needs into the complex machine language of the computer.

Designed initially for mainframes and then for minicomputers, database management systems have been around for a long time. The systems for larger computers are very efficient once designed. They allow the user the ability to design a unique, custom system for each application, thereby making it very fast. Such an efficient design running on a fast computer gives the best of all worlds. However, the systems were complex to develop or modify and required that the developer be an experienced database programmer. The backlog of applications grew as the need for more systems increased.

Once database management systems were adapted to microcomputers, they had the advantage of being much easier to use. The user interface was friendlier and designed for the nonprogramming user. They had the disadvantage, however, of yielding a less efficient design, running, as they were, on a computer slower than the mainframes and minicomputers. Over time, the microcomputer has become larger and faster, and the microcomputer-based database management systems have become more sophisticated to allow the programming of more efficient systems design. In addition to programming DOS-based systems, we now have the ability to program applications to run in the Windows User Interface (UI) Environment. The result has been very exciting. Increased end-user computing and programming has caused a decline in the backlog of systems. Although mainframe systems are still stronger, we can now design and run many systems on smaller computers rather than having to wait in the queue of the centralized data processing systems.

The sophistication of microcomputer database programming languages has also been improved. Fortunately, they are considerably easier to learn and use than traditional languages like FORTRAN, COBOL, and BASIC. Before the advent of these languages, database programming had to be left to the centralized computer programming staff. Now, the end user can learn to successfully program both DOS and Windows database applications.

DEFINITION OF TERMS

Before moving ahead, it is important to learn the terms used in database management systems. As in all disciplines, you must speak the language. The following terms are those most commonly used:

- **Enterprise** The organization about which a database is to be constructed—for example, a company, university, or segment of a government agency. The Case System in this text builds a database system for a video retail store. The video store is the enterprise.
- **Entity** Real-world things within an enterprise about which data will be recorded. For example, in our video store system, there are real, living, breathing customers and real, physical videotapes. The thing may be an activity, such as the sale of a videotape.
- **Attributes** Facts or characteristics about an entity type. For example, three attributes of a customer are name, address, and phone number.
- **Bit** The smallest unit of information in a data processing system. A single magnetized spot on a disk or in main memory. A binary digit.
- **Byte (character)** Characters are made up of bits. The 8-bit module of memory representing a character is called a byte. It is usually considered one character though it might be used in other forms to represent numeric data. For example, think of one megabyte as one million characters of data and one kilobyte as one thousand characters. (See Appendix D.)
- **Field** A field is used to store an attribute. A field is made up of characters and is the smallest unit of meaningful data. It is possible for a field to be only one character in length if that character is meaningful, such as a single-character transaction code. Characteristics of a field are its name, length, and data type (character, numeric, float, date, logical, and memo). We present the types of data Visual dBase allows in Chapter 3. A field may also be referred to as a word. A set of fields in a file creates a *column* of data.
- **Record** Records are made up of fields. A record is a group of related fields treated as a single unit. Also referred to as a row or a tuple (rhymes with couple).

- **File** Files are made up of records. A file is a group of records within the same classification. Think of it as a two-dimensional table of rows and columns (records and fields). Because it is only two-dimensional, it is called a flat file. Also referred to as a table or, because it contains related records, a relation.
- **Database** A self-describing collection of interrelated data. A complete selection of data, pointers, tables, indexes, and dictionaries. It may be more than one flat file linked (related) to form a multidimensional database. We discuss the relational aspects of Visual dBase in more detail later in the chapter.
- **Data dictionary** A complete description of the data in the database (data about data). Visual dBASE refers to it as the structure of the file. It contains the name, type, length, and so forth for each field.
- **Index** A file containing record numbers and data values. The data value is a word, or field value, that leads to the desired record in the database via the associated record number. For now, think of an index file as you would the index files of a library. To find a book, you search the index file. The located index card contains information that "points" to where the book is located on the shelf.
- **Key** A unique identifier for a record. A key is an attribute that sets that record aside from all others; for example, a social security number or an employee number.
- **Pointer** An indicator that signifies the current record being operated on. It can be looked at, moved, or otherwise manipulated as needed to accomplish a file manipulation procedure. In Visual dBASE, a command may either act on the single record under the pointer or automatically move the pointer to other selected records.
- **Query system** An element of a DBMS that allows the user to make ad hoc requests from the keyboard in the language of the DBMS.
- **System** A group of interrelated components acting together to perform a common goal.

Figure 1.1 displays a simple name and address card file. Figure 1.2 shows the same file in the form of a computerized file. Note the terms from the definition list as they apply to the file. The manual file will become a single DOS file when entered through the DBMS. The shaded areas in the picture of an automated file denote a single record, field, or column within the file. The index files are also single DOS files (and act similarly to those found in your public library). The analogies in the next section further demonstrate the concept of indexed files.

FIGURE 1.1 MANUALLY MAINTAINED ADDRESS FILE

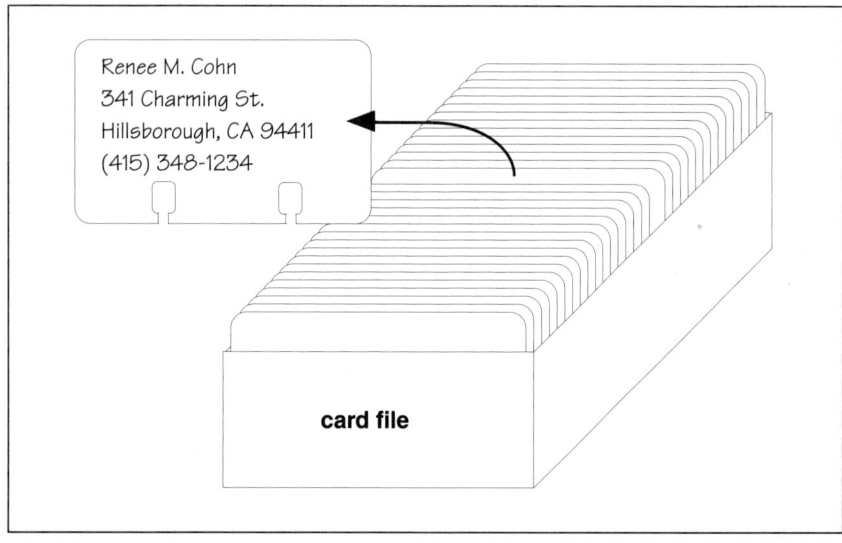

DATABASE MANAGEMENT SYSTEM ANALOGIES

We present the following two examples of manual data processing systems to assist you in learning electronic data processing, specifically the concepts of computerized database management. The computer is a cybernetic device in that it was designed to simulate data processing functions as performed by humans. Because we already have a good understanding of the process and terminology of manual data processing—and the computer operates the same way, only faster—these analogies should speed up the learning process.

LIBRARY ANALOGY

An analogy of a noncomputer file management system is a library. It exemplifies the need to manage a large group of records (books). Updating of the library occurs continually. Books are being added and deleted every day. Moreover, searching by many different topics occurs daily. Index files are maintained to assist in these searches. Following are some of the database management problems generated in this environment:

FIGURE 1.2 AUTOMATED ADDRESS FILE

FILE HEADER:

REC. NO.	FIRST	MI	LAST	ADDRESS	CITY	ST	ZIP	PHONE
1	Robert	J	Stacey	137 North Street	Burlingame	CA	94311	(415) 573-7746
2	Phillip	R	Jones	234 Los Prados	San Mateo	CA	94402	(415) 573-6066
3	Renee	M	Cohn	341 Charming St.	Hillsborough	CA	94411	(415) 348-1234
•	•	•	•	•	•	•	•	•
•	•	•	•	•	•	•	•	•
•	•	•	•	•	•	•	•	•
500	Joan	J	Albert	313 Clinton St.	Sacramento	CA	95834	(916) 648-7772

(Record, Row, or Tuple)

(Field)

(Column)

INDEX FILE

Key Field: last

REC NO.	LAST
500	Albert
•	•
•	•
•	•
3	Cohn
2	Jones
1	Stacey

INDEX FILE

Key Field: city

REC NO.	CITY
1	Burlingame
3	Hillsborough
•	•
•	•
•	•
500	Sacramento
4	San Mateo

INDEX FILE

Key Field: zip

REC NO.	ZIP
1	94311
2	94402
3	94411
•	•
•	•
•	•
500	95834

1. Perform updates (additions, changes, and deletions) as rapidly as possible to keep the library current.
2. Update indexes as rapidly as possible to ensure they cover all updated books in the library.
3. Design placement of books; for example, by author or title.

I recently searched a local bookstore for a book. I did not know the author, only the title. When my search began, it was frustrating to discover the books were arranged on the shelves alphabetically by author. Of course, the indexes (card catalogs) in a library solve this problem. We do not need many libraries with the same selection of books sorted by different keys. We use these same concepts of index searches in computerized database management system.

DESK ANALOGY

Almost all of us work at a desk. The manual data processing performed at a desk closely resembles a computerized file management system, especially as it relates to the basic concepts of computer hardware, software, and the management of computer files.

Refer to the diagram shown in Figure 1.3 as you follow through the analogy. Probably the most important definition we will study in this book is that of a system: a group of interrelated components acting together to achieve a common goal. We are using a computer hardware system. The hardware is driven by a software system. In this book, we are studying the programming of a database management system.

FIGURE 1.3 DESK ANALOGY OF A DATABASE MANAGEMENT SYSTEM

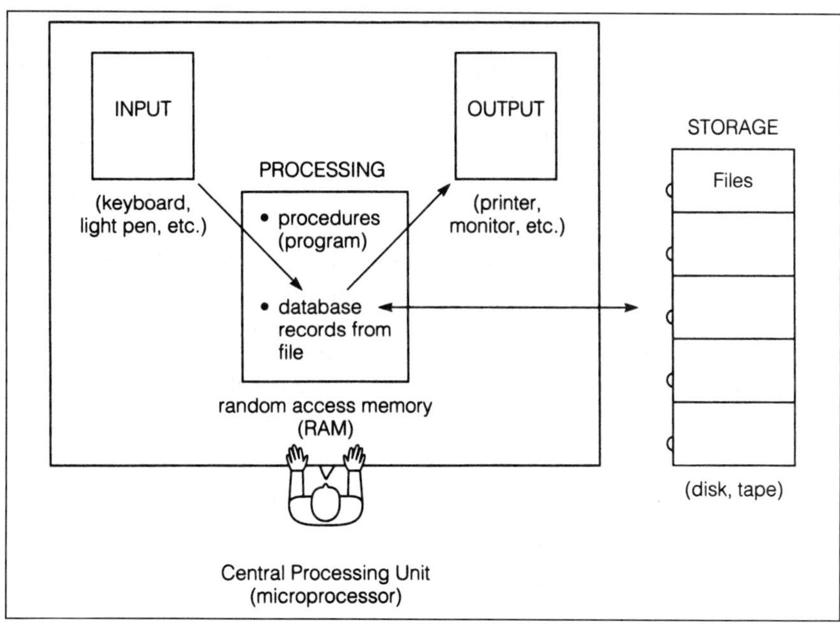

The *components* of either a manual or computerized hardware system are (1) input, (2) processing, (3) storage, and (4) output. In our desk analogy, these components are related to a computerized system as follows:

1. **Input.** The in-basket or telephone is the mode of data entry into the processing area. This may be simulated in the computer with a keyboard, light pen, or modem. Data can be manipulated only in the processing area. A computer system will have input *devices* to transmit input *data*, just as an in-basket may be the device to transmit an input transaction in a manual system.
2. **Processing.** The processing portion of the system is the person sitting at the desk and the work area in front of the person. The person sitting at the desk is simulated by the computer system's central processing unit (CPU), which is also referred to as the primary microprocessor in the microcomputer. The person sitting at the desk manipulates data according to procedures placed in the work area. This work area in the computer is called random access memory (RAM). The procedures executed are called software.
3. **Storage.** The file cabinets and bookcases are the storage components of the desk system. We place our files to be managed here until some type of data manipulation takes place. It is important that these files are designed to facilitate access, fast searches, and efficient updates and to be free of redundant data. Also important is to be able to generate reports readily from the data stored in the files. The computer simulates file cabinets with magnetic disks and tape. The objectives of manual file design with file cabinets are similar to file design on computers using disk and tape storage devices.
4. **Output.** The out-basket or telephone is the way we move information from the processing area. This may be simulated in the computer with a printer, plotter, screen, or modem.

Although there is more to a computerized database management system than presented here, it becomes apparent from the analogies that we already know a good deal about data processing and database management. If the application was a personnel, payroll, or inventory system, the thinking processes of building, manipulating, and reporting from files would be the same. It also becomes apparent that effective database management—whether of a small manually maintained card file or of a large computerized database—is essential.

Again, the thinking process of storing data in a manual file cabinet is similar to the method involved in designing data structures for automated disk storage. The primary purpose is to use minimal space and to facilitate fast access. Unfortunately, it is difficult to reduce data redundancy when minimizing the total file space used in a manual system. For example, in a manual filing system, the personnel, payroll, and training files all contain an employee name and address. The need to create and modify the same data in each file causes consistency problems across the files.

The redundancy problem was not solved in early computer systems—those using punched cards and magnetic tape as a storage media. The employee names and addresses were still contained in separate, sequentially accessed flat files. However, when direct access storage devices were added to computer systems, the problem began to be solved. Devices such as high-speed disks allowed database designers the ability to *integrate* files. An integrated file provides consistent data for multiple users, with potentially redundant data elements such as name and address appearing only once in the file system.

Generally, three models are used to accomplish file integration in database management systems: (1) the hierarchical model, (2) the network model, and (3) the relational model. Since the first two types are not often used in microcomputer database management systems and are beyond the scope of this book, we discuss them only briefly.

HIERARCHICAL MODEL

This model type is shaped like an upside-down tree. It is similar to the hierarchical directory system used in DOS—with the root node at the top. Another often used analogy is the organizational chart. See Figure 1.4. Each intersection in the diagram is called a node. For example, there is a President node, a Dept. A node, and a Branch B1 node. Some nodes are subordinate to others. The highest-level node is called the root node (President). Parent and child labels are given to designate subordinateness; for example, Branch A1 and Branch A2 are children of the parent node Dept. A.

FIGURE 1.4 HIERARCHICAL MODEL ANALOGY

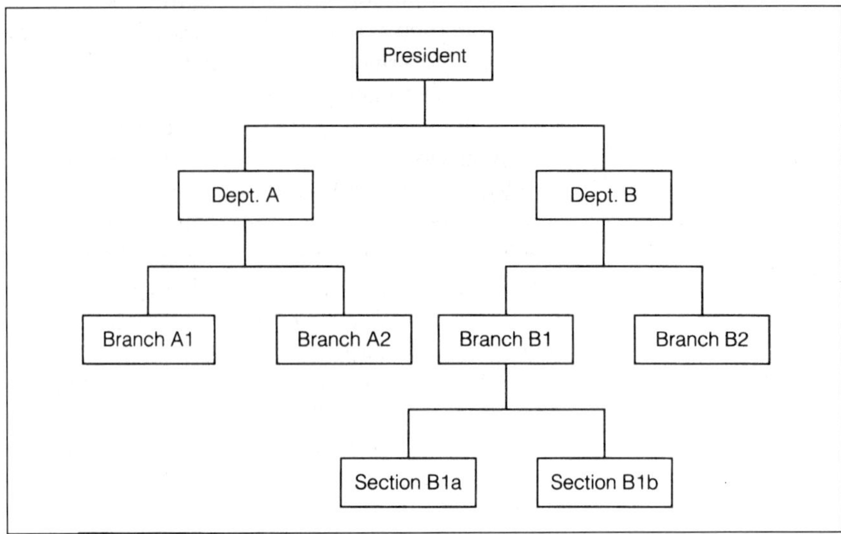

In this hierarchical model the President, or any node, has to be displayed only once, thereby eliminating its redundancy. If this were a hierarchical file structure, each node would represent a record and include information about its relationship to the other nodes in the file. Another characteristic of this structure is that each child node has only one parent node. Access is from the top down.

NETWORK MODEL

The network model is similar to the hierarchical model in that relationships are stored with the record at each node. The difference is that each child node may have multiple parents. For example, a good friend of mine, Fred, operates both a computer retail store and a hi-fi/stereo shop. If you look under computer retail stores in the telephone directory, you will find Fred. If you look under hi-fi/stereo shops, you will also find Fred. However, the Fred record needs to be stored only once in the network structured database. See Figure 1.5.

Hierarchical and network structures require large amounts of storage because relationships are stored with the records. Moreover, they are complex to build and usually require an experienced programmer. The relational model has become popular in micro-based database management systems because it uses less storage and is much simpler to develop.

FIGURE 1.5 NETWORK MODEL ANALOGY

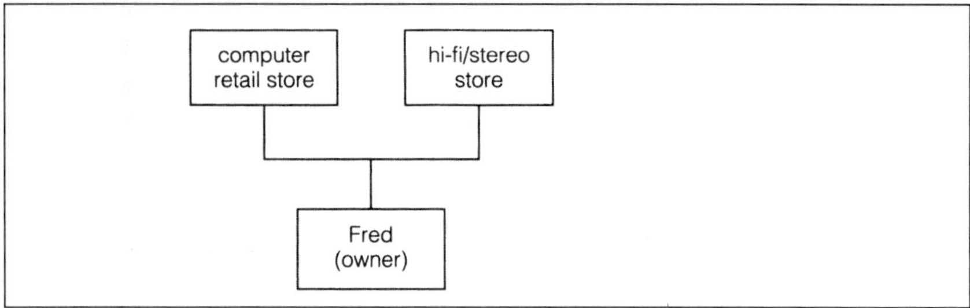

RELATIONAL MODEL

The relational model is made up of multiple flat files, which are related to one another by a key field. The physical pointer relationships between records are not stored with the records. This reduces total storage and gives the programmer the ability to establish new *virtual* files using command syntax. See Figures 1.6 and 1.7.

FIGURE 1.6 RELATIONAL DATABASE MODEL

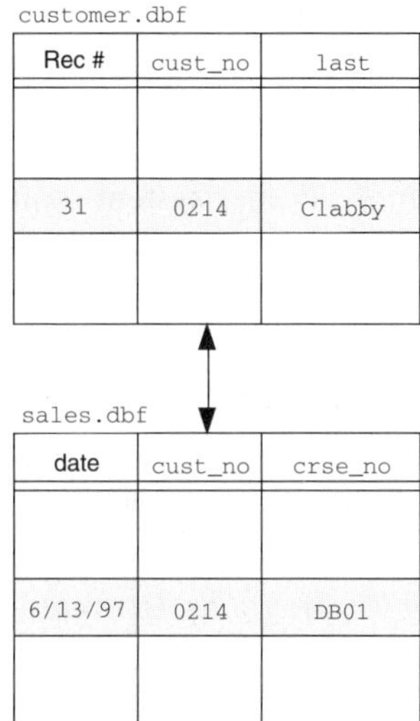

FIGURE 1.7 VIRTUAL MULTIDIMENSIONAL DATABASE

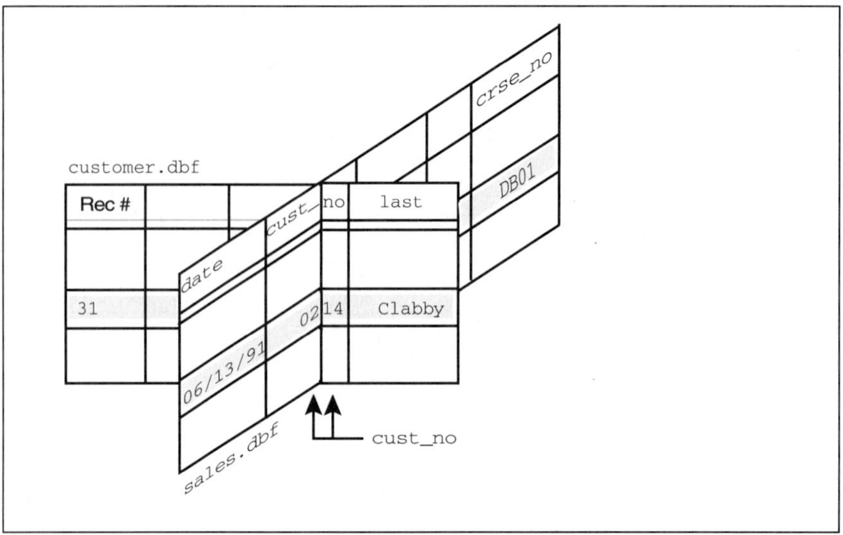

The customer file contains the last name and other pertinent information about each customer. Rather than storing the sales transactions associated with each customer in the same file, a separate sales file is established. When a report needs to be generated that matches sales to a customer, such as an invoice, the two files are linked on the common customer number field. The resulting virtual file establishes a view of the system required for that particular report. New virtual multidimensional files can then be formed by the programmer as other system requirements dictate.

We discuss programming of the Visual dBASE relational model in greater depth in Chapter 11.

NONINTEGRATED FILE MANAGEMENT SYSTEMS

There are less complicated multiple file systems on the market. However, these systems do not have the file integration capabilities of the models we have discussed here. They will be found in a number of spreadsheet programs, in certain mailing list programs, in other less sophisticated file management systems (FMS).

A BRIEF HISTORY OF dBASE

dBASE was conceived and originally developed by Wayne Ratliff, a mainframe database programmer on assignment in Pasadena, California. In his evenings, he assembled a microcomputer from a kit and wrote a microcomputer database management system containing a built-in structured programming language. (We discuss structured programming in more detail in Chapter 4.) Though this early version could not be called a relational model, it did contain limited file linkage syntax. Ratliff decided to market his new product by placing an ad in a computer periodical, though its initial purpose was to assist in the management of his football pools. He called his product Vulcan and sold about 60 copies the first year.

Ratliff then sold the rights to his program to Ashton-Tate, a software marketing firm in Southern California. He also joined the company as vice president in charge of new products, and the name Vulcan was replaced with dBASE II. The first major new product Ratliff developed was dBase III, which was written in the C programming language so that it could easily be recompiled on any computer using a C compiler. A major problem with dBASE II was that it was written in assembly language and had to be rewritten each time it was placed on a computer with a different machine language.*

Many advances in the dBASE language have occurred since. More sophisticated syntax and design screens were added, sort and index routines became faster, and a general acceptance of the language by the end computer user began to occur. Assembly and C-language interfaces could be built if an application needed a routine not covered by dBASE syntax. Many third-party vendors began to develop add-on products. These included report generators, application generators, speed enhancements, file repair packages, debugging aids, program documenters, and compliers. These products added to the popularity of dBASE and enhanced its usage.

Wayne Ratliff believed programming should be simple and straightforward. He also wanted his language to be structured and very capable, especially in the handling of database management. His language has become accepted today largely because he designed it with these attributes in mind.

---

* Wayne Ratliff left Ashton-Tate and formed his own company, Ratliff Software Production, Inc. (RSPI). He markets a DBMS product called Emerald Bay, which contains Vulcan™, an Xbase-type language.

Borland International, Inc. has since purchased Ashton-Tate and dBASE. Borland completed and released version 1.5 shortly after the acquisition, subsequently released version 2.0, and finally, DOS dBASE 5.5. The Professional Compiler promised by Ashton-Tate was released by Borland and is referred to as the Borland dBASE Compiler for DOS. Further, Borland has made all prior versions of dBASE upward compatible to Visual dBASE. This allows the DOS dBASE programmer the ability to move gradually into the Windows environment without having to learn a completely new language.

Visual dBASE is a complete rewrite of all prior DOS versions of the product. It is an excellent language for any Xbase programmer to develop Windows applications. This is true for the following reasons:

- It is easy to learn and is upward compatible from all prior versions of dBASE.
- Though the language is compatible with earlier versions of dBASE, many extensions have been added to it, including object-oriented programming commands and functions that take full advantage of the Windows environment. These include Dynamic Link Libraries (DLL), Windows API functions and calls, Windows printer and font support, Object Linking and Embedding (OLE), Dynamic Data Exchange (DDE), and multimedia support.
- A compiler is available to produce stand-alone user systems.
- It has the sophisticated syntax needed to solve a multitude of database programming problems in a Windows environment.

Table 1.1 lists the features and specifications of Visual dBASE.

TABLE 1.1 VISUAL DBASE FEATURES AND SPECIFICATIONS

Features	Specifications
Number of records	1 billion
Number of characters	2 billion
Maximum record size	32,767 bytes
Maximum number of fields	1024
Maximum field size	
Character type	254 bytes
Date type	8 bytes
Logical type	1 byte
Memo type	Unlimited
Numeric F/N type	20 digits (include sign/dec)
Number of open files	250
Number of open tables	255
Number of index files open	11(10 `.mdx/.ndx` plus 1 production `.mdx`) 47 tags per `.mdx`
Number of format files open	1 per active database
Numeric accuracy	
F type	
Largest number	15.9 digits (0.9 × E + 308)
Smallest number	0.1 × E – 307
N type	
Largest number	20 digits (0.9 × E + 308)
Smallest number	0.1 × E – 307
Number of memory variables	Up to 15,000
Length of command line	254 (1024 in edit window)
Source language	C++
Copy-protected	No
Command line editor	Yes
Editor size `(MODI COM)`	Unlimited
Command line length	4096
Maximum nesting level	Unlimited
Procedures per file	193
Procedure Size	Unlimited
Active procedure files	Unlimited
Sort levels	16
Number of printer drivers	Unlimited
Number of work areas	225
Number of programmable function keys	29

REVIEW EXERCISES

1. What qualities of the micro-based DBMS made it feasible to use as an alternative to a mainframe system?
2. What features distinguish a database management system (DBMS) from a file management system (FMS)?
3. Define the following terms:
   Enterprise
   Entity
   Attribute
   Byte
   Pointer
   Data dictionary
   Field
   Query system
   Key
4. Describe the difference between a flat file and a multidimensional file.
5. What is the difference between a hierarchical file structure and a network file structure?
6. How does a relational data structure minimize data redundancy?
7. Give two reasons why a programmer would select Visual dBASE to build an application.

CHAPTER SUMMARY

In this chapter, we presented the basic concepts of database management systems. The following topics were discussed:

- Database management systems have long been used on large computers. Though highly efficient, they are expensive to build and require an experienced mainframe or minicomputer programmer to develop.
- Current microcomputers are large enough and fast enough to make DBMS usage feasible.
- File redundancy, and the associated data consistency problem, is reduced by file integration. Database management systems use three basic models to accomplish this: (1) the hierarchical model, (2) the network model, and (3) the relational model. Most micro-based database management systems use the relational model.

The following terms were defined:

- Enterprise
- Entity
- Attributes
- Bit
- Byte (character)
- Field
- Record
- File
- Database
- Data dictionary
- Index
- Key
- Pointer
- Query system
- System

We also examined the history of the dBASE language. The following key points were covered:

- The language was authored by Wayne Ratliff.
- dBASE is relational database management system.
- Because of its growing popularity, Visual dBASE has become a popular choice for the development of Windows applications.

CHAPTER TWO

TOPICS

Introduction to Using Visual dBASE

- How to boot Visual dBASE
- The Visual dBASE desktop
- Adjusting the desktop windows
- Using the Command window
- DOS-type commands within Visual dBASE
- The Visual dBASE RUN/! command
- Edits within the Input pane
- Getting help from Visual dBASE
- Configuring Visual dBASE

Review Exercises

Chapter Summary

Getting Started with Visual dBASE

CHAPTER OBJECTIVES

In this chapter, we introduce Visual dBASE. After studying this chapter, you should be able to boot Visual dBASE from the Windows desktop, enter commands from the Command window of the Visual dBASE desktop, get help, and configure the system for your individual needs.

It is important that the student have access to a computer with Microsoft Windows 3.1 or higher that has Visual dBASE installed. Beginning with this chapter, all the sessions should be hands-on. Ideally, students will work through the various exercises with an instructor and then program the Case System on their own. All the exercises relate to, or are part of, the continuing Case System.

HOW TO BOOT VISUAL dBASE

We assume you have a working knowledge of DOS and its hierarchical directory system. You should also have a working knowledge of Windows 3.1 or higher. Visual dBASE is installed by default in the DOS subdirectory `C:\VISUALDB`. Begin your first session of Visual dBASE by double-clicking on the Visual dBASE icon from the Windows desktop. The icon was installed by the product in the Visual dBASE program group on the Windows desktop. Visual dBASE will boot up to display the product desktop (see Figure 2.1). This is a typical Windows Graphical User Interface (GUI) used by the programmer and the non-programmer.

THE VISUAL dBASE DESKTOP

We will look briefly at the main window of Visual dBASE, then examine it in more detail using each element in our exercises. Notice that the main window is a standard movable, sizable window with a title of *Visual dBASE*. Just under the main window title are the bars of the *menu system*. These menu items vary according to the desktop window selected and will be discussed in more detail as they are used.

The desktop also contains a *speedbar* located just below the pull-down menu system. The purpose of a speedbar is to get to an action faster than by going through the pull-down menu system. This allows both the programmer and the non-programmer more efficient use of the Visual dBASE desktop. As with the menu system, items on the speedbar vary according to the task.

There are two major windows on the desktop within the main window. Their titles are *Navigator* and *Command*, respectively. If the Navigator or Command windows are minimized, double-click on their icons on the lower part of the Visual dBASE desktop.

NOTE: The compass icon on the right side of the speedbar will maximize and/or give focus to the Navigator window. Also, on the right side of the speedbar, the genie lamp icon will open and/or give focus to the Command window.

FIGURE 2.1 VISUAL dBASE DESKTOP

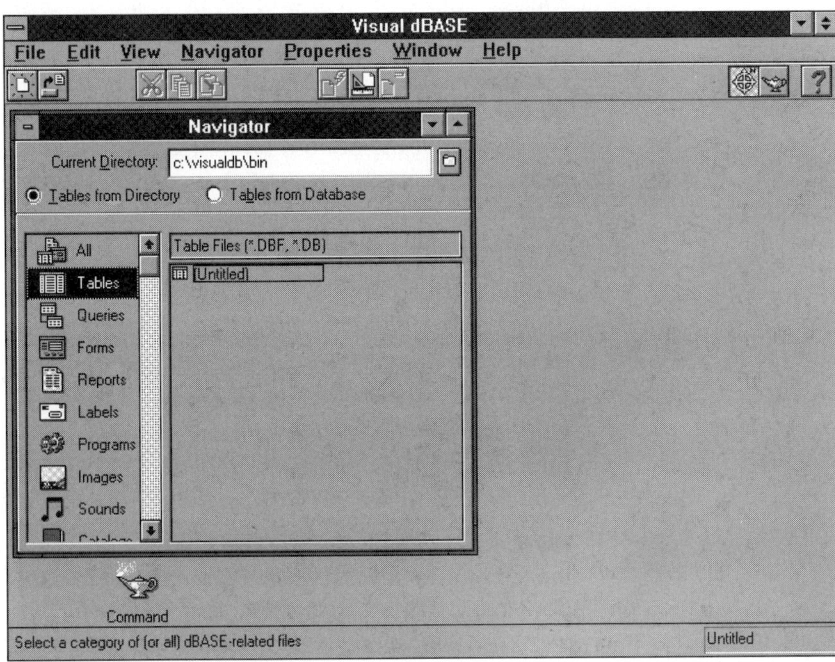

You can use the navigator to catalog, build, and execute the various objects of your system. The object icons are displayed vertically in the Navigator window and include Tables, Queries, Forms, Reports, Labels, Programs, Images, Sounds, and Catalogs. There is also a custom icon made visible by scrolling the Navigator window. If you have used the dBASE IV Control Center, the Navigator is similar in function.

You will discover that the Navigator is an excellent tool for the Visual dBASE programmer. It will allow quick access to the design tools of the product and direct execution of various objects. Initially, most of your commands will be entered from the Command window because you will need to learn command syntax as a prerequisite to programming. However, use of the Navigator will also be demonstrated.

The Command window consists of two panes, the *Input pane* and the *Results pane* (see Figure 2.2). The Input pane allows interactive use of Visual dBASE. Each command typed into the Input pane, followed by pressing <**enter**>, is executed immediately. The results will be displayed in the Results pane. Prior DOS versions of dBASE use a dot prompt for this type of user interaction. In either case, this interactive capability greatly enhances the developmental environment of the product. The programmer can test individual command sequences before entering them into a program module.

The Results pane displays the results of each command individually entered. Commands are retained in the Input pane until deleted and can be reused if needed. The results of programs written in prior DOS versions of dBASE and executed by Visual dBASE are also displayed in the Results pane.

Finally, at the bottom of the main window is the *status bar*. It displays prompts and other messages along with system information such as file status and pointer position.

ADJUSTING THE DESKTOP WINDOWS

You may need to resize or move the windows of the desktop to fit your needs as a programmer. For example, you may want to make the Command window a bit larger than its initial settings and the Navigator window a bit smaller. You may also want to change the relative size of the Input and Results panes (see Figure 2.2). This is done by using standard Windows mouse or keystroke sizing and moving operations.

NOTE: To resize a window, place the mouse cursor on either side and press the left mouse button. While the button is pressed, move the side of the window to the desired position. Release the button when finished. You can move two sides simultaneously by placing the mouse cursor on the corner of the window. To move a window, place the mouse cursor on the title bar, and press the left mouse button. While the button is pressed, move the window to the desired position.

Practice moving/resizing the Navigator and Command windows. Do this using standard Windows moving/sizing mouse movements described in the previous note. You can also use standard Windows keystrokes to move/resize a window.

Resizing the Navigator and Command Windows. Initially, there will not be many files displayed in the Navigator. Begin by making the Navigator window slightly narrower and the Command window slightly wider after giving focus to each window respectively (see Figure 2.2).

Resizing the Input and Results Panes of the Command Window. Make the Results pane slightly larger than the Input pane (see Figure 2.2). To adjust the relative size of the panes, click and drag on the divider between the two (just below the scroll bar at the bottom of the Input pane). Double-click on the same border line to restore it to its default position. Visual dBASE will remember any final adjustments you make and use them the next time the product is booted.

FIGURE 2.2 RESIZED DESKTOP WINDOWS

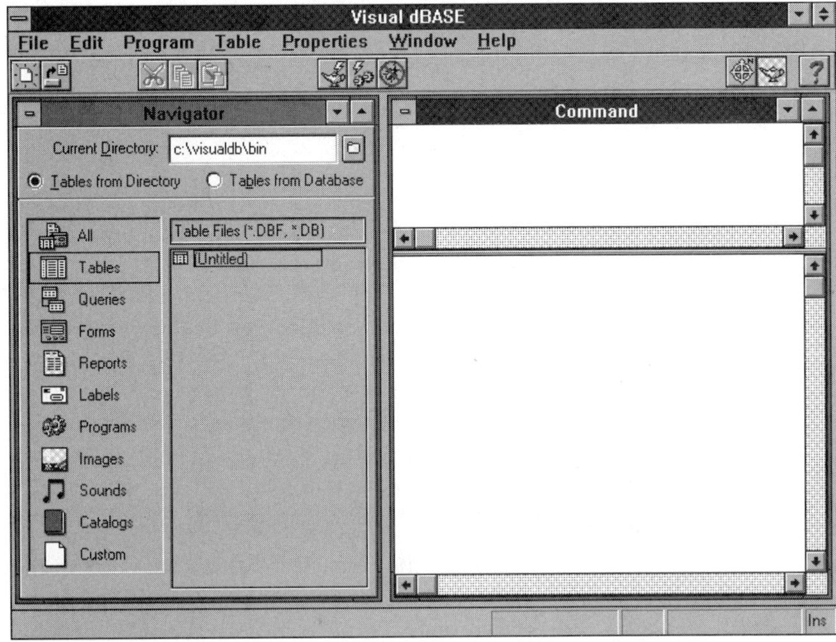

Your screen should now appear similar to Figure 2.2. Notice that the Command window is now larger than the default setting, and the Input pane within the Command window is now smaller than the Results pane. We will be using Visual dBASE in an interactive mode from the two panes of this window in most of our exercises. You will use this method of command entry as you build programs, test and debug programs, use DOS commands, and do housekeeping functions. Readjust these windows as needed as you proceed through the exercises of this text.

USING THE COMMAND WINDOW

As with any standard window, control is given to a dBASE window by giving it *focus*. When a window gets focus, its title bar is highlighted. There are several ways to give either the Navigator window or the Command window focus:

- Click on the window title bar.
- Pull down the Window menu and select Navigator or Command.
- Click the Command window icon in the Speedbar.

We can now begin to enter Visual dBASE commands in the interactive mode. The following sequence of commands will create a student files directory on your hard drive and make that directory the working directory for your student files. After giving focus to the Command window, type the following commands followed by an **<enter>** keypress at the I-bar prompt (Insertion point) in the Input pane:

```
SET TALK ON
MKDIR C:
CD C:
```

The first command in the sequence toggles the `TALK` feature on. Though the default setting of `TALK` is `ON`, it may have been turned `OFF` before this session. The command tells Visual dBASE to echo and display the results of most commands in the Results pane. A subdirectory for the student files is created with the second command. The third command makes that directory the working directory. Notice the directory change in the Results pane in the Command window and in the Current Directory text box of the Navigator window. An important feature of the Visual dBASE user interface is that there will usually be several ways to accomplish a task. For example, the directory change could also be accomplished as follows:

- Click on the Current Directory text box in the Navigator window and enter the directory change.
- Click on the browse icon to the right of the Current Directory text box. This will open the Choose Directory dialog box and allow the user to browse directories for a selection.

Settings made from the Current Directory text box in the Navigator will be remembered by Visual dBASE and used the next time the product is booted. Directory changes made from the Command window will not be remembered. This can be useful when making temporary directory changes that you do not want to affect the boot directory.

NOTE: The `SET DIRECTORY TO` command would accomplish the same results as the `CD` command with one exception. `CD` typed by itself without a path will cause Visual dBASE to remain in the current directory. `SET DIRECTORY TO` typed without a path will cause Visual dBASE to return to the Working directory specified at the dBASE icon level on the Windows desktop.

DOS-TYPE COMMANDS WITHIN VISUAL dBASE

Rather than exiting Visual dBASE, you can execute many DOS-type commands from the Input pane. I say DOS "type" because some Visual dBASE commands operate a bit differently from their corresponding DOS commands. Here is a partial list:

- **DIR (or DIRECTORY) [<drive>][<path>[<skeleton>]**
  Displays a list of files on the specified disk drive. DOS wildcards apply. If **DIR** is used with no option, only database files are listed. Type the following series of commands to exemplify the use of the **DIRECTORY** command. As you type each command, note the display (insertion point) in the Results pane.

```
CLEAR
DIR C:\VISUALDB\SAMPLES\
DIR C:\VISUALDB\SAMPLES\*.*
DIR C:\VISUALDB\BIN\DB*.*
```

The first command clears the contents of the Results pane. The next command displays an inventory of all database table files in the **SAMPLES** subdirectory and the third command displays all files in the **SAMPLES** subdirectory. The final command displays all files beginning with the letters "DB" in the **BIN** subdirectory under the **VISUALDB** subdirectory.

NOTE: The portions of a command supplied by Visual dBASE are called reserved words (for example, DIR, SUM, AVERAGE, and APPEND). A good program documentation practice is to capitalize all reserved words in a command and leave all words supplied by the programmer in lowercase (for example, all field names, filenames, and memory variable names). Though most commands in this book are displayed using this practice, Visual dBASE is not case sensitive. Commands can be entered in either upper or lower case from the Input pane.

- **RENAME <current filename> TO <new filename>** Renames a file. Again, note that it operates a little differently from its DOS equivalent. The DOS RENAME command does not require a **TO** clause.

EXAMPLE

```
RENAME ctest.prg TO ctest2.prg
```

This example shows the basic pattern of the DIR and RENAME commands. Appendix A includes all Visual dBASE DOS-type commands. Here are a few more DOS-type commands:

- **COPY FILE <filename> TO <filename>** Works the same as the DOS COPY command. It is used to copy a file from one subdirectory to another, either using the same filename or changing the name of the copied file. DOS does not use the reserved words **FILE** or **TO** in the command. The reason for this slight variation is that Visual dBASE has its own **COPY** command for copying database table files.
- **ERASE (or DELETE FILE) <filename>|?|<file skeleton>**
  Erases the specified file. If DOS wildcards are typed for the file skeleton or if the **?** clause is typed, the Visual dBASE Files Dialog box will appear for file selection. You can only erase one file at a time. Again, this is slightly different from the DOS equivalent.

- TYPE MORE<filename> [TO PRINTER/TO FILE <\filename>] [NUMBER] Writes an ASCII file to the screen, printer or disk.

THE VISUAL dBASE RUN/! COMMAND

If the programmer needs to execute an actual DOS command or other external program to Visual dBASE, the **RUN** command can be very useful. As an example, type the following from the Input pane to use the DOS DIR command (note the two forms of the command):

```
RUN DIR C: \VISUALDB\BIN
! DIR
```

NOTE: If the Visual dBASE RUN Command window closes immediately after the command has completed execution, the results may be difficult to read. To have this window remain open, you may want to modify the dBASEWIN.PIF file. To do this, go to the Windows desktop and select the **Main** program group **\ PIF Editor**. From the PIF Editor, **File** menu, **Open** option, choose C:\VISUALDB\BIN\DBASEWIN.PIF from the Open dialog box. From the PIF Editor window, clear the check box from the Close Window on Exit option (lower left-hand corner).

If an external program is executed with **RUN/!**, ensure that it is resident in the Visual dBASE subdirectory or has a path set to the proper subdirectory. You can also access the DOS prompt by typing the **DOS** command from the Input pane. Typing **EXIT** at the DOS prompt will then allow closing of the DOS window.

EDITS WITHIN THE INPUT PANE

Each command entered into the Input pane window can be recalled and edited simply by returning the cursor to the desired command using the cursor keys or by mouse cursor movement. Once you return the cursor to a command, that command can be edited or re-executed by pressing the **<enter>** key from any position on the command line. A few of the editing keystrokes are the **Ins** key to insert, **Del** to delete, **Home** to move the cursor to the beginning position, **End** to move the cursor to the end of the command line, and **Esc** to delete the entire command line. This editing ability is especially useful when reentering a very lengthy command that needs only slight modification.

You can use the Windows cut/copy and paste feature from the Input pane to delete a command or group of commands or write that group of commands to a file. This feature can be useful when testing a block of commands interactively, then moving that block to a program file.

To delete a command, press **Esc** on that command line. To delete a block of commands, mark the block and press **Delete** or choose **Delete** from the **Edit** menu.

NOTE: These Input pane deletions mentioned here are temporary and will be restored when the next command is executed. All commands entered throughout a session are retained as part of a session history of commands.

- **Re-execute a command:** Move the cursor back to a few of the DOS commands you have already entered. Once you have moved the cursor to a prior command, try making a few modifications before re-execution.
- **Erase a block:** Using the mouse, block the last two commands entered. Delete either by using the **Delete** key or by choosing **Edit | Delete**.
- **Erase all prior commands:** Choose **Edit | Select all**, then choose **Edit | Delete**.

GETTING HELP FROM VISUAL dBASE

Visual dBASE offers an extensive help system. We strongly recommend that you load the entire help system on your hard drive if space is available. You can view a help topic any time during a session, return to Visual dBASE, or search for a new topic.

Viewing the Help System. To view the general help system, select **Help | Contents** (see Figure 2.3). You can go directly to the Contents section of Help by pressing **Shift-F1** from the main window. A good place to start with Windows Help is to select **Help | How to Use Help**. At your leisure, you may want to browse the help system from this Contents screen. It will take you through the basics of using the help system of Visual dBASE and give you much insight on how a typical Windows help system operates. Close the Help window when finished.

Searching for Specific Topics. To search for help on a specific command or topic, select **Help | Search**. A typical Windows style dialog box should now appear on your screen as in Figure 2.4. The list of subjects contains commands, functions, and concepts. For example, type the word `basics` in the text box, then press **<enter>** or click **Show Topics**. Notice the sublist of topics that now appears. You can select a topic from this list with either a double mouse click or by pressing **down-arrow** and **<enter>**.

FIGURE 2.3 CONTENTS WINDOW FROM HELP MENU

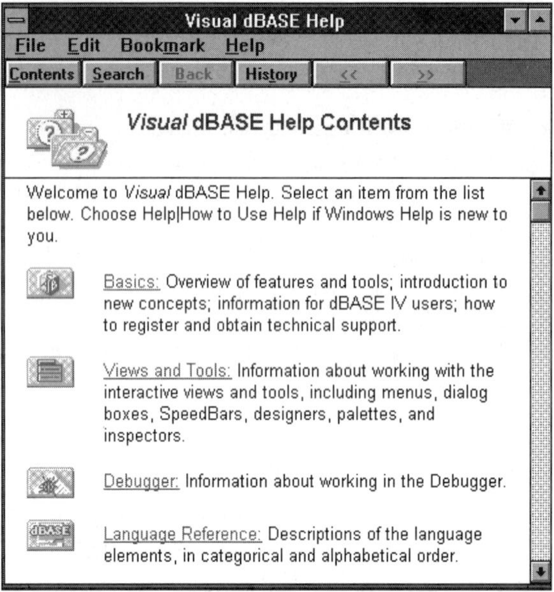

FIGURE 2.4 TOPIC SEARCH UNDER HELP

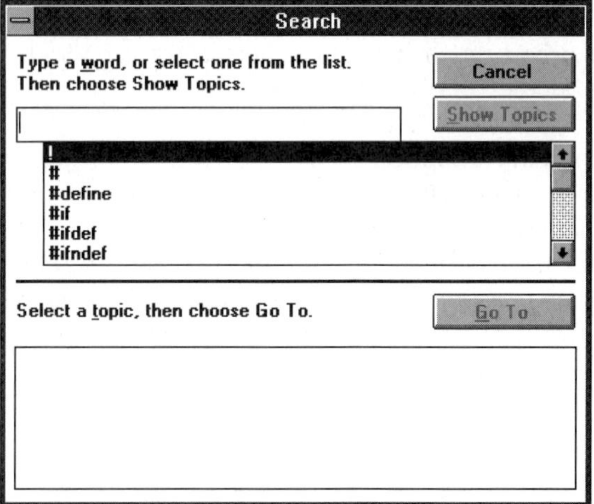

Getting Help from the Command Window. Help can also be obtained from the Command window. Remove the Help window from the screen by double clicking on the control-menu box in the upper left-hand corner of the window or select **File | Exit**. Then, give the Command window focus and enter the following command:

```
HELP
```

This will open the Visual dBASE Help window at the Contents level. From there, you can find the topic of your choice. You can also go directly to a topic from the command window. For example, type the following from the Command window:

```
HELP LIST
```

Additional Help Features. Visual dBASE help is context-sensitive. For example, from any dialog box or active window, pressing **F1** or clicking the question-mark speedbar icon will move you to the help on that topic. Also, notice that as you move the mouse cursor along the Speedbar or activate a menu item, a brief description of that item will appear in the message line at the bottom of the Visual dBASE desktop. Finally, there is a set of *Interactive Tutors* available by choosing **Help | InteractiveTutors**. You may want to browse through them if they are installed on your computer. To print a help topic, choose **File | Print Topic**. Visual dBASE utilizes the print facility of Windows.

CONFIGURING VISUAL dBASE

There are several components involved in configuring Visual dBASE. Prior users of dBASE used the `config.db` file. Setting the working environment with `SET` commands such as `SET DIRECTORY` as demonstrated earlier are still used but the `config.db` file is no longer present. Moreover, Visual dBASE operates through Windows and uses many Windows resources, such as printer drivers and fonts.

The `dBASEWIN.INI` File. As with all Windows applications, Visual dBASE is configured with a Windows initialization file. The name of this file is `dBASEWIN.INI` and it is located in the Visual dBASE home directory. To view the `dBASEWIN.INI` file in use on your system, type the following command from the Input pane:

```
TYPE MORE C:\VISUALDB\BIN\DBASEWIN.INI
```

The `MORE` option to the `TYPE` command will allow you to view the file one screen at a time. Your listing may contain a different number of segments, but should be similar to the sample file displayed in Figure 2.5. The commands in each segment establish parameters such as the location of the user interface objects like windows and dialog boxes. The settings are used each time the product is booted, and changes to the file are recorded as changes are made from within Visual dBASE. Though you can edit the file directly using a standard text editor, it is not advisable to do so.

Setting the Desktop and Command Window Properties. The **Properties** menu of the Visual dBase main window allows the programmer to modify default environmental settings. All property changes made through this menu will be recorded in the `dBASEWIN.INI` file. As an example, if you needed to change the default setting of the left margin for program listings, you would do the following:

1. Choose **Properties | Desktop Properties** from the main window.
2. Click on the Programming page tab at the bottom of the Desktop Properties dialog box (see Figure 2.6).
3. Click the Margin text box scroll arrows to change the value to 10.
4. Click the OK pushbutton.
5. Type the following command from the Input pane:

   ```
   TYPE MORE C:\VISUALDB\BIN\DBASEWIN.INI
   ```

   Scroll down to the [Command Settings] section. Notice that the `MARGIN` setting has been modified to 10.

REVIEW EXERCISES

1. What is the purpose of the Command window? What are the names of the two panes of the Command window?
2. What is meant by giving a window focus? Describe at least two ways to give a window focus. What would be the purpose in resizing the panes on the Command window?
3. How do you return the border line between the Input and Results panes of the Command window to its default position?
4. Minimize and then maximize both the Command and the Navigator windows.
5. What command do you use to execute an actual DOS command from within the Command window?

FIGURE 2.5 VISUAL DBASE dBASEWIN.INI FILE

```
[Fonts]                    **Settings for several of the non-Modal windows
1=Times New Roman,12,ROMAN
2=Arial,10,SWISS
3=Arial,24,SWISS
4=Ariston,24,SCRIPT

[CommandSettings]          **Determines STYLE settings for the ?/?? commands
_dbwinhome=C:\VISUALDB
directory=C:\DBDATA
Margin=0

[CustomClasses]            **Custom Class file/s
CC0=C:\VISUALDB\SAMPLES\BUTTONS.CC

[Install]                  **User ID information
Username=Robert L. Buchanan
Company=RLB & Associates

[Desktop]                  **Forms designer settings
Maximized=1
Position=11 48 631 469

[CommandWindow]            **Command window settings
Maximized=0
Minimized=0

[Navigator]                **Navigator window settings
Maximized=0
Minimized=0

[MRU_Files]                **Settings for Most Recently Used (MRU) files and sets order in which displayed
Order=bdeca
a=C:\DBDATA\YVIDEO.WFM,14,3

[Dialogs]                  **Coordinates of dialog boxes
More=24 124 237 242
FindText=170 177 605 315

[ControlsWindow]           **Settings for the Form Designers' Control Palette.
Position=472 0 640 388
Minimized=0

[FormDesigner]             **Settings for the Form Designer
ShowGrid=1
```

(Continues)

FIGURE 2.5 VISUAL DBASE dBASEWIN.INI FILE (continued)

```
[ObjectProperties]          **Settings for Object Properties window
CenterLine=125
Position=353 63 609 357

[ProcedureEditor]           **Settings for the Procedure Editor
Position=0 160 640 388
Minimized=0

[ProgramEditor]             **Settings for the internal text editor
Position=16 6 625 367

[OnOffCommandSettings]      **On/off settings, primarily from the Desktop Properties dialog box.
EXCLUSIVE=ON
DELETED=ON
EXACT=OFF
```

FIGURE 2.6 DESKTOP PROPERTIES DIALOG BOX

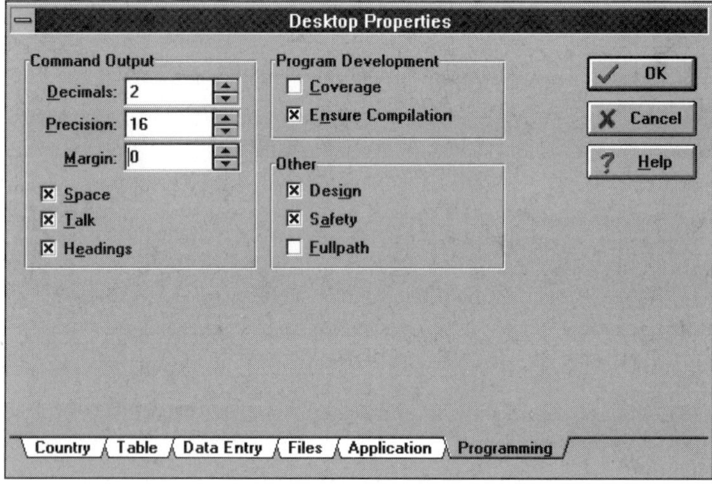

6. Using the proper Visual dBASE DOS type command, display the root directory of your hard drive in the Results pane. Display the same directory using the actual DOS directory command.

7. Display a description of the Visual dBASE `DIRECTORY` command from the help system. If your printer is connected, print the `DIRECTORY` command topic.

8. Erase all the commands currently in the Input pane.

9. Present the opening screen of the Visual dBASE on-line Tutorial System.

10. In the hands-on section of this chapter, you changed the left margin for program listings to 10. Reset the margin to 5 in the dBASEWIN.INI file. Make the change from the Desktop Properties dialog box.

CHAPTER SUMMARY

In this chapter, we booted and explored the desktop of Visual dBASE. The following topics were discussed:

- Visual dBASE was booted from its subdirectory. The parts of the Visual dBASE desktop (main window) were discussed.
- The Navigator and Command windows of the desktop were adjusted to meet the needs of a work session.
- The Command window was discussed in detail. Commands similar to DOS commands were entered from the Input pane of the Command window and the results observed in the Results pane. The RUN command was used to execute DOS commands from within Visual dBASE.
- Edits from within the Command window were discussed and executed. Commands were retrieved from prior entry, edited and reexecuted.
- We discussed and explored the extensive help system contained in Visual dBASE. This included looking at the general contents, searching for individual commands and subjects, and opening the contents screen of the built in tutorial system.
- The default settings stored in the `dBASEWIN.INI` file were viewed and modified using the Desktop Properties dialog box.

In the next chapter, we discuss command syntax from the Command window in more detail—actually building, manipulating, and listing database tables.

CHAPTER THREE

TOPICS

Visual dBASE Command Syntax

Visual dBASE Expressions

- Definition of an expression
- Components of an expression
- Usage of expressions

New Commands

Using Commands from the Command Window

- Creating the table structure
- Modifying the table structure
- Appending the table
- Listing the table

Introduction to the Case System

Review Exercises

Chapter Summary

Visual dBASE Command Syntax

CHAPTER OBJECTIVES

In this chapter, we introduce the use of Visual dBASE commands. If this were a book about chess, we would learn here how to set the board and how each piece moves. (We begin to learn to "play" chess in the next chapter.) We build and perform basic manipulations on a database table using commands entered from the Command window. Our goal is to become completely familiar with the form of Visual dBASE command syntax before writing programs using that syntax. We also introduce the ongoing Case System.

After studying this chapter, you should be able to build and do basic manipulations and to list data from a database table using commands entered from the Command window.

VISUAL dBASE COMMAND SYNTAX

Before entering commands from the Command window, we briefly discuss the parts of the Visual dBASE command syntax. Syntax in any programming language is very exacting and unforgiving, and Visual dBASE is no exception. Though some commands may deviate from a standard format, there are generally five major parts to a Visual dBASE command:

1. **Verb**: Tells dBASE *what* you want to do. The verb is always required. All other parts of the command may be optional. A verb may consist of multiple words.

EXAMPLE `EDIT, CREATE, LIST, DEFINE MENU`

2. **Scope**: Tells dBASE *how much* of the table the verb is to act on.

EXAMPLE `ALL, NEXT 5, REST`

3. **Expression list**: Tells dBASE *what to operate on*. The expression list can be a single field, a group of fields, or a group of calculated fields.

EXAMPLE `mail,  item_no, rate * 1.10`

4. **Condition**: Tells dBASE which records are to be selected from a table. In Chapter 6, we discuss both *search* and *scope* conditions.

EXAMPLE `FOR City = "Las Vegas"`

5. **Miscellaneous**: This segment is for the various options unique to certain commands.

EXAMPLE `TO PRINT, OFF, STYLE, ADDITIVE`

All commands that operate on an entire table have the above format. An example is the `LIST` command. Examine the following command series (do not type these commands in the Input pane at this point).

EXAMPLE
```
USE cphone
LIST NEXT 5 cust_no, city, amt_due FOR city = "San Mateo"
```

The `USE` command will open the cphone master table. This will automatically place the record pointer on record no. 1. The following will occur when this `LIST` command is executed (see Figure 3.1).

1. The pointer will move sequentially from record no. 1 to record no. 5. This is the defined scope.
2. When a record meets the search condition, only the customer number (`cust_no`), city (`city`), and amount due (`amt_due`) will be listed. (Though not a field, the record number is also listed.)

3. Within the scope of the first five records, only the customers from San Mateo will be listed.

Notice in this command that the city field is part of both the field list and the condition portion of the command. dBASE will search through the scope of five records. When a customer record is located from San Mateo within the scope, only the three fields from the field list in that record will be listed (**cust_no, city, amt_due**).

Notice in Figure 3.1 that the command has created a new *view* of the table. The scope limited the records we view to the first five (shaded area). The expression list further limited the view to certain fields within each record (fields within double line boxes). Finally, the condition portion of the command limits the view to only certain records within the scope. We discuss the programming of views in more detail in Chapter 11.

FIGURE 3.1 VISUAL dBASE COMMAND SYNTAX EXAMPLE

Verb — Scope — Noun (field list) — Condition

```
.LIST NEXT 5 cust_no, city, amt_due FOR city = "San Mateo"
```

Rec	cust_no	first	last	city	amt_due
1	0011	Robert	Jones	Sacramento	
2	0012	Janice	Murphy	San Mateo	50.00
3	0071	Phillip	Anderson	San Mateo	250.00
4	0034	Adrean	Dunfey	San Mateo	550.00
5	0022	Benjamin	Smith	San Francisco	300.00
6	0023	Jeanne	Gordon	San Mateo	450.00
7	0035	Kyle	Simlar	Sacramento	150.00
8	0077	Kevin	Howard	San Mateo	200.00
9	0018	Lorraine	McCarthy	San Francisco	350.00
10	0021	Andrea	Scwabbe	San Bruno	240.00

scope (records 1–5)

New VIEW of database resulting from command execution:

2	0012	San Mateo	50.00
3	0071	San Mateo	250.00
4	0034	San Mateo	550.00

Another important principle of Visual dBASE command syntax can be demonstrated from the previous example. *The verb operates on the open table.* We opened the table, then applied the **LIST** verb to it. The following would be in error:

EXAMPLE
```
APPEND cphone
LIST cphone
```

There must be an open (active) database table for commands to operate on. The correct sequence would be as follows:

EXAMPLE
```
USE cphone      && Open the table.
APPEND          && Append the currently open table.
LIST            && List the currently open table.
```

NOTE: The double ampersand symbol (&&) in a command signifies a command line comment; it is not included in the execution of the command. Do not include the comment when typing commands into the Command window.

VISUAL dBASE EXPRESSIONS

All programming languages use expressions as part of their command syntax. An understanding of expressions is a prerequisite to learning any command language. In this section, we define an expression, list its various components, and then discuss the usage of expressions.

DEFINITION OF AN EXPRESSION

An expression is a group of simple items and operators that can be evaluated to form a new simple value. There are four types of expressions in Visual dBASE: (1) numeric, (2) character, (3) logical, and (4) date.

COMPONENTS OF AN EXPRESSION

When a Visual dBASE expression is constructed within a command, it uses combinations of field variables, memory variables, constants, functions, and operators.

Field Variables. Field variables are the field names assigned at the time the table structure is created and may be included in an expression. When evaluated, the field value will be taken from the record at the current pointer position. Characteristics of field variables are as follows:

- **Name:** Names may be as long as 10 characters. They may contain letters, numbers, or the underscore character (_), but no blank spaces. They must begin with a letter. Do not use dBASE database alias names `(A–J)` or `M` or reserved words (`SUM, AVERAGE, COUNT`, and the like).
- **Data types:** Visual dBASE field variables can contain the following types of data.

  Character: Items that will not be calculated.
  Numeric: Values that will be calculated.
  Float: Calculated values that will be very large or very small.
  Logical: Values to be coded either true (`.T.`) or false (`.F.`). You may also use `.Y.` (yes) or `.N.` (no). The values may be either uppercase or lowercase.
  Date: Dates stored in this format will allow for date arithmetic.
  Memo: Allows coding of up to 32,766 characters of ASCII data associated with each record. Data is stored in a separate file with a `.dbt` extension. The 10-digit memo field in the database record contains a pointer to the memo data in the `.dbt` file. As with other field names, memo field names may be up to 10 characters in length.
  Object Linking and Embedding (OLE): Allows the integration of an OLE document in a table field. The document can be a graphic image, a sound, or a text document. The document can be embedded directly into a dBASE table field or linked from an external source.
  Binary: Data stored in a binary format. Examples are bitmap image data and sound data. Binary types supported are .BMP and .PCX images and .WAV sounds.

Memory Variables. Memory variables are storage modules outside the database. You might think of them as a scratch pad to keep track of items not included in database tables. Rules governing memory variables are as follows:

- **Name:** Names follow the same constraints as field variables.
- **Number active:** Limited only by available memory.
- **Types:** The values contained in memory variables are evaluated expressions. The data type of the memory variable becomes the data type of the expression. For example, if a numeric expression such as `6+1` is assigned to a memory variable `xValue`, the data type of the variable will become numeric.
- **Scope:** The *scope* of a memory variable determines its availability and duration in a program. Memory variable scopes will be discussed in more detail in Chapter 4.

Constants. A *constant* is a value that cannot be changed. A constant may be placed within an expression to become part of its evaluation. It is literally the value you want to appear rather than a field or memory variable that contains that value. For this reason, constants are sometimes called *literals*. The following constant data types are available:

- **Character:** Character type constants, also called character strings, must be contained within delimiters in an expression. The delimiters are required to distinguish a literal constant from a field or memory variable name. Delimiters may be double quotes (" "), single quotes (' '), or square brackets ([ ]). Three delimiter characters are available to allow one of the three to be included as part of the character string.

EXAMPLE

```
? "Hello" && Returns the following
Hello
? [Hello, "Bob"] && Returns the following
Hello, "Bob"
```

- **Numeric:** Any number with an optional decimal point (for example, 3.14). Delimiters are not used.
- **Logical:** `.T.   .F.   .t.   .f.   or .Y.   .N.   .y.   .n.`
- **Date:** Must be contained within braces delimiters (for example, {`10/10/95`}).

Functions. Functions are subprograms contained within Visual dBASE to perform more complex operations not covered by commands. One or more *arguments* are sent to a function from an expression. The function will operate on the arguments and then return the result to the expression for inclusion in its evaluation. Arguments are also referred to as *parameters*. In addition to a complete set of built-in functions, Visual dBASE allows the user to define his or her own functions as needed. We discuss user-defined functions in Chapter 10. Appendix B includes a complete list of built-in (internal) Visual dBASE functions.

EXAMPLE

```
? SQRT(49)        && Returns a value of 7
```

Operators. Operators are symbols used by Visual dBASE to link constants, variables, and functions together within an expression to form a single unit for evaluation. The symbol tells dBASE how to relate the components to determine its evaluation.

- **Comparison:** Symbols used to compare character, numeric, float, or date type data to obtain a single logical result (true or false).

=	equal
<= or =<	less than or equal to
<	less than
>	greater than

`>= or =>`	greater than or equal to
`<> or #`	not equal to
`$`	substring compare
`()`	parentheses for grouping

- **Logical:** Symbols used to compare two or more logical expressions to obtain a single logical evaluation (true or false). dBASE syntax uses period delimiters here.

  ```
  .AND.
  .OR.
  .NOT.
  ```

- **Arithmetic:** Symbols used to obtain the numeric evaluation of the components of an expression.

`+`	plus
`–`	minus
`/`	division
`*`	multiplication
`** or ^`	exponent
`()`	parentheses for grouping

- **String:** Symbols used to concatenate (add) two or more character components of an expression to form a single character type string. The minus concatenation symbol (–) causes all trailing blanks between strings to be moved to the end of the last string.

USAGE OF EXPRESSIONS

We have defined and identified the components of expressions. The following numeric, character, and logical expression examples are designed to reinforce your understanding of what an expression is and how its components are formulated.

Numeric Expressions

- `5 + 3` is a numeric expression. It contains two numeric constants (`5` and `3`) and an arithmetic operator (+). The expression evaluates to a simple value of `8`.
- `x = 5 + 3` is a Visual dBASE command containing the above expression. The equal sign in this command does not mean algebraically equal. It means "is replaced with (or assigned) the following expression, evaluated." The = sign may also be referred to as the assignment operator. The command might read as follows: "Establish a memory variable labeled **x**, and replace whatever is currently in the variable with the expression (`5+3`), evaluated." The = sign in this case is most often referred to as the *assignment operator*.

Early versions of dBASE did not use the equal-sign assignment operator. The **STORE** command was used instead and is still available for use.

The preceding command would then read as follows:

```
STORE 5 + 3 TO x
```

Some programmers prefer this format because it seems to read more naturally: "Store the expression `5 + 3`, evaluated, to **`x`**." The tradeoff is that it requires more coding keystrokes and is slower to execute. Either way, the command will cause the following three things to happen:

1. Set aside a module of memory.
2. Assign a label of **`x`** to the module.
3. Replace whatever is currently in the module labeled **`x`** with the evaluated expression, 8. (See Figure 3.2.)

To continue the discussion of numeric expressions, note the following series of commands and how they read:

```
x = 5               && Initialize a memory variable x to the
                    && value 5.
x = x + 1           && Replace x with the expression x + 1.
                    && evaluated (6).
y = (x / 2) *4      && Initialize a memory variable y.
                    && Replace with the expression (x / 2) *
                    && 4, evaluated (12).
```

The second statement, `x = x + 1`, is not algebraically true. But remember, = does not mean equal, it means is replaced with or is assigned.

A numeric expression can also contain functions and database variables. Consider the following:

```
x = 49
y = SQRT (x) + value
```

FIGURE 3.2 MEMORY VARIABLE INITIALIZATION

numeric-type data

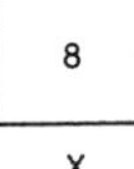

If **value** is a field variable from the record at the current pointer position in the open database and has a value of 10, these two statements would read as follows: (1) "Initialize a memory variable labeled **x**, and replace its current value with a numeric value of **49**" and (2) "Initialize a memory variable labeled **y**, and replace its current value with the numeric expression **SQRT (x) + value**, evaluated." In the expression, the memory variable argument **x** would be sent to the square root function. The square root (7) would be computed by the function and then returned to the expression to be included in the evaluation (7 + 10 or 17).

Character Expressions. Character constant strings and character variables may also be added together to form expressions. For example, consider the following:

```
greeting = "Hello"  && Initialize a memory variable
                    && labeled greeting.
first = "Joan"      && Initialize a memory variable
                    && labeled first.
? greeting + first  && Print the character expression,
                    && greeting + first, evaluated.
```

We've introduced the **?** print command a bit early here to help in our explanation of expressions. If we evaluate the character expression to be printed in the example, we get:

```
HelloJoan
```

We have added the two variables, back to back. This is called a string concatenation. If we want to separate the two variable values with comma and a space, we could add a character constant to the expression as follows:

```
? greeting + "," + first
```

This would evaluate to

```
Hello, Joan
```

Logical Expressions. All commands containing any type of condition will use logical expressions. When a logical expression is evaluated, the simple value generated is either true or false. The Visual dBASE logical constants are **.T.** and **.F.**. The period delimiters act the same as character string delimiters in that they differentiate between a variable and a constant. Consider the following command:

```
LIST FOR city = "San Mateo"
```

city = "San Mateo" is a logical expression. As the pointer moves through the table, this expression is evaluated for each record (is the city field equal to **"San Mateo"**). If it evaluates as **.T.**, the record will be listed. Now we will add another logical expression with a logical operator:

```
LIST FOR city = "San Mateo" .AND. amt_due > 500
```

For the total expression to evaluate as true, the city must be San Mateo and the amount due must be greater than $500. If we change the logical operator in the expression to **.OR.**, the evaluation criteria changes:

```
LIST FOR city = "San Mateo" .OR. amt_due > 500
```

Now if the city is San Mateo or the amount due is greater than $500, the expression will evaluate as true (**.T.**).

This has been a brief look at expressions. We introduce more complex expressions when we begin programming. All expressions, however, follow the principles outlined here.

NEW COMMANDS

The following is a listing of the syntax of each command introduced in this chapter. To avoid confusion, we often show only that portion of the syntax of a command that is necessary to do the exercises in this chapter. Appendix A shows the full syntax of the commands.

COMMAND `SET DIRECTORY TO [[<drive:>][<path>]]` or `CD[<path>]`

Specifies the operating system working drive and subdirectory.

COMMAND `CREATE <filename> /MODIFY STRUCTURE`

Provides a design screen to develop or modify the structure of a table.

COMMAND `SET EXCLUSIVE on/OFF`

Controls whether dBASE opens tables and their associated index and memo files in exclusive or shared mode. In Visual dBASE, multiple openings of the same table can occur. It is therefore necessary to have exclusive use of a table if modifications are to be made such as a modification of its structure. A table can also be opened exclusively by using the **EXCLUSIVE** option of the **USE** command. If **SET EXCLUSIVE ON** is used, it must precede the **USE** command. The default status of **EXCLUSIVE** can be set in the **dBASEWIN.INI** file by selecting **Properties** | **Desktop Properties** | **Table Tab**.

COMMAND `USE <database filename> EXCLUSIVE`

Opens an existing table. If a memo field is in the structure, the associated **.dbt** file will also be opened. **USE** by itself will close the open table. See previous command for use of **EXCLUSIVE** option.

COMMAND `LIST/DISPLAY STRUCTURE [TO PRINT/TO FILE]`

Lists or displays the field specifications (structure) of the open table.

COMMAND `MODIFY STRUCTURE`

Allows user modification of a table structure.

COMMAND `APPEND`

Provides data screen for adding new records to the open table.

COMMAND `APPEND FROM <filename>`

Appends the open table from another table.

COMMAND `LIST/DISPLAY [FIELDS] <expression list> [OFF] [<scope>] [FOR/WHILE <condition>] [TO PRINTER/TO FILE <filename>]`

Lists or displays the open table in an unformatted, columnar format.

COMMAND `GOTO <expN>`

Moves the pointer to the record number developed by the evaluation of the expression (for example, **GOTO 5 + 2** moves the pointer to record number 7).

USING COMMANDS FROM THE COMMAND WINDOW

This discussion is designed to give you experience in using commands from the Command window. The table built will be one of three to be used in the ongoing Case System. You will be creating, manipulating, and reporting from a database mangement system program—the Case System.

CREATING THE TABLE STRUCURE

The first task is to build the customer master table. Enter the following command sequence from the Input pane of the Command window:

```
CD c:\dbdata
CREATE ycustm
```

The first command will change to the drive and subdirectory created in the preceding chapter. If you prefer placing your exercise files in another subdirectory, change the command accordingly.

The **CREATE** command will open the Table Structure window. Each line entered here will define a single field in the database file. The definition includes the field name, the type of data to be entered into the field, the width of the field and number of decimal places if the data type is numeric. Ignore the Index column for now. Use **Tab/Shift-Tab** to move the cursor across or back from one item to another. Notice that a drop-down list box is available for the data Type selection. A mouse click will select a type from the list box. Also, overwrite the default field width of 10 as necessary. Type the file structure as shown in Figure 3.3. After you type the structure, your screen should appear as in Figure 3.4. To abort a design, either choose **File | Abandon and Close** or press the **Esc** key. Save the design using any of the the following techniques:

- Double-click the Table Structure window Control-menu box
- Choose **File | Save and Close**
- Press **Ctrl-W**

NOTE: You can exit and save from all Visual dBase design screens using the above techniques. **Ctrl–W** has been an exit and save method since dBASE II, and is still probably the easiest. Choosing **File | Abandon and Close** or **Esc** can be used to abort any design work surface.

MODIFYING THE TABLE STRUCTURE

Enter the following command sequence from the Command window:

```
USE                           && Close customer master table.
USE ycustm EXCLUSIVE          && Open customer master table.
DISPLAY STRUCTURE
MODIFY STRUCTURE
```

To demonstrate how to close the active table, we begin this segment by closing the customer table and reopening it. Notice that the name of the table disappears from the status bar when you execute the `USE` command by itself. Then, when you `USE ycustm EXCLUSIVE`, it reappears as the open table. The `EXCLUSIVE` option is necessary to modify the table structure.

FIGURE 3.3 CUSTOMER MASTER TABLE STRUCTURE `ycustm`

Field	Field Name	Type	Length	Dec	Index
1	FIRST	CHARACTER	10	0	N
2	MIDDLE	CHARACTER	1	0	N
3	LAST	CHARACTER	15	0	N
4	ADDRESS	CHARACTER	20	0	N
5	CITY	CHARACTER	10	0	N
6	STATE	CHARACTER	2	0	N
7	ZIP	CHARACTER	5	0	N
8	PHONE	CHARACTER	14	0	N

FIGURE 3.4 TABLE STRUCTURE WINDOW ycustm

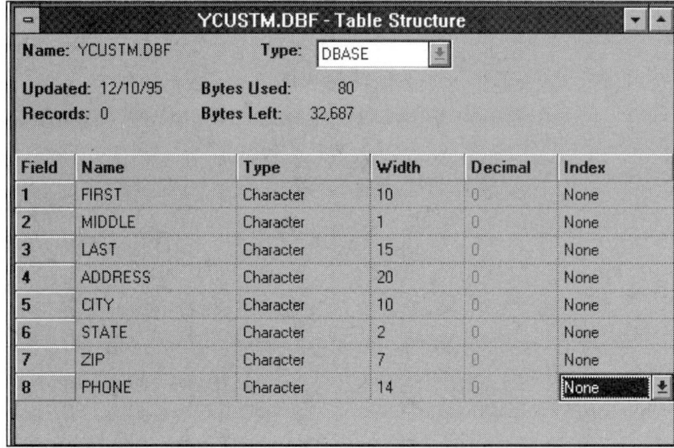
YCUSTM.DBF - Table Structure

Name: YCUSTM.DBF Type: DBASE

Updated: 12/10/95 Bytes Used: 80

Records: 0 Bytes Left: 32,687

Field	Name	Type	Width	Decimal	Index
1	FIRST	Character	10	0	None
2	MIDDLE	Character	1	0	None
3	LAST	Character	15	0	None
4	ADDRESS	Character	20	0	None
5	CITY	Character	10	0	None
6	STATE	Character	2	0	None
7	ZIP	Character	7	0	None
8	PHONE	Character	14	0	None

The `DISPLAY STRUCTURE` command is useful to examine the structure of the open table. When you create a table, it remains open until closed by another command. Use the `TO PRINT` option if you want a hard copy of the structure of the customer master table, `ycustm.dbf`:

1. Add the following field as the first field in the record, just before the `FIRST` name field. Place the cursor on the `FIRST` name field. Choose **Structure | Insert field** or press **Ctr-N** to insert a new line above the current line. You can also delete a field from the Structure menu or press **Ctrl-U**.

```
CUST_NO      Character     4
```

2. Increase the length of the `CITY` field to 15.
3. Add the following fields after the `PHONE` field:

```
CHARGE       Character     1
NO_RENTS     Numeric       3
AMT_RENT     Numeric       7     2
```

Care should be taken when modifying the structure. For example, if a field length and name are both changed, data could be lost. Visual dBASE automatically makes a backup of your table prior to saving the new structure. Only those fields that are still in the structure can be copied back when the modification is complete. A field name and length change of the same field should be done in two passes. Save the modifications to the Table

Structure window using any of the methods described above after the original structure was created.

APPENDING THE TABLE

Appending Records from the Keyboard. **To add records from the keyboard, enter the following command sequence from the Command window:**

```
DISPLAY STRUCTURE
APPEND
```

It is a good idea to display the structure of your table after making changes to verify that all changes have been made properly. The modified table structure should now be displayed in the Results pane. You may need to resize the Command window for this display. The **APPEND** command allows you to add records to the table. As you enter commands from the Command window, you will be working either in a *design* mode or in a *data* mode. The **CREATE** command placed you in a design work surface. The **APPEND** command places you in data mode screen for adding records to the open table.

The initial format of the Table Records window for data entry from **APPEND** will be the Form Layout. Records can also be added to the open table using the Column Layout or the Browse Layout format (see Figure 3.5). Press **F2** to toggle between the different layouts. For this exercise, toggle to the Form Layout and enter the record shown in Figure 3.6. When complete, the Form Layout Table Records window should appear as in Figure 3.7. Use **Tab/Shift-Tab** to move from field to field.

To save and exit, double click on the Control-menu box of the in the upper left-hand corner of the Table Records window.

Appending Records from Another Table. In addition to appending records from the keyboard, you can append a table from another table. You will need the data diskette provided with this textbook to execute the **APPEND FROM** command. Place the diskette into drive A, then enter the following command sequence from the Command window:

```
APPEND FROM a:zcustm   && Or b: drive if applicable
LIST
```

The structure of the two tables must be the same. The **APPEND FROM** command will copy all the records in **zcustm** to **ycustm**. This will give you a complete table to work with through the remainder of the exercises.

The **LIST** command without options will list the entire table. Don't be concerned at this point that the display of each record may be wider than the Results pane of the Command window.

FIGURE 3.5 LAYOUT WINDOWS FOR APPENDING RECORDS

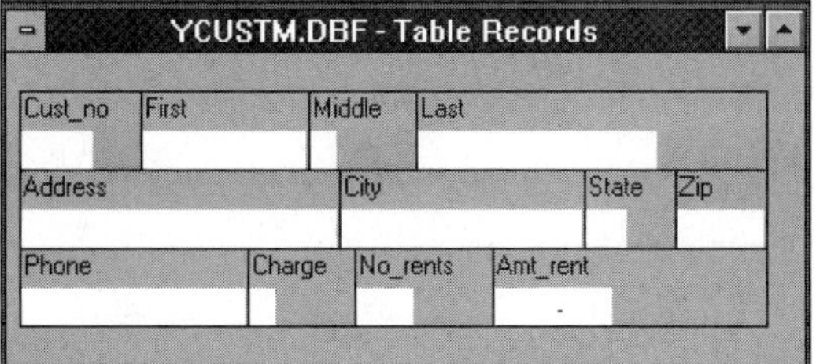

Form Layout

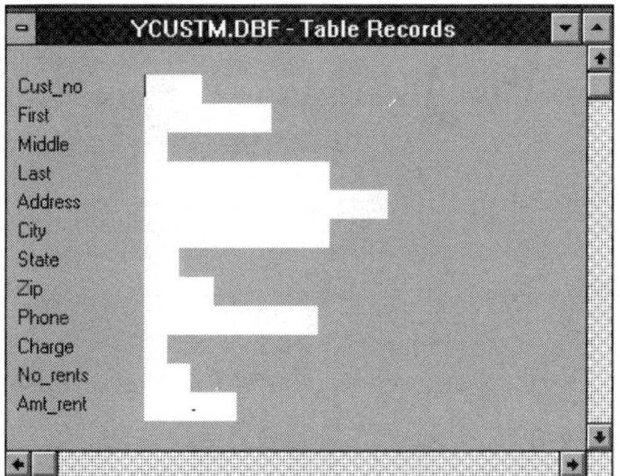

Column Layout

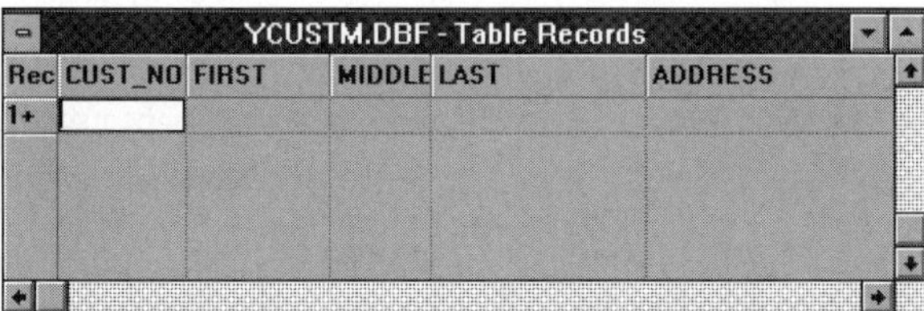

Browse Layout

FIGURE 3.6 INPUT RECORD--CUSTOMER MASTER TABLE

```
CUST_NO:      0001
FIRST:        Robert
MIDDLE:       K
```

```
LAST:           Bowers
ADDRESS:        3149 Los Prados
CITY:           Bakersfield
STATE:          CA
ZIP:            91001
PHONE:          (818) 927-1175
CHARGE:         M
NO_RENTS:       12
AMT_RENT:       51.35
```

FIGURE 3.7 COMPLETED EDIT/APPEND WINDOW

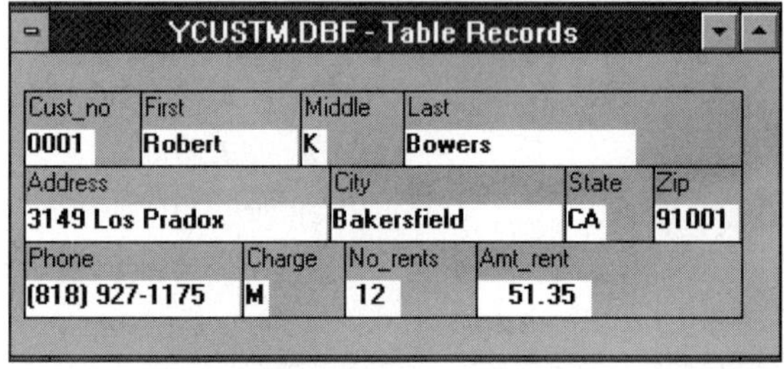

LISTING THE TABLE

For this exercise, you may again need to resize the Command window. Type the following command sequence from the Command window:

```
LIST OFF cust_no, last, first, amt_rent, amt_rent*1.10
LIST cust_no, last, city FOR city = "San Mateo"
GOTO 10
LIST NEXT 11 cust_no, city, amt_rent, charge
     FOR city = "San Mateo" .AND. charge = "V"
```

The first **LIST** command lists all the records in the table but only selected fields within each record. The **OFF** option suppresses the record number.

The second **LIST** command adds a condition. Only records containing customers living in San Mateo are listed. When each record meeting the condition is listed, only selected fields from within that record are listed.

The next two commands move the pointer to the 10th record and then list records 10 through 20 for individuals from San Mateo who have `V` (Visa) as a charge method.

INTRODUCTION TO THE CASE SYSTEM

As you do the exercises in this book, you build a complete, programmed system. The Case System involves the partial automation of certain accounting subsystems of a small video rental store. We develop only the initial segment in this book. It should provide the following:

- A banner about screen
- A password-protected menu system
- Custom **APPEND** (add) screen
- Custom editor capabilities
- Custom reporting
- A system utilities menu

In broad terms, the owner has asked you to develop a database management system to handle the maintenance of the customer master file, sales file, and film inventory file. There are also a few marketing and management information reports needed periodically.

As we move through the chapters of the book, we discuss new concepts. Using those concepts, you then build and appropriate module for the Case System. In this chapter, we develop the three database tables used by the system.

REVIEW EXERCISES

The purpose of these exercises is to build the remaining two tables needed in the Case System. Besides the customer master table, the system will require a film table and a sales table. These tables will store the film inventory and sales against that inventory.

PART 1: BUILD AND LIST THE FILM TABLE

1. From the Command window, **CREATE** a table with the following specifications:

- Name the table **yfilm**
- Build the structure as follows:

Field Name	Type	Width	Dec
FILM_NO	Character	4	
RATING	Character	1	
TITLE	Character	32	
TIMES	Numeric	0	
PRICE	Numeric	5	2

2. **DISPLAY** the structure to verify it has been developed properly.

3. **APPEND** the database table from the keyboard with the following record:

```
FILM_NO.:  0001
RATING..:  G
TITLE...:  Best Friends
TIMES...:  0
PRICE...:  3.95
```

4. **APPEND** the table **FROM zfilm.dbf**, which is provided on your student work disk.

5. **LIST** to the Results pane the entire database table.

6. **LIST** only the records containing G-rated films.

7. **LIST** only the records containing H-rated films within the scope of the first 25 records.

PART II: BUILD AND LIST THE SALES FILE

1. From the Command window, **CREATE** a table with the following specifications:
   - Name the table **ysales**.
   - Build the structure as follows:

Field Name	Type	Width
CUST_NO	Character	4
DATE	Date	8
FILM_NO	Character	4
RETURNED	Logical	1

2. **DISPLAY** the structure to verify it has been developed properly.

3. **APPEND** the table from the keyboard with the following record:

```
CUST_NO..:   0011
DATE.....:   01/10/96
```

```
FILM_NO..:   0037
RETURNED.:   T
```

4. `APPEND` the table `FROM zsales.dbf`, which is provided on your student work disk.

5. `LIST` the entire table.

6. `LIST` only the records representing February transactions.

7. `LIST` only the records representing films not yet returned (for `returned = .F.`) for the month of February.

The two tables developed here are part of the Case System. In Chapter 13, all three tables will be linked to form a multidimensional database.

CHAPTER SUMMARY

In this chapter, we introduced the syntax of the Visual dBASE commands. The following topics were discussed:

- Command syntax has the following five components: verb, scope, noun, condition, and miscellaneous option.
- An important segment of a command is the expression. Visual dBASE uses numeric, character, dates, and logical expressions as part of its command syntax.

The following commands were discussed and used:

- `SET DIRECTORY`
- `CREATE`
- `SET EXCLUSIVE`
- `USE`
- `DISPLAY STRUCTURE`
- `MODIFY STRUCTURE`
- `APPEND`
- `APPEND FROM`
- `LIST`
- `GOTO`

In the next chapter, we begin our discussion or programming using the command syntax of Visual dBASE.

PART TWO

Fundamentals of dBASE Programming

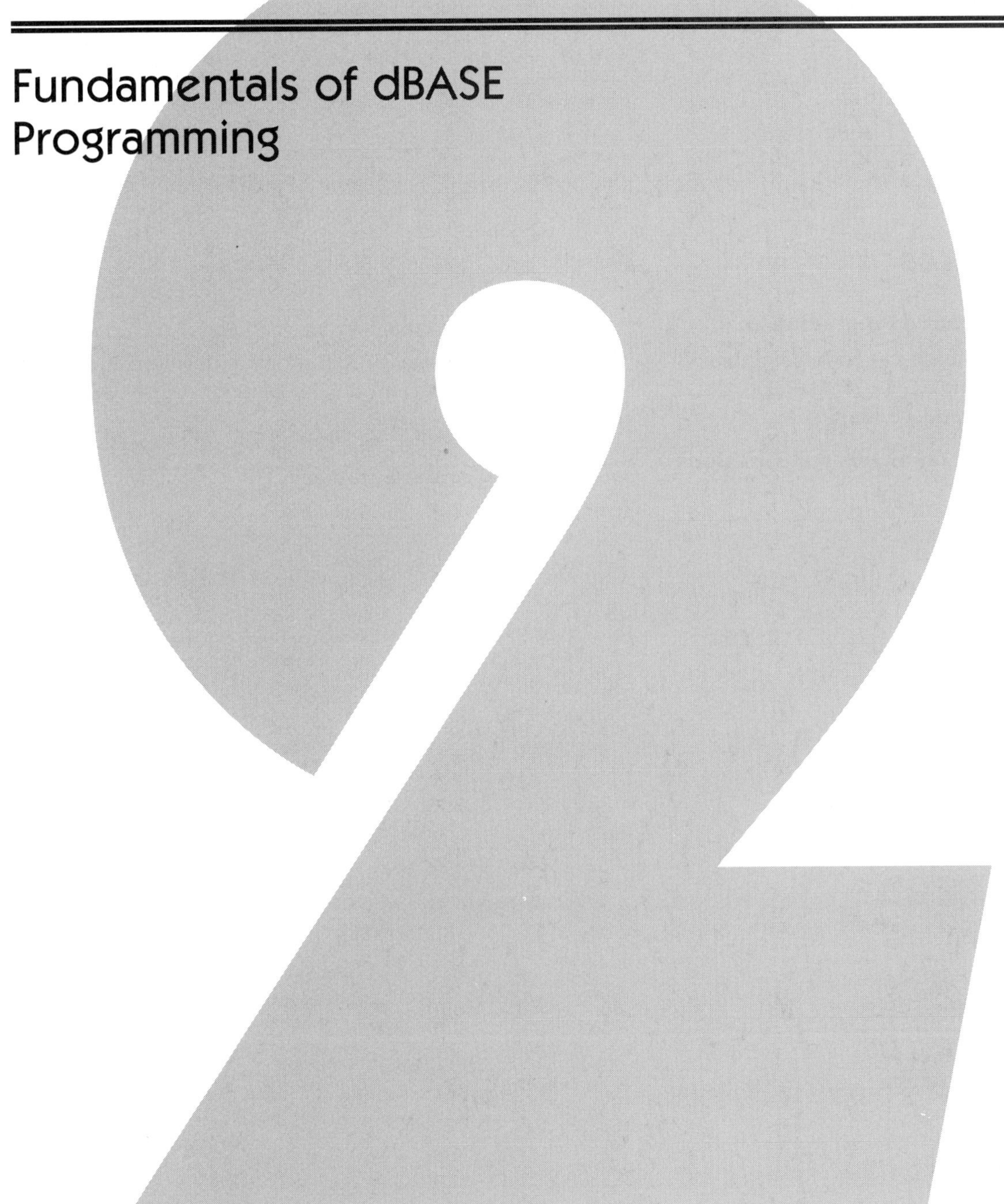

CHAPTER FOUR

TOPICS

Structured Programming

The structured building blocks
Single entry, single exit
Pseudocode

New Commands and Functions

Concepts

Visual dBASE program development cycle
Program documentation

Review Exercises

Chapter Summary

Introduction to Visual dBASE Programming Syntax

CHAPTER OBJECTIVES

In this chapter, we introduce Visual dBASE programming concepts and syntax. The objective is to learn and begin structured procedural programming with the building blocks of process, looping, and logic in a single program module. We also introduce and demonstrate Visual dBASE control statements supporting the building blocks. In Part III of this text, we will introduce object-oriented programming, trace its evolution, and discuss the integration of structured and object-oriented programming into Visual dBASE.

After studying this chapter, you should be able to understand and use the building blocks of structured programming. The final exercise will ultimately become part of the Case System and demonstrate the inclusion of a structured module into an otherwise windowed, object-based system.

STRUCTURED PROGRAMMING

The last time I had a television set repaired, I watched as the technician simply replaced a modular circuit board. No longer do technicians need to search through a maze of wires resembling a bowl of spaghetti to find the problem. Fortunately, the advantages of modular design have affected not only electronic design but also computer programming.

Structured programming is a technique devised to break a program down into modules. Within each module, the programmer can solve problem segments using the control structures offered by the program syntax. The benefits of structured programming techniques are that a program module is easier to design, code, test, and modify.

THE STRUCTURED BUILDING BLOCKS

The syntax culprit in earlier languages was the GOTO statement. It allowed the programmer to go to any part of a program from any other part of that program. The logic diagrams of unstructured programs resembled the maze of wires in the earlier television sets. In fact, some larger unstructured programs have been referred to as spaghetti programs. Traditional languages such as BASIC, FORTRAN, and COBOL have a GOTO statement, but Visual dBASE does not. (There is a `GOTO` pointer movement command but none to move program control.)

Structured languages such as Visual dBASE provide three control structures that have been found to be mathematically sufficient to solve all problems: (1) process, (2) logic (also referred to as selection or choice), and (3) loop (iteration). They are called the structured building blocks.

1. **Process:** Process occurs when procedures are executed step by step. Process 1 is followed by process 2, process 2 by process 3, and so on.
2. **Logic (selection):** Logic syntax gives the ability to make selections based on conditions. For example, a Visual dBASE logic structure is the `IF..ELSE` construct. *IF* a certain condition is true, *THEN* one process will occur, *ELSE* another process will occur—but not both.
3. **Loop (iteration):** The loop building block allows the programmer the ability to accomplish repetitive tasks. For example, the Visual dBASE `SCAN..ENDSCAN` control structure allows the examination of the first record in a table and then repeats the process for each record until the end of file has been reached.

SINGLE ENTRY, SINGLE EXIT

Another concept of structured programming is single entry, single exit. In keeping with the modular concept, the syntax of a structured language will allow only one entry point into a logic or loop construct or into a process and only one exit point. This eliminates the temptation to branch or jump to another point in the program.

In addition, it is good practice to have only a single point of entry into each program module within a system and to have only a single entry–exit point into and from the system itself. We discuss this concept in greater detail as you begin programming the Case System.

PSEUDOCODE

Probably the most often asked question when beginning a new program is, "Where do I begin?" The concept of pseudocode became popular as structured programming was gaining popularity. Rather than diagramming the logic of a program as a way of getting started, we develop pseudocode. It is similar to writing a report. Using the English language instead of dBASE code, the outline is sketched in and then the subtopics.

NEW COMMANDS AND FUNCTIONS

At this point, we provide only that portion of the syntax of the commands required for the solution of the Case System. The remaining portions of syntax we discuss in later chapters, as needed. Appendix A lists the full syntax of all commands. Appendix B lists all functions.

Do not attempt to enter the commands provided in the following summary of commands and functions, just scan the description and examples of each. Later in the chapter, you enter all the commands into actual programs using the program editor.

COMMAND `?/?? [<expression1>], [<expression2>. . .], [ , ]`

Displays the evaluated expression or list of expressions on the screen or echoed to the printer. The single ? command causes a carriage return and line feed, and then the expression list prints. The double `??` command is the same without the carriage return and linefeed. Each expression is separated by a comma. The comma will create one blank space between the evaluated expressions unless the `SET SPACE` command is toggled `ON`.

EXAMPLE

```
x  = 50
?  x, x * 1.10, x * 1.20, x * 1.50
         50         50            60     75
```

Each item in the list is an expression. It is evaluated and then displayed as part of the print list.

COMMAND

```
NOTE/* <comment text>
and
[<command>] && <comment text>
```

Denotes a comment within a program. Coding either of the first two forms, **NOTE** or *****, as the first character within a line allows the remainder of the line to be a comment. The second form, **&&**, allows a comment to follow a dBASE command.

EXAMPLE

```
NOTE This is a program to compute the value x.
* ==== > Any character following an * is considered
*         a program comment for documentation purposes.
? x       && Print the value of x.
```

The first three lines of this sample program will be ignored by dBASE at execution time. The comment after the **&&** in the fourth line will also be ignored.

COMMAND

```
DO WHILE <condition>
  <commands>
  [LOOP]
  [EXIT]
ENDDO
```

This control structure is one of the loop building blocks. It will process commands between the **DO WHILE** and the **ENDDO** until the condition stated in the **DO WHILE** evaluates to false. The condition is a logic expression **<expL>**. See Figure 4.1.

- The **LOOP** option moves control back to the **DO WHILE**. This is necessary in structured commands for those situations where you do not want to move all the way down to the **ENDDO** to loop back up for the **DO WHILE** evaluation of the logic expression. (For example, if bad data is discovered, you will want to return to the **DO WHILE** for corrected data rather than processing the bad data.)
- The **EXIT** option moves control to the statement just after the **ENDDO**. This allows exit from the **DO WHILE** loop at any point rather than at the **DO WHILE** evaluation.

We give an example using **LOOP** and **EXIT** in this discussion of commands after introducing the **IF..ELSE** control structure.

FIGURE 4.1 DO WHILE..ENDDO CONTROL STRUCTURE

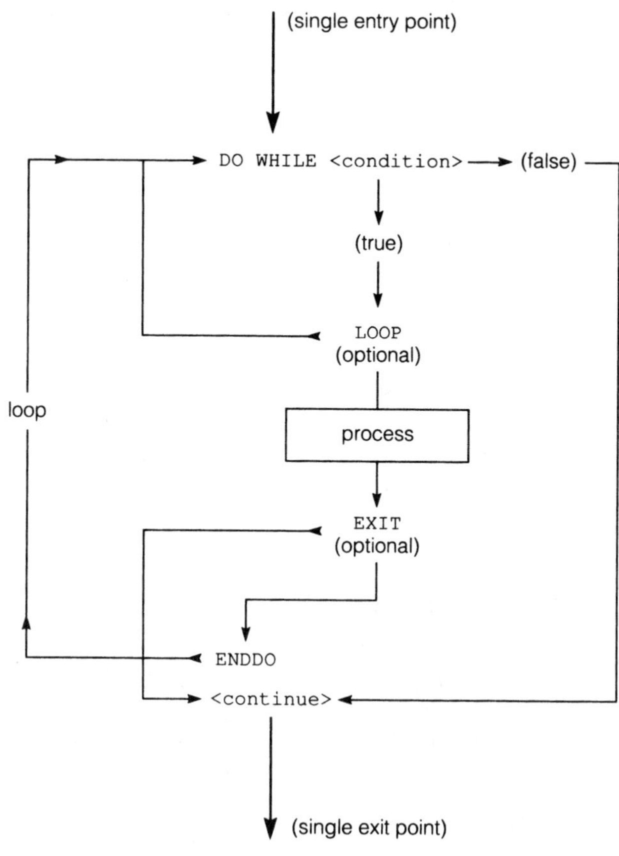

DO WHILE EXAMPLES

```
* ==== > A counting DO WHILE!
x = 0
DO WHILE x < 20
   x = x + 1
   ? x
ENDDO && x < 20
? "I am done counting!"
* ==== > End of program.
```

This **DO WHILE** introduces a counting technique. The initial value of **x** is set to zero just before executing the **DO WHILE**. The first time through the loop, the **DO WHILE** condition will be true (**x**, zero at this point, is less than 20). Therefore the process following the **DO WHILE** will be executed. Once inside the loop, the value of **x** is increased by 1 and then displayed on the screen. The next line executed is the **ENDDO**. The **ENDDO** *always* returns control to the **DO WHILE**.

The **DO WHILE** then evaluates the expression a second time. It will again evaluate to true (**x**, **1** at this point, is still less than 20), so the process will be executed again. This process will continue until **x** is equal to 20. The **DO WHILE** expression will then evaluate to false, causing control to transfer to the statement just after the **ENDDO** (the final **?** statement). Note the command line comment just after the **ENDDO** statement. This is handy to keep track of which **ENDDO** belongs to which **DO WHILE**.

It is possible to place a **DO WHILE** inside another **DO WHILE**. This is called nesting. Note the following segment.

```
* ==== > Another counting DO WHILE
x=0
y=0
DO WHILE x < 20
   DO WHILE y < 10
     y = y + 1
     ? y
   ENDDO && y < 10
   x = x  + 1
   ? x
ENDDO && x < 20
? ==== > End of program.
```

The outside **DO WHILE** (**x < 20**) will evaluate to true the first time through this program segment. Control will then move to the statement just inside the first **DO WHILE**, which is the next **DO WHILE**. It will be evaluated, just as the first was evaluated. The inside loop example will be repeated 10 times each time the outside loop is repeated. The number of loops inside loops (nesting) is limited only by available memory.

While nesting, each **DO WHILE** must be totally contained in the next highest level **DO WHILE**. The following is an example of improper nesting:

```
* ==== > Illegal Nesting.
┌── DO WHILE x < 10
│     ┌DO WHILE y < 20
└── ENDDO && x < 10
      └ENDDO && y < 20
```

This is illegal because the inside **DO WHILE** (**y < 20**) is not totally contained within the outside **DO WHILE** (**x < 10**). To correct it, the last **ENDDO** (**&&y < 20**) would have to be moved inside the **ENDDO** of the outside loop (**&&x < 10**).

NOTE: Though the DO WHILE..ENDDO is the traditional loop construct of the dBASE language, the SCAN..ENDSCAN and FOR..NEXT constructs are more efficient in most coding situations. They will be discussed and demonstrated in Chapter 6.

COMMAND

```
DO
    <commands>
    LOOP]
    EXIT]
UNTIL <condition>
```

Processes commands between the **DO** and the **UNTIL** clause until the condition stated in the **UNTIL** evaluates to true. The **LOOP** and **EXIT** clauses operate the same as in the **DO..WHILE** construct. This command will always process the commands between the **DO** and **UNTIL** at least once, whereas in the **DO..WHILE**, they may not be processed at all. This is because the condition to leave the loop is stated after the processing of the loop commands rather than before. In the following example, the **DO..UNTIL** loop will only execute one time.

EXAMPLE

```
xValue = 1
DO
    ? xValue
    xValue = xValue + 1
UNTIL x = 2
```

COMMAND

```
IF <condition
    <commands>
ENDIF
```

This is the first logic (selection) building block to be introduced. The construct is used if you want to either select or not select a process. If the expression evaluates to true, the ensuing process commands will be executed. If it evaluates to false, control moves to the **ENDIF** statement. The **ENDIF** *always* passes control to the next instruction in sequence; it does not loop back to the **IF** statement. See Figure 4.2.

EXAMPLE

```
* ==== > An IF statement inside a DO WHILE.
x = 0
DO WHILE x < 100
    x = x + 1
    IF x = 50
        ? " I'm half done!!!"
    ENDIF
ENDDO
? "Program segment complete."
* ==== > End of program segment.
```

In this example, the operator is notified by the program when it is halfway through the loop. Each time through the loop, the value of **x** is incremented, and then the **IF** expression is evaluated. When the expression evaluates to true (**x** is equal to 50), the **?** command displays the **"I'm half done!!!"** message on the screen.

FIGURE 4.2 IF..ENDIF CONTROL STRUCTURE

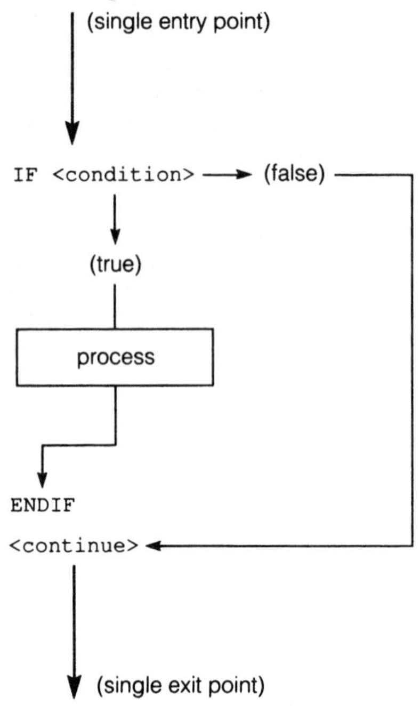

COMMAND

```
IF <condition>
  <commands for process A>
ELSE
  <commands for process B>
ENDIF
```

This logic building block control structure is used when you want to select either one process or a second process. It might read: "**IF** the condition is true, then do the first process, **ELSE** do the second process" (see Figure 4.3).

If the expression evaluates to true, process A will be executed, and then control moves to the **ENDIF**. If the expression evaluates to false, control moves to the **ELSE**, process B is executed, and then control moves to the **ENDIF**. Whenever an **ENDIF** is executed, control moves to the next instruction in sequence after the **ENDIF**. (Remember, don't try to make the **ENDIF** loop—that's the function of the **DO WHILE**, **DO..UNTIL**, or **SCAN** commands.)

EXAMPLE

```
* ==== > This program segment will demonstrate the
*        LOOP and EXIT syntax from within a DO WHILE.
DO WHILE .T.
   xinput = 0
   <commands to input value of xinput from keyboard>
   IF xinput > 500
      LOOP
   ELSE
      EXIT
   ENDIF
ENDDO && .T.
* ==== > Input validated -- continue.
<commands to process xinput>
* ==== > End of program segment.
```

FIGURE 4.3 IF..ELSE..ENDIF CONTROL STRUCTURE

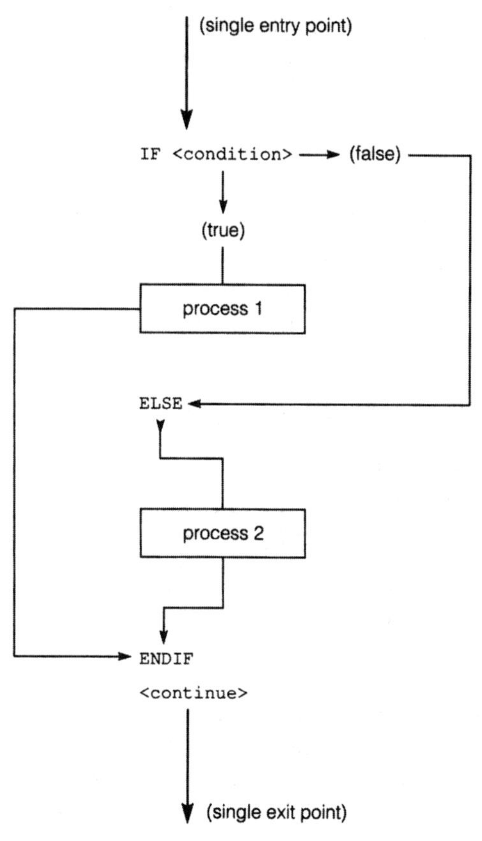

This is the type of segment a programmer might use to validate input from the keyboard. The expression in the **DO WHILE** is a logical constant of **.T.** and will always evaluate to true. It is used when you want to exit from within the loop and never at the **DO WHILE** statement. We haven't yet introduced commands to receive input from the keyboard, but we assume that just inside the **DO WHILE** a memory variable **xinput** is established by setting it equal to 0. The ensuing commands will allow an operator to replace the current value of 0 with a value from the keyboard. The **IF** expression will then test the contents of **xinput** to determine if it is greater than 500. If the expression is true, the **LOOP** command will return control to the **DO WHILE** (Figure 4.1). If the expression is false, control moves to the **ELSE** process, which executes the **EXIT** command, moving control to the statement just after the **ENDDO**.

When more than two alternatives are possible, **IF..ELSE**s can be nested.

EXAMPLE

```
* ==== > Nested IF..ELSEs
IF x = "1"
   ? "process no. 1"
   <commands>
ELSE
   IF x = "2"
      ? "process no. 2"
     <commands>
   ELSE
      ? "process no. 3"
      <commands>
   ENDIF
ENDIF
* ==== > End of program segment.
```

In the preceding example, further nesting could be used to achieve more than three options. However, this is not considered a good idea. The following **DO CASE** construct is a much better way to accomplish this.

COMMAND

```
DO CASE
   CASE <condition>
      <commands>
   CASE <condition>
      <commands>
   CASE <condition>
      <commands>
   OTHERWISE
      <commands>
ENDCASE
```

The **DO CASE** allows the selection of one course of action from a number of alternatives. Use this command if there are three or more alternatives. The two advantages the **DO CASE** has over nested **IF..ELSE**s are speed and less complex code. The **DO CASE** is easier to understand once coded and is more efficient when executed. See Figure 4.4.

FIGURE 4.4 THE DOCASE..ENDCASE CONTROL STRUCTURE

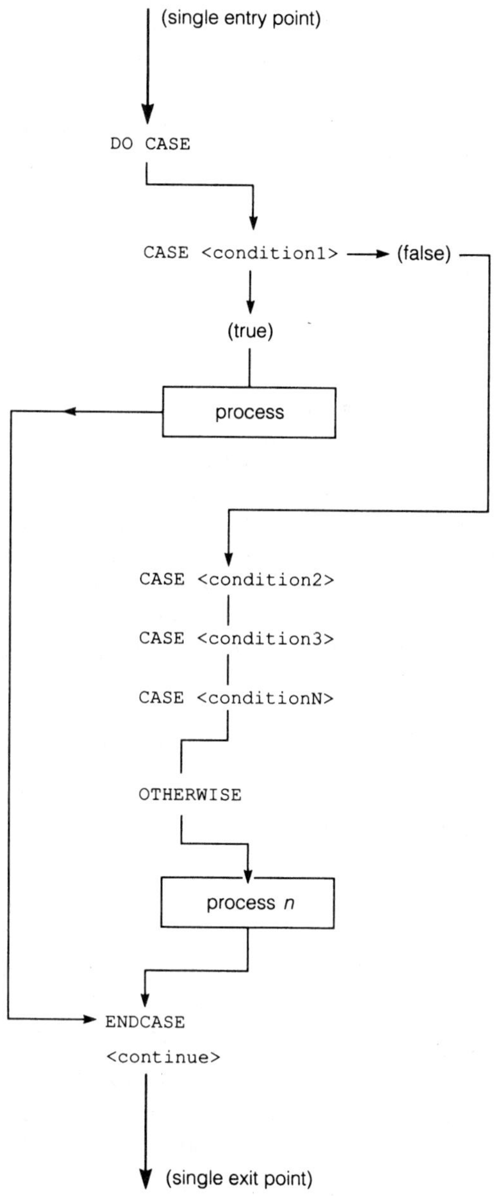

EXAMPLE

```
* ==== > A DO CASE nested inside a DO WHILE.
x = 1
DO WHILE x < 100
   DO CASE
      CASE x = 25
         ? "X is 25--I'm 1/4 finished."
      CASE x = 50
         ? "X is 50--I'm 1/2 finished."
      CASE x = 75
         ? "X is 75--I'm 3/4 finished."
      OTHERWISE
         ? x
   ENDCASE
     x = x + 1
ENDDO
? "Finished!"
* ==== > End of program segment.
```

In this example, the **OTHERWISE** clause is coded to represent (catch) the most frequent situation, and the **CASE** clauses are the exceptions. It could be the opposite in other routines. For example, a menu system is another use of the **DO CASE**. The operator selects an item, say 1 through 5, from the menu. The **DO CASE** in your program will then process that input value and select the proper routine to execute. The **OTHERWISE** option would be used to catch illegal responses. In the next chapter, you develop a main menu system for the Case System.

COMMAND `GO/GOTO BOTTOM/TOP or GO/GOTO <record number>`

Positions pointer to a specific record, either by record number or to the top or bottom of a table.

EXAMPLES

```
USE ycustm
GOTO 5                  && Move pointer to record number 5.
GO 10                   && Move pointer to record number 10.
15                      && Move pointer to record number 15.
GO TOP                  && Move pointer to first record.
GO BOTTOM               && Move pointer to last record.
```

Notice the example to move to record 15. Though it is not such a good idea from a documentation standpoint, you *can* code just the record number. This is especially useful from the Command window.

COMMAND `SKIP [<expN>]`

Moves the record pointer forward or backward in a table.

EXAMPLES

```
USE ycustm
SKIP          && Move pointer 1 record forward.
SKIP +15      && Move pointer 15 records forward.
SKIP -10      && Move pointer backward 10 records.
n = 5
SKIP n        && Move pointer 5 records forward.
```

COMMAND **CLEAR**

Clears the Results pane and homes the cursor. This command accomplishes the same thing as the DOS **CLS** instruction. It does not clear files, memory variables, and the like—just the Results pane.

COMMAND **SET TALK ON/off**

Toggles the talking feature **ON** or **OFF**. Visual dBASE responds to each command by displaying the evaluated expression. Usually, **TALK** is **OFF** within a program and **ON** in the Command window.

NOTE: The default toggle of each SET command is shown in uppercase in the command syntax.

COMMAND **MODIFY COMMAND/FILE <filename>**

Causes entry into the Visual dBASE full-screen editor. Though used primarily for program (**.prg**) file development, it can be used to develop any text file. If no extension is supplied, the default **.prg** extension is supplied. If no extension is desired, the **MODIFY FILE** form of the verb is used.

COMMAND **DO <program filename>**

Executes a dBASE command file. If the source file has not been compiled, the **DO** command parses it (deletes unnecessary blank lines, spaces, and comments and checks command syntax) and then compiles it into an object (**.pro**) file. The **.pro** file is then executed. In Chapter 7, we will also use the **DO** command to compile and execute a Windows form file.

COMMAND **SET DEVELOPMENT ON/off**

If toggled **ON**, activates a checking system that compares the time and date of the **.pro** file to its associated **.prg** file. If they are different, the **.pro** file will be deleted so that a current object file can be compiled. This makes it easier for a programmer to use an editor other than **MODIFY COMMAND** (which automatically deletes the last **.pro** file).

FUNCTION **EOF( )**

Indicates the end of file. This function returns a logical **.T.** when the pointer has passed the last record in the active table.

EXAMPLE
```
USE ycustm
GO BOTTOM
? EOF()
 .F.
SKIP
? EOF()
 .T.
```

FUNCTION `UPPER()`

Returns the uppercase of the argument to the expression for evaluation.

EXAMPLE
```
name = "christie"
? UPPER(name)
CHRISTIE
```

CONCEPTS

VISUAL dBASE PROGRAM DEVELOPMENT CYCLE

In this section, we begin developing structured programs. To become familiar with the program development cycle, we write a small program using the following four steps:

1. Program coding
2. Saving program to disk
3. Program testing
4. Rerun after testing

Program Coding. Visual dBASE has a built-in editor primarily for developing computer programs. We use it in this chapter to develop program file with a `.prg` extension. In Chapter 6, we will use it to edit windows form object programs developed using the Visual dBASE forms designer. You can invoke the editor either from the Input pane or from the Navigator. To begin our first programming exercise, type the following command from the Input pane:

```
MODI COMM mTest
```

NOTE: We have abbreviated the command verb `MODIFY COMMAND`. From the Input pane, it is necessary only to type the first four characters of any Visual dBASE reserved word used in a command. However, do not abbreviate reserved words when writing a program. Though the program would execute properly, it is not a good documentation practice.

This command opens the Program Editor window with an empty text file, `ytest.prg`. Your screen should appear as in Figure 4.5. You can move/resize the window as appropriate prior to entering a program. Table 4.1 contains a summary of the most often used editor keystrokes and Speedbar icons available when editing a program from the Program Editor window.

TABLE 4.1 CREATE/MODIFY COMMAND EDITOR KEYSTROKES

Keystroke	Function
Home or **End**	Moves cursor to beginning or end of line
Tab or **Shift Tab**	Moves cursor to next or previous tb stop
Ctrl–PgUp or **PgDn**	Moves cursor to beginning or end of file
PgDn or **PgDn**	Moves cursor to beginning or end of screen
F1	Help
F10	Accesses menu system
Del	Deletes character under cursor
Backspace	Deletes character to left of cursor
Ctrl–T	Deletes word under cursor
Ctrl–Y	Deletes a line
Ctrl–N	Inserts a blank line
Ctrl–W	Exits and saves file
Ctrl–Q or **ESCape**	Aborts edit without saving changes
	Create a new file
	Open a file
	Save this file
	Print from the active window
	Cut selected text, save to clipboard
	Copy selected text to clipboard
	Insert clipboard text at insertion point
	Find specified text
	Find and replace specified text
	Enter expression builder
	Execute current command or block of commands
	Execute a program
	Debug a program

FIGURE 4.5 PROGRAM EDITOR WINDOW

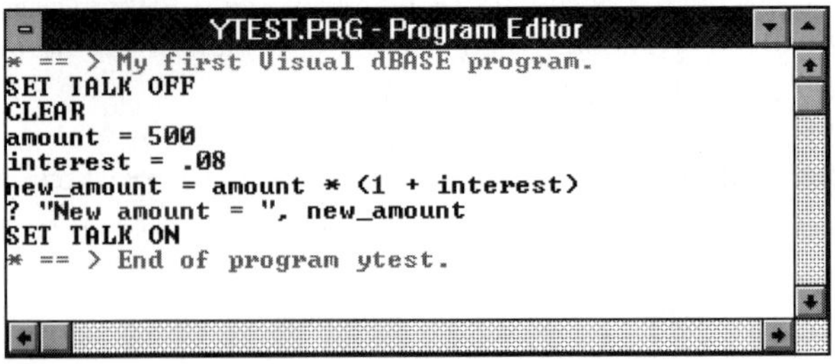

YTEST.PRG - Program Editor

```
* == > My first Visual dBASE program.
SET TALK OFF
CLEAR
amount = 500
interest = .08
new_amount = amount * (1 + interest)
? "New amount = ", new_amount
SET TALK ON
* == > End of program ytest.
```

Type the following program statements into the editor:

```
* == > My first Visual dBASE program.
SET TALK OFF
CLEAR
amount = 500
interest = .08
new_amount = amount * (1 +  interest)
? "New amount = ", new_amount
SET TALK ON
* == > End of program ytest.
```

NOTE: Notice the **Auto Colors** feature of the editor as you enter commands. Comments will be gray, commands black, and literals (constants) will be blue. When typing a character constant, each character will be red until delimiters are properly placed. You can turn this feature off from the Program Editor Properties dialog box together with word wrap, auto indent, right margin, line spacing, and editor font. To make these changes, select **Properties | Program Editor Properties** while the program editor is open.

Saving Program to Disk. It is a good idea to visually check your program at this stage. If it appears correct, save it to the disk using any of the following techniques (notice these are the same keystrokes used to exit and save from the Table Structure window):

- Double-click the Program Editor window Control-menu box
- Choose **File** | **Save** and close
- Press **Ctrl-W**

You should save your work to disk periodically to avoid data loss due to a power failure or similar problem. To do this from the program editor, choose **File** | **Save as**. You can also use this feature to retrieve a file, modify it, and then save it to disk using a different filename. The original file is unaltered.

Program Testing. Next, test the program with the DO command. When the DO command is executed, Visual dBASE first develops an *object* code file. You initially placed the dBASE commands in a `.prg` file, which is referred to as the source code file. dBASE converts that *source* code into a form that can be executed by the computer and places that code into the object file. The object code file has a `.pro` extension and is executed by the DO command.

To begin the first test of `ytest.prg`, type the following command from the Input pane:

```
DO ytest
```

If your program runs properly, the following results should be displayed in the Results pane:

```
New amount = 540.00
```

Rerun After Testing. The next step in the programming cycle is to correct any errors. If Visual dBASE encounters a problem during compilation of your source code, the Program Alert dialog box will appear on the screen (see Figure 4.6). Notice that you have a **Fix** option that will return you to the line of code in the Program Editor that is causing the problem. Once you have corrected it, you can save and exit once again to continue with compilation and program execution. If you do not want to fix the problem, you can **Ignore**, **Suspend**, **Debug**, or **Cancel** the edit and return control to the Visual dBASE desktop. **Ignore** will bypass the code in question and continue attempting a compilation of the source code. **Suspend** returns control to the Input pane, but does not close the program file. This will allow tests from the Input pane, such as current variable values and open file status. **Debug** transfers control to an internal testing utility that is discussed in detail in Appendix C. **Cancel** closes the program file and returns control to the Input pane.

NOTE: Errors may occur either during the compile process or at runtime. If a compile error occurs, **Suspend** and **Debug** are not available from the Program Alert window (as in the "Unterminated string" error demonstrated in Figure 4.6). The program can be suspended or debugged with the Visual dBASE debugger only during runtime execution.

FIGURE 4.6 PROGRAM ALERT DIALOG BOX

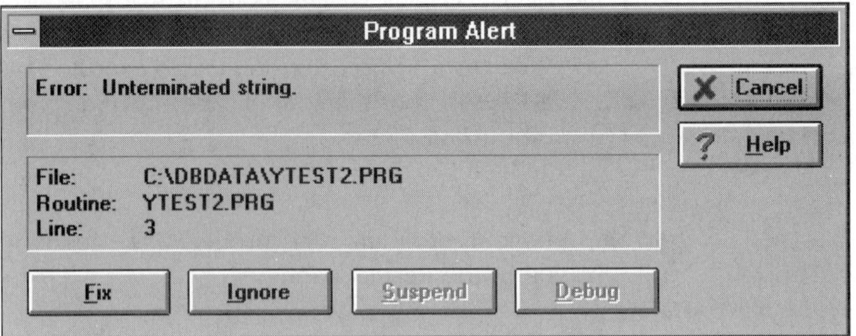

To demonstrate the use of the Program Alert dialog box, we will develop another short test program—and purposely place a bug within it. For this test, we will enter the Program Editor through the Navigator by performing the following sequence of operations:

1. From the Visual dBASE desktop, be sure that both the Navigator and Command windows are maximized.
2. Give the Navigator window focus.
3. Click the Programs icon from the icon list on the left-hand side of the navigator. Notice that an Untitled program icon and the `ytest.prg` program icon are now present in the Program Files list.
4. Double-click on the Untitled icon. The Program Editor window should now appear on your desktop.
5. Enter the following code into the editor—including the missing delimiter error:

```
SET TALK OFF
CLEAR
?"Hello World      && Omit the right delimiter
SET TALK ON
```

6. Save and exit by pressing **Ctrl-W**. At this point you will be asked to supply a program name. Call the program `ytest2.prg`.
7. From the Navigator, right-click on the `ytest2.prg` icon that now appears in the Program Files list. This will cause the Program Editor Speed menu to appear (see Figure 4.7). You can delete the program, execute a `DO` command, enter the debugger, return to the editor, or observe the current properties dialog box about the program. The debugger is discussed in detail in Appendix C.

FIGURE 4.7 PROGRAM EDITOR SPEED MENU

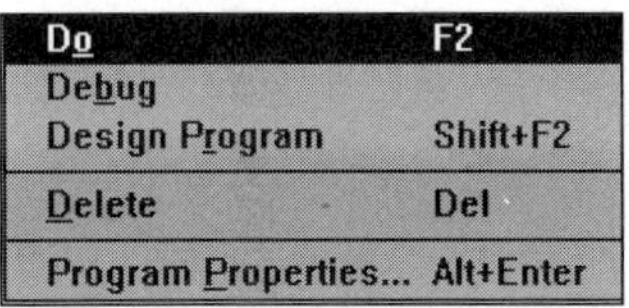

8. From the Program Editor Speed Menu, click on `DO`. dBASE for Windows will now attempt to run **`ytest2.prg`**. When the compiler encounters the missing delimiter bug, the Program Alert dialog box will appear (see Figure 4.6).

9. Choose **Fix** from the Program Alert menu. When control moves back to the Program Editor, place the missing right quote mark after the character string, **`Hello World`**. The string will turn blue when correct.

10. Choose **Program|DO** from the menu system. This will compile, execute, and return focus to the Command window in one step, rather than saving and then executing the `DO` from the Input pane. You can also compile without executing from the same menu if you want to complete a syntax check prior to executing the object file. After the compile, the Compilation Status window will appear (see Figure 4.8).

FIGURE 4.8 COMPILATION STATUS WINDOW

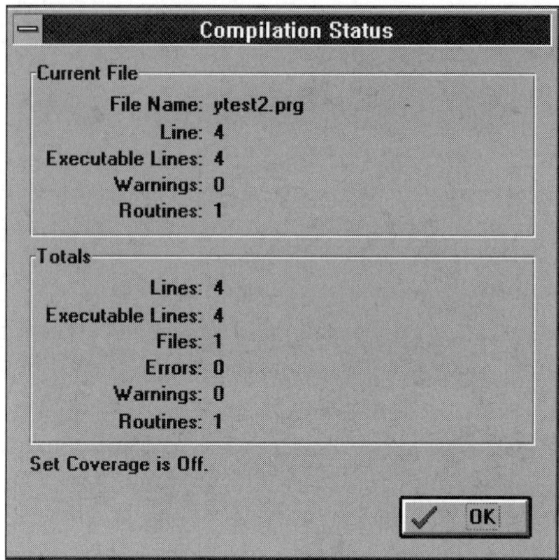

Finally, Speedbar icons can be used to compile and execute programs from the program editor. The following exercise will demonstrate this capability:

1. If the Program Editor is not already open with `ytest2.prg`, open it now—either from the Navigator or from the Input pane with `MODI COMM ytest2.prg`.

2. Notice the five program editor icons in the center of the Speedbar just above the Program Editor window (see Figure 4.5). The flashlight icon is used to find text within the editor. To its right is the find and replace text icon. The bug icon on the far right of center transfers control to Debug, the internal debugger utility.

3. To the left of the bug icon are the two lightning bolt icons. The genie lamp lightning bolt icon on the left will compile and execute a single line of code. For example, place the insertion point cursor on the `? "Hello World"` line of code—then click on the genie lamp icon. Each time you do this, `Hello World` appears in the Results pane. You may have to resize and/or move the Program Editor window to see the results. You could also give focus to the Command window after each icon mouse click to see the results.

4. Click the lightning bolt icon to the right of the genie lamp icon. This compiles and executes the program and gives focus back to the Command window.

5. Finally, to demonstrate the expression builder, place the insertion point cursor at the beginning of the last line of code. Open a blank line by pressing **Ctrl-N** and then type the question mark print verb without an expression as follows:

   ```
   ?
   ```

   With the cursor still on the `?` command line, click the formula icon in the center of the Speedbar to enter the expression builder. Refer to Figure 4.9.

6. Follow these steps within the Build Expression dialog box.

   - To insert a Visual dBASE expression into the command after the question mark verb, click on **Function** under the **Category** list at the bottom of the dialog box.
   - Scroll in the **Type** list and click **Numeric data**.
   - Scroll in the **Paste** list and double click on `SQRT`. `SQRT(expN)` should now appear in the Expression text box.
   - Delete `expN` from the within the parenthesis of the `SQRT()` function and replace it with a numeric constant of `49`. Then add a plus sign (+) and a numeric constant, `25`. Your expression should now appear as follows (see Figure 4.9):

     ```
     SQRT(49) + 25
     ```

FIGURE 4.9 BUILD EXPRESSION WINDOW

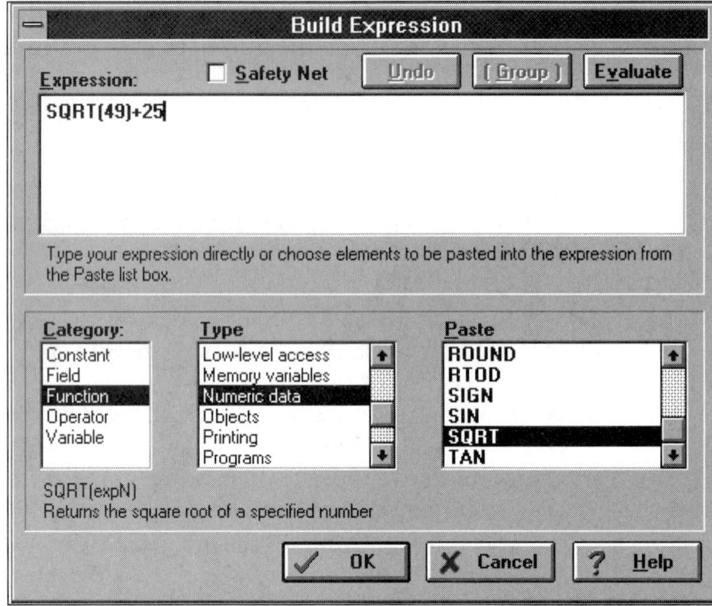

- Click on the **Evaluate** pushbutton on the top right of the Build Expression dialog box. A numeric `32.00` should appear under Result:, just under the Expression text box.
- Click on the **OK** pushbutton at the bottom of the dialog box to return the expression to the Program Editor.
- The completed expression should now appear after the `?` command in the `ytest2.prg` program. Click on the compile and execute SpeedBar icon to test the program containing the new line of code. Be sure that the evaluated expression, `32.00`, is displayed in the Results pane on the line after `Hello World`.

The Expression Builder is an excellent tool to construct an expression. It will allow you to quickly insert items such as functions, field variables, and memory variables without having to rely on your own memory, on-line help, or the reference manual for proper spelling. You can also insert items yourself rather than retrieving them—such as the plus sign numeric operator in the preceding example. Operators may also be retrieved from the Expression Builder.

NOTE: You will probably want to run a printed listing of your program during and after testing. This will assist you with program tests and also become part of your program documentation. You can print from the Program Editor either by choosing **File | Print** or by clicking on the print icon on the left side of the Speedbar. Either method will make the standard Windows print setup dialog box available if you need to change print settings for your particular printer.

As demonstrated in this group of hands-on exercises, Visual dBASE gives the programmer a number of alternative ways to use the Program Editor when moving through the programming cycle. As you continue to develop programs, you will be able to decide the best approach for yourself.

PROGRAM DOCUMENTATION

Program documentation is part of the total system documentation. The system document contains information for the system user as well as for the data processing personnel responsible for the operation of the system. Good program documentation is extremely important. One reason for frustration among data processing and microcomputer managers is the lack of good system and individual program documentation. Documentation is important for the current programmer and the future programmer responsible for program maintenance.

Logical Program Segments. Programs have various substructures, but usually they have the following general parts:

- **Program heading:** The program heading (sometimes called the preamble) is preceded by the comment symbol * and should include items such as the programmer's name or initials, the name of the program, a brief description of what the program does, memory variable names, and whether the program is called from a parent program.
- **Program initialization:** Each program requires some initialization of certain variables, toggles, and so on. For example, you may want to set the `TALK` toggle `OFF`, clear the screen, and set the environment for dBASE.
- **Open files:** If files are used in the program, they would be opened here. Further, indexes could be opened and relations between files established.
- **Data input:** Data entry from the keyboard, a file, or other medium may occur at this point.
- **Program execution:** This is the body of the program. The objective of the program happens here.
- **Data output:** If output to the printer, file, or other medium occurs, it would happen here.
- **Program close-out:** This is the opposite of program initialization. If toggles have been turned on, they are turned off here. If files were opened, perhaps they would be closed here.
- **Program footer:** This is a short footer message, preceded by the comment symbol. This message should indicate that the end of the program has occurred and to where program control is returning.

The parts of a program mentioned here are only a guideline. The application will dictate which parts are used and what they will contain. However, a well-structured program will clearly define each of the parts with appropriate subheadings.

General Documentation Guidelines. In addition to defining the parts of a program, other documentation guidelines are important. Here are some generally accepted rules:

- **Blank lines between logical blocks of code:** Each logical part of a program should be separated by a blank line. Each line of that logical block should be single-spaced. For example, the program initialization code should be separated by a blank line from the file opening section.
- **Indentation of control commands:** The body of logic and loop commands such as `DO WHILE` and `IF..ENDIF` should be indented. I recommend indenting just three spaces. If a five-space indent is used in a heavily nested segment, the command line begins to get very short.
- **Visual dBASE reserved words in uppercase:** All Visual dBASE reserved words should be in uppercase; all field names, memory variable names, and filenames should be in lowercase. Remember, reserved words are the dBASE words of a command, whereas filenames, field names, and memory variable names are supplied by the programmer.
- **Maintain a documentation book:** Set aside a binder to contain all documentation as the system progresses. This external documentation should include a listing of each program module of your system as well as other related information about your programs such as pseudocode, logic diagrams, and test data.

REVIEW EXERCISES

These exercises utilize the process, logic (selection), and loop structured building blocks to search a database for records meeting certain conditions. Part I is an introduction to programming. It introduces basic concepts of programming, use of pseudocode, and program documentation. Part II expands counting concepts and introduces nested `IF..ELSE`s. These exercises do not utilize the fastest search techniques available in Visual dBASE. We discuss fast searches in Chapter 6.

PART I: SELECTIVE TABLE SEARCH

The objective of this segment of the Review Exercises is to write a program to search the customer master table (`ycustm`) to locate and list to the screen the individuals from San Mateo (`city field`) who have rented five or fewer films (`no_rents field`).

- Name the program **`yparta`**.
- List to the screen the last name (**`last`**), address (**`address`**), and number of rentals (**`no_rents`**).

Pseudocode. The first step in the solution is to develop pseudocode from the problem specifications. As you can see from Figure 4.10, the initial pseudocode is very much like the parts of a program outlined under Program Documentation in this chapter.

Program Development. Enter the program editor by typing `MODI COMM yparta` in the Input pane. Enter the program as it appears in Figure 4.11.
When the program is entered, save it to the disk (press **Ctrl-W**).

Discussion. Notice that the pseudocode becomes the highest-level comments coded in the program. You may decide to open the program file with your editor and develop the pseudocode right there. Just be sure to precede each line with the comment character `*`. Let's discuss each part of the program (refer to Figure 4.11):

- **Program headings:** There will be additional items in future, larger programs. Information on memory variables and parent modules will be added.
- **Program initialization:** These two items are all that is needed for this program. However, the initialization will become much more extensive as the programs become more extensive.
- **Open tables:** We are using only one table in this program, with no indexes or relationships.
- **Search and list from the table:** The search routine consists of an `IF..ENDIF` nested in a `DO WHILE`. Note the following:
  1. The condition of the `DO WHILE` is `.NOT. EOF( )`. The function `EOF( )` will return a logic `.T.` when the last record has been passed.
  2. The `IF..ENDIF` will either print a record if the condition is `.T.` or bypass that record if the condition if `.F.`.
  3. The `UPPER( )` function will use the field variable `city` as an argument and return it to the expression in uppercase to be compared to the uppercase character string `"SAN MATEO"`. The value in the data base will not be altered because the uppercase string is being returned to the expression, not to the table.

FIGURE 4.10 PART I—yparta PSEUDOCODE

Program headings.
Program initialization.
Open database.
Search database.
Program close-out.
Program footer.

4. Notice the second **?** command verb. If the **?** is listed without an expression list, the result is a double-spaced report.
5. The **SKIP** command is outside the **ENDIF**. What would happen if it had been encoded inside the **ENDIF**? If the first record of the database creates a logic **.F.**, the **IF** process, including the **SKIP**, will never be executed, and an endless loop will be created. This is because the pointer can never move past the first record.

- **Program close-out:** We have closed the open table and set the **TALK** toggle back on. Remember, the **&&** symbol after the **USE** command designates a command line comment. Visual dBASE will ignore all characters after this symbol at execution. The close-out section will become larger as our programs become more complex.

- **Program footer:** This is a single program without children. When the system menu is developed, the footer will be expanded to mention that the program is "returning" to its parent module.

Program Testing. To test your program, type in the following from the Input pane:

```
DO yparta
```

If the program does not execute properly, check the source code and make any corrections necessary. Continue the rerun and test cycle until the program executes properly. Use the Input pane to recall previous commands when alternating between the **MODI COMM** and **DO** statements.

Program Modification. Modify program **yparta** to count the number of lines printed out. Double-space after the last line has been listed to include the following line:

```
*** TOTAL LINES PRINTED:    xx
```

The **xx** symbol will be the actual number of lines printed by your program.

FIGURE 4.11 PART 1—yparta VISUAL dBASE CODE

```
* Name of program: YPARTA.PRG
* Author.........: <student name>
* Description....: A program to search the customer master
*                  table.
* Origin date....: Today's date
* Last update....: 00/00/00

* ==> Program initialization
SET TALK OFF
CLEAR

* ==> Open master table
USE ycustm

* ==> Search and list from table
DO WHILE .NOT. EOF()
   IF UPPER(city) = "SAN MATEO" .AND. no_rents <= 5
      ? last, address, city, no_rents
      ?
   ENDIF
   SKIP
ENDDO

* ==> Program close-out
SET TALK ON
USE                         && Close master table
* ==> End of program YPARTA.PRG
```

This program modification involves the use of a counter. Type **MODI COMM yparta** to re-enter the program editor. *Note:* Each time you use **MODI COMM** on a program file, it deletes the previous **.pro** file automatically. Then, when the **DO <program filename>** command is invoked, it searches for a **.pro** file named **<program filename>**. If it finds one, it executes it. If it does not find one, it compiles the **.prg** file with the same name. In this manner, the **DO** command is able to execute the most current **.pro** file. Make the modifications as indicated in Figure 4.12.

A counter is a routine you will be using often in various programs. Three statements have been added to **yparta** as follows:

1. **xSum = 0**
Establish memory variable counter **xsum**.

FIGURE 4.12 PART 1—yparta WITH LINE COUNTER

```
* Name of program: YPARTA.PRG
* Author.........: <student name>
* Description....: A program to search the customer master
                   table.
* Origin date....: Today's date
* Last update....: 00/00/00

* ==> Program initialization
SET TALK OFF
CLEAR
xSum = 0                    && Establish counter memory variable

* ==> Open master table
USE ycustm

* ==> Search and list from table
DO WHILE .NOT. EOF ()
   IF UPPER(city) = "SAN MATEO" .AND. no_rents <= 5
      ? last, address, city, no_rents
      ?
xSum = xSum + 1             && Bump counter by one
   ENDIF
   SKIP
ENDDO

* ==> Program output
? "                    *** TOTAL NUMBER OF LINES: ", xSum

* ==> Program close-out
SET TALK ON
USE                         && Close master table
* ==> End of program YPARTA.PRG
```

2. `xSum = xSum + 1`
   Increase counter by one for each record listed. This statement is inside the **IF..ENDIF**, so only the records listed are counted. If it were placed just after the **ENDIF**, what would happen? It would count every record in the table rather than just those meeting the condition to be listed.

3. `? "          ***TOTAL NUMBER OF LINES: " , xSum`
   Print the total number of lines listed. This command is just after the **ENDDO**. When the **DO WHILE** is finished, all lines have been listed, and the counter contains that total.

FIGURE 4.13 SAMPLE OUTPUT--yparta

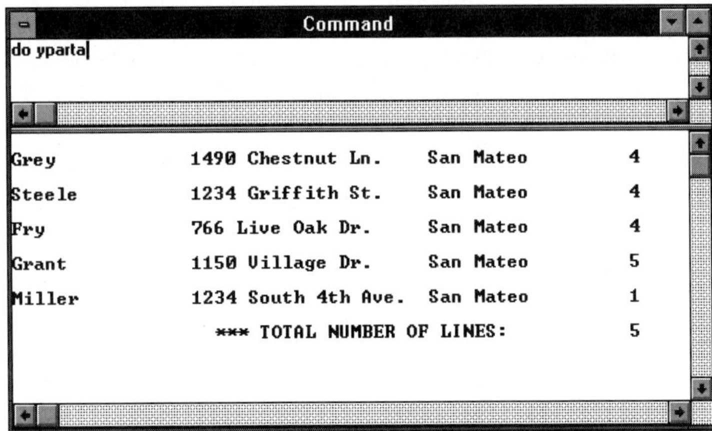

Rerun the program with the DO command. Continue testing until it executes properly.

When the program is correctly executing, the screen should appear as shown in Figure 4.13.

PART II. SEARCH USING NESTED IF..ELSEs

The objective of this segment of the Case System is to develop a program to count the number of customers using Visa, MasterCard, and other categories in the customer master file. The problem specifications are as follows:

- Modify the pseudocode of part I as necessary to solve part II.
- The three categories are in the character field charge. The field is one character in length.
- Name the program ypartb.
- Use nested `IF..ELSE`s to select the three categories. (The Case System exercise requires the use of the `DO CASE`.)
- List the output to the screen using the following format:

```
                    VIDEO EXPRESS
                Sales/Inventory System
--------------------------------------------------------------------
              CREDIT CARD INVENTORY SUMMARY


  o TOTAL CUSTOMERS USING MASTERCARD......:
  o TOTAL CUSTOMERS USING VISA............:
  o TOTAL CUSTOMERS IN "OTHER CATEGORIES".:
```

- The problem is very similar to **yparta**. To save time keying in the entire program, use a copy of **yparta.prg** as a boilerplate. After you enter the program editor with **MODI COMM ypartb**, select **Edit | Insert from file**. Choose **yparta.prg** from the **Insert from file** dialog box.
- Have your program present the three-line heading, VIDEO EXPRESS, Sales/Inventory System, CREDIT CARD INVENTORY SUMMARY, prior to entry into the **DO WHILE**. This will let the operator know that something is happening while the processing takes place.
- Initialize three counter memory variables, **xVisa**, **xMaster**, and **xOther**, to count each category.
- Inside the **DO WHILE**, establish nested **IF..ELSE**s to select by charge category for counting. (Refer to this chapter's discussions of nested **IF..ELSE**s.)
- Present the contents of the three counters to the screen as outlined in the specifications above.

PART III. MULTIPLE CONDITION SEARCH

The objective of this segment of the Case System is to introduce the **DO CASE** construct during a multiple condition search. This problem does not utilize the fastest search techniques available in Visual dBASE, which will be discussed in Chapter 6.

Modify Part II using the following specifications:

- Name the program **ypartc**.
- Use the **DO CASE** construct rather than nested **IF..ELSE**s.
- Add a fourth category for Diner's Club card members. Call the additional memory variable counter **xDiner**. Add the appropriate counter total line to the screen as output.
- After the Diner's Club total line, add another line to the screen containing the total of all categories. It should appear as follows:

```
*** TOTAL: (All Categories)            xx
```

xx is the total number inserted by your program.

This segment will become part of the Case System. In Chapter 7, a main application window menu will be developed for the Case System, and the segment you have just completed will be assigned as a main menu item. It will also be modified slightly to facilitate interaction with the menu. However, note that this module of the total system has been developed and tested independently of the total system. This modularity is a major benefit of structured programming.

CHAPTER SUMMARY

In this chapter, we began putting together the structured building blocks of process, loop, and logic. The problems solved used the looping and logic commands to search a database for records meeting given specifications. This is the foundation of database programming. In later chapters, you learn to do this with more complex systems, and you learn to search much more efficiently. However, all new structured programming skills will be built on what you have learned in this chapter.

The following topics were discussed:

- As in other disciplines, programming has become modular. By using the structured building blocks of process, loop, and logic, programs are easier to design, code, test, and modify. Each control structure segment of a module has a single-entry—single-exit point, as does the module itself as part of the system of modules. Pseudocode, or an English-language equivalent to computer code, is used to outline the logic parts of the program. Pseudocode may be general at the beginning of program design and more detailed when the logic becomes more complex.
- Visual dBASE provides an excellent editor to develop the source code of computer programs. Any other editor will suffice to build programs so long as it produces ASCII text files.
- As part of the total system documentation, program documentation is an important element in the programming process. General rules of program documentation, such as informative headings, space between logic blocks of code, indentation of logic instructions, and use of comment lines, should be adhered to.

The following commands and functions were discussed:

- `?/??`
- `DO WHILE..ENDDO`
- `DO..UNTIL`
- `IF..ENDIF`
- `IF..ELSE..ENDIF`
- `DO CASE..ENDCASE`
- `GO/GOTO`
- `SKIP`
- `CLEAR`
- `SET TALK`
- `DO`
- `MODIFY COMMAND`
- `SET DEVELOPMENT`
- `EO( )`
- `UPPER( )`

In the next chapter, we continue with procedural programming while learning the concepts of reorganizing the database.

CHAPTER FIVE

TOPICS

New Commands and Functions

Concepts

Sorting the table
The cascading sort
Creating a single key index file (`.ndx`)
Updating an index file
Rebuilding an index file
Changing the order of the indexes
Indexed sorts within sorts—the concatenated index
Creating a multiple key index file (`.mdx`)
Deleting an `.mdx` index `TAG`
The `.mdx` file versus the `.ndx` file
The trade-offs of updating versus rebuilding
Additional `.mdx` index file rules
A faster sort—copying an indexed table

Review Exercises

Chapter Summary

Reorganizing the Database

5

CHAPTER OBJECTIVES

In this chapter, we introduce methods used to reorganize the database. The output of your application may require the database to be organized in many different ways. The most efficient searches of a database are also a function of reordering. There are two ways to reorganize the database: sorting and indexing. Sorting is a physical method of reorganization. Indexing is the preferred method of reordering because sorting is too slow and is memory expensive. We will continue procedural programming of the Review Exercises from the Command window. There will not be any additions to the Case System until Chapter 7.

After studying this chapter, you should understand and be able to program the concepts of database organization.

NEW COMMANDS AND FUNCTIONS

We open this chapter by listing the new commands with only brief explanations. Detailed examples of each command and its usage are presented in the section headed Concepts, which follows.

COMMAND

```
SORT TO <filename> ON <field1> [/A][/C][/D]
     [,<field2>  [/A][/C][/D]. . . ]
     [ASCENDING] / [DESCENDING]
     TO <filename> [<scope>] [FOR/WHILE <Condition>]
```

Sorts the open table on the key field, producing another table sorted on that key. The various options allow cascading sorts on multiple fields, and ascending and descending sorts within those fields. The **/C** option allows dBASE to ignore case when sorting; therefore, it will not be a strict ASCII sort.

COMMAND

```
INDEX ON <key expression> TO <.ndx filename>
  TAG <tag name> [OF <.mdx filename>]
  [FOR <condition>] [UNIQUE] [DESCENDING]
```

Creates an index that allows the ordering of the database alphabetically, chronologically, or numerically. In dBASE II and III, a single index file was developed for each index key. The file created had an **.ndx** extension. This single key index file concept is still available in Visual dBASE, though it is no longer recommended. In addition to the single index file, Visual dBASE allows a multiple index file with the capability of containing as many as 47 indexes, called tags. This file has an **.mdx** extension. The **FOR** clause allows the building of conditional **.mdx** index tags, thereby decreasing the tag size and increasing its speed. This feature and the **SET KEY TO** command will be discussed in Chapter 6, Efficient Search Techniques.

COMMAND

```
SET INDEX TO [?/<filename>
     [ORDER [TAG] <.ndx filename>/<.mdx tagname>
     [OF <.mdx filename>]]]
```

Opens, or activates, an index file or files, both single index (**.ndx**) and multiple index (**.mdx**). The programmer has the option of specifying the controlling index or tag for an active table.

COMMAND

```
REINDEX
```

Rebuilds all active index files, both **.ndx** and **.mdx**.

COMMAND

```
SET ORDER TO <expN>
SET ORDER TO [TAG]
     <filename> / <.mdx tagname> [OF  < .mdx filename>]
```

COMMAND

```
ACCEPT [<prompt>] TO <memvar>
```

Prompts the operator for data. The data stored in the memory variable will be character type.

EXAMPLE

```
ACCEPT "ENTER LAST NAME: " TO ylast
ENTER LAST NAME: Jones <enter>
? ylast
```

Notice that delimiters are not required for **ACCEPT** command data entry. The character constant, Jones, will be stored in the variable, **ylast**.

COMMAND

```
INPUT [<prompt>] TO <memvar>
```

Prompts the operator for data. The data stored in the memory variable will be numeric type, unless delimiters are used.

EXAMPLE

```
INPUT "ENTER VALUE OF X: " TO x Value
ENTER VALUE OF X: 5 <enter>
? x Value
```

The **INPUT** command is used primarily for numeric data entry, but can also be used for character type data. If character type is desired, the character string must be typed within delimiters.

ACCEPT and **INPUT** are not used in the Case System. Though useful in DOS programs, they are not a means of input in a Windows application. In this chapter, we will use **ACCEPT** in our review exercises.

COMMAND

```
SET ORDER TO <expN>
SET ORDER TO [TAG]
    < filename> / <.mdx tagname> [OF  <.mdx filename>]
```

Establishes the master, or controlling, index file from a list of open index **.ndx** or **.mdx** files. When the indexes are first opened, the original order of the indexes is established. The **SET ORDER TO** command then selects a new master from that original order.

COMMAND

```
DELETE TAG <tag name> [OF <.mdx filename>]
       [,<tag name 2> [OF <.mdx filename> 2]]
```

DELETEs an index **TAG** from an **.mdx** file. If it is the production file, the filename does not have to be coded. You may delete more than one **TAG** in a single command. The production **.mdx** will be discussed in the Concepts section of this chapter.

COMMAND `WAIT [<prompt>] [TO <memvar>]`

Causes Visual dBASE to cease operations until any character is entered from the keyboard. The **WAIT** command differs from **ACCEPT** and **INPUT** in that it allows entry of only a single character from the keyboard by the operator after an appropriate prompt. The command is also different from **ACCEPT** and **INPUT** in that <**enter**> is not necessary from the operator after data entry. It is especially useful in menus and other situations that require only one character of input and when you don't want the operator to have to take the time to strike <**enter**> after input.

EXAMPLES `WAIT`

In this form (no prompt supplied), Visual dBASE will supply the prompt *Press any key to continue . . .*

`WAIT TO xConstant`

In this form (no prompt supplied), Visual dBASE will supply the prompt *Press any key to continue . . .* However, the single key pressed will cause the ASCII character to be stored, in character type format, in the memory variable for future reference.

`WAIT "ENTER A CHARACTER NOW" TO xConstant`

The prompt, as coded in the command, will appear on screen, and Visual dBASE will pause for operator input. The single character entered is placed in the memory variable as in the last example. The *Press any key to continue . . .* prompt will not be generated by Visual dBASE.

Here are some other **WAIT** considerations:

- To eliminate the Visual dBASE prompt, and not include your own in the command, code a zero-length character string prompt (`""`) in the command.
- After final testing of your completed system, **SET ESCAPE OFF** can be placed in a program to eliminate the problem of the operator inadvertently striking **Esc** during execution.

COMMAND `RETURN`

Returns control to the calling program. When a program module is completed, and no **RETURN** command is encoded, Visual dBASE will automatically supply one. If there is no calling program, Visual dBASE will return control to the Input pane.

The **RETURN** command should be encoded at the end of a module event though it is not needed at this natural return point to the calling program. If this is the single point of return to the calling program, it is good practice to encode the **RETURN** command to accentuate its position in the program.

COMMAND `CANCEL`

Stops execution of a program module and returns control to the Input pane. All open program files are closed.

COMMAND `QUIT`

Returns control to the operating system. All open files are closed. All memory variables are released.

COMMAND `SET EXCLUSIVE on/OFF`

Controls whether dBASE opens tables and their associated index and memo files in exclusive or shared mode. In a Windows environment, there may be multiple occurrences of the same event using the same table. If **EXCLUSIVE** is toggled to its default setting of **OFF**, changes such as indexing cannot occur. You can either toggle it **ON** at the beginning of each session, or set it to **ON** in the **dBASEWIN.INI** file.

NOTE: Prior to entering the exercises of this chapter, you will need to either toggle exclusive on in dBASEWIN.INI or type the command from the Input pane prior to each session. To modify dBASEWIN.INI, choose **Properties | Desktop | Table Tab** from the Visual dBASE desktop. Click the **Exclusive** check box. You will need to turn this toggle ON in each application as necessary, and not assume it is toggled one way or the other on a user computer system.

FUNCTION `CHR(<expN)`

Returns the character equivalent of a specified ASCII value.

EXAMPLE

```
? CHR(65)

A
? CHR(7)          && Rings computer bell.
```

FUNCTION `SPACE(<expN))`

Returns a character string composed of a specified number of space characters. The space character is ASCII code 32. The largest number of spaces you can specify is 32,766, the maximum length of a string.

EXAMPLE

```
? "Hello" + SPACE(5) + "WORLD"
```

FUNCTION `&`

This & symbol is called the macro substitution function. When Visual dBASE asks for a literal name, this function substitutes the contents of a memory variable for the literal name of that variable. The function works only with character type data.

EXAMPLE
```
xfile = "ycustm"
USE &xfile
```

The USE command requires a literal filename to open a file. The macro substitution function allows the programmer to store the name of the file in a memory variable and then use the memory variable to open the file rather than the literal filename.

FUNCTION `ORDER()`

Returns the master index file key or TAG from an .mdx file.

FUNCTION `IIF( <condition> , <exp1> , <exp2> )`

Duplicates the IF. .ELSE command. If the condition in the first argument evaluates to .T., expression 1 (argument 2 of the function) will be returned. If it evaluates to .F., expression 2 (argument 3 of the function) will be returned.

EXAMPLE
```
CLEAR
USE ycustm
LIST IIF (city = "San Carlos", "San Carlos", "Other City")
```

This example shows the usefulness of the IIF (Immediate IF) function. As the LIST command moves through the table, the city is compared to "San Carlos". If this condition is .T., "San Carlos" is listed; if .F., "Other City" is listed. You may also nest IIF( )s. To do this, use another IIF( ) for the third argument. In the above example, change the LIST command as follows:

```
LIST IIF(city = "San Carlos", "San Carlos",
     IIF(city = "San Mateo", "San Mateo", "Other City" ) )
```

This is useful for causing a print line to be displayed in different ways, depending on the conditions in that record.

CONCEPTS

To begin our discussion, we demonstrate the SORT function. Then we discuss the INDEX feature before briefly returning to the SORT to give an example of how to speed up the process by using an index file. Be sure you have the customer master table constructed in Chapter 3 in your data subdirectory. To ensure you have the proper table, DISPLAY the first three records to make sure the last names (last) are Bowers, Chambers, and Andrews, respectively. We use these records to demonstrate the INDEXing feature.

SORTING THE TABLE

To demonstrate physically sorting a table, type in the following from the Input pane:

```
CLEAR
USE ycustm
SORT TO ycsl ON last
USE ycsl
DISP ALL last
```

The `SORT` command in this example sorts the customer master table (`ycustm`) on the last name (`last`) field. The command has created a new table, `ycsl`, in sorted form. This is the first drawback of sorting: a table of the same size is created. For each new key sorted, a new table is developed. As you sort the table, notice how it takes some time even though it is a relatively small table. This is the second drawback of sorting: it is slow. After the indexing discussion, we introduce a faster sorting technique, but even that is unacceptably slow. The third drawback of sorting is that it creates redundant data as new sorted tables are generated. If a record is updated within the master table, all the sorted tables must be resorted to reflect the update.

NOTE: The **More** dialog will appear when commands such as `DISPLAY STRUCTURE` cause a list that is longer than the Results pane. You may either continue or cancel the display. You may want to move it to a more appropriate position if it overlays the Results pane. Once moved, it will retain its new position the next time you boot Visual dBASE.

THE CASCADING SORT

To illustrate the cascading sort, type in the following from the Input pane:

```
CLEAR
USE ycustm
SORT TO ycslf ON last /DC, first /AC
USE ycslf
DISP ALL last, first
```

In this example, the requirement is that the last name be in descending order and that the first name be in ascending order within the last name. Further, case is to be ignored. This is called a cascading sort.

The other option in the command is `[ASCENDING] / [DESCENDING]`. If included, all fields will be in the specified order. If an individual field in the cascade has a `/A` or `/D`, it will override the `[ASCENDING] / [DESCENDING]` option.

CREATING A SINGLE KEY INDEX FILE (`.ndx`)

We begin our discussion of **INDEX**ing using the single key index file.

The single key file index was used in dBASE III and though still available in Visual dBASE, its use is not recommended for new systems. Our discussion here will introduce the single key file index for the student that may be converting applications to Visual dBASE that were initially developed in dBASE III or other Xbase dialects that use the single key file index. The term Xbase is used to describe the various DBMS languages that are similar to dBASE in command syntax.

Make sure you have the proper table in your data subdirectory, and then type in the following from the Input pane:

```
CLEAR
USE ycustm
DISP ALL last, city, zip
INDEX ON last TO ycil
DISP ALL last, city, zip
```

Refer to Figure 5.1 as we discuss this example. The table is **DISPLAY**ed just after it is opened. The records at this point are sequential (note record numbers) and are in the order they were entered into the table, which is referred to as the *natural* order. The **INDEX** command builds a new file, the index file **ycil**, which contains the record number and field (**city**) ordered on the key field. All commands must now go through the index file to operate on the table. For example, the **DISPLAY ALL** command in our example displays the table in the last name order, the order of the index file. The record numbers in the output of the **DISPLAY** command are now in the order of the index file.

All pointer movement commands operate on the index file, not the database table. **GO TOP** will move the pointer to the first record in the index file. If a **SKIP** command is then executed, the pointer will move to the next record in the index file. If a **GOTO <record number>** command is used, the pointer will move to that record number; for example, **GOTO 10** will move the pointer to record 10 in the index file.

To continue the example, type in the following:

```
CLEAR
INDEX ON city TO ycic
DISP ALL last, city, zip
```

FIGURE 5.1 SINGLE AND MULTIPLE INDEX FILES EXAMPLES

CUSTOMER MASTER TABLE (ycustm.dbf)
(Natural Order)

REC NO.	LAST	CITY	ZIP
1	Bowers	Bakersfield	91001
2	Chambers	Baker	91000
3	Andrews	Asheville	91002
•	•	•	•
•	•	•	•
•	•	•	•
80	Gains	San Francisco	94838

INDEX FILE ycil.ndx

REC NO.	LAST
3	Andrews
1	Bowers
2	Chambers
•	•
•	•
•	•
68	Williams

INDEX FILE ycic.ndx

REC NO.	CITY
3	Asheville
2	Baker
1	Bakersfield
•	•
•	•
•	•
43	Westlake

INDEX FILE yciz.ndx

REC NO.	ZIP
2	91000
1	91001
3	91002
•	•
•	•
•	•
45	97609

PRODUCTION MULTIPLE INDEX FILE ycustm.mdx

TAG last

REC NO.	LAST
3	Andrews
1	Bowers
2	Chambers
•	•
•	•
•	•
68	Williams

TAG city

REC NO.	CITY
3	Asheville
2	Baker
1	Bakersfield
•	•
•	•
•	•
43	Westlake

TAG zip

REC NO.	ZIP
2	91000
1	91001
3	91002
•	•
•	•
•	•
45	97609

The table is now ordered by city. The **DISPLAY ALL** command moves the pointer to the top of the city index file, **ycic**, and begins to display the records in the order of the index file. The **DISPLAY** command must reach through the index file to operate on the table. The original table, `ycustm`, has not been altered. This is a major advantage over sorting. The original table remains unaltered regardless of how many index files are built. It can be reordered in many ways without needing the large amount of storage required by the `SORT` command.

Continue with the example by entering the following:

```
CLEAR
INDEX ON zip TO yciz
DISP ALL last, city, zip
```

Once again, the database has been reordered, this time in zip code order according to the zip code index file, `yciz`. We now have three index files to look at the original database in three ways: by last name, by city, and by zip code. The database remains unaltered.

UPDATING AN INDEX FILE

To understand the updating of single index files, type in the following:

```
CLEAR
APPEND
```

When the Table Records window is displayed, type the following fields into the record (we won't need all the fields for this example):

```
last: Aable
city: Asheville
zip.: 99999
```

While the cursor is still on the new record, press **Ctrl-W** to save and exit to the Command window.

```
GO BOTTOM
DISP last, city, zip
```

Notice that rather than scrolling through the many screens required to get to the last record via the `DISP ALL` command, we simply executed the `GO BOTTOM` command to `DISPLAY` the last record. The records are in zip code order. The new data is contained in the last record, as it should be because of the 99999 zip code. Now continue by typing in the following:

```
CLEAR
SET INDEX TO ycil
DISP ALL last, city, zip
```

Prior to pressing **cancel** to abort the continued display, note that the fields from the newly appended record are *not* present (the last name, Aable). When the record was appended, only the zip code index was open. The rule that applies here is as follows:

When a command is executed that alters the database (for example, EDIT, BROWSE, REPLACE, APPEND, DELETE, ZAP, and PACK) all active (open) indexes are automatically updated.

In our example, only the zip code (**yciz**) index was active (open) when the database was **APPEND**ed with the new record. When each **INDEX ON** command was executed to build each new index file, it automatically closed the index currently open. For example, when we created the city index (**ycic**), the last name index (**ycil**) was closed. That is why it was not updated with the **APPEND** and why the last name did not appear in the last **DISPLAY ALL** command above.

REBUILDING AN INDEX FILE

To fix the problem of all indexes not being current, type in the following:

```
CLEAR
SET INDEX TO ycil, ycic, ycil
REINDEX
DISPLAY ALL last, city, zip
```

Now the last name, Aable, appears in the display in the first record. Note that the **SET INDEX TO** command contains a list of index filenames. This list may include as many as 10 indexes per table. The first name in the list is called the *master* index and is the active or controlling index. The remaining indexes in the list are open and are there for updating purposes. If a command that alters the table is executed while all three indexes are open, they will all be updated automatically.

CHANGING THE ORDER OF THE INDEXES

Type in the following from the dot prompt:

```
CLEAR
USE ycustm INDEX ycil, ycic, yciz
DISP ALL last, city, zip
SET ORDER TO 2
DISP ALL last, city, zip
SET ORDER TO 3
DISP ALL last, city, zip
SET ORDER TO 0
DISP ALL last, city, zip
```

The **USE** command can open a table with indexes and establish the original order of the indexes. If the file is already open, as in earlier examples, the **SET INDEX TO** command opens the index files. The **SET INDEX** command could be used again to establish a new master index; however, this reopens each index each time the command is executed. Each time an index file is opened, or reopened, a time-consuming disk access must occur. By using the **SET ORDER TO** command, the index files are reopened only once; then, without reopening the files, the order is changed (that is, sets a precedence of indexes).

As you work through the above example, note that a new master index is established with each **SET ORDER** execution. Finally, **SET ORDER TO 0**, or **SET ORDER TO**, will set the database to its natural order without closing the index files. The files will continue to be updated.

INDEXED SORTS WITHIN SORTS—THE CONCATENATED INDEX

A cascading sort can be established with the options of the **SORT** command. This type of reordering is called a concatenated index when using the **INDEX** command. Type in the following:

```
CLEAR
USE ycustm
INDEX ON last + first TO ycilf
DISP ALL last, first
```

In this example, the Results pane displays the first name ordered within the last name (as in the Jones and Mason records).

As we previously mentioned, the **.ndx** file was used exclusively in dBASE II and III and the other Xbase dialects. It remains in Visual dBASE to maintain upward compatibility in the language. This is an excellent feature of dBASE because the programmer will often need to convert existing dBASE/Xbase systems to the Windows environment. For this reason, a knowledge of the **.ndx** file remains important.

CREATING A MULTIPLE KEY INDEX FILE (.mdx)

In the preceding examples we demonstrated the index file containing a single key. Now we build the *multiple index file*. This feature was added in dBASE IV and has several advantages over the single index file. It can contain up to 47 indexes (referenced by a **TAG** name) and requires only one file. You may have 10 indexes active using the **.ndx**, but that requires 10 open files. Further, the **.mdx** file opens automatically when the database table opens, thus eliminating the housekeeping chores involved in index updates. Finally, you will need exclusive use of a table to build an index tag.

To demonstrate the creation of an **.mdx** multiple index file, type in the following:

```
CLEAR
SET EXCLUSIVE ON
USE ycustm                    && Open master file.
INDEX ON last TAG last        && Build last name tag.
DISP ALL last, city, zip
INDEX ON city TAG city        && Build city tag.
INDEX ON zip TAG zip          && Build zip tag.
DISP ALL last, city, zip
SET ORDER TO city             && City tag to master.
DISP ALL last, city, zip
DISP STAT                     && Display status of files.
SET ORDER TO                  && Set to natural order.
DISP ALL last, city, zip
```

After opening the customer master file (**ycustm.dbf**), the **INDEX ON** command causes the following to occur:

- Establishes an **.mdx** file called the production **.mdx** file that has the same name as the database table.
- Builds the first **TAG** (**last**) in that file.
- Automatically assigns the same name to the index file (**ycustm.mdx**) as the database file (**ycustm.dbf**).
- In the future, any time this database is opened, the production **.mdx** file will also be opened. If the database is closed, the production **.mdx** file will also be closed.

When the table is displayed, you can see it has been reordered on the last name (**last**). Additional executions of the **INDEX ON** command, with the **TAG** clause, build additional **TAG**s in the **.mdx** file. You may want to think of the multiple index file as a big file containing as many as 47 index subfiles. Each subfile is given a reference name, or **TAG**, by the **TAG** clause of the command. The **SET ORDER TO** command sets a new **TAG** as the master, or controlling, index. **SET ORDER TO <enter>** will set the database to its natural order. The **.mdx** file remains open for updating purposes.

DELETING AN .mdx INDEX TAG

To demonstrate the removal of a **TAG** from an **.mdx** file, type in the following:

```
CLEAR
SET EXCLUSIVE ON
USE ycustm
DISP STAT
DELETE TAG zip
DISP STAT
INDEX ON zip TAG zip
DISP STAT
```

Note that the problems encountered when updating an **.ndx** file are eliminated with the **.mdx** file.

When the master file (**ycustm**) is opened, the production **.mdx** file (**ycustm**) is also opened. The **DELETE TAG** command deletes the zip **TAG** in the production **.mdx** file. The **INDEX ON** command places the zip **TAG** back in the production file; then we verify it is there with the **DISPLAY STATUS** command. The only way to close the production **.mdx** file is to close the associated **.dbf** table.

THE .mdx FILE VERSUS THE .ndx FILE

For programs developed in Visual dBASE, the **.mdx** file is the accepted way of applying indexes because of its increased efficiency over the **.ndx** file. However, the **.ndx** file is still in the language, not only because it maintains upward compatibility but also because it can still be useful. For example, to avoid time-consuming index updates in the **.mdx** file, separate **.ndx** files can be maintained for certain reports that do not require constant index maintenance.

Note, however, that nonproduction **.mdx** files may also be opened at the same time as the production **.mdx** file. Altogether, 10 files (**.mdx** or **.ndx**) may be opened in addition to the production **.mdx** file. For example, you could open five **.ndx** files and five nonproduction **.mdx** files. The nonproduction file is also a method of keeping **TAG**s that are used only occasionally.

THE TRADE-OFFS OF UPDATING VERSUS REBUILDING

The programmer must decide whether to update or rebuild an index. If an index is open when a command that alters the database is executed, the index will be automatically updated. If the index is not open when the updating command is executed, it must be opened and **REINDEX**ed (rebuilt). The important difference is that updating takes less time than rebuilding. Here are the trade-offs.

Advantages of updating

- Files are current for interactive processing.
- Updating takes less time than rebuilding (**REINDEX**ing).

Disadvantage of updating

- Though faster than rebuilding, updating can be too time consuming if there are a large number of indexes to update and the database is very large.

If the disadvantage is prevalent, rebuilding may be better. Even though rebuilding takes longer, it could be done on a second shift or during another opportune time when interactive processing is not taking place. Remember though, it won't be current until rebuilt. To solve this problem, you must experiment with benchmarks (time tests with application databases) for each application to examine the trade-offs, and then decide the best way to program that system.

ADDITIONAL .mdx INDEX FILE GUIDELINES

Here are some general rules about the `.mdx` file:

- The `OF [<.mdx filename>]` clause is used to designate a nonproduction `.mdx` file when using the `INDEX ON`, `SET INDEX TO`, or `SET ORDER TO` commands.
- `SET INDEX TO <enter>` will close all currently open `.ndx` files, but not the production `.mdx` file. The production `.mdx` file can be closed only by closing the database.
- `REINDEX` rebuilds all the `TAG`s in the `.mdx` file, as well as the indexes of all open `.ndx` files.
- A descending index `TAG` can be placed in an `.mdx` file by using the `DESCENDING` option, for example, `INDEX ON cust_no TAG CND DESCENDING`.
- Index files are easily corrupted when certain database operations take place, such as when making backups and moving data files from one area to another. It is therefore a good idea to give the user a utility to `REINDEX` after each of these types of operations to maintain file integrity.

A FASTER SORT—COPYING AN INDEXED FILE

A way to speed up the sort function, when a sorted file is needed, is to `COPY` an `INDEX`ed file. Type in the following:

```
USE ycustm
SET ORDER TO last
COPY TO ycsli
USE ycsli
DISP ALL last
```

By copying the `INDEX`ed file, pointer movement to the appropriate record occurs more rapidly than it does when reorganizing all records by the `SORT` command.

Here are examples of situations that might warrant `SORT`ing the database:

- It may be necessary to break a large sorted file into two parts so that it will fit on two floppy disks.
- When exporting data outside the dBASE environment, it may be better to have the file in sorted form because the receiving program may not understand the dBASE indexes.

REVIEW EXERCISES

PART I: DATABASE ORDERING FROM THE COMMAND WINDOW

In this exercise, the Visual dBASE command verb needed to solve the problem will appear in square brackets. The objective of this exercise is to construct the remainder of the command from the information presented earlier in the chapter.

1. Open the customer master table (`ycustm`) `[USE]`.
2. There should still be a production `.mdx` file, `ycustm.mdx`, on your disk as previously developed. Add to that production `.mdx` file a customer number (`cust_no`) tag. If for some reason you do not have the `.mdx` file, it will be created when the customer number tag is developed `[INDEX ON]`.
3. Display the customer number (`cust_no`) and the last name (`last`) of all records `[DISPLAY]`.
4. Place an index tag in the production `.mdx` file that will order the table with the first names in order within the last names `[INDEX ON]`. Call the tag `last first`. Display the first and last names to ensure the index is working properly `[DISPLAY]`.
5. Sort the table with the last names in descending order and the first names in ascending order within the last name `[SORT ON]`. Name the sorted file `ycslfd`. Display the result to ensure the sort was properly done (be sure you have the correct table open when the `DISPLAY` command is executed).
6. Make a sorted copy of the `ycustm` table in city order. Rather than using the `SORT` command, copy the table with the city tag as master `[SET ORDER TO]` `[COPY TO]`. Name the sorted file `ycsc`. Display the results to ensure the sort was properly done (be sure you have the correct file open when the `DISPLAY` command is executed).

PART II: PROGRAMMING SELECTIVE DATABASE ORDERS

The objective of this exercise is to build a program module using the reorganizing commands of Visual dBASE. This exercise module will not be added to the Case System.

Specifications. This module displays the customer master file to the screen in various orders. The program should contain an input screen for the operator to enter the order in which the table is to be displayed. Develop the module according to the following specifications:

- **Program name:** Call the module `yindex`.
- **Data entry:** Using the `ACCEPT` command, present an input screen as in Figure 5.2. The operator can enter one of the following field names, in upper or lower case:

  1. `LAST` For display in last name order.
  2. `CITY` For display in city order.
  3. `ZIP` For display in zip code order.

  Place the entered key value in a memory variable, `yKey`, as the `TO` clause of the `ACCEPT` command. The `ACCEPT` prompt is to read as follows:

  ```
  o ENTER A KEY VALUE FOR CUSTOMER LISTING:
  ```

  Using the `SET MESSAGE` command, place the following additional data entry prompt in the status bar (see Figure 5.2). Erase the message as soon as data entry is complete.

  ```
  Enter LAST, CITY or ZIP as key value...
  ```

FIGURE 5.2 DATA ENTRY SCREEN—PROGRAM MODULE `yindex`

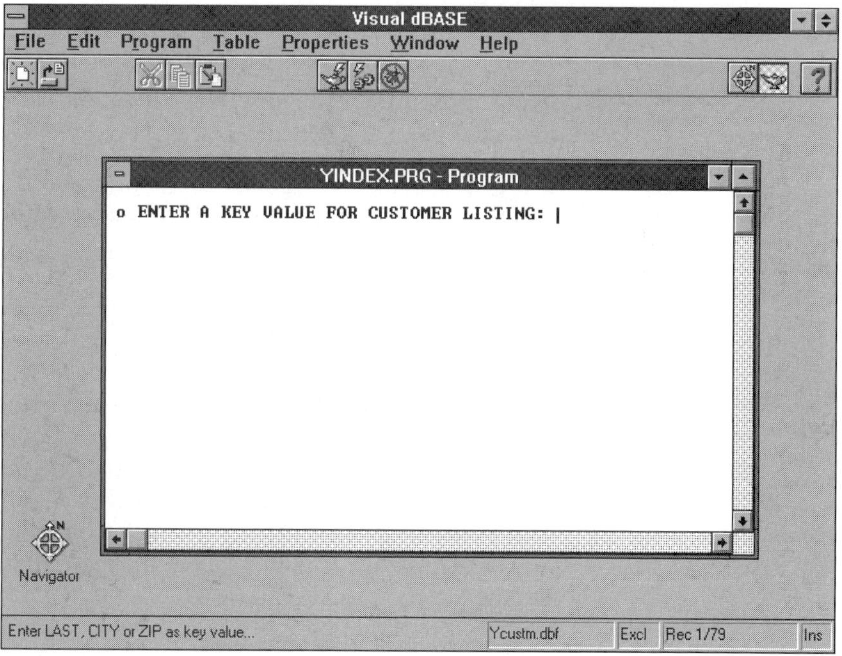

FIGURE 5.3 INITIAL OUTPUT SCREEN—PROGRAM MODULE `yindex`

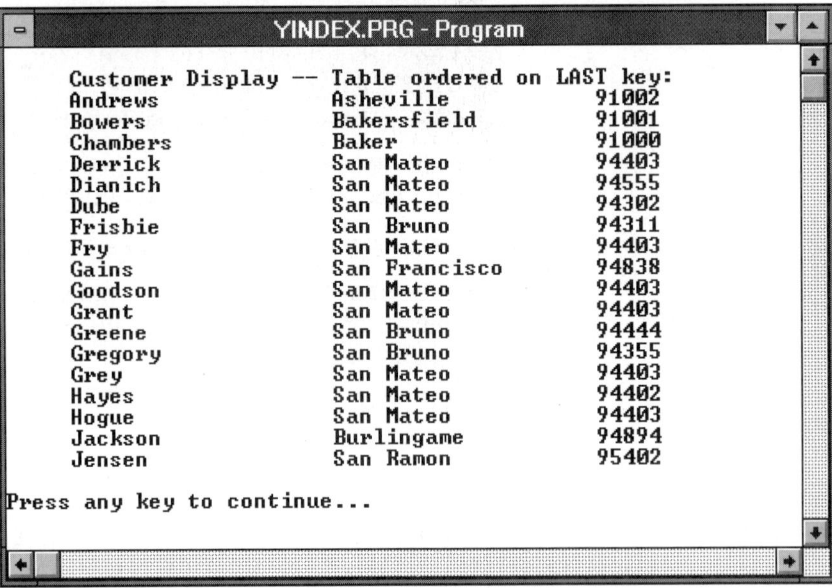

YINDEX.PRG - Program

```
Customer Display -- Table ordered on LAST key:
Andrews                Asheville         91002
Bowers                 Bakersfield       91001
Chambers               Baker             91000
Derrick                San Mateo         94403
Dianich                San Mateo         94555
Dube                   San Mateo         94302
Frisbie                San Bruno         94311
Fry                    San Mateo         94403
Gains                  San Francisco     94838
Goodson                San Mateo         94403
Grant                  San Mateo         94403
Greene                 San Bruno         94444
Gregory                San Bruno         94355
Grey                   San Mateo         94403
Hayes                  San Mateo         94402
Hogue                  San Mateo         94403
Jackson                Burlingame        94894
Jensen                 San Ramon         95402

Press any key to continue...
```

- **Heading display:** The first line of output should read as follows, and should appear only on the first page of the screen display (this line to replace the `ACCEPT` prompt line):

  Customer Display--Table ordered on <insert key field name here> key:

  The `<insert key field name here>` insert is to contain the key value as entered by the operator, in upper case (`LAST`, `CITY`, or `ZIP`). Insert a blank line after this title line, prior to the output detail lines. Use the `SPACE()` function to present a five-space left-hand margin.

- **Set order:** Establish the master index based on the value obtained from the `ACCEPT` command memory variable. For example, if the operator enters `ZIP`, order the table on the zip code. Use the macro substitution function (`&`) to reference the value in the memory variable initialized in the previous step. Because the record pointer remains on the record number of the previous master index tag after setting the table order, you will need to move it to the top of the table (`GO TOP`). The `DO WHILE` command does not reset it to the top of the table.

- **Detail display:** The ordered table record fields should appear one screen at a time (see Figures 5.3 and 5.4). Each screen is to contain 19 lines of data. Include the heading on the first screen only. As each screen is presented, your program should pause. Use the **WAIT** command for the pause and create one blank line between the last line of data and the *Any key to continue...* message. Use the **SPACE()** function to give each line a 5 space left margin and to separate each field with 5 spaces. Use the **DO WHILE...ENDDO** construct to loop through the table.

- **Line count:** Define a memory variable line counter to be bumped as each line is displayed, then reinitialized with each new screen. The following generic program segment demonstrates line counting as such. You may want to build the segment to better understand its operation.

```
* == > Begin program segment.
CLEAR
USE ycustm                   && Open table.
mLines = 1
DO WHILE .NOT. EOF()
   ? last, city, zip
   mLines = mLines + 1       && Bump line counter.
   IF mLines = 20            && Check for 19 line screen page.
      WAIT
      CLEAR                  && Clear screen for new page.
      mLines = 1             && Reset line counter.
   ENDIF
   SKIP
ENDDO
* == > End of program segment.
```

- **Test for additional displays:** After each listing of the table, ask the operator if another listing is desired (see Figure 5.4). Ask the question by placing an appropriate message in the status bar. Place a null in the **WAIT** prompt clause to eliminate the **WAIT** prompt. Loop back if the response is "**Y**" for yes. There are a number of strategies to test for loop completion. One would be an **IF** or **IF..ELSE** construct to test for the response to the Yes/No question. For example:

```
   * <prior code >
   WAIT "" TO mAsk       && Use null to eliminate WAIT
                         && prompt message.
   IF UPPER(mAsk) = "Y"
      LOOP
   ELSE
      EXIT
   ENDIF
   SKIP
ENDDO
```

However, what happens if the operator erroneously presses a key other than **"Y"** or **"N"**? In this situation, you could code an error routine as part of the **ELSE** clause—but usually, code that will exit on any key other than **"Y"** is sufficient. If this is the case, the following code is shorter and will do the same thing:

```
DO WHILE...
   * Process
   IF UPPER(mAsk) = "N"
      EXIT
   ENDIF
   SKIP
ENDDO
```

Now, any key other than **"N"** will return to the **DO WHILE**. An even shorter technique is to make the Yes/No memory variable, **mAsk**, the condition of the **DO WHILE**, as demonstrated in the following:

```
mAsk = "Y"
DO WHILE UPPER(mAsk)  = "Y"
   * <processing code>
   SET MESSAGE TO "End of File – ENTER ANOTHER KEY? (Y)/(N)"
   WAIT "" TO mAsk
   SKIP
ENDDO
```

In your exercise, code the latter technique.

FIGURE 5.4 FINAL OUTPUT SCREEN—PROGRAM MODULE `yindex`

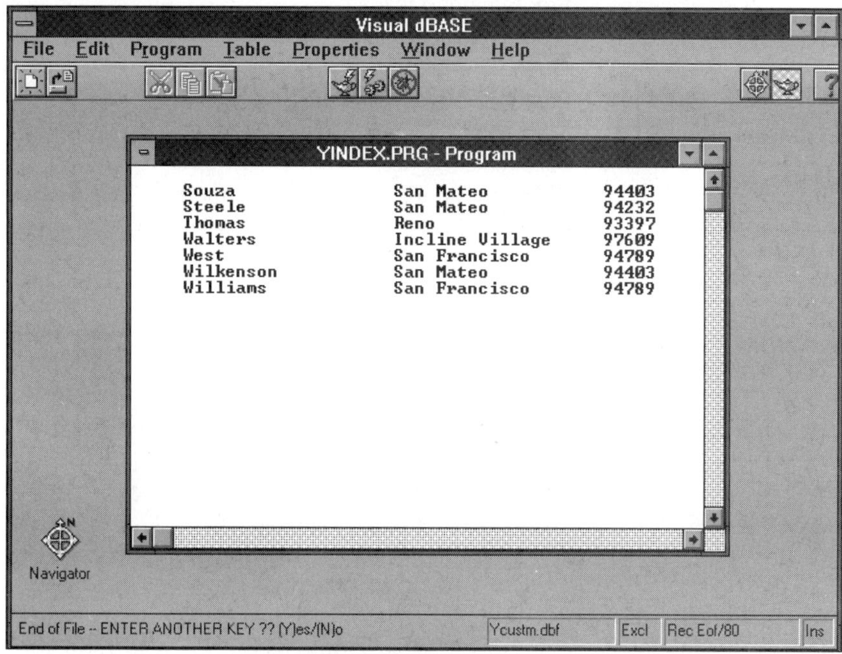

- **Data Validation:** Test the value entered into `xKey` to ensure it is either `last`, `city`, or `zip`. Use the `IF..ENDIF` construct to loop back to the `DO WHILE` if bad data is entered. Place an appropriate message in the status bar preceded by ringing the computer bell and the `WAIT` command.

NOTE: The primary purpose of this exercise is to code order changes in a database table. Concepts such as data entry and data validation in the Windows environment will be covered in detail in Chapter 9. However, the structured programming used here will be helpful as we begin programming object methods in Chapter 7.

Pseudocode Models. The pseudocode models for your problem solution appear in Figures 5.5 (general) and 5.6 (detailed).

FIGURE 5.5 GENERAL PSEUDOCODE—INDEXING MODULE `yindex`

Program headings.
Program initialization.
Open database.
Present input screen model.
Data entry.
Validity test.
Establish database order (from input).
Present output to screen, one screen at a time.
Program close-out.
Program footer.

FIGURE 5.6 DETAILED PSEUDOCODE MODEL—INDEXING MODULE `yindex`

- ________ Program identification.
- ________ Program initialization.
- ________ Open proper table.
- ________ Initialize loop exit variable.
- ________ Begin processing loop.
    - ________ Clear Results pane.
    - ________ Display prompt for data entry. Use the **`ACCEPT`** command prompt and a memory variable to receive requested field name for index order. Place prompt message in the status bar.
    - ________ Convert the entered data to upper case.
    - ________ Validate entered data.
    - ________ Set index **`ORDER TAG`** using the macro substitution function. Move the record pointer to the top of the table (**`GO TOP`**).
    - ________ Display output header message to screen. Place proper key field name from the **`ACCEPT`** variable into the message string.
    - ________ Initialize line count memory variable. Allow for header message line on first page.
    - ________ Begin loop for display of ordered database.
        - ________ Present a line of output.
        - ________ Bump line count memory variable by one.
        - ________ Begin logic to test for last line of single screen display.

FIGURE 5.6 (continued) DETAILED PSEUDOCODE MODEL—INDEXING MODULE `yindex`

__________ Print horizontal space prior to pause.
__________ Pause with `WAIT` command.
__________ Reset line counter to 1.
__________ `CLEAR` Results pane for next display.
__________ End last line logic.
__________ Move pointer to next record.
__________ End loop for display of ordered database.
__________ Place message: "**End of File-- ENTER ANOTHER KEY ?? (Y)es/ (N)o**" in the status bar.
__________ Use the `WAIT TO` command to place response in loop control memory variable. Use null variable for `WAIT` prompt.
_______________ End processing loop.
_______________ Present close-out messages.
_______________ Pause prior to return.
_______________ Close-out commands.
_______________ Return (single exit from module).

END OF PSEUDOCODE MODEL yindex.

Program Modification. Modify the program you created above to vary the format of each line of output data.

- Depending on the input key, vary the format of the output line of `yindex` as follows:
  1. If key is `LAST`, output in this order: last, city, zip.
  2. If key is `CITY`, output in this order: city, zip, last.
  3. If key is `ZIP`, output in this order: zip, city, last.
- Make a copy of program `yindex.prg`. Call the new program `yindex2.prg`. Change the heading and necessary code to accomplish the modification.
- Use nested `IIF()`s to modify the single output line in your program code.
- Use the `ORDER()` function as part of the condition expression in the `IIF()`, for example, `IIF(ORDER() = "LAST",. . . )`.

CHAPTER SUMMARY

In this chapter we learned the importance of reorganizing the database. The following topics were discussed:

- The reasons for reorganizing the database are to change the order of output or to facilitate more efficient searches.
- The `SORT` command is used to physically sort the database. The database should not be `SORT`ed unless a sorted copy is specifically needed. The `SORT` should be avoided because it is slow, memory expensive, and creates redundant data.
- There are two types of index files: the single index file with an `.ndx` extension and the multiple index file with an `.mdx` extension. The `.ndx` was used in earlier versions of dBASE and remains in the language to maintain upward compatibility.

The following commands and functions were discussed:

- `INDEX ON`
- `SET INDEX TO`
- `REINDEX`
- `SET ORDER TO`
- `DELETE TAG`
- `SET EXCLUSIVE`
- `&` (macro substitution)
- `ORDER()`
- `IIF()`
- `SPACE()`
- `CHR()`

Having learned the concepts of reorganizing the database, we can now begin our discussion of efficient search techniques. In the next chapter, we discuss the various search techniques available in Visual dBASE and how to program them as efficiently as possible.

CHAPTER SIX

TOPICS

New Commands and Functions

Concepts

- Sequential versus binary searches
- Visual dBASE search commands
- Scope versus search conditions
- Efficient search techniques

Review Exercises

Chapter Summary

Efficient Search Techniques

6

CHAPTER OBJECTIVES

One of the most important attributes of a database management system is the speed of information retrieval. A user wants a responsive system that will provide timely and useful information as quickly as possible. Unfortunately, not all programmed DBMSs work as speedily as a user would like. In this chapter, we begin our discussions of programming techniques designed to achieve the fastest possible searches of a database.

When I am asked to analyze an existing dBASE system to determine why it is so slow, I interview the user as part of the evaluation. Often, the user will say, "dBASE is really slow" or "I guess we need a faster computer." When moving an application to a Windows environment, the latter is often true. However, after examining the programming techniques used in the system, I usually find the culprit to be poor use of the language rather than a problem with the language.

After studying this chapter, you should understand the commands used to develop efficient searches of the database and how to program those commands into a system. This will be our final chapter of purely procedural programming from the Command window.

NEW COMMANDS AND FUNCTIONS

In this chapter, you should enter the examples as indicated. The discussion and examples that we present here will help you understand the concepts needed to solve the next segment of the Case System.

COMMAND `SEEK <expression>`

Searches the indexed table for the first occurrence of a key matching the expression clause. **SEEK** is very fast and is the focal point of most efficient search routines.

EXAMPLES

```
CLEAR
USE ycustm ORDER last
SEEK "Jones"
DISP last
lname = "Smith"
SEEK lname
DISP last
```

This example opens the customer master table with the **USE** command. The production **.mdx** file developed in the previous example, **ycustm.mdx** (see Chapter 5), was automatically opened at the same time. The **ORDER** can be set with the **ORDER** clause of the **USE** command, as in this example, or on a separate line with a **SET ORDER TO last** command. The database is now opened and ordered on last name. The **SEEK** expression is a character type constant, which, when evaluated, becomes the object of the search. dBASE stops on the first occurrence of **Jones**. **Jones** must be entered just as it appears in the database: for example, **JONES** will not locate **Jones**. The next **SEEK** in the example uses a memory variable expression as the object of the search. When evaluated, the variable becomes **Smith**. Most searches will be with memory variable expressions.

However complex the expression, when evaluated, the simple value becomes the **SEEK** search object. Though most searches will be with memory variable expressions, you may have need for a more complex expression. For example, **SEEK SQRT (49) + SQRT (81)** would search for the first occurrence of 16, which is the expression evaluated.

COMMAND `FIND <character string>`

Has the same function as the **SEEK** command. As in the **SEEK** command, the table *must* be indexed on the search key. However, the **SEEK** uses any expression as the search object, whereas the **FIND** can search only for a character string. This is another of those commands that was used in earlier versions of dBASE and is still included to make the language upwardly compatible. Unlike the **SEEK** command, **FIND** does not require delimiters around a character string, which makes it easier to use when working from the command window.

EXAMPLE

```
CLEAR
FIND Jones
DISP
```

You will probably prefer using the **SEEK** command in your programs. You can search for a memory variable object with the **FIND** command; however, you must precede the variable name with the macro substitution function, **&**, for example, **FIND &lname.**

COMMAND **SET EXACT ON/off**

When **SET EXACT** is set to **OFF**, you need place only the initial, unique characters after the **FIND**, **SEEK**, or **LOCATE** commands. This is useful to reduce the size of the search key.

EXAMPLE

```
CLEAR
SEEK "Jones"
SET EXACT OFF
SEEK "Jo"
DISP
```

COMMAND **LOCATE [<scope>] [FOR/WHILE <condition>]**

Searches the active table for the first occurrence of a record meeting a given condition. The table does not have to be indexed. The **LOCATE** command works in conjunction with the **CONTINUE** command.

COMMAND **CONTINUE**

Searches the active table for the next occurrence of a record meeting the condition specified in the **LOCATE** command.

EXAMPLES

```
CLEAR
SET EXACT ON
USE ycustm
LOCATE FOR city = "San Mateo"
DISP
CONTINUE
DISP
CONTINUE
DISP
SET EXACT OFF              && Set back to default.
```

After opening the customer master table, the **LOCATE** command searches for the first occurrence of a record with a city of **"San Mateo"**.

The **SET EXACT** command has been set to **ON**, so the complete field name must be encoded. The first **CONTINUE** command searches for the next occurrence of a record with a city of **"San Mateo"**. The next **CONTINUE** searches for the next occurrence, and so on.

COMMAND

```
SCAN [<scope>] [FOR <condition>] [WHILE <condition>]
   [<commands>]
   [LOOP]
   [EXIT]
ENDSCAN
```

This is a simplified alternative to the **DO WHILE** loop command. The **DO WHILE** requires an **IF..ENDIF** construct to select records to process and a **SKIP** command to move the pointer to a new record each time through the loop, whereas the **SCAN** command does not. **SCAN** will move through the active database, acting only on the records within the **SCAN <scope>** or selected by the **SCAN <condition>**. The **<commands>** between **SCAN** and **ENDSCAN** will operate only on those records selected. The **LOOP** and **EXIT** clauses have the same function as within the **DO WHILE**.

Here are examples of two program segments that accomplish the same result, one using the **DO WHILE** and the other using the **SCAN** command:

EXAMPLES

```
CLEAR
USE ycustm
* ==> This segment uses the DO WHILE construct.
DO WHILE .NOT. EOF()
    IF city = "San Mateo"
        ? last, city
    ENDIF
    SKIP
ENDDO
* ==> End of program segment.

* ==> This segment uses the SCAN construct.
SCAN FOR city = "San Mateo"
    ? last, city
ENDSCAN
* ==> End of program segment.
```

The first segment uses the **IF..ENDIF** construct and the **SKIP** to move the pointer to the next record to determine records with a **city = "San Mateo"**. The **SCAN** command eliminates these extra commands to accomplish the same task. Of course, the **SCAN** command is used only when moving through a database, whereas the **DO WHILE** can be used for other routines requiring the loop process. The **LOOP** and **EXIT** commands apply to the **SCAN** just as they do to the **DO WHILE**. **LOOP** transfers control back to the **SCAN** command, and **EXIT** transfers control to the statement just after the **ENDSCAN**.

COMMAND

```
FOR <memvar>=<start expN> TO <end expN>[STEP <step expN>]
    <statements>
    [LOOP]
    [EXIT]
NEXT
```

As with the **SCAN..ENDSCAN**, this command is a simplified version of the **DO WHILE**. It will execute the statements between the **FOR** and **NEXT** the number of times indicated by the **FOR** statement. The **STEP** option increments or decrements **memvar** each time the loop executes. **SCAN..ENDSCAN** is used with an open table, whereas **FOR..NEXT** is not. The advantages of **FOR..NEXT** over **DO WHILE** are speed and ease of coding.

EXAMPLE

```
FOR x = 1 TO 10
    IF MOD(x,3) = 0
        ? x          && Display values divisible by 3
    ENDIF
NEXT
```

The modules function, **MOD()**, allows the programmer to determine the remainder of one number divided into another. The loop in this example will execute 10 times. Each **x** value will be divided by 3 in **MOD()** to determine if the remainder is zero. If it is, it will be displayed.

COMMAND

```
SET KEY TO [<exp:match>/RANGE<exp:range>] [IN <alias>]
```

SET KEY TO turns off the current **RANGE** setting. This command allows only designated records to be seen in an index **TAG**. The records must be within a specified range.

FUNCTION

```
ELAPSED(<stop time expC>, <start time expC>)
```

Returns the elapsed time in seconds between the two time arguments.

FUNCTION

```
LIKE(<pattern>, <expC>)
```

Makes wildcard comparisons in a search command or function. If the pattern is in the character string, a logic **.T.** is returned. The two wildcard symbols are ***** for any group of characters and **?** for single character.

EXAMPLE

```
? LIKE ("*Market*","123 Market Street")
.T.
? LIKE ("?n*", "Anderson")
.T.
```

The first example asks: "Is the word **"Market"** contained anywhere in the second string?" The second example asks: "Is the second character in the string an **"n"**—ignoring the first character and the third and ensuing characters?"

FUNCTION **FOUND()**

Returns a logic **.T.** if the previous search command (**LOCATE**, **CONTINUE**, **FIND**, or **SEEK**) was successful. Notice the **FOUND()** example in the following **SEEK()** function discussion.

FUNCTION **TIME()**

Returns the system time.

FUNCTION **SEEK(<exp> [, <alias>])**

Searches the active or alias indexed database. The object of the search is the evaluated expression. This function performs just as the **SEEK <expression>** command, with a few advantages. Because it is a function, it can be included in an expression. If the object of the search is not found, it returns a logic **.F.** If you use the **SEEK** command, you must also execute either the **FOUND()** or **EOF()** function to determine whether the search was the successful. By using **SEEK()** instead the **SEEK** command, you eliminate this need. Further, **SEEK()** can do a search on an alias database, which we explore in a later chapter. Note the following program segment.

EXAMPLE

```
* ==== > Search using SEEK command.
CLEAR
USE ycustm
SET ORDER TO TAG last
SEEK "Jones"
IF FOUND()                    && Or IF .NOT. EOF()
  * ==== > GOOD data routine.
ELSE
  * ==== > BAD data routine.
ENDIF

* ==== > Search using SEEK() function.
IF SEEK ("Jones")
  * ==== > GOOD data routine.
ELSE
  * ==== > BAD data routine.
ENDIF
```

We have introduced the various commands involved in increasing the search and retrieval efficiency of systems developed with Visual dBASE. We now discuss how to use those commands to achieve that efficiency.

SEQUENTIAL VERSUS BINARY SEARCHES

A friend told me of a physics experiment he was asked to do in high school. The instructor gave the students a bucket of sand and a Geiger counter. He said that one grain of sand in the bucket was radioactive. They were to find that single grain with the Geiger counter. One solution to the problem would have been to take each grain of sand from the bucket, one at a time, and test it for radioactivity. In a database management system, this is called a sequential search. We would begin with the first record in the database and search every record until we found the one we were looking for. Needless to say, this could take a long time.

Another way to find the radioactive grain of sand—and this is the proper solution to the physics problem—would be to empty half the bucket of sand into another bucket, and then determine which bucket contained the radioactive grain. Then we would pour half of that bucket into another bucket, and once again test each bucket for the radioactive grain. We would continue this process of halving the sand until we located the proper grain. This is called a binary search. By using it, you can find a radioactive grain of sand very fast. If you are a Visual dBASE programmer, you will want to use the technique to retrieve records that meet a certain condition as quickly as possible.

The index file uses the binary method of storage and search. The information is stored forming an upside-down, treelike structure, as seen in Figure 6.1. If the tree is upside down, the root is at the top. Each intersection is called a node, so the topmost node is the root node.

As an example, if we execute the command `SEEK "Dole"`, the following steps take place. The search begins in the index tag `last` with the root node (rec 7, Jones). If the object of the `SEEK` is `Dole`, Visual dBASE decides, "Dole is to the left of Jones" and moves to the next node to the left (rec 4, Coster). At this point, it has eliminated everything to the right of the root node, or half the database. It then decides, "Dole is to the right of Coster" and moves to the next node to the right (rec 6, Dole). By doing this, it has eliminated half the remaining portion of the database. In our example, we have a "hit" on Dole. It now has the correct record number and key from the index file to move the pointer in the database file to the object record, Dole.

FIGURE 6.1 BINARY SEARCH MODEL (TREE STRUCTURE)

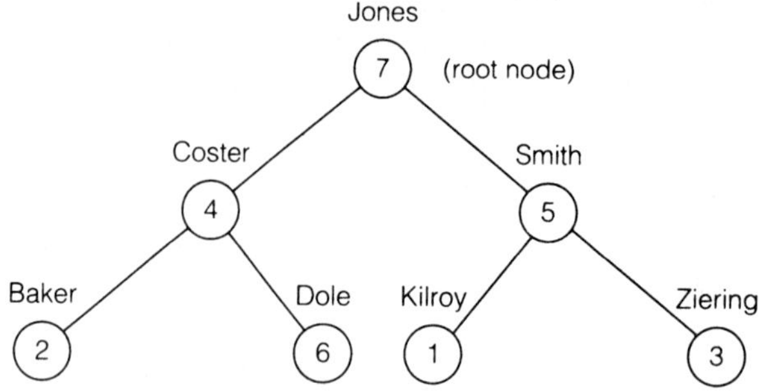

ycustm.dbf

REC	last
1	Kilroy
2	Baker
3	Ziering
4	Coster
5	Smith
6	Dole
7	Jones

ycustm.mdx

REC	TAG last
2	Baker
4	Coster
6	Dole
7	Jones
1	Kilroy
5	Smith
3	Ziering

The index file search is extremely fast and a major reason dBASE has been so successful. We therefore want to take advantage of it at every search junction.

VISUAL dBASE SEARCH COMMANDS

Now that we realize the binary search is fast and the sequential search is slow, we can examine again the search commands available in Visual dBASE. We can look at them in terms of the type of searches they provide and how to encode them properly to achieve faster searches. We first look at the commands that can produce the sequential search. Note the following:

```
CLEAR
USE ycustm
LOCATE FOR last = "Jones"
```

This sequence of commands will initiate the sequential search of the customer master file. The **FOR** clause in the **LOCATE** command will cause the pointer to move to the first record in the database. It will then test that record to see if it meets the condition (**last = "Jones"**). If it does not, it will move to the next record, and so on. If the first occurrence of **"Jones"** is at record number 50,000, we have sequentially examined 49,999 records prior to getting a hit.

Here's another example of a very slow sequential search (see Figure 6.2):

```
CLEAR
USE ycustm
LIST FOR last = "Jones"
```

FIGURE 6.2 SEQUENTIAL SEARCH MODEL

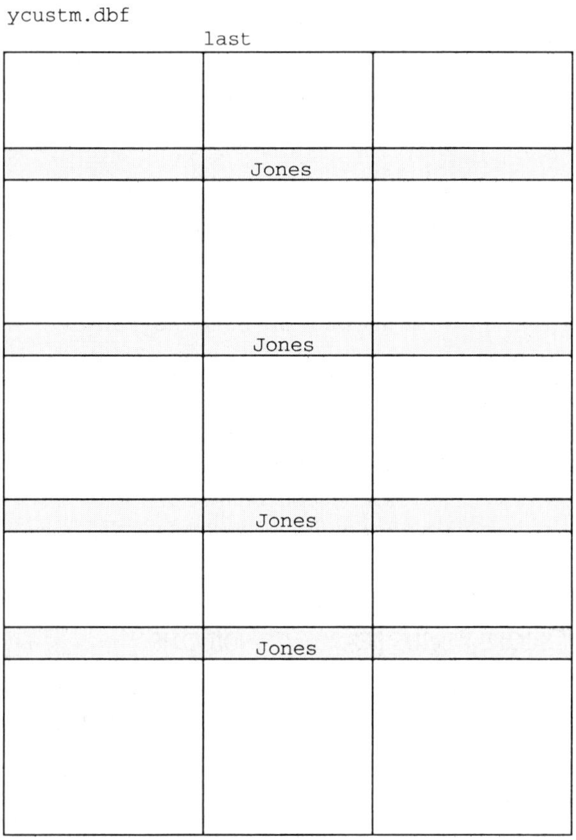

The **FOR** clause in the **LIST** command will move the pointer to the first record in the database. dBASE will then determine if that record meets the condition. It does not, so the pointer will move to the next record to examine the condition again. When a record is found that meets the condition, the **LIST** verb will print that record. It will then continue sequentially, examining every record until it finds another that meets the condition. If there are 1 to 100,000 records prior to the first record meeting the condition, it will examine each. The same is true between each occurrence, and what's worse, the same is true after it has **LIST**ed the last record meeting the condition. If there are 50,000 records after the last occurrence of **"Jones"**, dBASE will search every one of them—not knowing, of course, whether it has found the last one yet.

These are valid dBASE commands that will slow down many organizational systems. Let's continue this discussion with the **DO WHILE** and **SCAN** commands. Examine the following program segments:

```
* ==> Sequential Search Model (DO WHILE).
USE ycustm
DO WHILE .NOT. EOF()
   IF last = "Jones"
      ? last, city, state, zip
   ENDIF
   SKIP
ENDDO    && End of DO WHILE segment.
* ==> Sequential Search Model (SCAN).
SCAN FOR last = "Jones"
   ? last, city, state, zip
ENDSCAN     && End of SCAN segment.
```

As we demonstrated earlier, both these segments accomplish the same end. Both list the records having a last name of **"Jones"**. We introduced the **SCAN** command in this chapter on search efficiency because it does the same thing as the **DO WHILE**, with fewer steps. However, in our example, it does the same inefficient sequential search with fewer steps. This is not utilizing the command properly. In both cases, the pointer is being moved from the first record to the last, searching for records that meet the condition.

SCOPE VERSUS SEARCH CONDITIONS

Understanding the difference between the scope and search condition portion of the command syntax is important to our understanding of efficient searches.

The Search Condition Clause. The **FOR <condition>** is the search condition clause that asks: "What records do we want from the table?" It will cause the pointer to move to the top of the table and proceed searching sequentially, unless a scope or scope condition is present. For example, the command **LIST NEXT 10 FOR city = "San Mateo"** applies the condition only to the **NEXT 10** records in the table, regardless of where the pointer is when the search begins.

The Scope Condition Clause. The **WHILE <condition>** is the scope condition clause that asks: "How much of the table do we want to search?" The last example had a fixed scope (**NEXT 10**). However, what if we do not know how many records are in the scope? We want to search just while the last name is **"Jones"**, or perhaps we want to search while the city is **"Reno"**. These are examples of conditional scopes.

In the following example, our search objective is to list all records having a zip code beginning with 91. Let's assume we know that the 91s will be at the top of the table—if it is **ORDER**ed on zip code. However, we *do not* know how many there are. We have to use a conditional scope as follows:

```
CLEAR
USE ycustm              && The pointer is set to rec 1.
SET ORDER TO zip
```

Note: The pointer is still set to rec 1, which is *not* the first value in the **INDEX** file. **SET ORDER TO** does *not* reset the pointer.

```
GO TOP                  && Set pointer to top of index
                        && file.
LIST WHILE LIKE ("91*",zip)
```

The **USE** command opens the table in its natural order and sets the pointer to the top of the file. The order is then set to the **zip TAG**. After the **TAG** is set, the pointer remains on record 1, which is not the first record in the index file (review Figure 5.1 if you have a problem visualizing this). The **GO TOP** command moves the pointer to the top of the index file, which is the first occurrence of the **"91XXX"** zip codes.

The **LIST WHILE** command will begin with the current record and continue while the zip codes begin with **"91"**, as coded in the argument of the **LIKE()** function. This is a conditional scope.

Incidentally, the problem created by the **SET ORDER TO** command *not* resetting the pointer could also have been solved by the following form of the **USE** command:

```
USE ycustm ORDER zip
```

Notice in the status bar that the record pointer is now automatically on the first record in the index file. By coding the required **ORDER** in the **USE** command, we save a step. However, if you change the **ORDER**, the pointer will remain where it was in the previous **ORDER**. Fortunately, commands such as **FIND** and **SEEK** reset the pointer automatically to the first record in the **ORDER**ed table as they begin their search.

Finally, here is the key rule of pointer movement with the **FOR** or **WHILE** (**search** or **scope condition**) clauses.

> **The FOR clause will reset the pointer to the first record in the table, unless a scope or scope condition is present. If so, the pointer remains on the current record, and the search proceeds from that record to the end of the scope.**

EFFICIENT SEARCH TECHNIQUES

We can now put all this together to generate the proper coding to take full advantage of the efficient search techniques dBASE has to offer. These are the steps in conducting the efficient search:

1. **INDEX** on the key expression that will become the scope condition. For example, if using a scope based on a city, that would become the indexed field.
2. Execute a search with the **SEEK** command to locate the first record in the scope condition. If the search scope will cover the city of San Mateo, the **SEEK** search would rapidly find the first occurrence of that city.
3. Execute the dBASE verb using the **WHILE** clause to sequentially process the records within the scope.
4. Encode the **FOR** clause into the expression if a search condition is required within the scope condition.

Conditional Scope Search. The first example of the efficient search will be from the command window. Refer to Figure 6.3, and type in the following:

```
CLEAR
USE ycustm
SET ORDER TO city
SEEK "San Mateo"
LIST WHILE city = "San Mateo"
```

After opening the customer master file and ordering on the city field, the **SEEK** command searches for the first occurrence of **"San Mateo"**. Note from Figure 6.3 that the pointer is now at the first record meeting the search condition. The **LIST** command will begin from that record because of the **WHILE** clause. When the pointer moves past the scope, the search will end. We have moved the pointer to the first record in the scope as fast as possible using binary search techniques of the **SEEK** on an indexed file; we then sequentially listed the remaining records within the scope. Now sequential makes sense because the next record in sequence *is* the record we are looking for.

FIGURE 6.3 CONDITIONAL SCOPE SEARCH

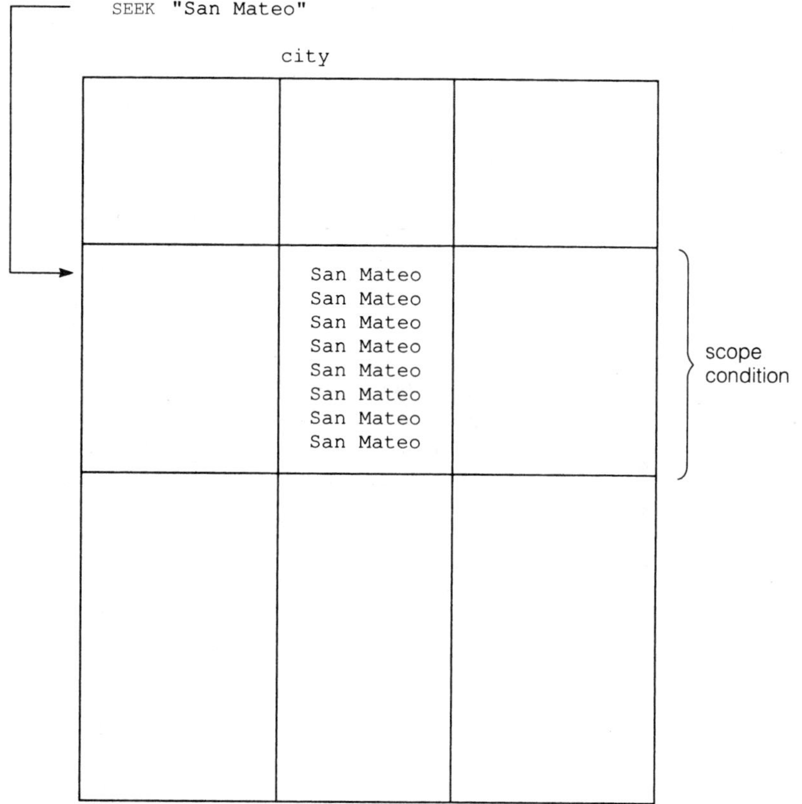

Search Condition Within a Scope Condition. It is also possible to search for only selected records from within the conditional scope. Refer to Figure 6.4, and type in the following:

```
CLEAR
USE ycustm
SET ORDER TO city
SEEK "San Mateo"
LIST last, city, no_rents
     FOR no_rents > 5
     WHILE city = "San Mateo"
```

FIGURE 6.4 SEARCH CONDITION WITHIN A CONDITIONAL SCOPE

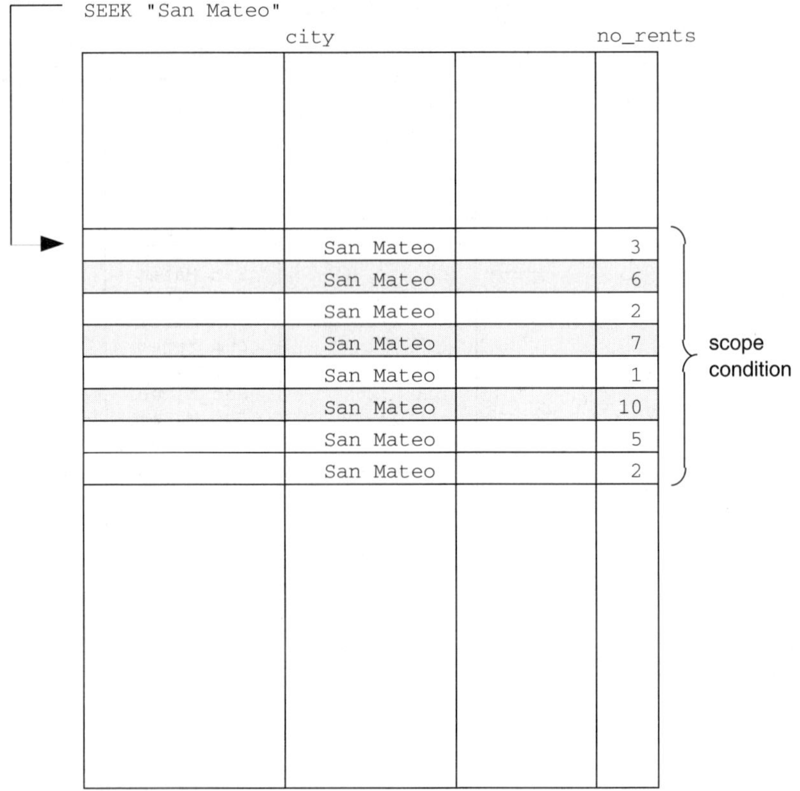

The requirement of this example was a listing of all customers from San Mateo who have rented more than five films. The scope condition is the same as in the previous example; however, we have added a search condition within the scope condition. Only those customers renting more than five films will be listed.

Note: The above search techniques can be applied to any command with a search or scope (`FOR` or `WHILE`) clause. Care should be taken when using commands that alter the table; for example, `REPLACE`—since you cannot `REPLACE WHILE` the field that is the key of the index.

Efficient Searches with `DO WHILE` and `SCAN`. So far, we have been working from the Command window with efficient search techniques. In your programs, search techniques will usually work in conjunction with the `SCAN` command. The same Command window examples from above could be programmed in segments with either the **DO WHILE** or the **SCAN**. Let's look at both because you may be called on to examine existing systems and need to speed up searches that now use **DO WHILE**s.

Note the following program segments:

```
* ==> Efficient Search -- DO WHILE and SEEK command.
USE ycustm
SET ORDER TO last
ACCEPT "ENTER LAST NAME: " TO mlast
SEEK mlast
IF .NOT. FOUND()
   * ==> Appropriate error routine.
ENDIF
DO WHILE last = mlast
   ? last, city, no_rents
   SKIP
ENDDO [last=mlast]
* ==> End of DO WHILE program segment.

* ==> Efficient Search -- SCAN with SEEK() function.
ACCEPT "ENTER LAST NAME: " TO mlast
IF .NOT. SEEK (mlast)
   * ==> Appropriate error routine.
ENDIF
SCAN WHILE last = mlast
   ? last, city, no_rents
ENDSCAN
* ==> End of program segment.
```

In both these segments, the **SEEK** command or **SEEK()** function moves the pointer extremely fast to the first record in the scope condition. The **DO WHILE** or **SCAN** then moves through the scope, selecting records based on the condition set forth in the command. You can see that the **SCAN** and **SEEK()** segments give a more concisely coded block to accomplish the same thing. Moreover, in most cases **SCAN..ENDSCAN** will execute faster than an equivalent **DO WHILE**.

Using the Conditional Index and SET KEY TO Commands. The conditional index and **SET KEY** commands produce even more efficient dBASE searches. An analogy might be a public library that uses index card files. To locate a book, you would first look through an index card file. To find a book by a certain author, you would search the author index card file first, then go to the book as directed on the index card. This is, of course, faster than sequentially searching for the book on the bookshelves. But think how much faster it would be if the library had an author index card file that contained *just* those cards on the author you are looking for. The conditional index gives us that capability in Visual dBASE searches.

Enter the following from the Input pane to illustrate the use of a conditional index:

```
USE ycustm
INDEX ON last TAG last75 FOR amt_rent > 75
DISPLAY ALL last, city, amt_rent
```

Notice that the **DISPLAY** verb selects only those records with an **amt_rent** greater than $75.00, in last name order. This creates an index **TAG** that contains *only* keys that meet those conditions. As in the library analogy, this creates a much faster search because, essentially, no search is necessary.

Though very fast, the conditional index has the drawback of requiring a number of **TAG**s for each search requirement. The **SET KEY** command allows the use of **RANGE**s within a single index **TAG** and reduces the need for many separate conditional **TAG**s and their associated housekeeping. Enter the following to illustrate:

```
USE ycustm ORDER last
SET KEY TO "Mason"
DISPLAY ALL last, city, amt_rent
GO TOP                 && Go to top of range.
GO BOTTOM              && Go to bottom of range.
```

In this example, only the last name **"Mason"** as a range is seen by dBASE. Notice that the **GO TOP** and **GO BOTTOM** commands take you to the top and bottom of the range, not to the top or bottom of the file as seen through the complete index **TAG**. All pointer movement is now restricted to the range. Continue with the following:

```
SET ORDER TO no_rents
SET KEY TO RANGE 3,6
DISPLAY ALL last, city, no_rents
GO TOP                 && First no_rents of 3.
GO BOTTOM              && Last no_rents of 6.
SET KEY TO RANGE 3, && All records >= to three.
DISPLAY ALL last, city, amt_rent
SET KEY TO RANGE, 6 && All records <= to six.
DISPLAY ALL last, city, no_rents
```

In this example, we have ordered the table on the numeric field **no_rents**. The first **SET KEY** sets the range greater than or equal to 3 and less than or equal to 6. The next two examples demonstrate the syntax used to set a lower or upper limit only.

Tests show that the conditional index is the fastest search and the sequential filter the slowest. The **SEEK( )/SCAN..ENDSCAN** and **SET KEY** searches should run at about the same speed. However, although the conditional index is slightly faster, **SET KEY** can look at many ranges within a single index **TAG** versus requiring multiple **TAG**s, as in the conditional index. Finally, **SEEK( )/SCAN..ENDSCAN** is effective in situations where various search objects must be located prior to viewing. This will be demonstrated in the chapter review exercise.

Benchmark Tests. When in doubt as to the efficiency of one coding scheme over another, you can build a benchmark test program. We have just explored four different ways of searching a database table, using (1) a sequential filter, (2) the **SEEK( )** function with a **SCAN..WHILE**, (3) a conditional index, or (4) the **SET KEY** search. Just how fast is one technique over another? To adequately test one coding scheme against another, you would need to construct a very large table. Additionally, a routine to record the starting and ending time of each test would be necessary.*

Additional Visual dBASE Efficiency Techniques. Here are a few additional thoughts on ways to increase processing speeds.

High Performance Filter Optimization. The sequential search takes on a new meaning with the use of the high performance filter optimization system in Visual dBASE. The sequential filters discussed earlier in this chapter should run dramatically faster than any using versions of dBASE prior to the dBASE IV 1.5 version. This is because later versions actually create an internal index based on the **FOR** clause and use this to optimize the search. Additionally, Visual dBASE will *learn* from prior searches of a file if an index **TAG** is not present and increase the optimization in subsequent searches of the same file.

Nevertheless, though optimized filters are dramatically faster than purely sequential filters, they should be avoided in program code that requires maximum efficiency. The indexed techniques discussed earlier will always be faster than setting a filter condition.

Efficient Use of Commands/Functions. In addition to the preceding techniques, the following general rules apply to the use of Visual dBASE commands and functions when used as part of search scenarios:

---

*A technical paper, *Efficient Search Techniques Using dBase IV*, was presented by Robert Buchanan at the Borland International Developers Conference in San Diego in 1993 and in Orlando in 1994. The paper is available from Borland, Inc. A diskette containing the demonstration files and benchmark test programs is also available.

- `IIF()` versus `IF..ENDIF`: The `IIF()` function will operate faster than the `IF..ENDIF` construct.
- UDFs versus Procedures: Procedures operate much faster than User Defined Functions. UDFs and procedures are discussed in Chapters 7 and 10.
- `SEEK()` versus `SEEK` versus `FIND`: `SEEK()` is faster than `SEEK` because the `FOUND()` function is built in. `SEEK` is faster than `FIND` because of the macro expansion required when using a `FIND` argument.
- Assign commands versus `STORE`: An assign command is faster than a `STORE` command. For example, `xvalue = 10` is faster than `STORE 10 TO xvalue`.

REVIEW EXERCISES

We will work a series of exercises and develop a short program module to reinforce the various search techniques discussed in the chapter. These techniques will also be utilized in the Case System.

PART I: EFFICIENT LISTINGS OF THE DATABASE

In this command window exercise, the dBASE verb needed to solve the problem appears in square brackets. The objective of this exercise is to construct the remainder of the command from the information presented in the chapter.

Problem A Specification. Using the efficient search techniques presented in this chapter, list the last names of all customers with the last name "Jones".

- Open `ycustm [use]`.
- `SET ORDER TO` the last name `TAG [SET ORDER To]`.
- `SEEK` the first occurrence of the last name `"Jones" [SEEK]`.
- `LIST` the last name and city of all customers with the last name `"Jones" [LIST]`.

Problem B Specification. List the last name, city, and number of rents (`no_rents`) of all the people from San Mateo who have rented more than six films.

To solve this problem, use a search condition (`no_rents`) within a scope condition (`city`).

PART II: PROGRAMMING EFFICIENT DATABASE LISTINGS

The objective of this exercise is to write a short program to list to the screen the number of rentals by all customers from a requested city.

Specification. Write the program according to the following specifications.

- Name the program **yfast.prg.**
- Build an index tag using the uppercase of the last name as a key. Name the tag **cityuc**. It will allow a search of the table with either an upper or lowercase key. The key entered by the operator will be made uppercase immediately after entry, regardless of its case on initial entry. It will then become the object of the **SEEK( )** function, which searches the uppercase index tag. Test using the following code example:

```
USE ycustm
INDEX ON UPPER(city) TAG cityuc
mKey = "sAn MaTeO"   && Data entry may be any case.
mKey = UPPER(mKey)
? SEEK(mKey)          && Returns .T.
```

- The program should be interactive with the user, allowing entry of the requested city from an input screen (Results pane) designed as in Figure 6.5.
- If the operator enters an invalid **city**, place the following message on the screen. Include the requested city `<invalid city>`.

  <invalid city> NOT IN DATABASE...TRY AGAIN (Y)es/(N)o ?

  Then give the operator the opportunity to either enter another city or exit the module.
- Output should appear as in Figure 6.6. Insert the input value of city into the output listing heading as shown.
- Each output line will appear as two columns. The first column contains the customer's first and last names, and the second column contains the number of rents (**no_rents**). Notice from Figure 6.6 that there is one space between the first and last name. If you trim the first name and concatenate it to the last name, the **no_rents** field will not be aligned down the page. How can this problem be solved? Use the negative string concatenation sign (–).

FIGURE 6.5 INITIAL DATA ENTRY SCREEN—PROGRAM MODULE `yfast`

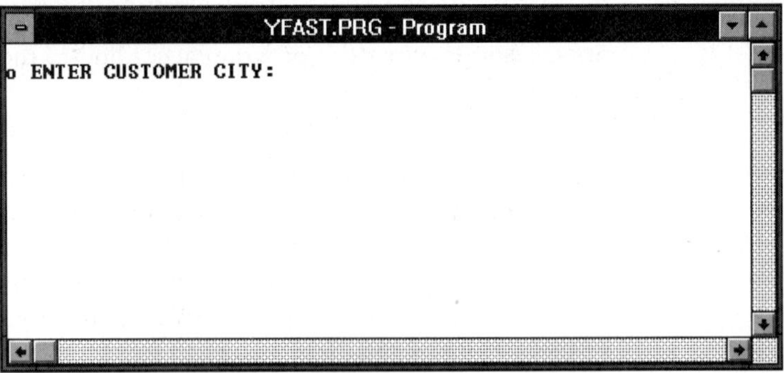

FIGURE 6.6 SAMPLE OUTPUT—PROGRAM MODULE `yfast`

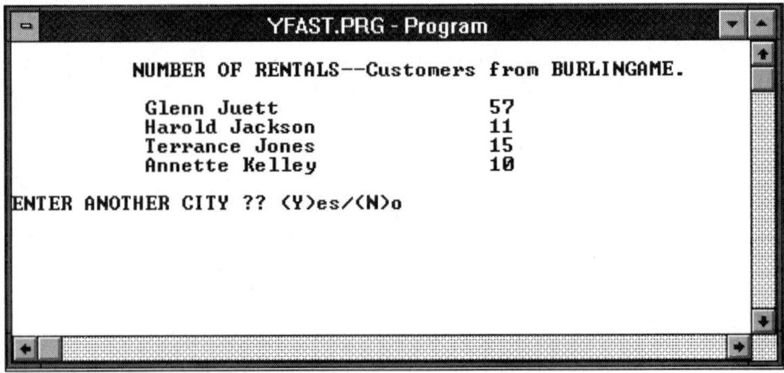

Pseudocode Models. The pseudocode models for your problem solution appear in Figures 6.7 (general) and 6.8 (detailed).

FIGURE 6.7 GENERAL PSEUDOCODE—EFFICIENT SEARCH MODULE `yfast`

Program headings.
Program initialization.
Open table.
Present input screen model.
Data entry.
Search for first occurrence of input city.
Present all cities matching input city to screen.
Program close-out.
Program footer.

FIGURE 6.8 DETAILED PSEUDOCODE—EFFICIENT SEARCH MODULE `yfast`

__________ Program identification.
__________ Program initialization.
__________ Open file to be used—set city **TAG**.
__________ Initialize loop control variable.
__________ Begin data entry loop.
    __________ Clear screen.
    __________ Display input screen model. Use the **ACCEPT** command for input city (Figure 6.5).
    __________ Begin logic to test for successful **SEEK**. Use **SEEK()** function for **IF** condition.
        __________ Clear screen. Place output listing heading on screen. Insert input city in heading as described in specifications (Figure 6.6).
        __________ Establish **SCOPE CONDITION** within **SCAN** command to list output to screen. Within the **SCAN..ENDSCAN** construct, place each line of data on screen using the **?** command in accordance with problem specification.

_**ELSE**_____

        __________ Procedure for unsuccessful search.

- Place error message on screen as described in problem specification.
- Use **IF..ELSE..ENDIF** construct to either **LOOP** back for new input, or **EXIT** to move to single exit point of module.

(continues)

FIGURE 6.8 (continued)

DETAILED PSEUDOCODE—EFFICIENT SEARCH MODULE **yfast**

__________ End logic to test for successful **SEEK**.

__________ Procedure for asking operator if another search is wanted. Place message in Results pane as described in the specifications. If operator responds with any character other than **"Y"**, **EXIT** to close-out.

__________ End data entry loop.

__________ Close-out commands.

__________ Return (single exit from module).

PART III: BENCHMARK TESTS

The objective of this exercise is to compare the speed of the **DO WHILE..ENDDO** to the **FOR..NEXT** construct. The benchmark program should allow the operator to enter the number of iterations each construct will execute and present the relative speeds in seconds.

Specification

- Name the program **ybchmk.prg**.
- Develop a **DO WHILE** to loop a variable number of times according to the numeric value entered by the operator. Use the **INPUT** command to get a numeric value from the operator to determine the number of iterations to use.
- Inside the **DO WHILE**, increment a memory variable, **xSum**, as follows:

  ```
  xSum = ySum + SQRT(200)/10
  ```

  Initialize the variable to zero prior to entry into the loop.
- Using the **TIME()** function, record the current system time just before entering the loop. Using the **ELAPSED()** function, record the difference between the recorded start time and the current time just after leaving loop.
- Develop a **FOR..NEXT** loop to accomplish the same calculation with **xSum**. Record the starting and elapsed time as with the **DO WHILE**.

The execution time between the two constructs will be only slightly different unless a large number of iterations is used. In systems using a smaller number, one is probably as appropriate as the other. However, in systems with highly iterative processes, the time difference may be appreciable and should be considered.

CHAPTER SUMMARY

In this chapter, we learned the types of searches available with Visual dBASE. We discussed all the search commands available in Visual dBASE as they relate to the building of efficient search models.

The following topics were discussed:

- There are two general types of searches: sequential and binary.
- Sequential searches are much slower than binary searches.
- The scope condition clause of a command defines how much of the database is to be searched. The search condition clause defines which records within the defined scope will be processed.
- The **SCAN..ENDSCAN** command was added in dBase IV and is a more efficient way to cycle through a database than the **DO WHILE** command.
- A fast way to search a table for a group of records meeting a given condition is to index the table on search key, move the pointer to the first occurrence of the group with the **SEEK** command or **SEEK()** function, and then sequentially process the remaining records in the group.
- To display a known range of records, use the **SET KEY** command or a conditional index **TAG**. The **SET KEY** command is slightly slower than a conditional index, but it requires fewer index **TAG**s to manage. The **SET FILTER TO** command should be avoided in most program code.

The following commands and functions were discussed:

- SEEK
- FIND
- SET EXACT
- LOCATE
- SCAN..ENDSCAN
- FOR..NEXT
- SET KEY
- LIKE()
- FOUND()
- SEEK()
- TIME()

In the next chapter, we will begin our discussions of object-oriented programming. Structured procedural programming will continue as you develop the programmed methods contained in the objects of the Case System.

PART THREE

Object-Oriented Programming with Visual dBASE

CHAPTER SEVEN

TOPICS

New Commands and Functions

Concepts

- Procedure files
- Memory variable management
- Object-oriented programming

Review Exercises

Chapter Summary

Introduction to Object-Oriented Programming

7

CHAPTER OBJECTIVES

In this chapter, we introduce Visual dBASE object-oriented concepts and syntax. We will trace the evolution of object-oriented programming and discuss both its compatibilities and its advantages over structured programming.

The management of memory variables and the use of procedure files become increasingly more important as we add object techniques to our structured programming concepts. We will discuss the types of memory variables available in Visual dBASE, their naming conventions, and their usage in object-oriented systems. Procedures and procedure files will be defined and used in the object programming exercises.

After studying this chapter, you should understand the basic terminology and concepts of Visual dBASE object-oriented programming and be able to build simple objects from the Command window and program editor.

NEW COMMANDS AND FUNCTIONS

COMMAND
```
PROCEDURE <procedure name> [(<parameter list>)]
<statements>
[RETURN [<return exp>]]
```

A procedure is a routine that may be used repeatedly. The **PROCEDURE** command identifies the name of a procedure, either within a program or within a procedure file. Although there is no restriction on the length given to a procedure name, only the first 32 characters are recognized. A procedure name can contain letters, numbers, or the underscore character. It will also optionally declare memory variables to represent parameters passed to the procedure. Parameter passing will be discussed in Chapter 9.

COMMAND
```
SET PROCEDURE TO <filename> [ADDITIVE]
```

Opens a procedure file.

COMMAND
```
PRIVATE <memvar list>
[ALL]
[ALL LIKE <Skeleton>]
[ALL EXCEPT <Skeleton>]
```

Allows the creation of a memory variable in a program module that has already been declared in a calling module—or declared **PUBLIC** in another module. This will be discussed in greater detail later in this chapter.

EXAMPLE
```
PRIVATE xValue1, xValue2
PRIVATE ALL LIKE x*
PRIVATE ALL EXCEPT g*
STORE 0 TO xValue1, xValue2
```

The wild-card symbol "*" allows declaration of all variables with the same first letter. Notice that **PRIVATE** does not initialize the variables, it only declares them. The last command in the example initializes the values of `xValue1` and `xValue2`.

COMMAND
```
PUBLIC <memvar list>
```

Allows creation of memory variables that will not be automatically released upon program module completion. See the discussion in the following section of this chapter for a more detailed explanation.

COMMAND `LOCAL <memvar list>`

Declares memory variables that are visible only in the subroutine in which they are declared. The lifespan of a **LOCAL** is limited to the module in which it was initialized.

COMMAND `STATIC <memvar list>`

Declares memory variables that are visible only in the subroutine in which they are declared. The lifespan of a **STATIC** is much like the **PUBLIC**.

COMMAND

```
RELEASE [<memvar list>]
[ALL]
[ALL LIKE <Skeleton>]
[ALL EXCEPT <Skeleton>]
```

Releases all memory variables in the memory variable list. **RELEASE ALL** from the Command window releases *all* live memory variables. **RELEASE ALL** from within a program releases only those variables **PRIVATE** to that module or to any of its children.

EXAMPLE

```
RELEASE xsum, ysum
RELEASE ALL LIKE r*
RELEASE ALL EXCEPT x*
```

The wild-card symbol allows release of all variables with the same first letter.

COMMAND

```
DEFINE <class name> <object name>
[OF <container object>]
[FROM <row,col> TO <row,col> | AT <row,col>]
[PROPERTY <stock property list>]
[CUSTOM <custom property list>]
[WITH <parameter list>]
```

Creates a new object from a class. The **NEW** operator can also be used to accomplish the same thing. This will be discussed in more detail in the Concepts section of this chapter.

COMMAND

```
CLASS <class name> [(<parameters>)] [CUSTOM]
   PARAMETERS <parameters>]
   [OF <superclass name [(<parameters>)]]
   [<constructor code>]
   [<member functions>]
ENDCLASS
```

Declares a custom class and specifies the member variables and functions for that class.

FUNCTION `INSPECT(<object reference>)`

Opens the Object Inspector window. The Object Inspector window is referred to as the Inspector. The Inspector lists object properties and lets you change their settings.

FUNCTION `STR(<expN>[,<length>][,<decimal>])`

Used to convert numeric type data to character type data.

EXAMPLE

```
CLEAR
mTotal = 6.30
? "THE TOTAL IS:", mTotal
? "THE TOTAL IS: " + STR(mTotal,3,2)
? "THE TOTAL IS: " + LTRIM(STR(mTotal,3,2))
```

The first print command **(?)** displays the character expression and numeric expression separated by a comma, because you cannot add character type data to numeric type. However, the extra space generated between the two expressions could create a problem. The second print command converts the numeric data to character type and shortens its length. This will reduce the spacing by allowing string concatenation. The **LTRIM()** function is used in the third example to get rid of any extra spaces caused by the whole number being smaller than the three spaces set aside as a **STR()** argument.

OPERATORS

`(.)` Dot reference operator **(.)**. Used to reference object properties.

`(::)` Scope resolution operator. Used to reference a method from a class.

`this` Object reference operator. Used in class declarations and methods to refer generically to objects without hard coding.

`NEW` The **NEW** operator creates an object of a specified class. The **DEFINE** command introduced earlier can also be used to create an object of a specified class. The **NEW** operator is used in the assign command syntax as follows:

```
<object name> = NEW <class name>([<parameters>])
```

CONCEPTS

The use of procedures and the management of memory variables is an important prerequisite to object-oriented programming. As we move through this chapter, we will build objects and then place procedures and memory variables inside those objects.

PROCEDURE FILES

One of the programmer's housekeeping tasks is to manage small but often used routines within a system. For example, you may have an error routine that presents a message to the operator from wherever that error occurs within a system. Rather than recoding the same routine over and over within the system, a short error program can be developed and called by the main program as needed.

In the early days of dBASE programming, such routines had to be placed in separate program files. In later versions, the procedure file was introduced and allowed for many separate procedures to be placed in a single DOS file. Once a procedure file is opened, any individual procedure from within the file can be accessed. In Visual dBASE, a single procedure file can contain as many as 193 procedures, and the number of procedure files open at one time is limited only by available memory.

Figure 7.1 displays an example of a procedure file, `globproc.prg`, global to all system modules. In this case, one of the procedures, `proc2`, is called by the program, `ysample2.prg`. Any procedure within the procedure file can be called from any program within a system of programs.

Beginning with dBASE IV, *in-program* procedures were made available. If a group of procedures is being used primarily by a single program, those procedures can be coded within that program file (see Figure 7.2). Later in this chapter, the same concepts will be used to access procedures within objects. In this case, various error messages are being called from the in-program procedures by the main program.

NOTE: Procedure files may also contain User Defined Functions (UDFs), which will be explained in Chapter 9. Both procedures and functions will be used extensively as we build the Case System.

MEMORY VARIABLE MANAGEMENT

Visual dBASE has certain rules governing the use of memory variables. These need to be discussed, especially as they apply to initialization and automatic release by a program module. Memory variable naming conventions are also important in that they will greatly ease the housekeeping chores related to memory variables.

FIGURE 7.1 SAMPLE PROCEDURE FILE

```
* == > PROGRAM ysample2.prg
<program commands>

* == > Execute procedure.
DO proc2

<program commands>
*   ==   >  End of program  ysample2.prg
```

```
* === > PROCEDURE FILE globproc.prg

* === > Procedure #1 description.
PROCEDURE proc1
  <procedure commands>
RETURN

* === > Procedure #2 description.
PROCEDURE proc2
  <procedure commands>
RETURN

* === > Procedure #3 description.
PROCEDURE proc3
  <procedure commands>
RETURN

* === > End of procedure file globproc.prg
```

FIGURE 7.2 PROCEDURES WITHIN A PROGRAM

```
* == > PROGRAM ysample.prg
<program commands>

* ==  > Program segment.
DO  CASE
     CASE item = "1"
     DO mess1
  CASE item = "2"
     DO mess2
  CASE item = "3"
     DO mess3
ENDCASE

<program commands>
* == > End of program segment.



* == >  BEGIN IN-PROGRAM PROCEDURES.

* == > Message procedure #1.
PROCEDURE mess1
 ? "Set toggle to 1 -- Any key to continue"
RETURN

* == > Message procedure #2.
PROCEDURE mess2
 ? "Incorrect data -- Try again ?"
RETURN

* == > Message procedure #3.
PROCEDURE mess3
 ? "Record not in database -- Try again ?"
RETURN

* == > End of Procedures.
* == > End of Program ysample.prg
```

Scoping Memory Variables. A memory variable scope consists of its *lifespan* and its *visibility*. Lifespan is the time between the creation of a memory variable and its final release from memory. Release may occur automatically or it may be forced by the programmer. Even though a memory variable is alive, it may not be available from all parts of a system. Its availability is referred to as its visibility.

Types of Memory Variables

1. `PUBLIC:` Variables so declared are alive and visible from anywhere in a system. They can be released only with the `RELEASE` or `CLEAR ALL` command. Variables scoped as `PUBLIC` can be used from anywhere within a system; for example, a variable containing the current path can be used by an application. However, because of its global visibility, a `PUBLIC` variable becomes susceptible to inadvertent destruction or modification and should be used sparingly in an object-oriented system.

2. `PRIVATE:` Visual dBASE allows the use of a module containing a variable with the same name as another variable that is used in a parent module. An example of this is when a module is used in a system that was previously developed for another system, and that module contains a memory variable name already alive in a parent module of the current system. To avoid having to change the names of all the affected variables in the subprogram, the names can be declared `PRIVATE` to that module and to all its children. The variables from the parent module having the same name, though still active, are *hidden* to the subprogram.

   A `PRIVATE` memory variable is automatically released when the program module in which it was created is closed. It is visible in the module in which created, and all the children of that module.

3. `LOCAL:` As with a `PRIVATE` memory variable, a `LOCAL` variable is automatically released when the program module in which it was created is closed. However, it is visible only in the module in which created, and not in the children of that module. Its purpose is to protect the variable against inadvertent overwriting within a child module. Also, when you create an object, all variables that are members of that object are automatically `LOCAL` in scope without the need for the `LOCAL` declaration.

   Counters such as those used in `FOR..NEXT` or `DO WHILE` loops are examples of variables that should be protected by a `LOCAL` scope.

4. `STATIC:` As with `LOCAL` variables, the `STATIC` memory variable is visible only in the module in which it was created, and not in the children of that module. However, its lifespan is similar to the `PUBLIC` memory variable and can only be released by program code. Its purpose is also to protect against inadvertent overwriting.

NOTE: When any type of memory variable is alive, but not as visible, it will be referred to here as out-of-scope. It should not be confused with hidden, which refers to a variable hidden from a lower level procedure by the `PRIVATE` declaration discussed previously.

Here are some additional rules governing the **STATIC** memory variable:

- The **RELEASE** command will only release a **STATIC** if executed within the module in which it was initialized. If an explicit **RELEASE** is executed somewhere else in the system, the memory variable that is **STATIC** to a module will remain alive, though not visible.
- The **CLEAR ALL** or **QUIT** command will release a **STATIC** memory variable wherever executed.
- A **STATIC** memory variable can be declared and initialized in the same statement. Type the following code segment into the program editor (call the program **ystatic**). After the segment is typed, press the **Run** button in the Speedbar to execute.

```
* ==> Begin segment
CLEAR
SET TALK OFF
LOCAL xVaL                 && Declare xVal
STATIC yVal = 10           && Declare and initialize yVal
xVal = 5                   && Initialize xVal
yVal = yVal + 1
SET TALK ON
RETURN
* ==> End segment
```

After this program has completed its execution, close the Program Editor and enter the following commands from the Input pane:

```
DISP MEMO         && Pause to verify status of yVal.
CLEAR ALL
DISP MEMO
```

DISP MEMO will verify that **yVal** is still alive after the procedure is closed. **CLEAR ALL** will finally release **yVal**.

- If a **STATIC** memory variable is both declared and initialized in the same statement, it will retain its final value when control returns to the routine in which it was initialized. For example, if you execute **ystatic** a second time, the initial value of **yVal** will be 11 versus 10. If run again, it will be 12, and so on. If the **STATIC** is declared in one statement and initialized in another, **yVal** will return to its initialized value each time control returns to the procedure.

- **RELEASE ALL** in a program or procedure will not release **STATIC** or **PUBLIC** memory variables. They must be explicitly released. In the preceding example, **RELEASE yVal** in the program segment would release **yVal**. **RELEASE ALL** in the program would not.

NOTE: In earlier versions of Visual dBASE, DISPLAY MEMORY may not display LOCAL and STATIC memory variable scopes properly. If they are alive, they will appear, but as PUBLIC or PRIVATE rather than LOCAL or STATIC. Further, if they are out of scope, they may not appear as such.

To better understand these definitions and rules, see the diagram in Figure 7.3. It displays a series of program modules, one calling another. Follow the diagram as we discuss how it applies to the above definitions and rules.

FIGURE 7.3 MEMORY VARIABLE MANAGEMENT

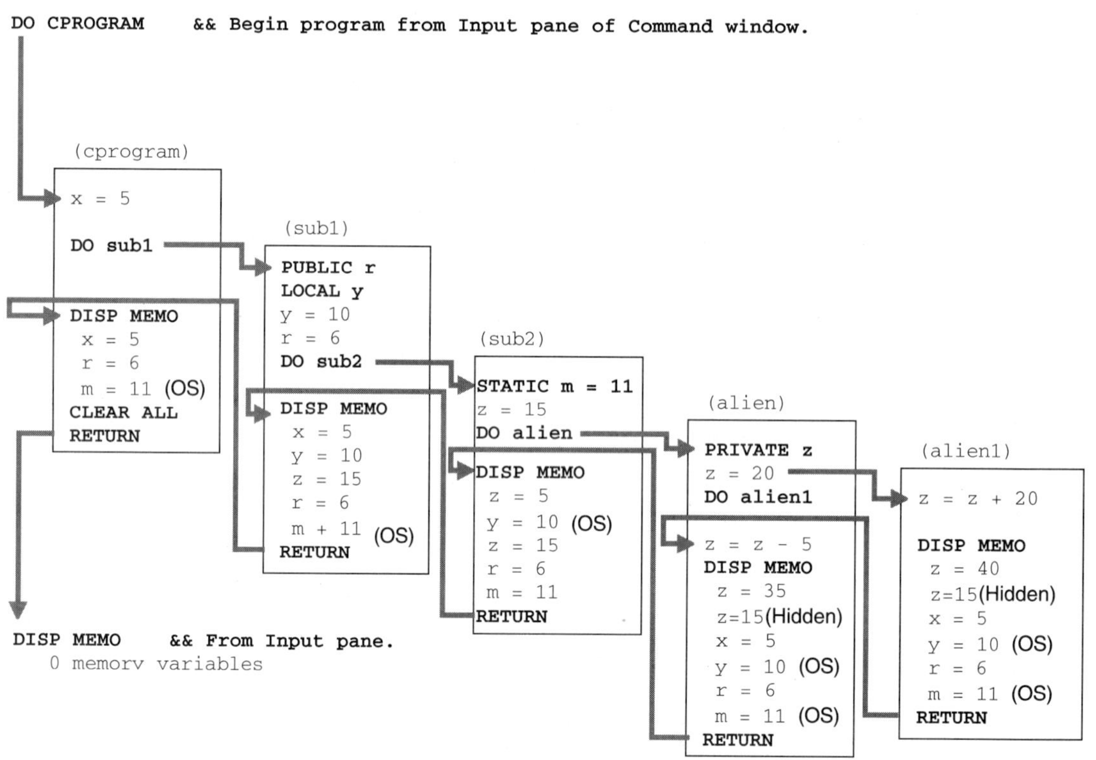

In Figure 7.3, the variable **x** is initialized in **cprogram**, and is therefore automatically **PRIVATE** in lifespan and visibility. It is alive in **cprogram** and alive in all the children, or called programs, of that module. It is only released when **cprogram** has been cancelled and control returned to the Input pane. You would consider **x PRIVATE** to **cprogram**.

The variable **r** is declared **PUBLIC** and the variable **y** is declared **LOCAL** in **sub1; y** will not be visible in all the children of **sub1**, though it will be alive in all the children of **sub1**. It will be released when **sub1** is cancelled and control returned to **cprogram**. Because **r** has been declared **PUBLIC**, it will not be released by **sub1**. It is now alive and visible to all modules, including the parent module, **cprogram**.

The variable **m** is declared **STATIC** and initialized in the same statement in **sub2**. It will not be released when **sub2** is cancelled and control returned to **sub1**. Because it is **STATIC**, it will not be visible in all the children of **sub2** but will be alive in those modules. Next, note the subprogram **alien**, a child of **sub2**; **sub2** and **alien** contain a memory variable **z**. To keep the **z** of **sub2 HIDDEN** while control is in **alien**—or its child, **alien1**—the **PRIVATE** statement is used to declare the new **z** of **alien** private to **alien** and **alien1**. If that sounds a bit tricky, just follow it through on the diagram!

Note the **DISPLAY MEMORY** command in each module. It displays the current values of the live memory variables in each module just prior to returning to the calling module. You may want to create the programs in Figure 7.3 using your **MODIFY COMMAND** editor; then execute them for a better understanding of their management of memory variables. Be sure to read the note in the next section on the shortcomings of the **DISPLAY MEMORY** command in early versions of Visual dBASE.

Memory Variable Naming Conventions. Certain guidelines for naming memory variables are used. We outlined some rules governing memory variable names in Chapter 3. However, within the rules, certain naming conventions can be applied to make the housekeeping and reference of variables an easier task. Once you decide which conventions to use, try to stay with them in a single system to maintain uniform documentation standards. Listed are some examples:

- Always preface a variable with an additional character to the name selected (for example, **xRate**, **mTime**, **rTitle**). This will help you distinguish between a memory variable and a field variable.
- Capitalize the first letter of multiple word names. For example, if you have a pay rate variable, name it **mPayRate**.
- If a memory variable is used to temporarily hold a value from a field variable, or if it will be in any way associated with a field variable, give both variables the same name except for the first letter. For example, a programmer may want to establish memory variable input

buffers. Buffers can be used to temporarily hold input values during validity tests. If you have a field variable **rate**, call its buffer memory variable **mRate**.

- Try to use names that are meaningful rather than single character names. For example, **xValue** rather than **x**.
- Certain variables may have unique characteristics. For example, you may want to indicate their data type and scope within the first letters of a variable name. Begin global (**PUBLIC**) variables with the letter **g**. Begin character type variables with a **c**, numeric type with an **n**, and logical type with an **l**. That will make them easy to recognize or store to a file with the **SAVE** command using the wild card character (for example, **SAVE TO xglobal ALL LIKE g*)**.
- A documentation rule listed earlier suggested making all memory variables, field variables, and filenames lowercase when coded in an instruction. Some programmers will also designate the first letter of a filename uppercase to distinguish it from a field or memory variable name (for example, USE Xmaster).

OBJECT-ORIENTED PROGRAMMING

Background. A few years ago, I purchased a new tract home and was able to observe its construction. It was interesting to note that the builder I purchased from did not actually build the home. He designed it, then subcontracted to many different companies to put the structure together. Each contractor specialized in a different aspect of the structure; for example, foundation, framing, water, sewer, heating, electrical, etc. This modular approach has been refined even further in prefabricated home building. Each module is built at a separate location, then moved to the construction site and integrated into the total structure. Unfortunately, the problems with purely modular design and construction became apparent when I asked the builder to make a change during construction. The expression on the builder's face indicated that change was neither necessary nor desirable in his daily schedule of work. Structured languages acknowledge the desirability of changeable and reusable code, but they do not offer code that will easily accomplish that goal.

Most computer information systems are in a constant state of change. Modular design and construction is very beneficial, but the ability to make changes while maintaining data and code integrity has become equally desirable. Object-oriented programming languages view change as both inevitable and desirable.

Traditionally, menu-driven computer systems have been strictly procedural. To execute an element of a system, a series of steps must occur to get to that procedure. For this reason, a *top-down* or *bottom-up* design approach was usually adopted. A more desirable system is *event driven*, in that from anywhere within a system, an event such as a mouse click or keypress will move control to another part of the system. Object-oriented languages are event-driven languages. Rather than only from top down or bottom up, design can now occur from almost any direction.

Object-oriented programming is not meant to replace structured programming, but rather to enhance it. Good structured programmers are already practicing object-oriented principles when they build procedures that share data and can be reused in other parts of the same system or in different systems. Object-oriented programming simply formalizes this process, while adding event-driven capability.

Introduction to Objects. Think of an object as a protected *container*. We can place both data and procedures inside the container. This is referred to as *containership*. The data memory variables in an object are referred to as *properties,* and the procedures in an object are referred to as *methods*. The properties and methods of an object are referred to as its *members*. An object can also contain another object or collection of objects (for example, a Windows application desktop contains a collection of objects).

There are two command structures available to create objects in Visual dBASE. First is the **DEFINE** command. It is similar to the dBASE IV define commands and is usually preferred by programmers experienced in dBASE IV. The **NEW** operator in an assign command can also be used to create an object and is more in keeping with traditional object-oriented syntax.

To build our first object, enter the following from the Input pane:

```
CLEAR
DEFINE OBJECT fred
? fred
```

The **DEFINE** command created a new object in memory named **fred**. Our communication with the object will be by way of its *reference variable*, **fred** (see Figure 7.4). The **?** command displays the reference variable as an object. **DISP MEMO** would also display it as an object.

Next, we will create a numeric, a text, and a logical data property within the **fred** object. We also create a numeric variable outside the object. Type the following:

```
fred.xValue = 10
fred.xText = "This is an Object"
fred.xLogic = .T.
yValue = 25
? xValue, xText, xLogic    && Creates an Alert error.
? fred.xValue, fred.xText, fred.xLogic, yValue
```

FIGURE 7.4 EMPTY OBJECT CONTAINER, `fred`

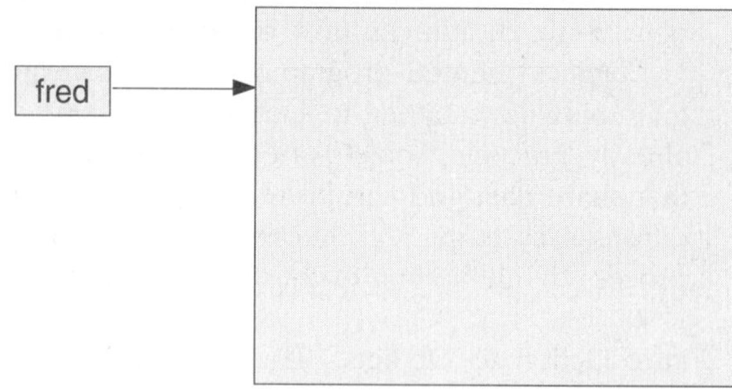

This series of commands introduces the *dot (.) reference operator*. The dot operator is a way of referencing properties and methods in much the same way as the backslash (\) is used to reference subdirectory and file names in a drive path. The first `?` command will create an error and demonstrates the protection an object holds for its members. The second `?` command properly displays the properties within the object because it contains their proper reference. The **`DISP MEMO`** command will not display the properties—only the object reference, **`fred`**. Figure 7.5 displays the object and its three data properties. Notice that **`yValue`** is outside of the **`fred`** object.

Using the Object Inspector. We queried the properties within our first object using the `?` command. Visual dBASE has an Object Inspector that not only lets you look at properties, but also lets you make changes to those properties. Type the following:

```
INSPECT(fred)
```

If not already there, click the **Properties** tab of the Inspector (don't be concerned with the **Events** or **Methods** tabs at this time). The three properties created should be displayed as in Figure 7.6. Using the mouse and keyboard, make the following changes to the properties:

`xLogic:` Click anywhere on the property. Click on the list box arrow. Select false (`.F.`) from the drop-down list.

`xText:` Click anywhere on the property. Change the text to uppercase.

`xValue:` Click anywhere on the property. Using your mouse, click on the spin box up-arrow to increase the **`xValue`** to 15.

FIGURE 7.5 OBJECT CONTAINING DATA PROPERTIES

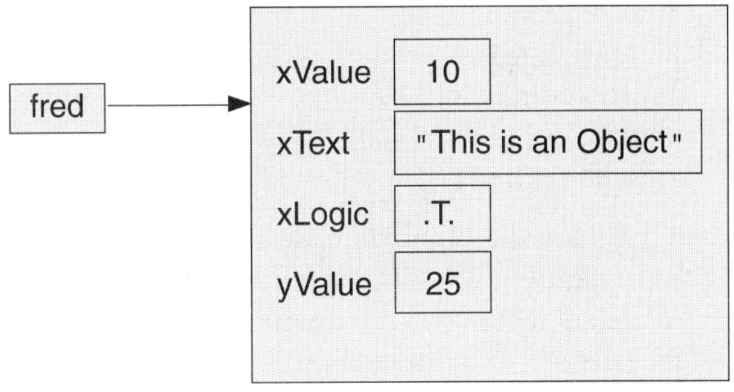

FIGURE 7.6 OBJECT PROPERTIES INSPECTOR EXAMPLE

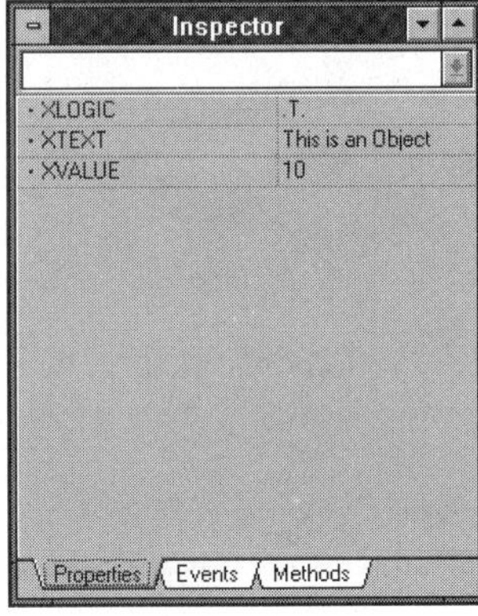

Save the changes by double clicking the Inspector control box. Check the results by retrieving and executing the following command from the Input pane:

```
? fred.xValue, fred.xText, fred.xLogic
```

Multiple Object References. An object can be referenced by more than one variable. If changes are made to the object by referencing either variable, those changes will be reflected when using the other variable. Type the following:

```
jean = fred
? jean.xValue
jean.xLogic = .T.          && change back to .T.
INSPECT(jean)
INSPECT(fred)
```

The same object is now referenced by two variables, **fred** and **jean** (see Figure 7.7). The change made to the logical property of **jean** is reflected when **fred** is inspected. Though it now has multiple references, there is still only one object.

FIGURE 7.7 ONE OBJECT WITH TWO REFERENCES

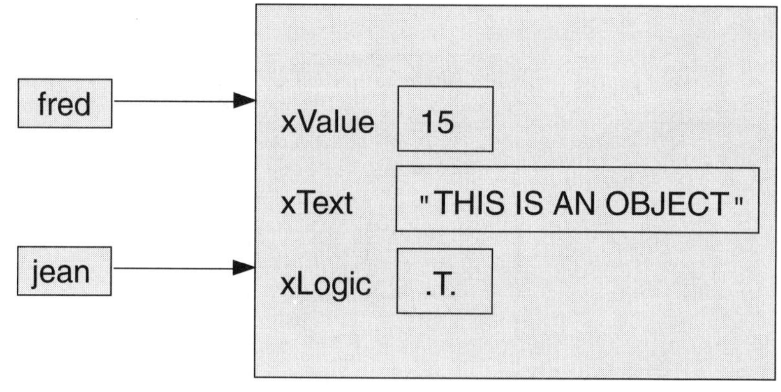

Classes. We have mentioned that object-oriented programming allows for ease of code modification. *Classes* give us that capability. If the procedural programmer needs a program module that is similar to an existing module, she/he will probably make a copy of the existing module for modification. We suggested this in Chapter 4 when developing the programming exercises. In object-oriented programming, we accomplish this with classes.

A class is a template or pattern of an object with which to build the actual object or objects. Each new object built from a class is called an *instance* of that class. To create an object is to *instantiate* that new object from a class. The new object will contain all of the member properties of the class. For example, if a blueprint of a home lists the width of the living room as 18 feet, a home built from that blueprint will contain a living room with a width of 18 feet. This is referred to as *inheritance*.

Every object you create is based on and inherits the characteristics of an existing class. Visual dBASE has many built-in (*stock*) classes. For example, the Object class that was used to develop the empty container object, **fred**, in the preceding exercise is a stock class. A complete list of the built-in classes in Visual dBASE is contained in Figure 7.8.

Creating New Classes. In addition to its own stock classes, Visual dBASE allows the programmer to build new classes. Subclasses can then be built from those new parent classes. To begin a demonstration of that capability, examine the following code segment. The **CLASS..ENDCLASS** command in the segment cannot be executed from the command window—only from a program file.

```
** Begin segment
x = NEW Parents()                      && Create new object
? x.HisFname+ " " + x.Lastname         && Query the operator
CLASS Parents
  this.HisFname = "John"               && Begin construction code
  this.HerFname = "Jean"
  this.LastName = "Jones"
ENDCLASS
** End segment
```

The sequence of events here may seem a little confusing to the procedural programmer. Actions in the code segment will occur in the following order:

1. The program file (**.PRG**) containing the sample code segment is compiled. As a result of the compilation, the **CLASS..ENDCLASS** construct creates the new class, **parents**. During the process, the property member assignment statements are executed. The code that assigns the properties to the class is called the class *constructor code*.

FIGURE 7.8 VISUAL dBASE STOCK CLASSES

```
ARRAY
ASSOCARRAY
BROWSE
CHECKBOX
COMBOBOX
DDELINK
DDETOPIC
EDITOR
ENTRYFIELD
FORM
IMAGE
LINE
MENU
LISTBOX
MENUBAR
OBJECT
OLE
OLEAUTOCLIENT
PAINTBOX
POPUP
PUSHBUTTON
RADIOBUTTON
RECTANGLE
SCROLLBAR
SHAPE
SPINBOX
TEXT
```

CLASS..ENDCLASS introduces the this reference operator. The this variable is created whenever a class is created or whenever an event-handler is executed (event-handlers are discussed later in this chapter). In this case, it refers to this object class rather than its actual name. The use of this allows generic coding of the object name. By so doing, you can develop many objects from a class without changing the first name in the assignment command reference list each time it is passed on to a new object.

2. The new object, x, is instantiated from the Parents class and inherits the member properties of the class. The NEW operator rather than the DEFINE command has been used to create the new object and assign x as its reference variable. Remember, both the DEFINE command and the NEW operator in an assign command do the same thing—create an object from a class.

3. The ? command queries the object and displays the first and last name of the father.

Creating Subclasses. The parents class created in the preceding example contains only information about parents. The children of the parents have different first names, but the same last name. If we develop a subclass, children, it will inherit all the properties of the parent class, parents, including the last name. To demonstrate this, examine the program yfamily, listed in Figure 7.9.

The yfamily program contains code similar to the segment listed above that created a new class, parents, and instantiated an object, x, from that class. In addition, yfamily creates a subclass, children, from the parents class, and instantiates an object, y, from that subclass. All of the properties of parents are inherited by children. The OF clause of the second CLASS..ENDCLASS construct references the parent class, parents, from which it creates the subclass, children. The first names of the children are assigned in the constructor code of children. Finally, the program queries both objects to list the family members in the Results pane (see Figure 7.10).

FIGURE 7.9 PROGRAM TO CREATE NEW CLASS , yfamily

```
                    YFAMILY.PRG - Program Editor

** NAME.........: YFAMILY.PRG
** DESCRIPTION..: A program to demonstrate the following:
**                o  Creating new classes
**                o  Creating a sub-class from a class
**                o  Instantiating an object from a class
**                o  Instantiating an object from a sub-class
**                o  Querying multiple objects

PUBLIC x, y
** Create parents object
x = NEW PARENTS( )

** Create children object
y = NEW CHILDREN( )

** Query parent and children objects
SET TALK OFF
CLEAR

** Family Names
? "Mother..: " + x.HerFname + " " + x.Lname
? "Father..: " + x.HisFname + " " + x.Lname
? "Son.....: " + y.SonFname + " " + y.Lname
? "Daughter: " + y.SisFname + " " + y.Lname
SET TALK ON

** Create parents class
CLASS parents
   this.HerFname = "Jean"
   this.HisFname = "John"
   this.Lname    = "Jones"
ENDCLASS

** Create children sub-class
CLASS children OF parents
   this.SisFname = "Jill"
   this.SonFname = "Sonnie"
ENDCLASS

** End of Program YFAMILY.PRG
```

FIGURE 7.10 OBJECT QUERIES OUTPUT—PROGRAM `yfamily`

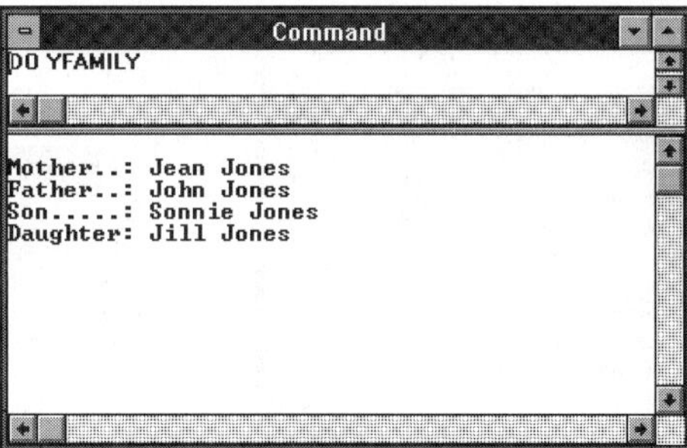

The inheritance of the last name from the **`parents`** object demonstrates the benefits of subclasses in object-oriented programming. In addition to data properties, methods can be inherited to further reduce the programming involved in system modification.

Creating Form Objects. The Form class will be the most used stock class of Visual dBASE. We will use it to develop most of the main window objects of the remaining exercises and the Case System. The objects we have created so far have contained only properties, and therefore have not demonstrated event-driven methods.

The following exercise demonstrates how to instantiate a Windows Form object from the stock class, Form. Type the following from the Input pane:

```
yform = NEW FORM()        && Create yform object
yform.top = 5             && Modify inherited
yform.left = 20           && object position properties
yform.height = 10
yform.width = 65
yform.text = "My First Form"
INSPECT(yform)            && Inspect new form object
```

The first command instantiates a new object from the Form stock class. The assignment commands modify the position properties inherited by the new object, **`yform`**, and change the title of the form window. By activating the Inspector window, you see that the new form object has inherited a number of properties and methods from the Form class. It contains all the elements of a standard Windows form. Click on each tab in the Inspector window to scan the Properties, Events, and Methods contained in the new form (see Figure 7.11). You can resize the window if necessary. We will explore these in more detail as needed in the solution of the Case System.

FIGURE 7.11 OBJECT INSPECTION OF `yform`

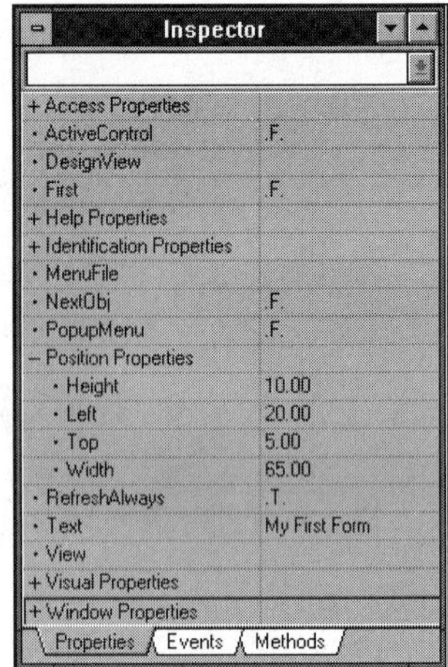

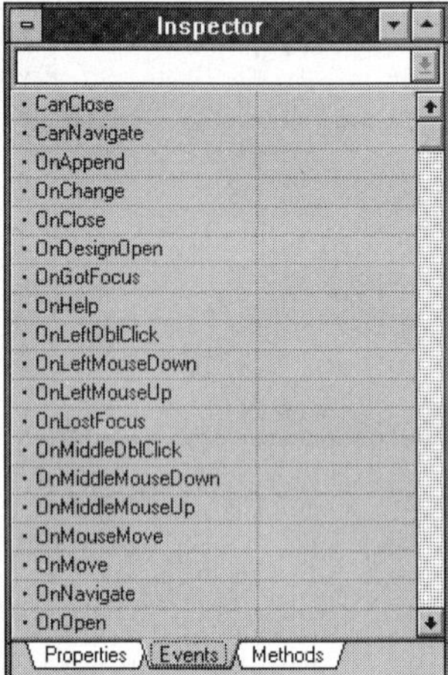

NOTE: The terminology of the Inspector may be misleading. Properties, Events, and Methods are all Properties of the class. As such, they could be referred to as Property properties, Event properties, and Method properties. This text refers to them as Properties, Events, and Methods—as do the Visual dBASE reference manuals and most other texts.

Under the Methods properties of the Inspector window, you will see a method named Open. A method is a procedure or function *encapsulated* within an object that performs a task. The Open method was inherited from the stock class, Form. From the Input pane, we will execute the Open method to open our new Form object. As you type the command, notice that we have used the forms object reference variable and dot reference to tell Visual dBASE where the Method is located. Close the Inspector window from its control button prior to typing the command.

```
yform.OPEN()
```

To close the form, double click on the Control-Menu box.

Creating Objects Within Form Objects. As we have noted, objects can contain other objects. This is common in Windows applications. Most of the stock classes listed in Figure 7.8 are used to instantiate objects within Form objects. Such objects in a Form are called *controls*. For example, Forms may contain text, pushbuttons, entry fields, spin boxes and so on. To demonstrate placing a control object within a Form object, proceed as follows:

- **Enter program into program editor:** Enter the program, `yform`, into the `MODI COMM` program editor (see Figure 7.12). The program places a text object control within a form object. The `AT` clause of the `DEFINE` command positions the upper left corner of the Text object relative to the form window. However, the Left property coding overrides that position (16 versus 10 units).
- **Test the program:** Test the program by clicking on the **Execute a program** button in the Speedbar. The program should place a form window in the center of your screen as shown in Figure 7.13. To close the form, either press the **Esc** key or click on the **Form control** button.
- **Save the program:** When the program executes properly, save it by selecting **File | Save and Close** or by double-clicking on the **Program editor window control** button.

FIGURE 7.12 PROGRAM PLACING AN OBJECT WITHIN AN OBJECT, yform

```
** NAME........: YFORM.PRG
** DESCRIPTION.: Create an object within another
**                object.

y = NEW YFORM()
y.Open()

** Define new class from Form class
CLASS YFORM OF FORM
   this.Text = "My First Form"
   this.Top = 5
   this.Left = 20
   this.Height = 10
   this.Width = 65

   ** Define text object within this class
   DEFINE TEXT ytext OF THIS AT 4, 10;
        PROPERTY;
           Height 1.4,;
           Left 16,;
           Width 30,;
           Text  "An Object in an Object",;
           FontName "Arial",;
           FontSize 12,;
           ColorNormal "B/W+",;
           Border .T.

ENDCLASS

** End of Program, YFORM.PRG
```

FIGURE 7.13 WINDOWS DISPLAY—PROGRAM `yform`

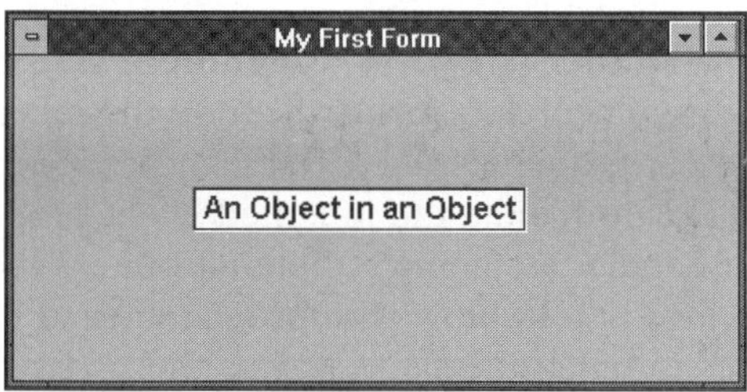

Remember, the class constructor code will occur first and create the new class, **`yform`**, from the stock class, Form. The **`DEFINE Text`** command is referring to the stock class, Text. It instantiates the text control, **`ytext`**, from the stock class, Text. Although **`ytext`** inherits all the properties of the Text stock class, we have used the **`PROPERTY`** clause of the **`DEFINE`** command to override several of those properties. For example, we have redefined the text property of the text control object and changed its position, the font it uses, its size, and its color.

Height	Height of the box containing the text
Left	Distance from the left side of the window, **`yform`**
Width	Width of the box containing the text
Text	A Character string to be contained in the text box
FontName	The font to be used when displaying the text
FontSize	The point size of the font to be used
ColorNormal	The foreground color (the text) and the background color (the text box)

Creating Methods Within Objects. Earlier in this chapter we examined the Properties, Events, and Methods of the **`yform`** form object by opening the Inspector window (Figure 7.11). So far, the only method we have used is the Open( ) method. It was used to open **`yform`**. Forms are event driven in the sense that actions initiated by the operator will cause events to occur. For example, a mouse click on a pushbutton may cause a form to close or a mouse click on a spin box up-arrow may increase the value in the spin box. Stock classes such as Form have many built-in events as shown in the Inspector. There are also built-in methods that can be initiated such as those used to open or close a form. Such methods are referred to as *event-handlers*. We can use built-in methods or create our own methods to be contained within a class.

To demonstrate this capability, modify the **yform** program to create a procedure that will beep the computer's bell two times whenever the OnClose event occurs within the form. Examine and enter the shaded code in Figure 7.14.

- **Event-handler property assignment statement.** Just as the property assignment statements override the inherited Form class position and color properties, the event-handler assignment statement assigns a method to handle the inherited event property, **OnClose**. The event-handler assignment code introduces the *scope-resolution operator* (**::**). It allows the programmer to reference methods within classes in much the same way as the **this** reference operator allows referencing of properties. The assignment statement could have been written either of the following ways:

```
this.OnClose = CLASS::TwoBeeps
this.OnClose = YFORM::TwoBeeps
```

CLASS here means *this* class. This particular class is **yform** so that name could be used instead of **CLASS**. However, by using **CLASS**, you do not have to repeat the name as more methods are developed. Moreover, the reference will remain valid as subclasses are developed. Methods can also be referenced in this manner from other classes—even though they are encapsulated within the other class.

FIGURE 7.14 EVENT-HANDLER CODE—PROGRAM `yform`

```
** NAME........:   YFORM.PRG
** DESCRIPTION.:   Create an object within another
**                 object.

y = NEW YFORM( )
y.Open()

** Define new class from Form class
CLASS YFORM OF FORM
   this.Text = "My First Form"
   this.Top = 5
   this.Left = 20
   this.Height = 10
   this.Width = 65
   this.OnClose = YFORM::TwoBeeps

   ** Define text object within this class
   DEFINE TEXT ytext OF THIS AT 4,10;
       PROPERTY;
          Height 1.4,;
          Left 16,;
          Width 30,;
          Text " An Object in an Object",;
          FontName  "Arial",;
          FontSize 12,;
          ColorNormal  "B/W+",;
          Border .T.

   PROCEDURE TwoBeeps
      ? CHR(7)
      ? CHR(7)
   RETURN

ENDCLASS

** End of Program, YFORM. PRG
```

- **Method (PROCEDURE) code.** The development of the procedure follows all the rules outlined earlier in this chapter. Notice that the procedure is completely contained within the `CLASS..ENDCLASS` statement. This ensures that it is a member of, and protected by, the newly formed `yform` class. The code within the procedure will ring the computer bell twice. Each time the form closing event occurs, the OnClose event-handler will execute and ring the bell twice.

We will be creating more elaborate forms as we build the Case System and code the related exercises. You will also begin using the Forms Designer of Visual dBASE to construct most of your forms. However, by discussing object theory first and hard-coding a few forms as we have done here, you should be able to better understand and appreciate the strengths of the Forms Designer, especially its use as a *two-way design tool.* The Forms Designer is two-way in the sense that if code generated by it is modified directly, those modifications will be intact when you return to the Designer.

REVIEW EXERCISES

PART I: REVIEW QUESTIONS

1. What is the content of a procedure file and what is its purpose?
2. What are the two parameters involving the scope of a memory variable?
3. What is the lifespan of a `STATIC`, a `LOCAL`, a `PUBLIC`, and a `PRIVATE` memory variable?
4. Name three ways to release a `STATIC` memory variable. Is a `STATIC` ever automatically released?
5. What is a hidden memory variable?
6. What is the difference between structured or procedural programming and object-oriented programming?
7. Define the following terms:
   a. Class
   b. Object
   c. Object reference variable
   d. Instantiate
   e. Property
   f. Method
   g. Containership
   h. Dot (.) reference operator
   i. Stock class

PART II. BUILDING AN OBJECT

In this exercise, you will build an object that contains two memory variables. You will also display the object contents to the screen. This exercise is to be completed from the Command window.

Specifications

1. Create a new, empty container object. Name the object reference variable `mydata`. Use the Visual dBASE stock class Object.
2. Place the following memory variables inside the object.

Variable name:	`xRate`	Value:	`15`
Variable name:	`xMessage`	Value:	`"THE RATE IS:"`

3. Using the `?` command, query the object to place the following information in the Results pane:

```
THE RATE IS: 15
```

Use the **`STR()`** function to convert the numeric variable, **`xRate`**, to character type data. Notice that there is only one space between the display of the text in **`xMessage`** and the first digit of the value in **`xRate`**. By converting **`xRate`** to a character string, you will find it easier to control the leading blanks in a display.

PART III: BUILDING A FORM OBJECT

In this exercise, we will create a Form object, modify several of its inherited position and visual properties, and build a method to handle its OnOpen and OnClose events.

Specifications. Create a Windows form that will ring the system bell five times as it opens and five times when it closes. Build the form according to the following guidelines:

1. Create the form
   - Using the **`MODI COMM`** program editor, open a file named **`yform2.prg`**.
   - Create a new Form class, **`myform`**, from the Visual dBASE stock class `Form`.

- Modify the following inherited properties in class **myform:**

  Visual: `ColorNormal = "W+/R"`
  You can specify two colors using the ColorNormal property; the foreground (text) and the background. The colors are declared using the color attributes as listed in Figure 7.15. You can also specify high intensity of a color using a plus sign after the attribute (+). In the next chapter, you will learn to design other colors using the Choose Color dialog box.

  Position: `Left = 18`
  `Top = 2`
  `Height = 10`
  `Width = 60`

  Text: `Text = "A BELL RINGING RED FORM"`

- Create a text object within **yform** from the Visual dBASE stock class Text. Modify the following properties inherited from the stock class Text.

  Text: `"PRESS ESCAPE TO CLOSE"`
  Position: `Width to 38`
  Font: `FontSize to 10`

- Develop a procedure within your new Form class, **myform**. Name the procedure **FiveBells**. Use the **FOR..NEXT** construct to develop a loop that will ring the system bell five times.

- Assign the procedure, **FiveBells**, as the event-handler for both the OnOpen event property and the OnClose event property of class myform.

FIGURE 7.15 VISUAL dBASE COLOR CODES

ColorNormal Attributes

Color	Attribute
Black	N or blank
Blue	B
Gray	N+
Green	G
Cyan	BG
Red	R
Magenta	RB
Brown	GR
Yellow	GR+
White	W
Blank	X

Note: A plus sign (+) after an attribute causes high intensity (unless the attribute already contains a plus sign).

- Instantiate a new object from the new form class, `myform`. Name the object reference variable for the new object `y`.
- Open your form, `myform`, using the forms `OPEN()` property.
- Save the program file, but do not close the program editor (**File | Save**).

2. **Test the form**
   Test your new form by clicking on the **Run** button in the speedbar. Correct any coding errors and continue testing until it executes properly. The form should appear as in Figure 7.16. As the form opens, the bell should ring five times. When the form is closed by either pressing the **Esc** key or by double-clicking on the **Forms Control** button, the bell should again ring five times.

3. **Print the program**
   Print a copy of the program file. Access the print menu either from the File menu or by clicking the **Print** button in the Speedbar.

FIGURE 7.16 OUTPUT, PROGRAM `yform2`

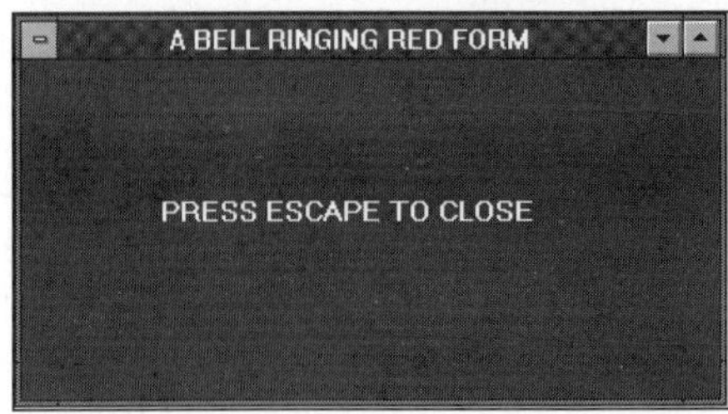

CHAPTER SUMMARY

In this chapter, we introduced object-oriented programming in Visual dBASE. We also discussed the management of memory variables and the use of procedure files, especially as applied to object-oriented programming. Topics included the following:

- **Procedure files**. Used to code routines that will be used more than once in a system, procedure files can be contained in a global procedure file or within a single program module. They are used as methods in objects.
- **Memory variable management.** The types of memory variables are `PUBLIC`, `PRIVATE`, `LOCAL`, and `STATIC`. Scoping a memory variable defines its lifespan and visibility. Names given to memory variables are designed to facilitate easier housekeeping and reference.
- **Object-oriented programming.** Objects are protected containers derived from templates called classes. Objects can contain properties (data) and methods (procedures). The following terms were derived and discussed:

Object
Class, stock class
Container, containership
Properties, methods, members
Reference variables
Dot (.) reference operator
Instantiate
Inheritance
Constructor code, (`this`) reference operator
Controls
Scope-resolution operator (`::`)
Two-way design tools

The following new commands were introduced:

- `PROCEDURE, SET PROCEDURE TO`
- `PRIVATE, PUBLIC, LOCAL, STATIC`
- `RELEASE`
- `DEFINE (object definition)`
- `CLASS..ENDCLASS`

Two new functions were introduced:

- `INSPECT()`
- `STR()`

The following object operators were introduced:

- Dot reference operator (.)
- `this` reference operator
- Scope resolution operator (::)
- `NEW` operator

In the next chapter, we will continue using the Visual dBASE Form class to build an application desktop for the Case System. The two-way Form Designer tool and Menu Designer will also be introduced.

CHAPTER EIGHT

TOPICS

Background

New Commands and Properties

Concepts

- Using the Form Designer
- Parts of the Form Designer work surface
- Placing controls on a form
- Changing control object properties
- Placing a pushbutton control on a form
- The Form Designer as a two-way tool
- Building a menu system in a form

Review Exercises

Chapter Summary

Creating an Application Desktop

8

CHAPTER OBJECTIVES

In this chapter, we introduce the very powerful Form Designer, the most important tool of the Visual dBASE programmer. Here, too, we introduce the Menu Designer, which you will use to build your Windows application menu systems. In Chapter 7, you began using Visual dBASE code to build forms. Now you will learn how to use the Form Designer to generate that code and to add controls that will create a professional and functional form.

After studying this chapter, you should be able to create fully functional Windows screens and menu systems using the Form Designer and Menu Designer.

BACKGROUND

Early in my programming career, I wrote programs in pure machine code—just one step above the 1s and 0s of the Central Processing Unit. I can still recall the extreme detail and housekeeping involved in the development of those programs. Over the years, many levels of languages have emerged that have made programming much less tedious. In addition, program design tools have evolved that generate code based on design specifications provided by the programmer. The Visual dBASE Form Designer is such a tool.

Unfortunately, most code generators produce volumes of code to do simple tasks. Further, their design work surfaces do not reflect changes made directly to the generated source code. The Form Designer solves both problems. It does not produce excess code and is a *two-way* design tool in that the design work surface reflects all changes that occur at the source code level, and the generated code reflects all changes that occur on the design work surface. Because of these features, we highly recommend use of the Form Designer in the development of Visual dBASE programs.

NEW COMMANDS AND PROPERTIES

The following list features new properties in addition to new commands. Properties are a part of the class constructor code commands and the `DEFINE <class name>` command introduced in the preceding chapter. The list includes method properties, such as **`READMODAL( )`**, as well as several properties that were used in the preceding chapter. They are listed here for further clarification.

COMMAND `CREATE/MODIFY FORM`

Opens the Form Designer to either create or modify a form.

COMMAND `CREATE/MODIFY MENU`

Opens the Menu Designer to either create or modify a menu.

COMMAND `KEYBOARD <expC> [CLEAR]`

Places the value of **`<expC>`** into the typeahead buffer. For example, the following command typed from the Command window will cause focus to move to the Navigator window.

```
KEYBOARD "{CTRL-TAB}"
```

PROPERTY `Text`

Designates a character string to display in or beside an object. The Text property of a Form object is the character string making up the title of the form. Property of Class: **BROWSE**, **CHECKBOX**, **FORM**, **MENU**, **PUSHBUTTON**, **RADIOBUTTON**, **RECTANGLE**, **TEXT**

PROPERTY `Alignment`

Positions text in a Text object or an Image in an image object.
Property of Class: **IMAGE**, **TEXT**

PROPERTY `FontSize`

Specifies the point size of a font in an object.
Property of Class: **BROWSE**, **CHECKBOX**, **COMBOBOX**, **EDITOR**, **ENTRY-FIELD**, **LISTBOX**, **PUSHBUTTON**, **RADIOBUTTON**, **RECTANGLE**, **SPIN-BOX**, **TEXT**

PROPERTY `UpBitmap`

Specifies the graphic image to display when a pushbutton is not selected.
Property of Class: **PUSHBUTTON**

PROPERTY `MDI`

Specifies whether a window conforms to the Windows Multiple Document Interface standard. The MDI standard allows the programmer to open multiple documents within an application window, if so desired. Visual dBASE uses MDI to manage multiple documents or views.
Property of Class: **FORM**

PROPERTY `READMODAL()`

Opens a form as a *modal* window. A modal form takes control of the user interface, much the same way a dBASE for DOS window controls. If a modal form is opened, no other form can be opened at the same time. An example of a modal form could be a dialog box that is to have control until it is closed. A modal form must be opened with the **READMODAL()** method property and the MDI property must be set to false (**.F.**). Aside from dialog boxes, most forms are *modeless* (non-modal).
Property of Class: **FORM**

PROPERTY `MenuFile`

Attaches a predetermined menu system to a form.
Property of Class: **FORM**

PROPERTY `ColorNormal`

Determines the colors of an object that is not selected. To differentiate between a selected and nonselected object, ColorNormal can be contrasted with the ColorHighlight property.
Property of Class: `BROWSE`, `CHECKBOX`, `EDITOR`, `ENTRYFIELD`, `FORM`, `LISTBOX`, `OLE`, `SPINBOX`, `TEXT`

PROPERTY `StatusMessage`

Specifies the status bar message while an object has focus.
Property of Class: `BROWSE`, `CHECKBOX`, `COMBOBOX`, `EDITOR`, `ENTRYFIELD`, `FORM`, `LISTBOX`, `MENU`, `OLE`, `PUSHBUTTON`, `RADIOBUTTON`, `SCROLLBAR`, `SPINBOX`

PROPERTY `SysMenu`

Specifies whether a form has a Control Menu.
Property of Class: `FORM`

PROPERTY `SETFOCUS()`

Gives focus to a form or an object in a form. Use SetFocus() to make a form or an object in a form ready to receive user input. When a form has focus, its title bar is highlighted. When an object in a form has focus, its border is highlighted.
Property of Class: `BROWSE`, `CHECKBOX`, `COMBOBOX`, `EDITOR`, `ENTRYFIELD`, `FORM`, `LISTBOX`, `OLE`, `PAINTBOX`, `PUSHBUTTON`, `RADIOBUTTON`, `SCROLLBAR`, `SPINBOX`, `TABBOX`

CONCEPTS

We will begin our discussion by creating a simple form. During the process, we will examine all the components of the Form Designer and how each is used. You should have both the Navigator and the Command window open and the data directory set to `C:\DBDATA`.

USING THE FORM DESIGNER

To open the designer, type the following command from the Input pane:

```
CREATE FORM yform3
```

As you can see, the initial designer work surface appears very busy. To get rid of some of the clutter and simplify the screen, do the following (use Figure 8.1 as your guide):

- Resize and move the Form Designer window.
- Give focus to, then minimize the Command window.
- Give focus to, then minimize the Navigator window.

FIGURE 8.1 FORM DESIGNER WORK SURFACE

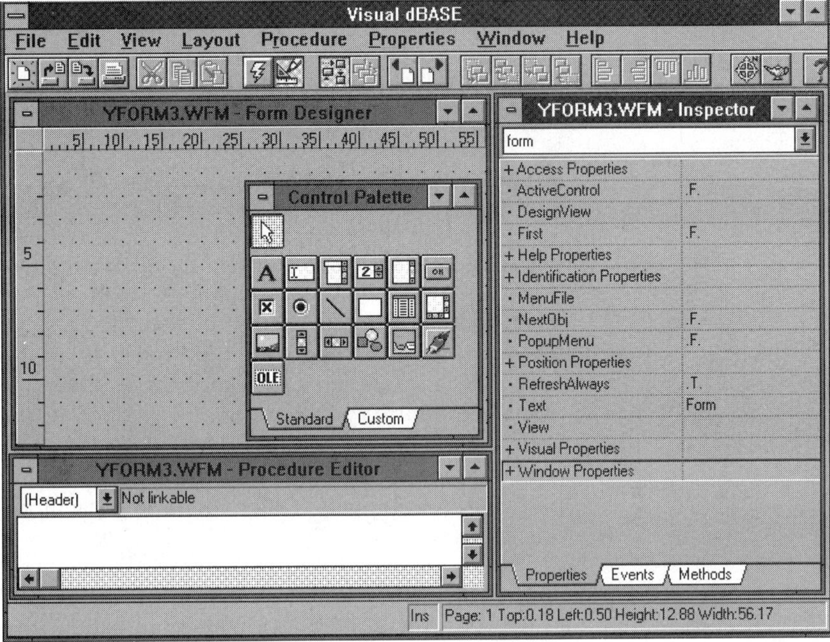

- If it is not currently displayed, display the Control Palette **(View | Control Palette)**.
- If it is not currently displayed, display the Procedure Editor window **(View | Procedure Editor)**.
- If it is not currently displayed, display the Inspector window **(View | Inspector)**. Give focus to the Inspector window.

There are a number of ways to enter the Form Designer. Each of the following will take you to the Form Designer by way of the *Form Expert*. From the New Form dialog, you then choose **Designer** to enter the Form Designer.

- From the Navigator, click the **Forms** icon, then double-click **Untitled** under the Form Files column.
- From the Speedbar, click the **Design** button (the triangle and ruler just to the left of center).
- Choose **File | New | Form**.
- Choose **Navigator | New Form**

NOTE: We will not be using the Form Expert. It is an excellent tool to design a generic form based on an open view or table. However, our approach is to design each element of a form from the Form Designer. After learning how to use the Form Designer, you may want to explore the Form Expert for generic designs that can be fine-tuned with the Designer itself. If you want to toggle the Form Expert off when entering the Form Designer, select **Properties | Desktop Properties | Application Tab**. Remove the check mark **(x)** from the **Form** checkbox under **Prompt for Experts**.

PARTS OF THE FORM DESIGNER WORK SURFACE

The following is a general overview of the Form Designer work surface. We will explore each component in more depth later in the chapter.

Menu System. Certain items of the menu system change and become unique to the work surface the user selects. In this case, they reference the Form Designer. As an example, choose **View | Form** to view the results of our new form, `yform3`. The basic shell of the form should appear on your screen. Now choose **View | Form design** to return to the design work surface. Notice also that pressing **F2** and then **Shift-F2** will accomplish the same results. Other menu items will be used as we design various forms.

Speedbar. As with other segments of Visual dBASE, the Speedbar is used in lieu of a menu item to expedite an action. For example, view our new form, `yform3`, as it will appear at runtime by clicking on the **Lightning Bolt** icon in the Speedbar. Return to the design work surface by clicking on the **Design** icon just to the right of the Lightning Bolt icon.

Form Window. This is the form itself. It is a "Visual" design work surface. As you place a control, you will be able to see the effects of placement, size, color, and so forth. It contains a grid and horizontal rulers to assist you in the placement of controls.

Inspector Window. This is the Object Inspector as described in the preceding chapter. We will use it to assign properties, events, and methods to a form.

Control Palette. We will use this tool to place objects on our form. We use Control objects to cause events to occur, place text on a form, receive data from an operator, display graphics or sound, and display lines or boxes to group other objects. Figure 8.2 displays a list of the controls in the Control palette, their icons, and a general statement as to the purpose of each. We will use most of these objects as we complete the remaining exercises and Case System modules of this text.

Procedure Editor. The procedures that are the events attached to controls such as pushbuttons or menu items will be developed in the Procedure Editor. We will begin using it later in this chapter.

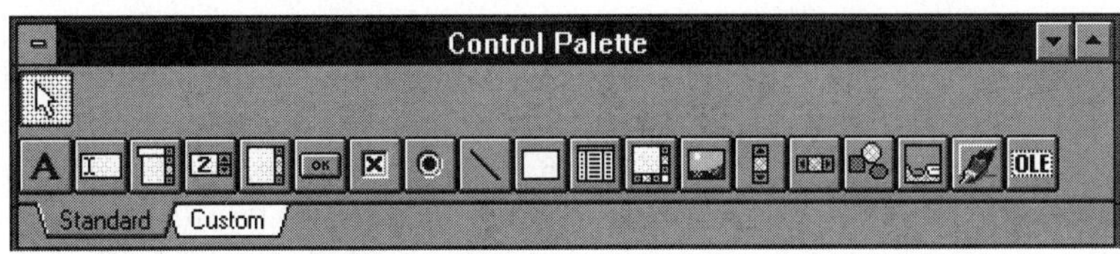

Control	Purpose
TextObject	Displays a title, description, or other verbiage on the form.
EntryField	To enter a single piece of data from an operator for use by the system.
ComboBox	Combines an entry field and a list box. Allows the operator to enter a new value or select an input value from a list of values.
SpinBox	Contains up/down buttons to increase or decrease a numeric or date input value. It is an entry field with a form of scroll bars.
ListBox	Allows selection of an input value from a list of values.
PushButton	Causes the occurrence of an event (e.g., a different record is displayed or a form closes).
CheckBox	Places boxes for the operator to check if a listed value is to be used or not used. Can also be thought of as a toggle between two opposing values. Any number of checkboxes can be checked within a group.
RadioButton	Used to select a single value from a group of values. As with a radio pushbutton, if one button in a group is pressed, the others revert to the opposite state.
Line	A line draw feature used to separate objects on a form or to add to the visual appearance of a form.

Control	Purpose
Rectangle	A box drawing feature to group objects on a form or to add to the visual appearance of a form.
Browse	Displays a table or view in the form of a browse screen object. As with the Table Records window, a Form or Columnar layout can also be used.
Editor	Places a box on the form to edit a text file or memo field.
Image	Displays a graphic image on a form.
Vertical ScrollBar	Allows selection of numeric or date values from a range of values in a vertically displayed scrollbar. A slider button within the ScrollBar increases or decreases the value.
Horizontal ScrollBar	Acts the same as a Vertical ScrollBar, but is displayed horizontally on a form.
Shape	A region of color in a form.
TabBox	Creates a tab-based form.
PaintBox	A generic UI object to be placed on a form.
OLE	Places an object developed by another application within a form; for example, a document from a text editor or a sound from a recording application.

PLACING CONTROLS ON A FORM

Our first exercise will be to demonstrate the ability to place textual data on a form. We will continue working with `yform3` to give it certain characteristics of a *banner screen* window. Banner screens are used to identify an application soon after it boots. Windows applications have *About* dialog boxes that serve this function. In addition to appearing when the application boots, **About** dialogs are also available from the Help menu.

You should still be within the Form Designer with `yform3` as the open form. The initial step is to select an object, then move it to the form. To do this, proceed as follows:

1. **Placing a Text control.**

   - **Select the control object.** In the Control palette, click the **Text** control icon, then move the pointer cursor to the Form window. The pointer becomes crosshairs when moved across the Form window.
   - **Set the control object on the form.** Click the crosshairs at the upper left point of the text location on the form, then drag to the lower right-hand corner. You could also just click the crosshairs to choose the default size of the object.
   - **Move/resize the control object.** When a control object has focus, handles (small square bullets) appear around its perimeter. Move the control by placing the pointer inside its perimeter, then dragging it to the new position. Resize by dragging the handles of the control as you would any Windows object. You can also move a control with the arrow keys and resize with **Shift** and the arrow keys. Choose the method that is the best for you. The text control should appear as in Figure 8.3.

2. **Placing a Rectangle control.** Using the preceding techniques, place a **Rectangle** control on the form as a frame around the **Text** object. First, click on the **Rectangle** control in the Control palette, then set the object on the form. Finally, resize it so that it appears as in Figure 8.3.

3. **Using the Layout menu.** The rectangle control currently overlays the text control. The layout menu will allow you to align controls on the form. It will also bring objects to the foreground or background as needed. To send the rectangle control to the background, proceed as follows (see Figure 8.3):

   - Give the rectangle, `Rectangle1`, focus by clicking on its perimeter.
   - Choose **Layout | Send to Back**.

FIGURE 8.3 TEXT AND RECTANGLE OBJECT PLACEMENT

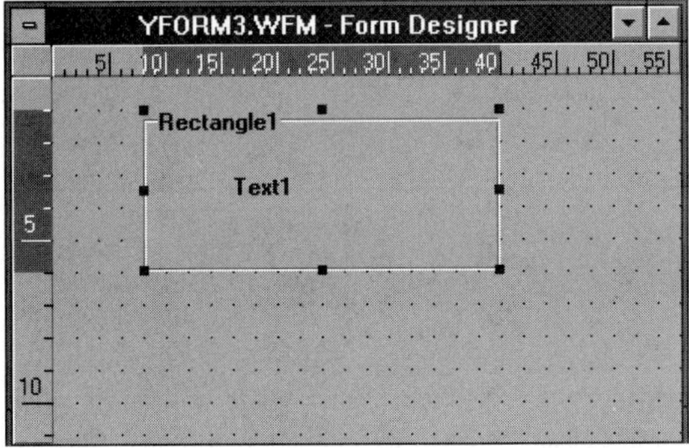

CHANGING CONTROL OBJECT PROPERTIES

Now that the text and rectangle control objects are on the form, we can change a few of their properties. Proceed as follows:

1. **Give focus to the Inspector window.** If the Inspector window is not open, right-click from anywhere within the form window. Choose **Inspector** from the drop-down speed menu that appears. If it is already open, either click its title bar or choose **Window | Inspector** to give it focus.
2. **Resize/move the Inspector window and Form window as necessary.** Ideally, they would be side-by-side versus one overlaying the other.
3. **Changing control properties.** Give focus to the Text control, `Text1`, in the Form window. As you move focus between the form, the text control, and the rectangle control, notice that the list of related properties change in the Inspector window. You can also change the focus of a form control by using the list box at the top of the Inspector window. Proceed as follows:
   - Text property. Click on the **Text** property in the Inspector window. Change the property text string to the following:

     ```
     MY BANNER SCREEN
     ```

You should be able to observe the Text property changes on the form as they are being typed.

NOTE: The Alignment property listed earlier can be very useful if the text inside the object is smaller than the size of the object itself. The text can then be centered or justified in any direction. In Part II of the Review Exercises, we will use this property to center a character string that will vary in length according to a button press by the operator.

- **Font Properties.** Double-click the **Font Properties** group in the Inspector window. The plus sign (+) prefacing the **Font Properties** group indicates there are a series of font properties available. The plus sign will change to a minus sign (–) when the double-click occurs and the entire group of font properties is displayed. Click the **FontSize** property within the group. Adjust the size of the font to 11 points by clicking the spinbox arrow.

4. **Modify the Rectangle control text property.** Give focus to the Rectangle control, `Rectangle1`, in the Form window. Click the **Text** property. Press the **Backspace** key to eliminate the current text, `Rectangle1`. We want this property to be blank.

5. **Test the final form.** View the final form to verify its appearance at run-time (either **View | Form**, or press **F2,** or click the **Run** Speedbar icon). If necessary, return to the design work surface (**View | Form design**, press **Shift+F2**, or click the **Design** Speedbar icon) to resize/move the Text and Rectangle controls on the form. The final view should appear as in Figure 8.4.

FIGURE 8.4 FINAL VIEW OF TEXT AND RECTANGLE CONTROLS

6. **Save your work so far.** Save your work so far, but remain in the Form Designer **(File | Save)**.

NOTE: Normally, when a banner screen window (**About** dialog box) is opened on the screen, it takes control of the screen in much the same way a dBASE IV window takes control. With such control, no other windows can be opened until the dialog box is closed. We will make the banner screen in Part II of the Review Exercises a modal form for that purpose.

PLACING A PUSHBUTTON CONTROL ON A FORM

The controls we have placed on the form so far have been visual with no related action. The next control we place on the form will cause an event to occur. The control will be a pushbutton that, when pressed or clicked, will cause the form to close. Proceed as follows:

1. **Open the Form Designer.** If not already open, reenter the Form Designer by typing the following into the Input pane:

```
MODI FORM yform3
```

You could also modify the form using the Navigator by clicking on the **Forms** icon, right-clicking on the **yform3** icon, choosing **Design Form** from the drop down menu (or more directly by pressing **Shift+F2** on the **yform3** icon).

2. **Placing the PushButton control.** Place the control using the same techniques that we used above on the Text and Rectangle controls. Click on the **PushButton** control icon in the Control palette and move it to **yform3**. Center it just below the rectangle control (see Figure 8.5A).

FIGURE 8.5 PUSHBUTTON1 ON FORM `yform3`

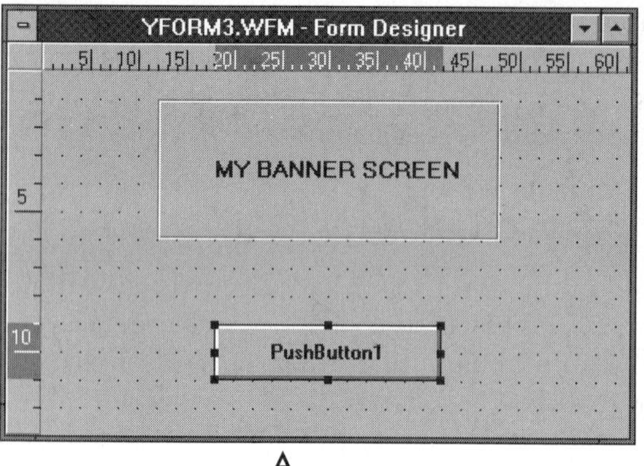

A

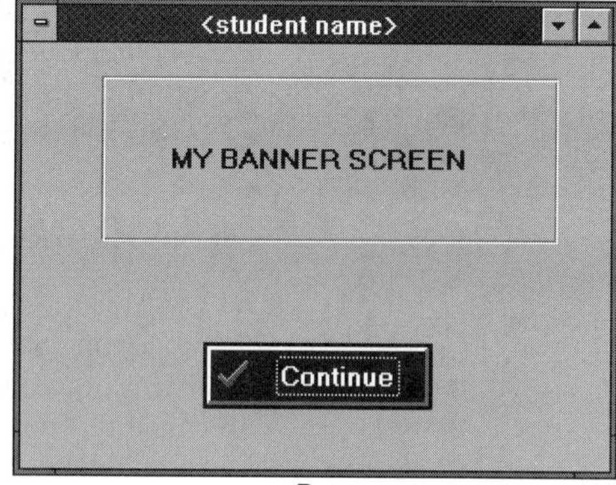

B

3. Change the PushButton properties. Change the inherited properties of the pushbutton control as follows:

- **Text property.** Change the Text property from `Pushbutton1` to the following:

  Continue

- **FontSize property.** Change the font size to 11.
- **ColorNormal property.** To begin, double click the **Visual Properties** group if it is preceded by a plus (+) sign. Click the **ColorNormal** property, then click the **Toolbar** that appears to the right of the text box. This opens the **Color Property Builder** dialog box (see Figure 8.6).

As demonstrated in the preceding chapter, a background and foreground color can be set. Choose one or the other by clicking the appropriate radio button at the top of the dialog box. You can select a background/foreground combination either from the Basic Colors palette or from the color spectrum at the right of the palette dialog. As you select a basic color, notice that crosshairs in the color spectrum move to that color in the spectrum. Most colors you will need can be selected from the Basic Colors palette—though you may want to experiment with custom colors if needed in your application.

FIGURE 8.6 COLOR PROPERTY BUILDER DIALOG BOX

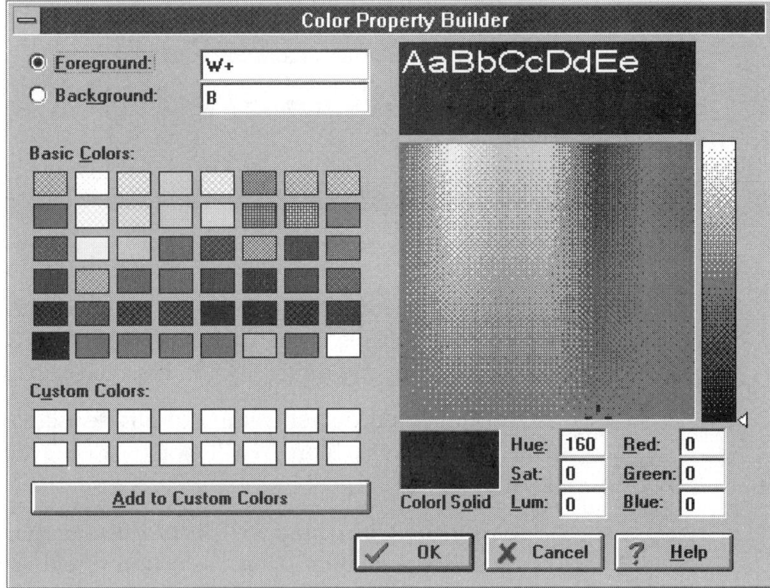

For our pushbutton control, select **Blue (B)** for the background color and **Bright White (W+)** for the foreground color. Though we are not modifying them on this form, the form itself, the text object, and the rectangle object also have a ColorNormal property. Click **OK** to return to the Form Designer.

4. **Bitmap property.** A bitmap image will add to the visual functionality of a control such as a pushbutton. For example, we could place a green checkmark just to the left of the text property, **Continue**, on our pushbutton. To do this, proceed as follows:

- **Inspector window.** Give focus to the Inspector window.
- **Selecting a bitmap.** Double-click the **Bitmap Properties** group if it is preceded with a plus (+) sign, click the **UpBitmap** property, then click the **Toolbar** in the text box. This will display the UpBitmap Property Builder dialog box (see Figure 8.7). UpBitmap refers to the property in effect when the button is in an up state. Other properties affected by the state of a pushbutton are the following:

  DownBitmap—the bitmap displayed when the button is pressed.
  FocusBitmap—the bitmap displayed when the button is in focus. It will not be displayed when the button does not have focus.

FIGURE 8.7 UPBITMAP PROPERTY BUILDER DIALOG BOX

DisabledBitmap—for times when you do not want a pushbutton available to the user. If a pushbutton is disabled (Disabled Property set to .T.), the DisabledBitmap will be in effect.

The inherited default setting of all the Bitmap properties is an empty string. Therefore a bitmap will not be displayed unless that property is modified.

- **Using the UpBitmap Property Builder dialog box.** The Location drop-down list box allows selection of either a Visual dBASE built-in bitmap (**Resource** selection) or a bitmap from an external file (**Filename** selection). For our pushbutton graphic, select **Resource** from the Location list box, then click the toolbar to the right of the Bitmap text box (see Figure 8.7).
- **Using the Choose Resource Bitmap dialog box.** Each bitmap has an ID number. Click on a few of the numbers to observe the corresponding bitmap in the adjacent Bitmap rectangle (see Figure 8.8). Finally, place the cursor on ID number 20 (a small green checkmark) and click the **OK** button at the bottom of the dialog box, then click the **OK** button on the UpBitmap Property Builder dialog box.
- **Save/View the form.** Save your work so far (**File | Save**) and then view the form (**View | Form** or press **F2**). The form should now appear as in Figure 8.5B. At this stage of the design, clicking or pressing the pushbutton will not cause an event to occur. Return to the design worksurface (**View | Form Design** or press **Shift+F2**).

5. **Assigning a PushButton event-handler:** The purpose of our pushbutton is to close the Banner window form. Usually, a Banner window will open for operator information prior to entry into an application. That is why our Banner window pushbutton text property is **Continue** as opposed to **Exit.** The operator will click it to close the Banner window, then continue into the application. To build a pushbutton event-handler to close the Banner window form, proceed as follows:

FIGURE 8.8 CHOOSE RESOURCE BITMAP DIALOG BOX

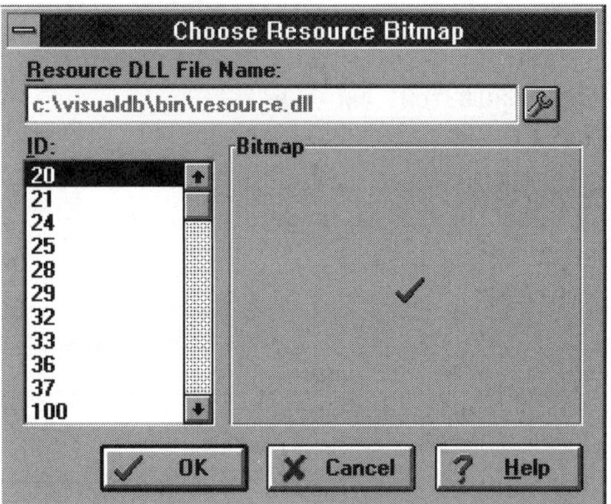

- **Entering the Procedure Editor.** To enter the editor, proceed as follows:

  Give focus to the Inspector window (click anywhere within its title bar).
  Choose **form.pushbutton1** from the Inspector window list box (just under the title bar).
  Click the **Events** tab of the Inspector window.
  Click the **OnClick** event, then Click the **OnClick** toolbar.

- **Using the Procedure Editor.** Our pushbutton event-handler will take the form of a procedure, as discussed and used in the preceding chapter. When the editor opens, the first line of code (`PROCEDURE` command), which names the procedure, is supplied for you. The name supplied corresponds to the event in question. As discussed in the preceding chapter, we will use the `CLOSE( )` method of the class Form to close the form. Finish entering the code as follows (see Figure 8.9):

```
PROCEDURE pushbutton1_OnClick
   form.CLOSE()
RETURN
```

Save the procedure by double-clicking the Procedure Editor control-menu button. The procedure is now complete, including its assignment to the `OnClick` event property.

FIGURE 8.9 PROCEDURE EDITOR

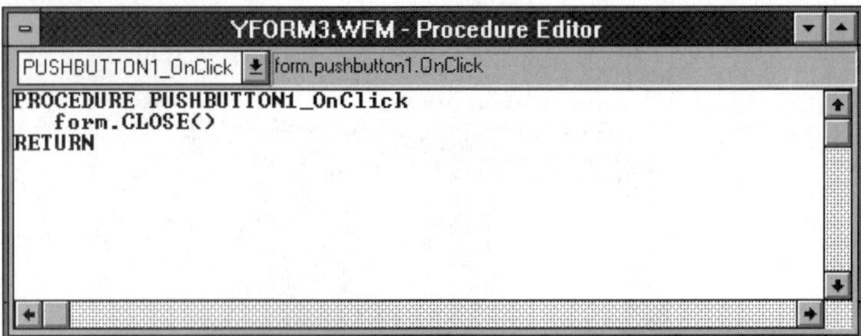

- **Final Save/View of the form.** Save your work so far (**File | Save**), then view the form (**View | Form** or press **F2**). After viewing the completed form on your screen, click the **Continue** pushbutton to execute the event-handler, which should close the form. If it works properly, control should return to the Command window. If we had entered the Form Designer from the Navigator window, control would return to the Navigator window.

THE FORM DESIGNER AS A TWO-WAY TOOL

In the preceding chapter, we created a form by entering Visual dBASE code into the program editor. In this chapter, we created a similar form using the Form Designer. Because the Form Designer is a two-way tool, we can also use combinations of the two. To demonstrate this, proceed as follows:

1. **Enter the program editor.** Type the following command from the Command window:

```
MODI COMM yform3.wfm
```

The Program Editor now contains the code generated by the Form Designer for our Banner screen form, `yform3.wfm` (see Figure 8.10). Notice that it follows the same general form as the code developed in the preceding chapter using the Program Editor.

FIGURE 8.10 VIEW OF yform3.wfm FROM THE PROGRAM EDITOR

```
** END HEADER -- do not remove this line*
* Generated on 07/21/95
*
parameter bModal
local f
f = new YFORM3FORM()
if (bModal)
   f.mdi = .F. && ensure not MDI
   f.ReadModal()
else
   f.Open()
endif
CLASS YFORM3FORM OF FORM
   Set Procedure To C:\DBASEWIN\SAMPLES\BUTTONS.CC
   additive
   this.Width =          51.666
   this.Text = "<student name>"
   this.HelpID = ""
   this.HelpFile = ""
   this.Height =          12.8232
   this.Left =          25
   this.Top =           3

   DEFINE RECTANGLE RECTANGLE1 OF THIS;
       PROPERTY;
         Width         40,;
         ColorNormal "N/W",;
         Border .T.,;
         Text "",;
         Height          5,;
         Left           7,;
         Top           1

   DEFINE TEXT TEXT1 OF THIS;
       PROPERTY;
         Width         26,;
         ColorNormal "N/W",;
         Border .F.,;
         FontSize          11,;
```

(continues)

FIGURE 8.10 (continued) VIEW OF yform3.wfm FROM THE PROGRAM EDITOR

```
          Text "MY BANNER SCREEN",;
          Height            1,;
          Left            13,;
          Top             3

    DEFINE PUSHBUTTON PUSHBUTTON1 OF THIS;
         PROPERTY;
          Width             20,;
          ColorNormal   "W+/B",;
          OnClick CLASS::PUSHBUTTON1_ONCLICK,;
          FontSize            11,;
          Text "Continue",;
          UpBitmap "RESOURCE #20",;
          Default .T.,;
          Group .T.,;
          Height            2,;
          Left            16,;
          Top             9
    PROCEDURE PUSHBUTTON1_OnClick
       form.CLOSE()
    RETURN
ENDCLASS
```

2. **Modifying the generated code.** We will make changes to the code that will center the form and place the student name in the form title bar. Make the following changes to the form constructor code of **yform3.wfm** (note shaded lines in Figure 8.10):

```
this.Left = 25.00
this.Text = "<student name>"      && Enter your name here.
this.Top  = 3.00
```

3. **Test the revised form.** To test the changes, click the **Execute the program** icon in the Speedbar. Make sure the form is centered and contains your name in the title bar. Press the **Continue** button to close the form. Finally, close the Program Editor (double-click the **Control** button).

NOTE: A form developed through the Form Designer will have a `.wfm` (windows form) extension. This extension is required to maintain the two-way tool capability of the Form Designer. It is also required when executing such a file from the Command window with the `DO` command or if editing with the `MODI COMM` command. It is not required when using `MODI FORM`.

4. **Return to the Form Designer.** We can now return to the Form Designer to see if the changes we made from the Program Editor are still intact. Type the following from the Input pane:

```
MODI FORM yform3
```

This command works only with a Windows form file and does not require use of the `.wfm` extension. The form should now be centered on the designer work surface. The form title does not appear unless you view the form (**View | Form** or **F2**). You can also look at the modified properties in the Inspector window. Of course, any changes you now make from the Form Designer will be intact when you return to the Program Editor.

5. **Close the Form Designer.** Close the Form Designer by choosing **File | Save and Close.**

BUILDING A MENU SYSTEM IN A FORM

A windows application usually contains a menu system. In Visual dBASE, we use the Menu Designer to add a menu to a form. Proceed as follows:

1. **Create an applications desktop form.** The highest order window in an application is referred to as its desktop. The system menu is part of that window. To create the form, type the following from the input pane:

```
MODI FORM yform4
```

2. **Create the menu system.** The Menu Designer window is very straightforward and easy to use. It virtually eliminates the need for the hard coding of menus in Visual dBASE systems. The Menu Designer is also a two-way tool, so modifications can be made at either level. Proceed as follows:

- **Open the Menu Designer.** Give focus to the Inspector. Click the **MenuFile** property, then double-click the **Toolbar** to access the Menu Designer. Prior to entry, you will need to supply the menu file name, `yform4.mnu`, in the MenuFile Property Builder dialog box.

  NOTE: You can also access the Menu Designer by typing `CREATE MENU` from the Command window. However, if already in the Form Designer, access via the MenuFile property toolbar is much more convenient. Further, when access is gained in this manner, the menu file name will be automatically inserted as the MenuFile property.

- **Create drop-down menu items.**

Develop a menu item. Type the first item, `&File`, at the cursor position. Press the **Tab/Shift-Tab** key to move horizontally and the **Up/Down-arrow** keys to move vertically. The ampersand (**&**) will cause the letter it precedes to be underlined. This is referred to as the *mnemonic key* of that menu item. An item can be selected at runtime by pressing **Alt+<mnemonic key>** . For example, **Alt+F,** will select our File menu. Every menu item in a menu system should contain a mnemonic key. Using **Tab/Shift-Tab** to move horizontally and the arrow keys to move vertically, type the following menu items:

```
&File          &Utilities          &Help
E&xit
```

Editing an existing menu. Edits can be made using the Menu menu of the Menu Designer. For example, place the cursor on the Exit item, select **Menu | Insert Menu Item**, then add the following two new menu items:

```
&File
Printer &Setup
&Print
E&xit
```

Continue editing by placing a separator bar between the `Exit` item and the `Printer` item on the File menu. With the cursor on the Exit item, select **Menu | Insert Separator.** To delete a menu item, select **Menu | Delete Current.** Your final view of the menu from the Menu Design work surface should appear as in Figure 8.11.

Close the Menu Designer. Double-click the **Menu Designer** control box.

FIGURE 8.11 THE MENU DESIGNER

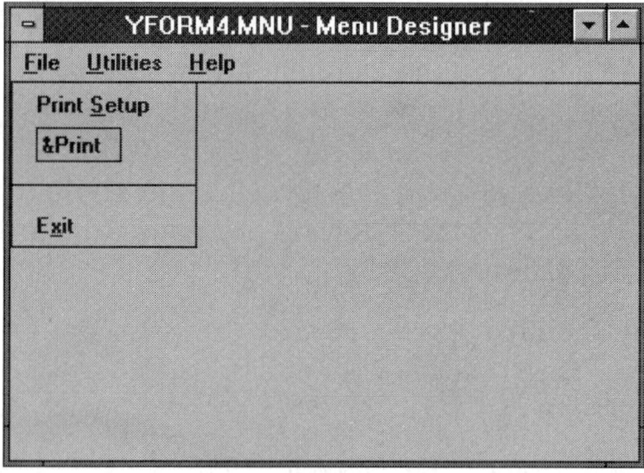

3. **Attaching the menu to the form.** The menu that we constructed with the Menu Designer is contained in a separate file, `yform4.mnu`. It will be automatically entered as the **MenuFile** property of our form, `yform4.wfm`. If the menu was created from the Command window, the file name could be inserted by double-clicking the **MenuFile** property toolbar and selecting the appropriate menu file name from the MenuFile Property Builder dialog box.

4. **Setting the Multiple Document Interface (MDI) property.** This property determines if a window conforms to the windows Multiple Document Interface standard. As discussed earlier, one element of the standard that we are concerned with is whether or not the form is modal.

   Another element of the MDI standard, and the one we are concerned with here, is the menu system of a form. If the MDI property is set to `.T.`, the menu system of a form replaces the Visual dBASE menu. If it is set to `.F.`, the menu is contained within the form itself. We want our menus to replace the Visual dBASE menus, so we want that property to be set to true (`.T.`). The default setting is `.T.`, so no action is required at this point. The MDI setting is part of the Window Properties group in the Inspector.

   NOTE: For more information on the characteristics of the Multiple Document Interface (MDI) windows standard, refer to a Windows reference manual or to on-line help in Visual dBASE.

5. **Attaching an action to a menu item.** Our next step will be to attach a procedure to the Exit item of the File menu. Its function will be to close the form. Proceed as follows:

- Place the menu design on the work surface. To do this, give focus to the Inspector, click on the Menufile property (`yform4.mnu`), then click on the toolbar. Finally, from the **Modify Menu File Property** dialog box, click the **Design Current Menu** radio button, and then the **OK** button.
- Give focus to the Exit item on the File menu with a mouse click or by using the down-arrow key.
- Give the Inspector focus. Press the **Events** tab, then click the **OnClick** property. Finally, click the **Toolbar** to open the Procedure Editor. Type the following procedure (the first line should appear automatically):

```
Procedure EXIT_OnClick
   form.CLOSE()
RETURN
```

Double-click the Procedure Editor **Control Box** to close the editor. Double-click the **Control Box** of the Menu Designer to close the designer and return to the Form Designer work surface.

6. **Test the form and menu system.** View the form by pressing **F2** from the Form Designer work surface. The menus should replace the Visual dBASE menus as opposed to being within the new form. Test the **File** item of the menu by pressing **ALT+F** or by a mouse click. Select the Exit item from the File menu to exit the form and return to the Command window.

7. **The Menu Designer as a two-way tool.** Menus in Visual dBASE are best created using the Menu Designer. However, the code generated by the Menu Designer can be modified directly. The Menu Designer is also a two-way tool in the sense that after direct modification of the code, you can return to the menu designer and find that modification intact. To review the code generated by the Menu Designer for menu `yform4.mnu`, enter the Program Editor (see Figure 8.12).

```
MODI COMM yform4.mnu
```

The menu model developed by the Menu Designer is similar to the form object model generated by the Form Designer. The main body of the model consists of a `CLASS..ENDCLASS` construct. In Visual dBASE, programmers do not specifically designate bar menus, pulldown menus, or cascading menus in their designs. The menu type will be a function of the location of the definition in the object hierarchy. For example, in `yform4.mnu`, the File menu item is at the top of the definition hierarchy. The Print option of the File menu is defined as an object inside of the File item object, and so forth down the hierarchy.

FIGURE 8.12 SOURCE CODE LISTING, MENU PROGRAM, `yform4.mnu`

```
** END HEADER -- do not remove this line*
* Generated on 07/21/95
*
Parameter FormObj
NEW YFORM4MENU (FormObj,"Root")
CLASS YFORM4MENU (FormObj,Name) OF MENU(FormObj,Name)
   this.Text = ""

   DEFINE MENU FILE OF THIS;
       PROPERTY
         Text "&File"

         DEFINE MENU PRINT_SETUP OF THIS.FILE;
             PROPERTY;
               Text "Print Setup"

         DEFINE MENU PRINT OF THIS.FILE;
             PROPERTY;
               Text "Print"

         DEFINE MENU MENU9 OF THIS.FILE;
             PROPERTY;
               Text "",;
               Separator .T.

         DEFINE MENU EXIT OF THIS.FILE;
             PROPERTY;
               OnClick CLASS::EXIT_ONCLICK,;
               Text "E&xit"

   DEFINE MENU UTILITIES OF THIS;
       PROPERTY;
         Text "&Utilites"

   DEFINE MENU HELP OF THIS;
       PROPERTY;
         Text "&Help"

   Procedure EXIT_OnClick
      form.Close()
   RETURN

ENDCLASS
```

REVIEW EXERCISES

The following exercises review the use of Form Designer and the Menu Designer. The final exercise builds an application desktop for the Case System, including an application banner screen.

PART I: REVIEW QUESTIONS

1. What advantages does the Visual dBASE Form Designer have over traditional code generators?
2. Name two ways to enter the Form Designer.
3. How do you prevent Visual dBASE from entering the Form Expert prior to entering the Form Designer?
4. How is a control placed on a form?
5. What Form Designer tool is used to change a property of a control?
6. Explain the difference between a FocusBitmap and an UpBitmap property?
7. Explain what an event-handler is and how to attach one to form control.
8. What is a mnemonic key and how is it coded when using the Menu Designer?
9. What is the purpose of a menu separator line?
10. What is the definition of a Modal form?

PART II: CREATING A FORM

Objectives: To use the Form Designer to design a form that will change background colors based on a pushbutton click by an operator. The form will demonstrate placing control objects on the form, changing inherited properties of a form and its objects, and assigning event-handlers to control objects. The code generated by the Form Designer will be modified using the Program Editor. The completed form should appear as in Figure 8.13.

FIGURE 8.13 REVIEW EXERCISE, PART II, `yform5.wfm`

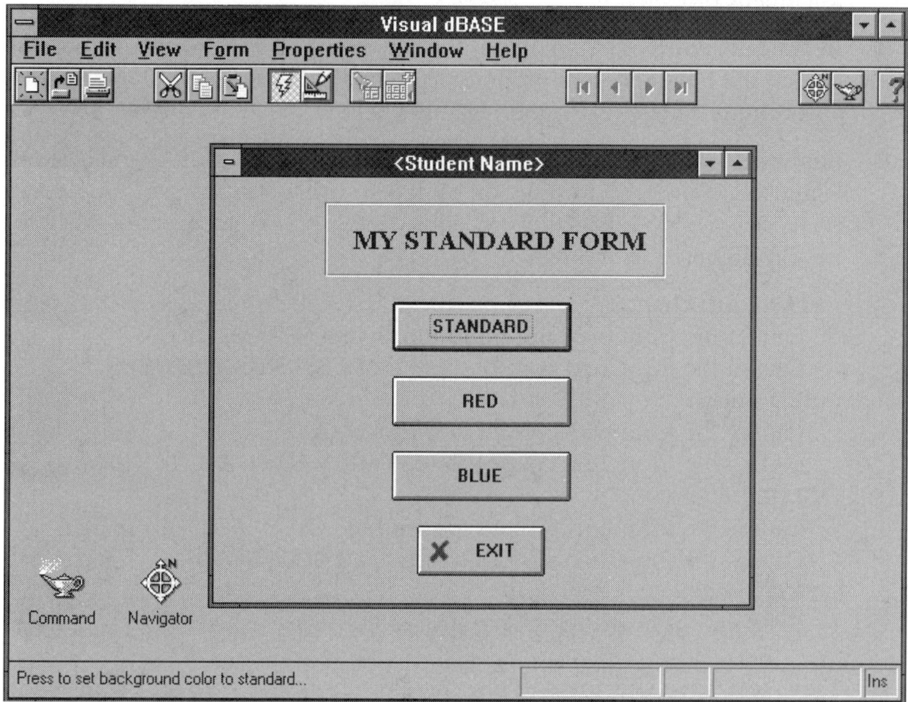

Specifications: Design the form using the following guidelines. Refer to Figure 8.13 during each phase of the design to visualize the general format of each control.

- **Form file name.** Call the form `yform5.wfm`.
- **Form title.** The form title is to contain the name of the student developing the form.
- **Text control.** Place a text control on the upper portion of the form. Use a Times New Roman font with a point size of 14. Center the Text within the object using Alignment under Position properties of the Text control (pick **center** from the drop-down list). Size the control so that it is just slightly larger than the character string listed below. It is to read as follows:

  MY STANDARD FORM

As the operator presses pushbuttons on the form, different sets of character strings will be placed in this object. They will be shorter in length than the standard string and centered appropriately by the original setting of the Alignment property.

- **Rectangle control.** Frame the Text control using a Rectangle control. Modify the inherited Text property to form a solid line around the perimeter of the rectangle. Place the rectangle behind the Text control.

- **Pushbutton controls:** Place four pushbuttons on the form as indicated in Figure 8.13. The text property on each is to use a MS sans serif font with a point size of 10. Using the Procedure Editor, code an event-handler for each pushbutton as follows:

  STANDARD button
  Causes the form background to turn white (**W**).
  Causes the form Text control to read **MY STANDARD FORM**.
  RED button
  Causes the form background to turn red (**R**).
  Causes the form Text control to read **MY RED FORM**.
  BLUE button
  Causes the form background to turn blue (**B**).
  Causes the form Text control to read **MY BLUE FORM**.
  EXIT button
  Exits the form and returns control to the Input pane.

- **View/test/save the form.** View the form from the Form Designer work surface. If it is working properly, save and exit to the Command window.

- **Modify the form from the Program Editor.** Modify the generated code in `yform5.wfm` to add a StatusMessage property to each pushbutton. The messages should read as follows:

  STANDARD: Press to set background color to standard ...
  RED: Press to set background color to red ...
  BLUE: Press to set background color to blue ...
  EXIT: Press to exit form ...

- **View/test/save the form.** View the form from the Program Editor. If it is working properly, save and exit to the Command Window.

In this exercise, we build the Case System application desktop form, place a menu system within the form, and present an application banner screen. We will also link the exercise created in Chapter 4. That program module, `ypartc.prg` was developed and executed through the Command window, and as such it is not a Windows application. This will demonstrate a technique to temporarily run a dBASE III or IV DOS program from your Visual dBASE application until conversion takes place.

Specifications:

- **Enter the Form Designer.** Enter the Form Designer and name your form `yvideo`.

- **Modify form properties.** Modify the following properties of the desktop form:

  Make the background color of the form bright white (**W+**). Modify the title of the form (the Text property) to read as follows:

  VIDEO EXPRESS SYSTEM

  The menu system that you will be creating for the desktop is to replace the Visual dBASE menu system. This will require that the MDI property of the form be set to false (.T.).

- **Create the menu system.** Enter the Menu Designer from the Form Designer work surface and create a menu system named `ymenu.mnu` for the Video Express System as follows:

&File	**&Add Records**	**&Utilities**	**&Dos Modules**	**&Help**
Printer &Setup	**&Customer Table**		**&Credit Card Summary**	
&Print	**&Film Table**			

&Exit				

- **Create a status bar prompt message.** Using the StatusMessage property, assign a prompt message to the form as follows:

  Select a menu item ...

- **Attach an action to the Exit menu item.** Create a procedure that will close the desktop form and attach it to the **Exit** item of the desktop File menu. Use the **OnClick** property of the Exit item.

- **Resize the desktop.** The application desktop will be the highest-order form in the Video Express system. As such, it should be almost a full screen form. It should not cover the status line at the bottom of the screen or the Visual dBASE menu/speedbar (See Figure 8.14). From the design work surface, resize the default size of the form. You may not be able to complete this resizing with the mouse cursor. If not, complete the resizing by adjustment of the Height and/or Width properties of the form.

  NOTE: When the form size has been adjusted to cover most of the design work-surface, it will also cover the Inspector and Control Palette. To give focus to either of these, select **Window I Controls** or **Properties** or press a series of **Ctrl-Tabs**. If they are not currently open, right-click on the form itself to select **Form Designer Properties** (drop-down menu) **I Inspector** or **Controls**.

- **View the form.** At this point the form should appear as in Figure 8.14. View the form to verify your work so far. After viewing the form, return to the Form Designer.

FIGURE 8.14 VIDEO EXPRESS DESKTOP, `yvideo.wfm`

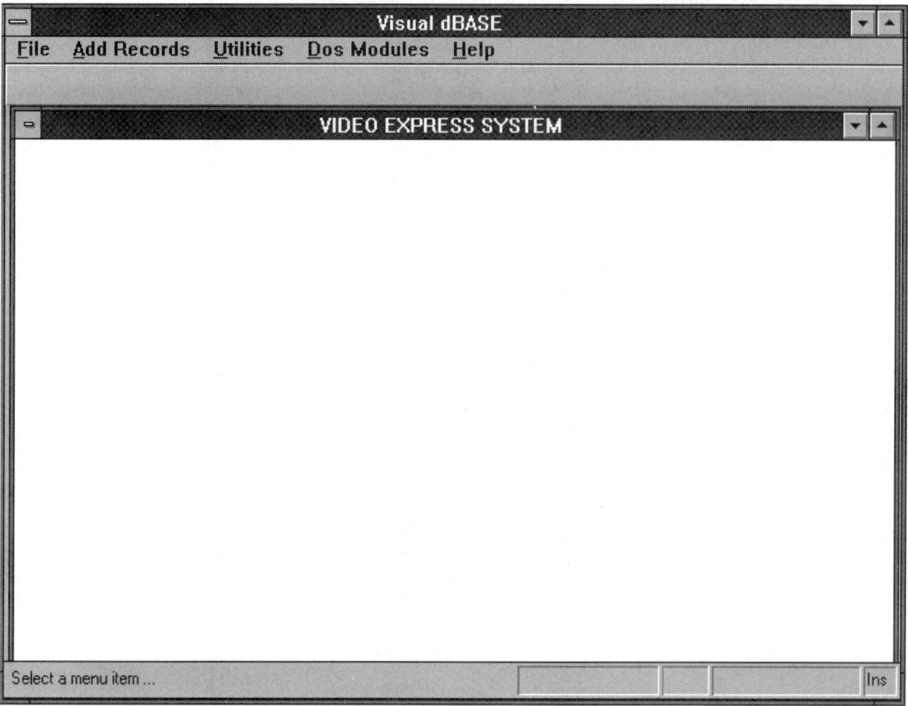

- **Add a banner screen to the desktop.** The next step will be to create a banner screen to be presented as the OnOpen handler of the desktop form (see Figure 8.15). The banner screen is to be centered on the desktop and closed by the PushButton OnClick handler. Using the Form Designer, proceed as follows:

  File name. Name the banner screen form file, `ybanner.wfm`.
  Fonts and font sizes. The main Text item, "VIDEO EXPRESS SYSTEM," is to be a 14 point Arial font. Use a 10 point Arial font for the remaining Text items.
  Give the banner form a title. Replace the current Title property with the following:

  About Video Express

  Assigning a prompt message. Modify the StatusMessage property of the form as follows:

  Press continue button to access main menu ...

FIGURE 8.15 APPLICATION DESKTOP WITH MENU AND BANNER SCREEN

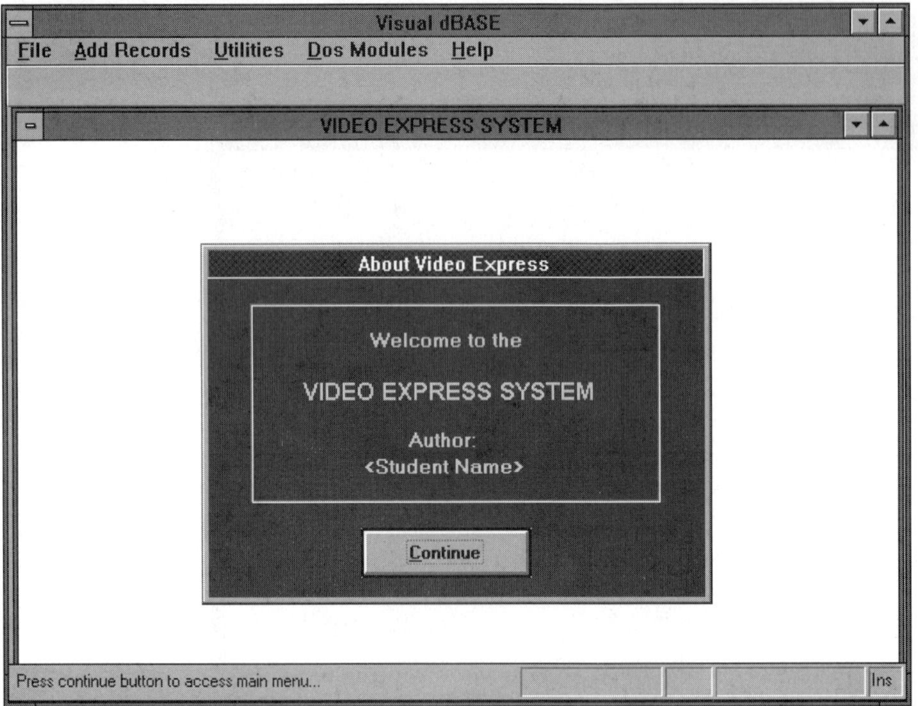

PushButton. Attach an OnClick event-handler to the **Continue** pushbutton that will close the form. Additionally, place a checkmark icon (Resource 22) on the pushbutton.

Remove the control menu. We want this form to be closed only from the **Continue** pushbutton, so we want to remove the control menu. To do this, go to the Inspector, then select the Window Properties group. Set the SysMenu property to .F.

Make the form modal. The banner screen window is to be a modal form. We want it modal so that no other actions can take place until it is closed. To do this, we want the form to be opened using the `READMODAL()` method rather than the `OPEN()` method and we want the MDI property to be set to **`.F.`** One solution would be to go directly to the source code of `ybanner.wfm` and change the `form.OPEN()` command to `form.READMODAL()` plus change the MDI property to **`.F.`** However, those changes would not be honored by the two-way tools of the forms designer.

Fortunately, the code generated by the Form Designer allows us to create a modal form. Review the following code taken from our **About** screen, `ybanner.wfm`, source code. This code segment is generated by the Form Designer for all forms.

```
parameter bModal
local f
f = new YBANNERFORM()
if (bModal)
   f.mdi = .F. && ensure not MDI
   f.ReadModal()
else
   f.Open()
endif
```

The `PARAMETERS` command and the ability to pass parameters to programs will be discussed in detail in Chapter 10. However, we will briefly introduce the concept here to demonstrate opening a modal form. If we pass a parameter of a logical `.T.` to the generated code, it will cause the form to open as a modal form. The variable, `bModal`, will accept the passed parameter causing the `IF` condition to be true. This will cause the MDI property to be set to `.F.` and the form to be opened using `form.READMODAL()`. In the next step, we will see how to pass the parameter to `ybanner.wfm` as the Video Express desktop window opens.

Running the banner screen as the desktop opens. When the desktop form is opened, the banner screen is to appear. To accomplish this, use the OnOpen event-handler of the desktop form, `yvideo.wfm`. Code the OnOpen event-handler as follows:

```
Procedure Form_OnOpen
   DO ybanner.wfm WITH .T.  && Run program with
                            && passed parameter.
RETURN
```

If the `WITH` clause is omitted and no parameter is passed, the variable, `bModal`, in `ybanner.wfm` will be `.F.` by default causing the form to be opened modeless. Most of your forms will be run as modeless.

Test the forms. Test both the desktop form, `yvideo.wfm`, and the banner screen, `ybanner.wfm` together using the following command from the Input pane:

```
DO yvideo.wfm
```

If everything is working properly, the Video Express application desktop form will be displayed on the Visual dBASE desktop. The banner screen form will be centered inside the application desktop (see Figure 8.15). The banner screen should disappear when the **Continue** button is pressed. Clicking anywhere else on the form other than the **Continue** button should have no effect on the form. Close the desktop form by selecting **File | Exit** from the desktop menu system.

- **Attach DOS application module to the desktop menu.** Visual dBASE allows for parallel conversion of DOS applications. You can temporarily attach dBASE for DOS modules to the application desktop until time permits their conversion. Because a DOS application can only be executed from the Input pane, a few extra commands must be added to the attaching code. Proceed as follows:

Modify DOS program module. When we developed the DOS module, `ypartc.prg`, it was executed from the Command window. After execution, control returned to the Command window and the output remained in the Results pane. We are now going to connect that module to the menu system of Video Express. Unless we cause the DOS program to pause after presenting the output to the Results pane, control will immediately return to the application desktop—and the user will not be able to view the Results pane because it will be under the application desktop. To solve this problem, type `MODI COMM ypartc` into the Commands window and then add the following two commands just prior to the `RETURN` command in the program:

```
WAIT
CLEAR
```

This will cause `ypartc.prg` to pause and present a **Press any key to continue...** message. When the operator presses any key, the results pane will clear and control will return to the applications desktop.

Open the Menu Designer. It is not necessary to open the Form Designer if your modifications only apply to the menu system. From the Input pane, enter the following command:

```
MODI MENU ymenu.mnu
```

After entering the Menu Designer, place the cursor on the **Credit Card Summary** item of the **Dos Modules** menu. Finally, click the **OnClick** event property in the Inspector window, then click the **OnClick** toolbar.

Attachment code. The procedure code to attach the DOS module to the windows menu item is as follows:

```
Procedure Credit_Card_Summary_OnClick
    KEYBOARD "{CTRL-TAB}"
    DO ypartc.prg
    form.SETFOCUS()
RETURN
```

Before running the program, **`ypartc.prg`**, we must give the Command window focus. This must be done because DOS programs can only run in the Command window. Unfortunately, Visual dBASE does not give us a handle to the Command window to give it focus programmatically. However, the **`KEYBOARD`** command will allow us to move focus from one object to the next by supplying the **`Ctrl-Tab`** keypress of windows. Without this statement, the results of the credit card summary program would be displayed in the Command window behind the desktop. The command following the `DO` statement uses the SETFOCUS( ) method property of the form to give focus back to the application desktop after completion of the credit card summary.

Prior to running the DOS module, you may want to make the Results pane larger and perhaps minimize the Navigator. This will better accommodate the output of the DOS module. Unfortunately, Visual dBASE does not give us an easy way to do these chores programmatically.

Test and save updates. All aspects of the Video Express desktop should now execute properly. Run the application from the Command window as follows:

```
DO yvideo.wfm
```

If the credit card summary program is running properly, its output should be displayed in the Results pane when that item is selected from the main menu. After the operator responds to the **Press any key to continue...** message at the end of the program, focus should return to the application desktop. Clicking the Exit item from the File menu should close the Video Express application and return control to the Command window.

CHAPTER SUMMARY

In this chapter, we introduced the Form Designer and the Menu Designer. These design tools are very important to the Visual dBASE programmer because they are two-way tools and do not generate any excess code. Their use can greatly increase programming productivity.

The following topics were discussed:

- **Using the Form Designer.** We learned how to enter the Form Designer from both the Command window and the Navigator.
- **Parts of the Form Designer work surface.** The Form Designer contains a menu system, speedbar, form window, Inspector, and Control palette.
- **Placing controls on a form.** Controls are moved to the Form Designer work surface from the Control palette. In this chapter, we placed a Text, Rectangle, and PushButton control objects on a form. Once on the form, the objects were moved and resized.
- **Changing control object properties.** Once controls are placed on a form, their inherited properties can be modified as required.
- **Placing a PushButton control on a form.** Control objects such as Text and Rectangle do not necessarily cause actions to occur, whereas a control such as PushButton can cause an event to occur. Controls such as PushButton cause the form to be event driven.
- **The Form Designer as a two-way tool.** The two-way nature of the Form Designer allows the programmer to create and modify form objects either from the designer work surface or from the generated source code.
- **Building a menu system.** The Menu Designer relieves the Visual dBASE programmer from the tedious job of developing menu system source code. This design tool is also a two-way tool. It can be accessed either from the Form Designer or directly from the Command window.

The exercises of this chapter added an application desktop, banner screen window, and menu system to the student Case System. Also introduced was a technique that allows the programmer to temporarily attach a DOS program module to a Windows menu system.

The following commands were discussed:

- `CREATE/MODIFY FORM`
- `CREATE/MODIFY MENU`
- `KEYBOARD`

The following object properties were discussed:

- `Text`
- `Alignment`
- `FontSize`
- `UpBitMap`
- `MDI`
- `ColorNormal`
- `StatusMessage`
- `SysMenu`
- `SETFOCUS( )`

In the next chapter, we begin programming custom data entry screen forms. We add an input screen to the Case System and learn the concepts of buffered input and data validation as new records are added to the various tables of the system.

CHAPTER NINE

TOPICS

New Commands, Functions, and Properties

Concepts

- Data entry form design guidelines
- Buffered data entry
- Data entry pseudocode
- Designing a data entry form
- Data validation coding
- Transferring validated data to a table

Review Exercises

Chapter Summary

Data Entry Windows Design

9

CHAPTER OBJECTIVES

In this chapter, we introduce the concept of programming to add records to system tables. Data that is entered from the keyboard by an operator poses several problems for the programmer. Data validation must be included in the design of append windows to avoid table data corruption. Moreover, the generic append windows provided by Visual dBASE GUI are not designed adequately for the nontechnical operator. In a customized system, append windows should be designed to satisfy the ergonomic needs of the user-operator.

After studying this chapter, you should understand the concepts of append window design and how to develop code for proper validation of data.

NEW COMMANDS, FUNCTIONS, AND PROPERTIES

COMMAND `SET CUAENTER ON/off`

If set to **ON**, causes the enter key to move focus and activate the last item on a form as opposed to the next item in sequence. In a Windows application, the enter key is typically used to submit the form by moving control to the last item on the form. However, on a data entry form, it is usually more convenient for the operator if the enter key is used to move focus to the next data entry item.

COMMAND `SET CONFIRM ON/off`

Controls the cursor's movement from one entry field to the next. To change the default, set the **CONFIRM** parameter in **dBASEWIN.INI**. When **SET CONFIRM** is **OFF**, dBASE moves the cursor immediately to the next input area when the current one is full. When **SET CONFIRM** is **ON**, the cursor moves to the next input area only when you press <**enter**>. Use **SET CONFIRM ON** to prevent moving the cursor from one input area to the next automatically, thus avoiding data entry errors such as the overflow of contents from one input area into the next. Use **SET CONFIRM OFF** when input speed is more important.

COMMAND `APPEND [BLANK]`

Adds a new record to a table. Moves the pointer to the blank record. This command was introduced in an earlier chapter to add records either from the keyboard or from another table. Our use here is to append a blank record to a table. New data will then be added to the blank fields of that record.

COMMAND

```
REPLACE <field1> WITH <exp1> [ADDITIVE]
  [,<field2> WITH <exp2> [ADDITIVE]...]
  [FOR/WHILE CONDITION][REINDEX]
```

Replaces the contents of specified fields in the current table with data from specified expressions. We will use it in this chapter to move data from entry field Value properties to an appended blank record.

FUNCTION

```
TAGNO([<tag name expC> [,<.mdx filename expC>
     [,<alias>] ] ] )
```

Returns the index number of the specified index. Useful in conjunction with other functions that reference tag numbers.

```
USE ycustm
? TAGNO("last")
2
```

FUNCTION **KEYMATCH (<exp> [,<index position expN> | [<.mdx filename expC>,]<tag expN> [, <alias>]])**

Indicates if a specified expression is found in an index. Especially useful in preventing duplicate records from being added to a table.

```
USE ycustm                && Table is in natural order
? KEYMATCH ("0040",TAGNO ("cust_no")), RECNO()
.T.       1
```

The first command opens the file and places the record pointer on record number 1. It does not set an index order. **KEYMATCH()** in the next command searches for a **cust_no** number of "0040" in the **cust_no** index tag. The second parameter of the function asks for the numeric position of the tag in the production **.mdx** file. We have used the **TAGNO()** function to determine that position number. Because there is a "0040" customer number in the table, **KEYMATCH()** returns a logical **.T.**, which is displayed on the screen by the **?** command verb.

The advantage of using **KEYMATCH()** rather than the **SEEK()** function is that **KEYMATCH()** does not alter the position of the record pointer. **SEEK()** will leave the pointer on the located record or at the end of file if a duplicate key does not exist. In this example, the pointer remains on the first record in the table after the **KEYMATCH()** search.

PROPERTY **VIEW**

Specifies the name of a query or table on which a form is based.

Property of class: **FORM**

PROPERTY **SelectAll**

Determines if the value contained in an entry field or a spin box initially appears selected (highlighted).

Property of class: **ENTRYFIELD**, **SPINBOX**

PROPERTY **Value**

The value that an object contains.

Property of class: **CHECKBOX**, **COMBOBOX**, **EDITOR**, **ENTRYFIELD**, **LISTBOX**, **RADIOBUTTON**, **SCROLLBAR**, **SPINBOX**

PROPERTY **MaxLength**

Specifies the maximum scrolling width of an entryfield.

Property of class: **ENTRYFIELD**

PROPERTY `Width`

Determines the width of an object. In the case of a Line object, it specifies the thickness of the line to be drawn. The Width property will vary according to the font used. Therefore, the Width property may be different than the width of the field specified in the table structure.

Property of class: **BROWSE**, **CHECKBOX**, **COMBOBOX**, **EDITOR**, **ENTRYFIELD**, **FORM**, **IMAGE**, **LINE**, **LISTBOX**, **OLE**, **PUSHBUTTON**, **RADIOBUTTON**, **RECTANGLE**, **SCROLLBAR**, **SPINBOX**, **TEXT**

PROPERTY `Group`

Starts an object group in the tabbing order of the parent form. For example, the first Radio Button in a group should have Group set to **.T.** Succeeding Radio Buttons to be included within the group will have Group set to **.F.**, and are to be moved to the form sequentially after the first one has been placed.

Property of class: **CHECKBOX**, **PUSHBUTTON**, **RADIOBUTTON**

PROPERTY `RangeMax`
`RangeMin`
`RangeRequired`

RangeMax determines the upper limit for values the user can enter in a spin box or scrollbar. RangeMin sets the lower limits. RangeRequired determines whether the range specified in RangeMax and RangeMin are enforced.

Property of class: **SCROLLBAR**, **SPINBOX** (RangeRequired applies only to a spin box)

PROPERTY `Picture`
`Function`

Determines the format of data typed into an entry field or spin box object and data displayed in a Text object. The **?/??** command that we use from the Command window can also contain both Picture and Function clauses.

Property of class: **ENTRYFIELD**, **SPINBOX**, **TEXT**

PROPERTY `Valid`

An event property. It specifies a condition that must evaluate to true (**.T.**) before the user can remove focus from an object. Valid can be in the form of a procedure, code block, or function. In this chapter's Review Exercises, we will use procedures. User defined functions (UDFs) and codeblocks will be discussed in the next chapter.

Property of class: **ENTRYFIELD**, **SPINBOX**

PROPERTY `EscExit`

Determines whether user can exit a form by pressing **Esc**. The default setting is a logical `.T.` If the designer does not want a form to be closed using the **Esc** key, this property must be set to `.F.`

Property of class: `FORM`

PROPERTY `ValidErrorMsg`

Displays a character string to display in an error message dialog box when the Valid property of a data entry field returns a `.F.`

Property of class: `ENTRYFIELD`, `SPINBOX`

CONCEPTS

The design of the various windows of your system represents the system's interface with the user. If the programmer disregards this important interface, even though the rest of the system is programmed to perfection, the system may fail. Assumptions about a system are usually based on reaction, whether justified of not, to the user interface.

In general, you can group the forms of your system into two categories—data entry and dialog. Data entry forms mimic data entry paper form documents and are required to add records to the tables of a system. Dialog boxes are required to give information to the user and to receive instructions from the user on how to proceed to an ensuing step. Some forms may overlap the two, but these criteria for each will normally hold true. Our discussions in this chapter are concerned primarily with data entry forms.

DATA ENTRY FORM DESIGN GUIDELINES

There are general rules to follow when designing a form window. We begin our discussion of proper form window design with the add records function (`append`), then continue with more advanced techniques as we develop other modules of the Case System. Here are some guidelines to consider during the design of a window:

- **User involvement.** Involvement by the user in the screen design is the first rule of good form design. *Alpha testing* of the program is the programmer's tests; *beta testing* is the user's tests. Get feedback and redesign the forms accordingly if necessary.

- **Window titles.** Have a simple, centered title for each form for immediate recognition.
- **Screen syntax.** Use language that is simple and familiar to the user. For example, the generic Visual dBASE append screens display field variable names that are usually somewhat meaningless to the user. A field name such as `Amt_rent` should read **Amount Rent** on a form.

  Dialog with the user is very important. Instructions should be clear and concise. Further, take care not to be abrasive in any way. For example, when an error such as invalid data entry is pointed out to an operator, constructive comments are appropriate. You will find that users tire very quickly of abusive sounds, color changes, or verbiage in error dialogs.
- **Placement of items.** The user reads a screen form much the same as any other document. Information should therefore flow from left to right and from top to bottom. The user should not have to jump around on a form to locate the next item.
- **Pushbuttons.** Most forms have at least one pushbutton that is used for form exit. Here are some general guidelines for the usage and placement of pushbuttons on a form:

  Try to make them all the same size and use the same font and font size for each.

  Their placement should be along the bottom or right-hand side of a form.

  If many pushbuttons are required, separate them by category and place like groups within rectangles or separate with lines.

  Make the spacing between multiple pushbuttons even and align them on the form along their left or top borders.

  The text labels on a pushbutton should be only one word if possible. Labels for forms with multiple buttons should contain a mnemonic key. The label should describe what event will occur if the button is pressed.
- **Use of Enter and Tab.** Most touch typists use the **<enter>** key extensively. It is difficult for them to adjust to using the **Tab** key to move from one item to the next. Because of this, the **<enter>** key should be programmed to move the cursor to the next item, as opposed to the last item. The last item on a form should submit the form, which is appropriate on a dialog box but not a data entry form. The `SET CUAENTER` command is used for this purpose.

  Generally, data entry should be possible without the need for operators to remove their fingers from the keyboard. Having to bounce back and forth between the keyboard, the mouse, and the **Tab** key during the entry of a record will reduce operator productivity—and enthusiasm for the system.

BUFFERED DATA ENTRY

Data validation is a very important part of data entry screen design. Ideally, your program will validate each piece of information entered by the operator prior to its addition to a database table. The data entry controls of Visual dBASE provide the facility to receive data from the operator and perform various validation tests on that data.

Visual dBASE provides syntax to link a table or view directly to a form. Data entry controls can then be linked to individual fields within the table. Unfortunately, this gives the operator direct access to the table. A better approach is establish a buffer between the operator and the database.

Various techniques can be used to buffer input data prior to its addition to a table. A popular technique used by dBASE for DOS programmers is to establish a memory variable to act as a buffer for each field in the table. Data is initially entered into the memory variable, validated, then transferred to a blank record that has been appended to the table. Memory variables can still be used as buffers in Visual dBASE, but the coding is somewhat cumbersome. For example, memory variables cannot be defined in Class constructor code and still maintain two-way use of the Form Designer. Variables can be defined in an event-handler, then datalinked to the Value property of the data entry control. If not datalinked to the Value property, variables are local in scope to the handler and are not available to the Valid property. As we discussed previously, making them Public is also not desirable. Fortunately, the Value property of an entry field provides a buffer much the same as using a memory variable and provides adequate buffering of data. This will be the technique used in the exercises of this text.

DATA ENTRY PSEUDOCODE

The design of data entry screen code will follow this general format:

- Design and code data entry fields on the form. Use the Value property of each entry field as a temporary buffer during data validation.
- Code the data validation properties of each data entry field.
- Add a blank record to the table.
- Transfer validated data from the input buffer to the new blank record in the table.

DESIGNING A DATA ENTRY FORM

In this hands-on discussion, we will build a data entry form for the customer master table of the Video Express System. Because this is a discussion and demonstration of the many aspects of individual controls on a data entry form, we do not use all the fields in the table.

We will build the form, then link it to the menu system of the Video Express desktop. Proceed as follows:

- **Enter the Form Designer.** Enter the Form Designer by typing the following command from the Input pane:

  ```
  CREATE FORM yinputcm
  ```

- **Add a Text control.** Using the Control palette, place a Text control across the top of the form as a form title. Modify the inherited properties of the control as follows (see Figure 9.1):

  Text: DATA ENTRY – Customer Master File
  Font/FontSize: Arial, 14 point
  Height: 1.00
  Alignment: Center

- **Add a Line control.** This is our first use of the Line control. Move an instance of this object to the form using the same techniques used with other objects. Place the Line Control just under the Text object and make it the same length (see Figure 9.1). Resize as necessary. Modify the current Width property of the Line Control to 3. The Width property of a Line control designates its thickness.
- **Add an Abort/Exit Pushbutton.** In the lower right-hand corner of the form (see Figure 9.1) place a Pushbutton control that will allow the operator to abort the current record, then exit the form and return to the menu system of the desktop. During your tests and until linked to the menu system, this pushbutton will return control to the Command window.

  Use the techniques discussed in the preceding chapter to place the control on the form.

  Assign a red "abort" bitmap, ID#24, to the Pushbutton UpBitmap property. Include a mnemonic on the letter "**x**" of the Text property (**Abort/E&xit**).

  Assign an OnClick event handler to the pushbutton that will close the form. Give focus to the Inspector. Select **Pushbutton1** from the Inspector combobox. Choose the Inspector Events tab, click the OnClick event property, then click the OnClick toolbar. Type the following code into the Procedure Editor:

  ```
  Procedure FORM_CLEANUP
     USE                  && Close the table/view
     form.CLOSE()         && Close the form
  RETURN
  ```

The Procedure Editor automatically assigns a procedure name. In this case, we changed the assigned name to `FORM_CLEANUP`. Because this method will be used each time we close the form, regardless of the event, `FORM_CLEANUP` becomes more descriptive than `PUSHBUTTON1_OnClick`. Double click the Control button of the Procedure Editor to save the procedure.

- **Add a Text control descriptor.** This control will be used to describe the entry field. Place it on the form as shown in Figure 9.1. Modify the inherited properties as follows:

  Text: Customer No.
  Font/FontSize: Arial, 10 point
  Alignment: Bottom left

- **Add an Entryfield control.** Move the entry field from the Control palette to a position on the form just to the right of the Text control descriptor (see Figure 9.1). Modify the inherited properties of the entry field as follows:

  MaxLength. This property is in the Edit Properties group and is to be set to `4`, which corresponds the width of the customer number field, **cust_no**, in the table, **ycustm.dbf**. This will prohibit the operator from entering a value that is longer than required for a valid customer number.

  FontName/FontSize. Change the default value to a 10 point Courier New font. A monospaced font such as Courier New willbe much easier for the operator to read and work with than the default entry field font of MS Sans Serif.

  Width. In the Position properties group, change the default value of Width to `6`. The width of an entry field is not necessarily the same as the width of the corresponding field in the table. This is because of the varying size of the font used for the entry field value. You will have to try different widths for each entry field based on the font and font size used and the corresponding field width in the table.

  Value. The Value property will be used to store the data entered by the operator and will become the buffer for that value during the validation process. Change the default value to four ASCII spaces. Press the backspace key to remove the current text in the Value property, then press the spacebar four times followed by **<enter>** to insert the required ASCII spaces. This will cause the entry field to be blank when it receives focus.

  Placing a Rectangle control. Place a Rectangle control around the perimeter of the Entryfield. We will be placing other entry fields on the form, so make it large enough to include several more (see Figure 9.1). Change the Text property of the Rectangle to a *null* (zero length) string. To do this, remove all characters from the Text property.

Controls such as rectangles and entry fields are stored in layers. This may cause a situation where one control is on top of another control, thereby hiding it on the form. To push the Rectangle control behind the Entryfield control on this form, make sure the Rectangle control has focus, then select **Layout | Send to back**. The entry field will now be visible within the rectangle when the form is viewed. We will discuss setting the order of controls on a form in greater detail later in this chapter.

- **Set the form properties.** Give focus to the form itself. Using the Inspector, modify the properties of the new form as follows. You can begin with the Position properties listed here, but you may need to adjust them in the Form Designer by using standard resizing techniques.

  Text: ADD RECORDS
  Top: 4.5
  Left: 15.5
  Height: 20.00
  Width: 71.50
  MDI: .F.
  View: `ycustm.dbf.` This property attaches the table, `ycustm.dbf`, to the data entry form.
  OnOpen event-handler: Each time the form is opened, we want the `CUAENTER` toggle to be set to `OFF` and the `CONFIRM` toggle set to `ON`. This will allow the operator to press <**enter**> to move to the next entry field and will cause the cursor to automatically move to the next entry field if the field is filled during data entry. Also, we do not want the operator to be able to exit the form by pressing the **Esc** key. Finally, we want focus to be placed on the first entry field of the form. From the Inspector, click the **Events** tab, click the **OnOpen** event, then the **Toolbar**. Code a Form level OnOpen event-handler in the Procedure Editor as follows:

```
Procedure Form_OnOpen
    SET CUAENTER OFF SET CONFIRM ON
    form.EscExit = .F.
    form.ENTRYFIELD1.SETFOCUS()
RETURN
```

Double-click the **Control** button of the Procedure Editor to save this procedure.

FIGURE 9.1 INITIAL DATA ENTRY FORM, `yinputcm.wfm`

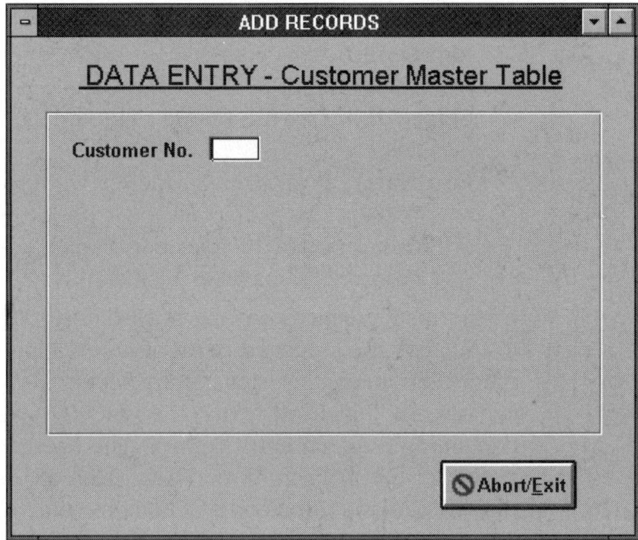

- **Save/View/Test the form.** Save your work so far (**File | Save**). View the form (**View | Form**). It should appear as in Figure 9.1. Test the following aspects of the form:

  Focus should be on the Entry field control when the form opens.

  Type any four-digit number into the entry field. Focus should automatically move to the **Abort/Exit** pushbutton after the last digit is typed.

  The form should close with focus returning to the Command window when the **Abort/Exit** pushbutton is clicked.

- **Add remaining pushbuttons.** Position the remaining two pushbuttons on the form as indicated in Figure 9.2. We will not assign events to these pushbuttons until later in the exercise. Include a mnemonic on the text properties of each pushbutton as follows:

  Save/&Next
  Save/E&xit

  The first of these pushbuttons will allow the operator to save the current record and begin entering another record. The second will allow the operator to save the current record and then exit the append form and return control to the desktop.

- **Add the remaining entry fields.** Add an entry field for the data entry of a first name, last name, phone, and amount of rent. Refer to Figure 9.2 for the placement of each. Modify the properties of each Entryfield control as follows:

  MaxLength: First Name = 10, Last Name = 15, Phone = 14, Amount Rent = 7

  SelectAll: .F. for the phone field and .T. for the remaining entry fields

  FontName, **FontSize:** Courier New, 10 point (for each)

  Width: First = 14, Last = 21, phone = 20, amount rent = 10

  Value: First = 10 spacebar blanks, Last = 15 spacebar blanks, Phone = 14 spacebar blanks.

Unfortunately, early versions of Visual dBASE do not have the ability to initialize the Value property of an entry field to any data type other than character using the Inspector. However, Value properties can also be initialized within the OnOpen event-handler of the Form containing the data entry control. This method still allows complete design of the form from the Form Designer as opposed to going directly to the source code to initialize the values.

We will initialize the Amount Rent field, **Entryfield5**, using the OnOpen handler. Earlier in this exercise, we created an OnOpen event-handler at the Form level. From the Form Designer work surface, enter the Procedure Editor with **Right-click | Procedure Editor** and modify the `Form.OnOpen` procedure to add the following command. Be sure to add the command *prior* to the `SETFOCUS()` command:

```
form.Entryfield5.Value = 0.0
```

Save your work (**File | Save**).

FIGURE 9.2 FORM yinputcm WITH ALL CONTROLS PLACED

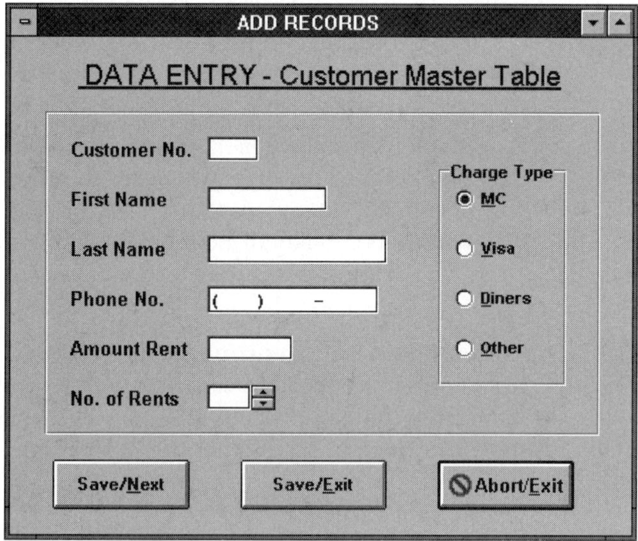

NOTE: An alternative for placing entry fields on a form is the Fields Palette (**View | Fields Palette**). It was introduced in Visual dBASE and can save keystrokes for the designer. For example, if you click and drag a numeric field from the Fields Palette versus from the Controls Palette, the datalink property will be set automatically for that field. The type of control associated with a field can be declared from the Associate Control Types dialog (**View | Associate Control Types**). The View property must be set for a form prior to usage of the Fields Palette.

- **Add final Text descriptors.** Add Text descriptors for the remaining entry fields. Refer to Figure 9.2 for the placement of each. Modify the properties of each Text control as follows:

  FontName, FontSize: Arial, 10 point
  Alignment: Bottom left
  Text: First name = **First Name**, Last name = **Last Name**, Phone = **Phone No.**, Amount Rent = **Amount Rent**, and Number of Rents = **No. of Rents**

  Save your work (**File | Save**).

- **Add a Spin Box.** When a customer opens an account, the initial number of videos rented is entered into the `no_rents` field of the new customer master record. As additional films are rented, this field will be automatically updated by the system. The minimum number of films initially rented may be 1, but never more than 10.

  Place a Spin Box control on the form just under the Amount Rent Entryfield (see Figure 9.2). Modify the inherited properties as follows:

  Statusmessage: "Enter amount this customer pays for a rental ..."
  FontName/FontSize: Courier New, 10 point
  SelectAll: .F.
  Value: 0 (Unlike an Entryfield control, a Spin Box control can be initialized to a numeric zero from the Inspector)

- **Add a Radio Button group.** Radio buttons are used to select one item from a group of items. The operator can select only a single item from the group. We will use a radio button group to enter the payment method a customer uses to charge a video. The operator can select MasterCard, Visa, Diners Club, or Other as a source of credit for a particular customer.

  Begin the group placement by moving a single radio button from the Control palette to the form. Next, move three more radio buttons to the form and place them just under the initial button. The placement of these three buttons should occur sequentially after the placement of the first button. Do not place any other object until all four buttons have been placed. Refer to Figure 9.2 for their position.

  Modify the inherited properties of the four Radio Button controls as follows:

  Group property: Radio buttons are treated as a group by Visual dBASE. A group is defined using the Group property (Access Properties group). The first button in a group contains a setting of **.T.** for the Group property and the ensuing buttons contain a setting of **.F.** for the Group property. The default setting of the Group property is **.T.** After a button is placed, all ensuing buttons will default to **.F.** When another **.T.** is set, a new group begins. If you placed the four radio buttons as described in the preceding step, the Group property settings should be correct. If not, you can change them to their proper setting from the Inspector. You could also make the changes directly to the source code using the Program Editor.

FontName/FontSize: Arial, 8 point (for each radio button)
Text:
1st button = **&MC**
2d button = **&Visa**
3d button = **&Diners**
4th button = **&Other**
StatusMessage:
MC = **Select MasterCard ...**
Visa = **Select Visa ...**
Diners = **Select Diners Club ...**
Other = **Select if other than MC, Visa, or Diners ...**
Value:
MC = `.T.`
Visa, Diners, Other = `.F.`

- **Place a Rectangle control around the Radio Button group.** Place a Rectangle control around the radio buttons as shown in Figure 9.2. Change the inherited properties of the control as follows:

  Text = `Charge Type`

  We now have a control order problem. When this Rectangle control is placed on the form, it is on top of the Radio Button controls. If we use **Layout | Send to back**, it will then be under the previous rectangle, and thereby hidden. Prior to continuing with the form, we must discuss the order of controls on the form in more depth.

- **Modifying the z-order of Form controls.** Each control on a form occupies its own plane. A control is positioned on the flat surface of an individual plane using its x- and y-axis coordinates. Planes representing two or more controls are stacked on top of one another and represent the z-axis (depth) of the form (refer to the on-line Help diagram in Figure 9.3). For this reason, the order in which the planes are stacked is referred to as the *z-order* of the form. The z-order affects the visual characteristics of controls on a form and their tabbing order.

  The visual aspects of the z-order are very important because one control can be hidden by another if not ordered correctly. For example, if a group of radio buttons are placed within a rectangle, the rectangle control plane must be placed behind the radio button planes. If not, the radio button group will not be visible. The *tabbing order* is of equal importance. Tabbing order is the order of focus movement from one control to the next as the operator presses the tab key. The default order is the order in which the controls are placed on the form by the programmer.

  In this segment, we will set the z-order and corresponding tabbing order of the customer master file append form, `yinputcm.wfm`. Proceed as follows:

FIGURE 9.3 Z-AXIS DISPLAY OF CONTROLS FROM ON-LINE HELP

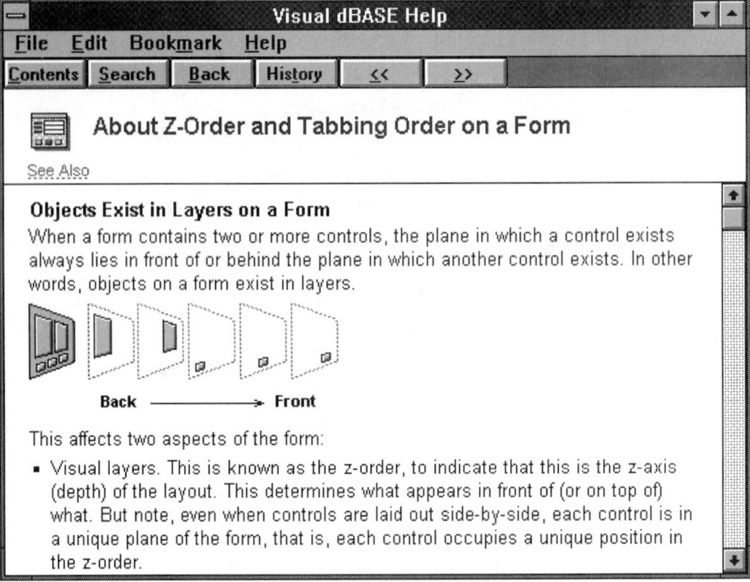

Bring the form, `yinputcm.wfm`, into the Form Designer if it is not already there. Select **View | Order View**. Though your controls are probably not in the same order, your order view should now appear similar to the Order View window in Figure 9.4.

Select **Layout | Set Control Order** to bring the Set Control Order window onto the design work surface (see Figure 9.4).

We begin by placing the large rectangle control plane on the bottom of the stack. Click the `RECTANGLE1` control in the list box within the Set Control Order window. Click the Up or Down button (or drag and drop the control name) to move this control to the top of the list. Notice that the control number located in the upper left-hand corner of the Rectangle object, `RECTANGLE1`, is now 1. When a control number on the form is changed in this manner, all of the succeeding numbers will change accordingly.

After assigning `RECTANGLE1` as control 1, continue by order the remaining controls as follows. Your control names may differ somewhat from the following list. If so, make sure the descriptions of the controls are in the correct order. For example, the **Save/Exit** button should follow the **Save/Next** button, regardless of whether they are named `PUSHBUTTON1`, `PUSHBUTTON2`, or `PUSHBUTTON3`.

Control	*No.*	*Description*
RECTANGLE1	1	Entryfield Border
RECTANGLE2	2	Radio Button Group Border
TEXT1	3	Form Title
TEXT2	4	Customer No.
TEXT3	5	First Name
TEXT4	6	Last Name
TEXT5	7	Phone No.
TEXT6	8	Amount Rent
TEXT7	9	No. of Rents
ENTRYFIELD1	10	Customer Number Entryfield
ENTRYFIELD2	11	First Name Entryfield
ENTRYFIELD3	12	Last Name Entryfield
ENTRYFIELD4	13	Phone Number Entryfield
ENTRYFIELD5	14	Amount Rent Entryfield
SPINBOX1	15	Number of Rents Entryfield
RADIOBUTTON1	16	MC Radio Button
RADIOBUTTON2	17	Visa Radio Button
RADIOBUTTON3	18	Diners Radio Button
RADIOBUTTON4	19	Other Radio Button
PUSHBUTTON2	20	Save/Next Button
PUSHBUTTON3	21	Exit/Save Button
PUSHBUTTON1	22	Exit/Abort Button

The Line control, `LINE1`, is not listed. Though it is included in the order, it does not contain an order number in the Order view. The controls will appear in the source code in the same order as listed above, with Line1 appearing prior to `RECTANGLE1.`

Click the **OK** button to close the Set Control Order window.

- **Save/View/Test the form.** Save your work so far (**File | Save**). View the form (**View | Form**). It should appear as in Figure 9.2. Test the form as follows:

  Focus should be on the Customer Number entryfield control when the form opens.

  Pressing the **Tab** key should move focus sequentially through all the entry fields, to the spin box, then to the radio button group. Test the radio button group with the arrow keys. Each arrow keypress should move focus from one radio button to the next while displaying the proper status line prompt message. Finally, pressing **Tab** again should move focus from the radio button group to the **Save/Next** push button, then to the **Exit/Save** push button, and then to the **Exit/Abort** push button. Press **Tab** once again to return focus to the Customer Number entryfield.

FIGURE 9.4 ORDER VIEW SCREEN, `yinputcm.wfm`

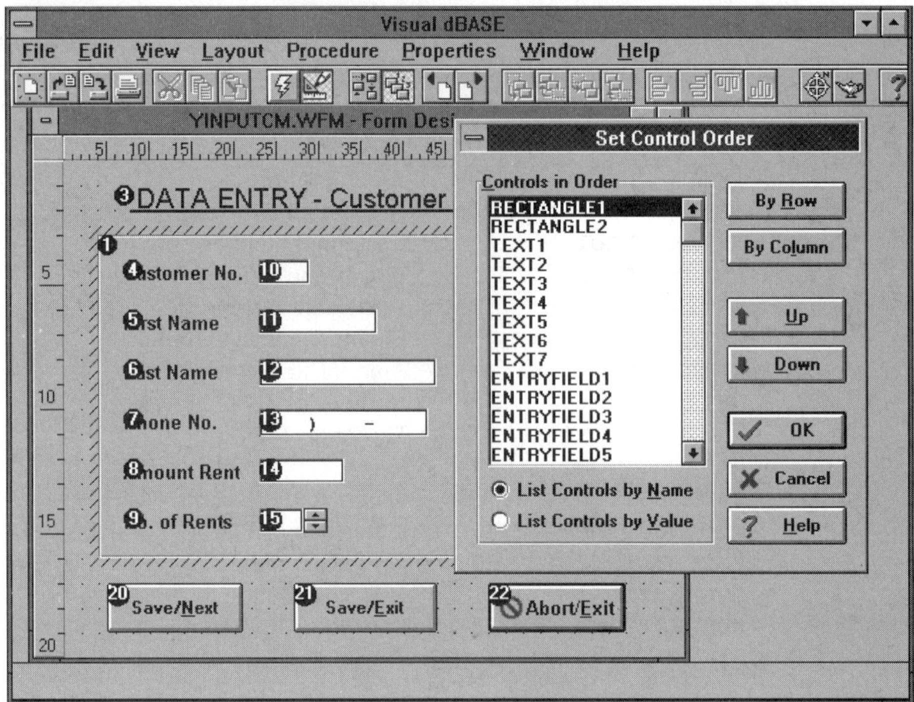

Type `1245` into the Customer Number entryfield. Control should automatically move to the First Name entryfield. When an entry field is completely filled, control should automatically move to the next field. If the data entered does not fill the field, press **<enter>** to move to the next field. Type the remaining Entryfield and Radio Button tests as follows:

```
First Name     Mary
Last Name      Rossi
Phone No.      (415) 123–4567
Amount Rent    3.00
No. of Rents   4
Charge type    Diners (Click proper radiobutton)
```

Exit the form by clicking the **Abort/Exit** pushbutton. Control should return to the Command window when this pushbutton is selected. The data that was typed in the preceding test has been lost at this point. We will discuss and demonstrate how to transfer the entered data to the Customer table later in this chapter.

DATA VALIDATION CODING

The next step in the data entry process is the validation of the data entered by the operator. In the preceding test, the data was entered into the Value property of the entry fields and radio buttons. The data would remain in the Value property while data validation checks are being made. Once validated, the data will be transferred to the proper table.

Several types of validation are available. Data can either be restricted upon entry or tested against programmed criteria after it is entered. It is also possible to test a preset condition prior to the entry of a data element. Restrictions can also be placed on output data. This allows exact formatting of screen and printed reports.

- **Picture and Function properties.** The Entryfield and Spin box controls have Picture and Function properties to assist in the validation of data. For example, we may want to restrict an entry field to all uppercase, or establish the format of a numeric field.

  Picture and Function clauses are also properties of the Text control and are clauses in the `?/??` command. To demonstrate the use of the Picture and Function clause in an output command, type the following into the Input pane of the Command window:

```
xText = "shirley"
? xText FUNCTION "!"
SHIRLEY
? xText PICTURE "!AAAAAA"
Shirley
xVal = 12345
? xVal PICTURE "99,999.99"
12,345.00
? "abc   " PICTURE "@J !XXXXX"
   Abc
```

  The difference between a Picture and a Function property is that a Function symbol applies to the entire data field, whereas a Picture symbol applies to each individual character within the field. The display of each character of a field within the Picture clause is referred to as a picture *template*. The first example demonstrates the use of a Function clause. The **!** function restricts display of the entire **xText** field to all uppercase. In the second example, the Picture template, **"!AAAAAA"**, restricts each character individually. The first character is restricted to uppercase using the **!** symbol and the second and ensuing characters are restricted to any alphabetic character using the

A symbol. The final example demonstrates using both a function symbol and picture symbols in a single Picture template. We have used the **J** function to right-justify the field and used the same template as in the second example to capitalize the first character. For this to work, you must code an **@** symbol prior to the function and separate the function and the template by a space. Notice in the first example that the **@** symbol is not required in the Function clause—only when coded in a Picture clause. Complete lists of all Picture and Function property symbols are contained in Figures 9.5 and 9.6.

FIGURE 9.5 FUNCTION PROPERTY SYMBOLS

Function	Operation
^	Display numbers in scientific notation.
!	Display in uppercase. Any character allowed.
$	Display in currency format.
A	Allow only alphabetic characters.
B	Left-justify text within a field.
D	Current **SET DATE** format for date display.
E	Date in European format.
I	Center text within a field.
J	Right-justify text within a field.
L	Display leading zeros.
M	Sequentially displays predefined options.
R	Display literal values within a field, but do not include in the stored value.
S<n>	Limit field width to <n> characters. Scroll characters horizontally within the limited field.
T	Trim both leading and trailing blanks from a field.
V<n>	Wraps a character string within a <n> width.
X	Display DB after negative numeric value.
Z	Display a zero numeric value as blanks.

FIGURE 9.6 PICTURE PROPERTY SYMBOLS

Function	Operation
`#`	Allow only digits, blanks, and signs.
`!`	Convert letters to uppercase. No effect on other characters.
`$`	Display current **SET CURRENCY** string rather than leading zeros.
`*`	Display *s rather than leading zeros.
`.`	Designates decimal position.
`,`	Display as necessary in numeric field. Limited by leading zeros.
`9`	Only numbers allowed in character type data. Allow numbers and signs for numeric type data.
`A`	Allow only letters.
`L`	Allow only logic type data.
`N`	Allow letters and digits.
`X`	Allow any character.
`Y`	Allow only logical `Y`, `y`, `N`, `n`. Lowercase `y` or `n` converted to uppercase.

- **Entryfield and Spinbox formatting.** Picture and function properties are used in Entryfield and Spinbox controls to format data as it is entered by the operator. To demonstrate this capability, open `yinputcm.wfm` in the Form Designer. Proceed as follows:

  Give focus to the Inspector. Using the Inspector Combobox, select the customer number entryfield, **Entryfield1**. You could have also given focus to **Entryfield1** directly on the form prior to giving focus to the Inspector.

  Selecting a Function property. From the Edit Properties group, click the FUNCTION property. Remember, if a group header is preceded by a plus sign (+), it must be double-clicked to display the group properties. A second double-click will remove them.

  Using the Template Properties Builder dialog box. Open the **Template Properties Builder** dialog by clicking the **Toolbar** icon to the right of the Function property.. We want to use the `J` Function symbol to right-justify input into the field. Locate the `@J` symbol in the **Template Symbols and Format Functions** list in the dialog, then double-click to select (see figure 9.7). Click the **OK** button to finalize the operation. As you return to the Inspector, notice that the `@` sign has been stripped from the Function symbol in the Function property text box. This could have been accomplished by simply typing the `J` after the Function property in the Inspector.

FIGURE 9.7 TEMPLATE PROPERTIES BUILDER DIALOG BOX

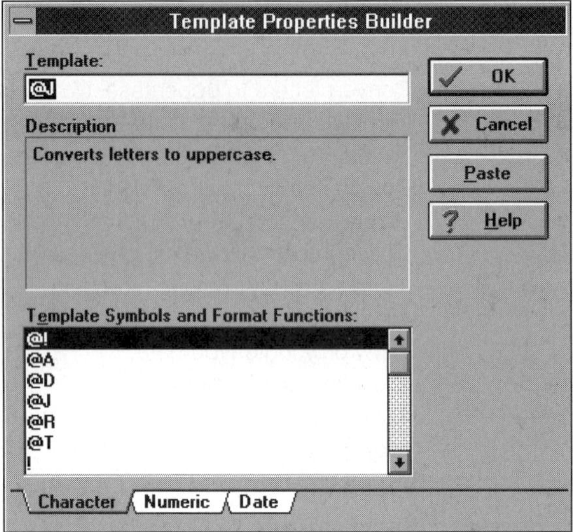

Coding a Picture Template. With **Entryfield1** still selected, click Picture in the Edit Properties group from the Inspector. Type the template, `9999`, into the text box. This will restrict data entry to all numeric characters. In the initial portions of this exercise, we saw that delimiters are needed around both a function symbol and a picture template. They are not coded in the Inspector but are inserted when the source code is generated.

Test the Entryfield1 Picture/Function properties. Select **View | Form** to test your work so far. You should not be able to type alphabetic characters into the Customer Number entryfield. Further, if you type fewer than four numbers, they should become right-justified. Return to the Form Designer by selecting **View | Form Designer**.

Create a Phone No. Entryfield Picture Template. From the Inspector, select the Phone No. entryfield, **Entryfield4**. Click Picture under Edit Properties. Type the template, `(999) 999–9999`, into the text box. This will restrict input to numeric characters, and automatically place the parentheses, space, and dash.

Create an Amount Rent Entryfield Function and Template. From the Inspector, select the Amount Rent entryfield, **Entryfield5**. Click Function under Edit Properties. Type the two functions, `JZ`, into the text box. This will right-justify the entryfield and suppress zero entries from the entryfield display. Notice that you can place two or more function symbols together. Zero suppression is a cosmetic feature that displays a numeric field as blanks the same way a character field is displayed as blanks prior to data entry.

Click Picture under Edit Properties. Type the template, `9999.99`, into the text box. This will restrict input to numbers and set the decimal point location.

Create a No. of Rents Spin Box Function and Template. From the Inspector, select the No. of Rents spin box, **Spinbox1**. Click Function under Edit Properties. Type the two function symbols, `JZ`, into the text box. This will right-justify the entry field and suppress zero entries from the entry field display.

Click Picture under Edit Properties. Type the template, `99`, into the text box. This will restrict input to two numeric characters.

Using the RangeMax, RangeMin, and RangeRequired Spin Box properties. It is usually a good idea to set maximum and minimum values on a spinbox control. From the Inspector, select the **No. of Rents** spinbox, **Spinbox1**. Click RangeMax under Edit Properties. Type a maximum value of `10` into the text box. Click RangeMin under Edit Properties. Type a minimum value of `0` into the text box. Click RangeRequired under Edit Properties and set the value to `.T.`. RangeRequired must be set to `.T.` if RangeMax and/or RangeMin is used.

Test the Entryfields and Spin Box validation properties. Select **View | Form** to test the next group of entryfield properties as follows:

Phone No. Entryfield: Type `9166481234`. You should be restricted to numeric characters. The template should automatically place parentheses, space, and dash.

Amount Rent Entryfield: Type `2.50`. The field should be blank until data is entered (no zeros). Data should be right-justified after entry. Decimal position should be two places from the right.

No. of Rents Spin Box: Type `11`. This value should be rejected and modified to `10`, which is the upper limit set by RangeMax. Using your mouse, click the Spinbox arrows to test both the upper the lower limits. When the value reaches zero, the display should be blank. When you press `<enter>` after a valid value is entered, the value should become right-justified in the Spinbox.

Save the form and return to the Command window by selecting **File | Close**.

- **Using the Valid Event property.** The data validation properties we have used so far are excellent in restricting data as it is entered by the operator. However, they will not cover all the situations you will encounter. Suppose, for example, we want to determine whether a duplicate customer number already exists in the customer table. The Valid Event property allows the programmer to test the data entered against predetermined criteria. To demonstrate this, enter the Form Designer with `yinputcm.wfm`, then proceed as follows:

  Selecting the Valid Event property. Give focus to the Inspector, select the **Events** tab. Using the Inspector Combobox, select the Customer Number Entryfield, **Entryfield1**. Click the Valid Event.

  Coding a Valid Event-handler. A Valid event-handler must return a logical `.T.` or `.F.`. Valid will not allow the operator to remove focus from an entry field or spin box unless the handler returns a `.T.`

To enter the Procedure Editor, click the Valid Event toolbar to enter the Procedure Editor. Enter the following code:

```
Procedure ENTRYFIELD1_Valid
  IF KEYMATCH (form.EntryField1.Value,TAGNO("Cust_no"))
     RETURN .F.
  ENDIF
RETURN .T.
```

Double-click the **Procedure Editor Control Box** to exit and save the procedure.

This procedure uses the `KEYMATCH()` function to search the customer table and determine if the number the operator entered is already in the table. The first parameter of `KEYMATCH()` is the customer number character value entered by the operator. The second parameter is the number of the `Cust_no` index `TAG` in the production `.mdx` file of the customer master table, `ycustm.dbf`. The table was opened when we coded the View property at the Form level in the Class constructor code. The `TAG` number is returned by the `TAGNO()` function. `KEYMATCH()` returns a `.T.` if it finds a duplicate customer number in the table. If this is the case, the next statement, `RETURN .F.`, returns a logical false to the Valid property for the event-handler procedure. If `KEYMATCH()` returns a `.F.`, the data entered by the operator is valid (there is no duplicate customer number). Control then moves to the last statement in the procedure, `RETURN .T.`, which returns a logical true for the event-handler procedure. If this is the case, the data entered by the operator is valid and will be accepted.

NOTE: This is the first procedure we have used that actually returns a value. Such a procedure is useful as an event handler that requires a `.T.` or `.F.` returned to satisfy a Valid condition. In the next chapter, we will discuss Procedures and User Defined Functions (UDFs) in more depth, and their ability to return values to expressions. We will also discuss Codeblocks, which will allow a shortcut method to code an event-handler.

Coding the ValidErrorMsg property. When the Valid condition does return a `.F.`, a message box will automatically appear. ValidErrorMsg determines the message that will appear in the dialog box. To code the error message, click the ValidErrorMsg property of the Edit Properties group in the Inspector. Make sure you have selected the Customer Number entry field, **Entryfield1**. Code the following message:

DUPLICATE EXISTS – PLEASE RETRY ...

Test the Valid property and error dialog. Test the Valid property by selecting **View | Form**. When the form appears, type `0010` as a customer number. This number should already exist in the customer table and should trigger the Valid error and associated dialog box (see Figure 9.8). When the message dialog appears, press the **OK** button to return to the entry field. Next, type `0123` as a customer number. This number does not already exist in the table and should be accepted by the Valid property. Focus should then move to the next entry field.

TRANSFERRING VALIDATED DATA TO A TABLE

The final step in the data entry process is to transfer the validated data to the table. Our form has three pushbuttons. The first button allows the operator to append the current record to the table and then return focus to the Customer Number entry field to begin entry of the next record. The second button allows the operator the ability to append the current record to the table and then exit the form. The third button allows the operator to abort the current record and exit the form.

- **Coding the Save/Next pushbutton handler.** There will be several methods involved in the OnClick handler of this pushbutton. Here are the tasks we must accomplish:

  Final data validation. Code any additional data validation procedures. For example, you may want to check to see if any field has been left blank. If so, you could inform the operator and then give focus back to the field in question. We will not do this in our exercise.

  Add new record to table. Append a blank record to the table. Replace the fields of the blank record with entryfields and spinbox values entered by the operator.

FIGURE 9.8 VALID ERROR MESSAGE DIALOG BOX

Initialize the form for the next record. Initialize the Value properties of each data entry field. This would involve setting the character string fields back to blank spaces and the numeric fields back to zero. However, there may be times when you will want to retain a value from the preceding record, such as a date field. In that case, you would omit the date Value property from the initializing routine. Then, when focus returns to the field for entry of the next record, the date from the preceding record would already be contained in that date entry field.

Return focus to the first entry field. Give focus back to the first entry field, **Entryfield1**, for entry of the next customer number.

Enter the Form Designer with the form file, **`yinputcm.wfm`**. Proceed as follows to begin coding the **Save/Next** pushbutton methods.

Coding the SAVE_RECORD method. Open the Procedure Editor by selecting **Procedure | New Method**. This allows you to bypass the Inspector to enter the Procedure Editor, which is useful when building a procedure that is not directly attached to an event property.

```
Procedure SAVE_RECORD
   APPEND BLANK
   REPLACE cust_no  WITH form.Entryfield1.Value,;
           first    WITH form.Entryfield2.Value,;
           last     WITH form.Entryfield3.Value,;
           phone    WITH form.Entryfield4.Value,;
           amt_rent WITH form.Entryfield5.Value,;
           no_rents WITH form.Spinbox1.Value
   DO CASE
      CASE form.Radiobutton1.Value
         REPLACE charge WITH "M"
      CASE form.Radiobutton2.Value
         REPLACE charge WITH "V"
      CASE form.Radiobutton3.Value
         REPLACE charge WITH "D"
```

```
        CASE form.Radiobutton4.Value
            REPLACE charge WITH "O"
    ENDCASE
RETURN
```

The first command in the procedure will append a blank record to the open table, **ycustm.dbf**, and move the record pointer to that record. The next command replaces each field in the appended blank record with the Value property of each of the entry fields on the form. The DO **CASE..ENDCASE** construct is used to determine which radiobutton in the radiobutton group contains a **.T.**. The charge field in the blank record is then replaced with the appropriate charge type.

Double-click the control Procedure Editor control button to save the method.

Coding the INIT_FORM method. The next method will initialize all the values on the form back to their original blank or zero values. It will also set the MC radiobutton to **.T.** and the remaining buttons in the group to **.F.**. Open the Procedure Editor by selecting **Procedure | New Method**. Type the following code into the procedure editor:

```
Procedure INIT_FORM

    form.Entryfield1.Value   = SPACE(4)

    form.Entryfield2.Value   = SPACE(10)

    form.Entryfield3.Value   = SPACE(15)

    form.Entryfield4.Value   = SPACE(14)

    form.Entryfield5.Value   = 0.00

    form.Spinbox1.Value      = 0.00

    form.Radiobutton1.Value = .T.

    form.Radiobutton2.Value = .F.

    form.Radiobutton3.Value = .F.

    form.Radiobutton4.Value = .F.

RETURN
```

Coding the Save/Next pushbutton OnClick Event-handler. We can now code the OnClick handler for the **Save/Next** pushbutton, **Pushbutton2**. Give focus to the Inspector. Choose **Pushbutton2** from the Inspector Combobox. Choose the **Inspector Events tab**, click the **OnClick** event property, then click the **OnClick toolbar**. Type the following code into the Procedure Editor:

```
Procedure PUSHBUTTON2_ONCLICK
    form.SAVE_RECORD()
    form.INIT_FORM()
    form.Entryfield1.SETFOCUS()
RETURN
```

The first command calls the **SAVE_RECORD** method that we coded earlier. The second command calls the **INIT_FORM** method that we coded earlier. The last command gives focus back to the first entry field in the form for entry of the next record. We have divided this into several methods because they may be called by another event-handler of the form. This modular approach will reduce the redundant coding otherwise required.

- **Coding the Save/Exit pushbutton handler.** This pushbutton will cause the current record to be saved, but will exit the form rather than setting up the form for new record entry. The OnClick handler will be similar to the preceding button handler, but it will not be necessary to initialize the form.

  Give focus to the Inspector. Select **Pushbutton3** from the Inspector Combobox. Choose the Inspector Events tab, click the OnClick event property, then click the OnClick toolbar. Type the following code into the Procedure Editor:

```
Procedure PUSHBUTTON3_OnClick
    form.SAVE_RECORD()      && Generic save method
    form.FORM_CLEANUP()     && Pushbutton1 event handler
RETURN
```

  This is the last pushbutton we need to code. The **Abort/Exit** pushbutton was coded earlier in the exercise.

- **Final testing of the form.** We can now make a final test of the form to make sure all the pushbuttons are functioning properly. Select **View | Form** and test the pushbuttons as follows:

  Enter the record from the earlier test into the form as follows:

```
Customer no.   0234
First Name     Mary
Last Name      Rossi
Phone No.      (415) 123-4567
Amount Rent         3.00
No. of Rents      4
Charge type    (Diners -- click proper radiobutton)
```

FIGURE 9.9 FINAL TEST OF DATA ENTRY FORM

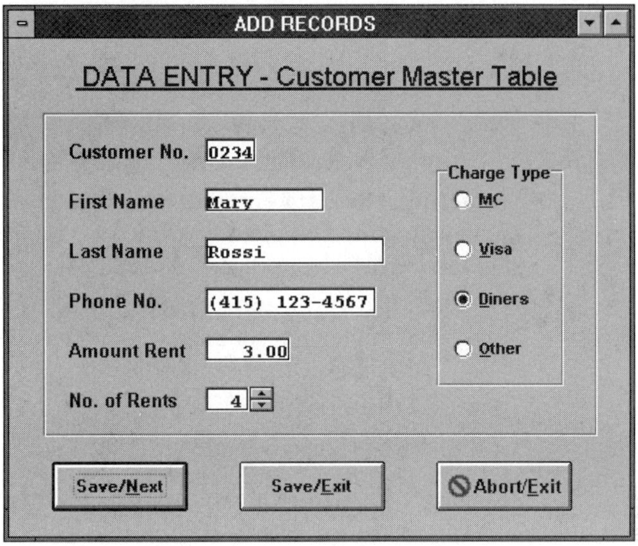

Your screen should appear as in Figure 9.9. When you press **<enter>** from the Radiobutton group, focus should move to the **Save/Next** pushbutton. Make sure that all fields are readable and right-justified where applicable.

Click the **Save/Next** pushbutton. Focus should return to the customer number entryfield, and all entryfields on the form should be blank.

Enter the following new record:

```
Customer no.    0456
First Name      Charles
Last Name       Hatfield
Phone No.       (916) 921-1212
Amount Rent          2.50
No. of Rents       1
Charge type     (Visa -- click proper radiobutton)
```

Click the **Save/Exit** pushbutton. Focus should now return to the Command window. There should not be an open table name displayed in the status bar.

From the Command window Input pane, type the following command:

```
USE ycustm
GO BOTTOM
SKIP -1
DISP REST
```

This series of commands should display the last two records in the table in the Results pane. Make sure that both new records were entered correctly. Remember that our form does not include all the fields in the structure of the table.

- **Attaching the data entry form to the desktop menu.** We can now attach the completed form to the application desktop menu. To accomplish this, proceed as follows:

  Place the application desktop into the Form Designer. Type the following command from the Input pane. This will enter the Form Designer with the application desktop form, `yvideo.wfm.`

  ```
  MODI FORM yvideo
  ```

  Enter the application desktop menu system. From the Form Designer, give focus to the Inspector. Your form covers the entire window, so the best way to do this is to right-click on the form window, then choose **Inspector** from the drop-down menu. Next, click the **MenuFile** property, then click the **MenuFile toolbar**. Finally, click the **Design Current Menu** radio button from the Modify Menu File Property dialog, then click the **OK** button.

  Attach the data entry form to the menu. We will attach the data entry form to the Customer Table item of the Add Records menu. To do this, click **Add Records**, then click **Customer Table**. This could also be accomplished from the Inspector by choosing the correct menu item from the Inspector Combobox. Click the **Events** tab, click the **OnClick** property, then click the **Toolbar**. This will place you into the Procedure Editor. Type the following procedure:

  ```
  Procedure CUSTOMER_TABLE_OnClick
     DO yinputcm.wfm
  RETURN
  ```

  Double-click the Procedure Editor control button to save the procedure. Double-click the Menu control button to save the menu file.

  Test the menu attachment. To make sure the data entry form has been attached properly, choose **View | Form** from the Form Designer. From your application desktop, choose **Add**

Records | Customer Table. This should call the data entry form. Click the **Abort/Exit** pushbutton. This should return control to the application desktop. Finally, click **File | Exit** to return control to the Command window.

REVIEW EXERCISES

The following exercises review the development of a data entry form. In Part II you will add to the Case System by building a data entry form for the film table of the Video Express system.

PART I: REVIEW QUESTIONS

1. What is the difference between alpha and beta testing of an application? Why is beta testing important?
2. Where should pushbuttons be placed on a form?
3. Why should input data be buffered prior to adding to a table?
4. Which property of an entry field or spin box can be used as a data buffer when entering data into a system?
5. Name the general pseudocode steps involved in building a data entry form.
6. Define the z-order of a form.
7. What is the difference between a Picture and a Function property of an Entryfield or Spinbox control?
8. When would a Valid event property be used instead of a Picture or Function property to restrict input data?
9. Name the two Visual dBASE commands used when transferring validated data from input buffers to a table (to create a blank record and to move data to that record).
10. What is the purpose of the `ValidErrorMsg` property?

PART II: BUILDING A FILM TABLE DATA ENTRY FORM

In this exercise, you will build a data entry screen for the Film table of the Video Express system. As new films are received, they are entered into the system by an operator. As with the customer table data entry form, your data entry form will include a partial list of the fields in the table. Proceed according to the following specifications.

FIGURE 9.10 FILM TABLE DATA ENTRY FORM, `yinputfm.wfm`

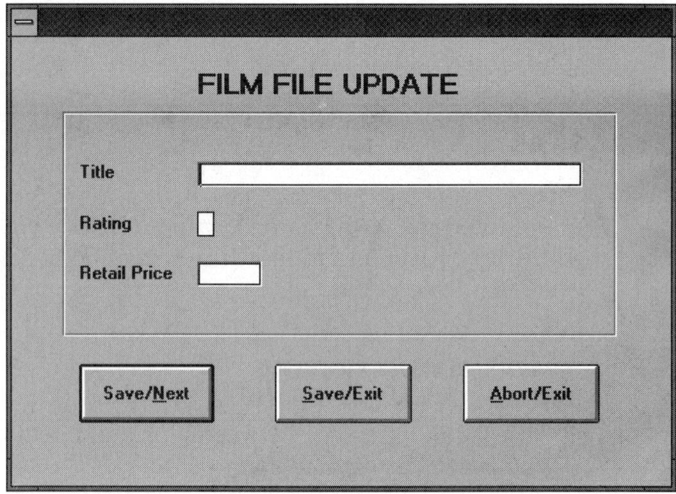

- **Design the form layout.** Your form should be designed to appear as in Figure 9.10. It is to contain the film title (`title`), the film rating as assigned by the retailer (`rating`), and the retail price of the film (`price`). Further, it is to have a form heading line, `FILM FILE UPDATE.`

  Use the same property settings on that were used on the customer table data entry form. For example, use an Arial font for text data and Courier New for entry fields. Other properties that are important to the form are as follows:

  The title bar of the form (Text property) should read `ADD RECORDS`.
  The form View should be the film table, `yfilm.dbf`.
  Establish an OnOpen event-handler for the form. Ensure that `CUAENTER` is properly set and that the first Entryfield receives focus when the form is opened. Further, do not let the operator exit the form using the **Esc** key.
  Initialize character Entryfield Value properties to blanks and numeric to zero.
  Place three pushbuttons on the form as shown in Figure 9.10.
  Place an appropriate operator prompt message in the status bar for each entry field.

- **Set the z-order of the form.** Stack the form controls with the rectangle at the bottom of the plane layers to be followed by the text, entry field, and the pushbuttons. The tabbing sequence should begin with the Film Title

Entryfield. It should then move sequentially to the remaining entryfields. Finally, the tabbing order should move across the three pushbuttons from left to right. The highest-order control in the stack will be the **Abort/Exit** pushbutton.

- **Data Validation (Picture/Function properties).** Using the Picture and/or Function properties, ensure that following restrictions apply to the Form Entryfields:

  Film title: Restrict to uppercase.
  Film rating: Restrict to uppercase. Restrict to alphabetic data only.
  Film Price: Right-justify the field and set the field to blank if the value is zero. Restrict entry to numeric data only and set the decimals to two places.

- **Data Validation (Valid properties).** Using the Valid property, restrict data entry as follows:

  Rating: Valid ratings are (G)eneral, (H)orror, (X)-rated, or (K)iddie. Any other rating entry is invalid and should cause the Valid error message dialog to appear. Place an appropriate error message into the dialog box.
  Price: The price should never be less than 0 or greater than $5.00. Restrict data entry to this range of values using the Valid property. Present an appropriate error message in the error message dialog box if the value entered is outside this range.

- **Pushbutton event-handlers.** Code the event-handlers for each pushbutton control as follows:

  Save/Next: Append a blank record to the table. Transfer the validated data from each Entryfield Value property to the appended blank record. After the data transfer to the table is complete, initialize the Character Type Entryfields to blank and the Numeric Entryfield to zero. Finally, give focus to the Film Title Entryfield for entry of the next record.
  Save/Exit: Append a blank record to the table. Transfer the validated data from each entryfield Value property to the appended blank record. Finally, exit the form and return focus to the application desktop.
  Abort/Exit: Abort the current entry and return focus to the application desktop.

- **OnClose event-handler.** This event-handler is to be executed whenever the form is closed. It should close the open file and close the form.

- **Testing of the form.** Test your form by entering the following films into the film file table:

Title	*Rating*	*Price*
THE LION KING	K	4.95
THE FLY	H	2.95
ABSENCE OF MALICE	G	2.95

After entering the data, return to the Command window and verify that the film data was properly added to the film table, `yfilm.dbf.`

PART III: CODING A DUPLICATE RECORD CHECK

Code a Valid event-handler for the Film Title Entryfield, **Entryfield1**, of Part II to test for duplicate entries. If a title already exists, place an appropriate error message in the Valid property Alert box. The operator should have the ability to press the **Esc** key to exit the form if a valid title cannot be entered. Consider the following in your solution:

- When you use the `KEYMATCH()` function, the field to be searched for the duplicate key must be indexed. Do not have the handler index the field. It should be indexed from the Command window prior to running the application.
- The Value property that is entered by the operator must be left- and right-trimmed prior to the search. Otherwise, the search will be including any leading or trailing blanks in the entered title.
- The `EXACT` command toggle should be off on this type of search.

CHAPTER SUMMARY

In this chapter, we introduced the concepts of data entry form design. We discussed and demonstrated input data form design criteria and data validation techniques. The following topics were discussed:

- **Data entry form design guidelines.** We discussed items such as the importance of user involvement, alpha and beta testing, language to use within screens, guidelines for pushbutton design and placement, and the ergonomics of form design such as limiting the use of the **Tab** key in place of the **<enter>** key.
- **Buffered data entry.** The operator should not be given direct access to the database tables. Data entry should occur through buffers such as memory variables or the Value property of entry field controls.

- **Data entry pseudocode.** The steps involved in data entry form design are (1) design of the form and form controls, (2) code validation of entry field controls, (3) adding a blank record to the table, and (4) transferring the validated data to the table.
- **Designing a data entry form.** We designed two data entry forms—one with the assistance of the instructor and one as a student exercise. The exercises demonstrated the various aspects of data entry form design using Text, Line, Rectangle, Entryfield, Spinbox, and Radiobutton controls.
- **Data validation coding.** Picture and Function properties are used to restrict data entry. If further validation is necessary, the Valid property is used to establish entry field conditions.

The data entry form exercises in this chapter added a customer table and film table data entry form to the student Case System. The following commands were discussed:

- `SET CUAENTER`
- `APPEND BLANK`
- `REPLACE`

Two functions were introduced:

- `TAGNO()`
- `KEYMATCH()`

Also discussed were the following properties:

- View
- SelectAll
- Value
- MaxLength
- Width
- Group
- RangeMax, RangMin, RangeRequired
- Picture, Function
- Valid
- EscExit
- ValidErrorMsg

In the next chapter, we begin programming User Defined Functions (UDFs) and Code Blocks. This will introduce more efficient techniques to code event-handlers that are to be used by only a single control in a form object. We will also develop a password encryption module for the Case System.

CHAPTER TEN

TOPICS

New Commands, Functions, and Properties

Concepts

- Parameter passing
- Building a password encryption procedure
- Using codeblocks

Review Exercises

Chapter Summary

Using Codeblocks and User-Defined Functions

10

CHAPTER OBJECTIVES

An important concept of modular programming is the ability to reuse modules from prior systems. This is equally important in object-oriented programming. A module is a small, concise, and self-contained unit. The programmer attempts to avoid rewriting modules, or portions of modules, whenever possible. Fixed routines that are reusable without modification can be maintained as methods in an object or in global procedure files. Certain routines are suitable to be compiled into user-defined functions, which can also be contained in procedure files. In this chapter, we learn a major benefit of object-oriented programming in Visual dBASE: the ability to develop and maintain a library of various routines to use in future systems development.

After studying of this chapter, you should understand the commands and concepts involved in building reusable modules. You also begin building a library of reusable procedures and user-defined functions contained in a global procedure file. We will then demonstrate the concepts by a series of exercises and by adding a password encryption module and a password decryption module to the Case System.

NEW COMMANDS, FUNCTIONS, AND PROPERTIES

COMMAND `DO <filename> WITH <parameter list>`

We introduced this command earlier, but we now add the **WITH** clause. In addition to executing the designated program file, the **WITH** clause passes parameters to that file. The parameters are manipulated by the subprogram, then returned to the passing module.

COMMAND `PARAMETERS <parameter list>`

Assigns local variable names to variables passed from a calling program. This command is used in conjunction with the `DO <filename> WITH <parameter list>` command. It is a dBASE IV command that is still in the language to maintain upward compatibility.

COMMAND

```
PROCEDURE <procedure name> [(<PARAMETER LIST>)]
   [<statements>]
[RETURN [<return exp>]]
```

Defines a procedure in a procedure or program file and optionally declares memory variables to represent parameters passed to the procedure. Introduced earlier without using the **PARAMETER LIST** clause. The variables in the **PARAMETER LIST** are local in scope, protecting them from modification in lower-level routines.

COMMAND `CLOSE PROCEDURE`

Used to close the currently open procedure file.

COMMAND

```
FUNCTION <UDF name> [(<parameter list>)]
   [<statements>]
[RETURN [<return exp>]]
```

Used to identify a user-defined function within a procedure file. Not used as extensively as a **PROCEDURE** because Visual dBASE makes no distinction between UDFs and procedures.

COMMAND `SET SAFETY ON/off`

Determines whether a confirmation dialog is presented before overwriting a file or when using the **ZAP** command to erase records from a table.

COMMAND `SAVE TO <filename> [ALL LIKE/EXCEPT <skeleton>]`

Saves all, or a specified group, of memory variables to a memory file. The file has an **.mem** extension.

```
** Save all active variables to yallvars.mem
SAVE TO yallvars
** Save variables that begin with g to yglobal.mem.
SAVE to yglobal ALL LIKE g*
```

COMMAND

```
RESTORE FROM <filename> [ADDITIVE]
```

Loads and activates all memory variables from the named memory file. All current variables are released unless the **ADDITIVE** clause is used. **ADDITIVE** will cause the variables from the file to be added to the current active variables.

```
** RESTORE all global variables.
** Add to current variables.
RESTORE FROM yglobal ADDITIVE
```

COMMAND

```
SET DECIMALS TO <expN>
```

Determines the number of decimals displayed as a result of numeric functions and calculations.

```
SET DECIMALS TO 5
? 5.3 * 32.44
     171.93200
```

FUNCTION

```
LEN(<expC>)
```

Returns a numeric type value representing the length of a character string.

```
CLEAR
x = "THIS IS A TEST OF THE LEN() FUNCTION"
? LEN(x)
   36
```

FUNCTION

```
SUBSTR(<expC>,<starting position>
[,<number of characters>])
```

Used to extract a substring or series of characters from a string. The starting position of the extraction is required. The number of characters is optional. If the number of characters is not entered, the extracted string will begin with the starting position and end with the last character of the original string.

```
CLEAR
name = "Roberta"
? SUBSTR(name,3,4)
bert
? SUBSTR({10/12/96},7,2)       && Extract year.
96
? SUBSTR(TIME(),7,2)           && Extract seconds.
45
```

FUNCTION `ASC(<expC>)`

Returns the ASCII decimal code for the first character of the evaluated character expression. The returned value is numeric type. Refer to Appendix D for a complete list of ASCII codes.

```
CLEAR
? ASC("—")              && The "—" character is decimal 45.
45
```

FUNCTION `STUFF(<expC1>,<expN1>,<expN2>,<expC2>)`

Used to replace a character or series of characters in a string with another character string. The four arguments are defined as follows:

- `expC1`: String to receive the replacement.
- `expN1`: Starting position of **`expC1`** where replacement begins.
- `expN2`: Number of characters to be **`STUFF`**ed into string.
- `expC2`: String to be **`STUFF`**ed into original string.

```
CLEAR
name = "Joan R. scott"
? STUFF (name,9,1,"S")      && STUFF uppercase "S"
                            && into name.
Joan R. Scott
```

FUNCTION `VAL(<expC>)`

Used to convert numbers stored as character type data into numeric expressions. The number of decimal places is set by the **`SET DECIMALS`** command.

```
CLEAR
SET DECIMALS to 3
x = "123.1"
? VAL(x)
   123.100
```

FUNCTION `LOWER(<expC>)`

Returns the lowercase of the character expression argument. If the characters are already lowercase, they remain lowercase.

```
? LOWER("GEORGE")
george
```

FUNCTION `PROPER(<expC>)`

Converts a character string to proper noun format.

```
? PROPER("alice r. jones")
Alice R. Jones
xName = "mary mccarthy ii"
? PROPER(xName)
Mary Mccarthy Ii
```

The second example demonstrates that **PROPER()** does not cover all the situations you might encounter. In this chapter, you will build a procedure that will add more functionality to **PROPER()**.

FUNCTION `SET (<expC>)`

Returns the current setting of a **SET** command or function key. Use **SET ()** to learn a **SET** or function key setting so that you can change it or save it.

EXAMPLE

```
? SET ("TXK") && To determine current setting of TALK.
```

PROPERTY `ValidRequired`

Determines if the Valid event property applies to all data or to new data only. If set to **.T.**, the Valid property will be tested even though no data has been entered.

Property of class: **ENTRYFIELD**, **SPINBOX**

PROPERTY `ColorHighLight`

Sets the color of the object that has focus.

Property of class: **ENTRYFIELD**, **LISTBOX**, **OLE**, **SPINBOX**

PROPERTY `OnChange`

An event property. Executes a procedure or codeblock when the user changes the value displayed in an object.

Property of class: **ENTRYFIELD**, **SPINBOX**

PROPERTY `OnLostFocus`
`OnGotFocus`

An event property. Executes a procedure or codeblock when focus is removed from or given to an object.

Property of class: **BROWSE**, **CHECKBOX**, **COMBOBOX**, **EDITOR**, **ENTRYFIELD**, **FORM**, **LISTBOX**, **OLE**, **PUSHBUTTON**, **RADIOBUTTON**, **SCROLLBAR**, **SPINBOX**

PROPERTY `Enabled`

Determines if an object can be selected. When the Enabled property of an object is set to true, the user can select and use it. When the Enabled property is set to false (`.F.`), the object is dimmed and the user cannot select or use it. The default setting is a logical true (`.T.`).

Property of class: `BROWSE`, `CHECKBOX`, `COMBOBOX`, `EDITOR`, `ENTRYFIELD`, `FORM`, `LISTBOX`, `MENU`, `OLE`, `PAINTBOX`, `PUSHBUTTON`, `RADIOBUTTON`, `SCROLLBAR`, `SPINBOX`, `TABBOX`

CONCEPTS

In modular programming, subprograms were defined as routines within larger programs or systems of programs. A subprogram could be developed as a separate program file, as an in-program procedure, or as a procedure in a global procedure file. It was not the solution to an application; it was only part of a system of programs designed to solve an application.

In Visual dBASE, subprograms are not used as they were in dBASE for DOS. Procedures and/or user-defined functions (UDFs) become the method properties of objects. Procedures were introduced in Chapter 7 and we have since used them as handlers for the various events of the Form class and form controls. However, we have not as yet communicated with procedures. In Chapter 3, we passed a numeric parameter to the square root internal function, **`SQRT()`**. The function then returned the square root of the numeric value to the expression that included the function. We communicate with procedures and UDFs the same way we communicate with the internal functions of Visual dBASE—by passing parameters to them. We can also receive values from procedures and functions. For example, in the preceding chapter we coded a Valid event procedure that returned a logical **`.T.`** or **`.F.`** to the Valid event property.

In addition to the ability to communicate with a procedure to control how it will perform, the object-oriented language of Visual dBASE allows the programmer to build procedures that will act in different ways without parameter communication. They perform actions that are common and most appropriate for any object in a hierarchy of objects. This is referred to as *polymorphism*, which literally means "having many shapes." A command analogy might be **`SKIP`** in that the same command moves to different records according to current pointer placement and number of records in a table.

PARAMETER PASSING

We communicate with a procedure or function by passing parameters to it. Parameter values dictate how the procedure will perform. As we mentioned, this is done in much the same manner as we pass parameters to internal functions such as **SQRT()**.

Building a Global Procedure file. The procedures and UDFs that we define must either be part of a program file or placed in a separate file referred to as a procedure file. We will create such a file here, and it will be the beginning of the file in which we can place the global procedures we will use throughout our system. We will also use it to develop procedure and UDF exercises. To create this file and to demonstrate parameter-passing procedures, enter the Program Editor from the Command window:

```
MODI COMM  yproc      && Create a procedure file
```

Type the following code into the editor. The first segment is the header for the procedure file. The code that follows is a sample procedure that receives three parameters, then uses them to adjust the area value of one of the parameters. Notice that we separate each procedure with a commented divider line.

```
** Name.......: YPROC.PRG
** Description: My global procedure file.
** Author.....: <student name>

* ========================================================= *

** PROCEDURE NAME: AdjustArea
** Description...:  Parameter passing exercise #1.
** Author........: <student name>
** Date..........: <today's date>
PROCEDURE AdjustArea (area, length, width)
  length = length * 1.10 && Increase length by 10%
  area = length * width
RETURN
** End of Procedure, AdjustArea

* ========================================================= *
```

Save and exit the Program Editor. To test the procedure, type the following commands from the Command window:

```
SET PROCEDURE TO yproc ADDITIVE && Open the procedure file.
OldArea = 100
DO AdjustArea WITH OldArea, 10, 10
? OldArea
  110
```

The first command of the test opens the procedure file. The **ADDITIVE** clause adds the file to any procedure files already open. There is no limit on the number open at one time. The next command assigns a value of `100` to `OldArea`. That value is then adjusted to `110` by the procedure.

In the procedure file code, the **PROCEDURE** statement names the procedure, names the variables that will receive the passed parameters, and declares the parameters local in scope to the procedure. The local variable scoping will protect the variables from external variables by the same name. The current value of `OldArea` was sent to the `AdjustArea` procedure. It became `area` in the procedure. After the calculation of `area` in the procedure, using the two values of `length` and `width` also passed, the result was returned to the calling program variable, `OldArea`. Notice that you did not have to tell the procedure what value to return. Visual dBASE knows what to return by following these rules:

- If a defined memory variable is passed to a procedure with a variable defined in the parameter list to receive it, it will be returned to the original variable whether or not it was modified by the subprogram. When a constant is passed as a parameter, no values are returned.
- The parameter lists must match in data type. The number of parameters does not have to match.
- All local variables in the procedure are released when a **RETURN** occurs.
- If the parameter passed is an expression, it will first be evaluated to a simple value and then will become a memory variable in the procedure.

Though no value is specified to be returned by the preceding procedure example, we can see that a parameter passed to a procedure by a variable is automatically returned to that variable. This concept will help explain how procedures operate when a return value is specified.

Creating a Procedure that Returns a Value. In Visual dBASE, we can build a procedure that will return a value specified in the **RETURN** statement. For example, we might want to pass the number of iterations a benchmark procedure is to perform. To demonstrate, reopen the procedure file, `yproc.prg`, using the Program Editor. Add the following procedure to the file:

```
** PROCEDURE NAME: TimeSpent
** Description...: Parameter passing example
** Author........: <student name>
** Date..........: <today's date>
PROCEDURE TimeSpent (Iterations)
  ** Capture current talk value--turn talk off.
  IF SET("TALK") = "ON"
     SET TALK OFF
     xTalk = "ON"
  ELSE
     xTalk = "OFF"
  ENDIF
  ** Begin test
  StartTime = TIME()
  x = 1
  DO WHILE x <= Iterations
     DoSomeCalc = SQRT(1000*1000)/2
     x = x + 1
  ENDDO
  SET TALK &xTalk
RETURN ELAPSED(TIME(),StartTime)
** End of Procedure, TimeSpent
```

* == *

As in the first procedure exercise, the **PROCEDURE** statement defines the name of the procedure plus the name of the variable to receive the passed parameter and declares that variable local to the procedure. The **TIME()** function is used to record the start time of the loop, and then **TIME()** coupled with **ELAPSED()** is used to determine the total running time. Finally, the **RETURN** command returns the elapsed execution time for the loop.

At the beginning of the procedure, we have captured the current setting of **TALK**, using the **SET()** function. If **TALK** is **ON** during this type of iterative procedure, all of the assign commands will be displayed in the Results pane, which can be time consuming. Notice that we tested the current value of **TALK**, turned it off if it was on, *then* assigned **OFF** to **xTalk**. This was necessary so that the assign command would not be displayed in the event that **TALK** was **ON** prior to calling the procedure. At the conclusion of the procedure, we reset **TALK** to its original state using the macro substitution function (**&**).

To test the procedure, type the following commands from the Command window:

```
SET PROCEDURE TO yproc ADDITIVE
SET TALK ON
? TimeSpent (10000)
? TimeSpent (10000) + 5
```

We have tested this procedure using commands different from those used when we tested the first procedure. That is because the first procedure did not return a value. Though it did modify the contents of the passed parameter, `OldArea`, it did not return a value. If a procedure returns a value, it must be called from an expression such as in the **?** command. **RETURN** is returning a value to the expression that called the procedure. Only one value can be returned from a procedure. The **DO** command should not be used to call a procedure that returns a value. In the current example, the first **?** command calls the procedure using **10000** as the passed parameter. The second **?** command further exemplifies the use of the procedure within an expression. After the elapsed time is returned, it is included in the final evaluation of the expression that adds **5** to the elapsed time.

The parentheses that contain the parameters are referred to as the *Call Operator*. The name of the procedure that is being called is referred to as a *Function Pointer*. For example, the above procedure call takes the syntax form of , `<function pointer> ([parameters])`—or as used here, `TimeSpent (10000)` .

NOTE: If a procedure does not return a value, the RETURN statement is not required. In dBASE IV, all procedures required a RETURN. In Visual dBASE, it is left to the discretion of the programmer. In this text, we have coded the RETURN after all procedures for the sake of form. From a documentation standpoint, RETURN denotes the specific end of a procedure.

Procedures that Modify a parameter. We have seen that we can build a procedure that returns a value to an expression. Care must be taken if the value returned has modified the passed parameter. As an example, add the following procedure example to your global procedure file, `yproc.prg`:

```
** Procedure Name: PLUS10
** Description:  Procedure example that modifies a parameter.
PROCEDURE Plus10(InitVal)
  InitVal = InitVal + 10
RETURN  InitVal
```

Test the program from the Command window as follows:

```
CLEAR
SET TALK OFF
SET PROCEDURE TO yproc
xRate = 100
? Plus10(xRate) + 50
   160
? xRate
   110
```

Our procedure worked, but it contains a very subtle bug. The passed number, **100**, should not be altered by the procedure. A complete explanation follows.

We first opened the procedure file, cleared the Results pane, and turned the **TALK** toggle off. After assigning a value of 100 to the variable, **xRate**, we passed it to the procedure. The procedure received it as the parameter **init_val**, increased it by 10 percent, and then returned it to the calling expression for inclusion in its evaluation. The final evaluation is **160**. However, this is where our subtle little bug occurs. Notice that the number in the variable **xRate** is now **110** instead of its original value of **100** prior to being passed to the procedure.

An internal Visual dBASE function does not alter the value passed as a parameter. It does not return a value to a variable for replacement, it returns a value to an expression to be included in the evaluation of that expression. For example, using the internal Visual dBASE function **UPPER()**, type the following:

```
mLast = "jones"
? UPPER (mLast)
JONES
? mLast
jones
```

In this example, the variable **mLast** contains the lowercase name **jones**. The **?** command verb in the next line displays the expression **UPPER(mLast)** evaluated. **mLast** is passed to the function as a parameter, converted to uppercase, returned to the expression to be evaluated, and then displayed by the **?** verb. It is *not* passed back to the variable **mLast**; it is passed to the expression to be evaluated and acted on by the command verb.

From this, we can develop an important rule of procedures:

Within a procedure, do not modify a parameter passed as a variable if that parameter is the one to be returned.

If you break this rule, the original passed variable will be altered. To correct this in our previous example, we will give the calculated value in the procedure a different variable name and then name that value to be returned to the expression. Modify the procedure as follows:

```
PROCEDURE Plus10(InitVal)
  NewVal = InitVal + 10
RETURN NewVal
```

In this particular example, another solution would be to place the expression itself in the **RETURN** statement:

```
PROCEDURE Plus10 (InitVal)
RETURN InitVal + 10
```

In the second example, the expression is evaluated to a simple value. Then that simple value is returned to the expression, leaving the original variable **xRate** unchanged.

Procedures Versus User-Defined Functions. prior versions of dBASE, the preceding example would be developed a user-defined function (UDF). Examine the following code:

```
FUNCTION Plus10
  PARAMETERS InitVal
RETURN InitVal + 10
```

The only difference between this routine and the preceding routine is the use of the **FUNCTION** command rather than the **PROCEDURE** command. Visual dBASE does not make a distinction between a UDF and a procedure. Moreover, the Form Designer uses procedures exclusively. Therefore it is recommended that you use procedures and not UDFs in Visual dBASE applications. You can still use UDFs developed in prior versions of dBASE and you can still develop UDFs using Visual dBASE. The **FUNCTION** command remains in the language primarily for upward compatibility with prior versions of dBASE. Also, the **PARAMETERS** command was used in earlier versions of dBASE to name parameters. It is not necessary in Visual dBASE but remains in the language to maintain upward compatibility. This makes it possible to use both UDFs and procedures developed in prior versions without modification.

BUILDING A PASSWORD ENCRYPTION PROCEDURE

As we mentioned previously, procedures may be contained either within a program file or in a separate file. The programmer will want to build an extensive library of procedures to use in future projects. You can have more than one procedure file library, and you can open as many procedure files as needed by an application. In this segment, we will add a password encryption procedure to our procedure file, **yproc.prg.**

There are many strategies for system protection. In our system, we will require the Video Express system operator to enter a password to gain access to the application desktop and main menu. The system should also provide the operator the facility to change the password once entry has been achieved. If such a routine were not necessary, password programming would be relatively simple. The system password could be embedded in the system as a memory variable and then compared to the operator supplied password from the keyboard. However, if it is to be a changeable password, the variable must be stored in a memory file (an **.mem** extension file used to store memory variables), which leaves it exposed to any intruder with even limited DOS knowledge. Our sample procedure exercise will be to encrypt the system password prior to its storage in a memory file.

We will build a complete password entry module for the Case System in this chapter and in this section we will build a procedure to be used by that routine. Refer to the procedure in Figure 10.1 and the encryption diagram in Figure 10.2 as we discuss the encryption routine.

It's important to remember that the procedure must be placed in a procedure file or be contained within a program. Our procedure file can be constructed with **MODIFY COMMAND** and will be added to the file, **yproc.prg**. It will be the beginning of our student library of procedures. Within the procedure file, the **PROCEDURE** statement defines the procedure, **encrypt**. We will want to pass two values: (1) **xPass2**, to receive the unencrypted password, and (2) **xPlus**, the incremental number to add to the ASCII value to form the encryption. To ensure the passed variable is unchanged, the next statement stores the passed value to another variable, **xPass**.

The initialized memory variables are used as follows:

- **xStop**: The procedure is designed to handle variable length passwords. The **LEN()** function is used to determine the length of the password contained in **xPass**. It is then stored in **xStop**.
- **xPointer**: Indicates the position of the character currently being encrypted. It will begin with **"1"** and end with the value contained in **xStop**.

The procedure now proceeds through the password, encrypting a single character with each pass through the **DO WHILE**. The encryption command is a series of embedded functions. dBASE will begin its evaluation from the center and then move outward as it completes the total evaluation to replace the current value in **xPass**. For example, if the password to be encrypted is **"PASSWORD"** and the value passed in **xPlus** is **60**, the first execution through the loop will evaluate as follows:

FIGURE 10.1 PASSWORD ENCRYPTION PROCEDURE, ENCRYPT

```
** Procedure...: Encrypt
** Description.: A procedure to encrypt (encode) a password.
** Author......: <student name>
** Date........: <today's date>

** Procedure initialization
PROCEDURE encrypt (xPass2, xPlus)
   xPass = xPass2              && Store parameter to different
                         && local variable so passed
                         && parameter, xPass, will not
                         && be modified.

   ** Initialize loop variables
   xStop = LEN(xPass)
   xPointer = 1

   ** Encrypt loop
   DO WHILE xPointer <= xStop

      xPass = STUFF(xPass,xPointer,1, ;
            CHR(ASC(substr(xPass,xPointer, 1))+ xPlus))
      xPointer = xPointer + 1

   ENDDO  && [WHILE xPointer <= xStop]
RETURN xPass

** End of procedure, Encrypt

** ==================================================== **
```

- **SUBSTR(xPass,xPointer,1):** SUBSTR selects the character to be encrypted from **xPass** (current value of **"PASSWORD"**), at the **xPointer** (current value of 1) position, 1 character in length. The first time through the loop, this evaluates to **"P"**.
- **ASC("P"):** ASC ( ) will convert the "P" returned from SUBSTR to its ASCII number from the ASCII table. Appendix D contains the complete ASCII table of characters. After the first time through the loop, this numeric character is 80.

FIGURE 10.2 PASSWORD ENCRYPTION DIAGRAM

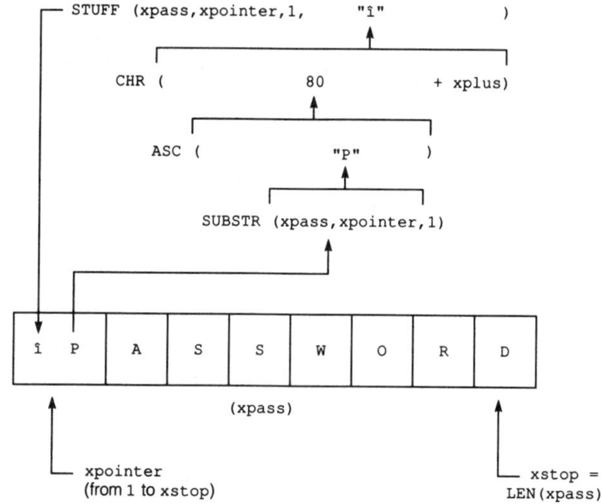

encryption command statement:

```
xpass = STUFF (xpass,xpointer,1,CHR (ASC (SUBSTR (xpass,xpointer,1) ) + xplus))
```

Explanation: As the pointer moves to each character, it is (1) extracted with SUBSTR, (2) converted to ASCII decimal with ASC, (3) increased by the value in xplus, and (4) converted back to the incremented ASCII character with CHR. The encrypted character then becomes the fourth argument of STUFF that places it back into the pointer position of the string. This process continues until each character is converted.

- **80 + xPlus:** XPlus, the incremental value (60) passed to the procedure, can now be added to the numeric 80, returned from ASC(). This numeric value (140) becomes the argument to the CHR() function.
- **CHR(140):** The CHR() function does the opposite of the **ASC** function. It converts a numeric value to its equivalent ASCII character. In this case, 140 numeric is converted to the "î" character. (Refer to the ASCII table in Appendix D).
- **STUFF(xPass,xPointer,"î"):** The STUFF() function places the character, "î", into the **xPointer** (current value of 1) position of xPass (current value of "PASSWORD").
- **xPass = "îASSWORD":** The current value in **xPass** ("PASSWORD") is replaced with the completed expression evaluation ("îASSWORD"). This completes the encryption of the first character of the password.

As **xPointer** is incremented, the process will continue. Each character will be replaced with its ASCII value plus **60**, until **xPointer** is equal to **xStop**. When completed, the encrypted password contained in **xPass** will be **"î}ÅÅôïÄÇ"**.

This is the first reusable procedure to be placed in your global procedure file. It should be entered into the **MODIFY COMMAND** editor by the student and tested as follows:

```
CLEAR
SET PROCEDURE TO yproc         && Must be opened for test.
password = "PASSWORD"
? ENCRYPT(password,60)
î}ÅÅôïÄÇ
```

Note that the procedure file must be opened prior to using the **ENCRYPT()** procedure. Each time you modify the procedure file, be sure to execute **SET PROCEDURE TO yproc** again. The object program file (.pro extension) must be recompiled to reflect the change.

The decision to build the encryption routine as a procedure versus a subprogram was based on the need to have the encrypted password returned to an expression. The password entered by the operator from the keyboard will be encrypted by this procedure in a logic expression comparing it to the valid password encrypted within your system.

Password Decryption Procedure. The decryption routine is equally important in our password security system. In your password modification utility exercise, the encrypted password in the memory file will be decrypted prior to being displayed for the operator. It is very similar to the encryption procedure; however, rather than adding the incremental value, you will be subtracting it from the ASCII value of each character of the encrypted password. Your decryption procedure will be in Part IV of the Review Exercises at the end of this chapter.

There are more sophisticated methods of password encryption. The encrypted password could be placed in other types of files, or even hidden in extra space in a file header. Also, the encryption algorithm could be made more complex. For example, a different incremental value could be used for each character of the password. For another degree of complexity, **xPlus** could be developed by a random number generator each time the system is entered, encrypted, then stored with the encrypted password. The strategy used in our encryption procedure will be adequate for most nonsensitive data systems in that it will keep most intruders out—and at least slow the serious intruder down a bit.

USING CODEBLOCKS

We have constructed procedures that contain only a single command. We have constructed others that were not only very short, but also used only one time by a form control. If a procedure is going to be used only once, or if it is very short, its code can be placed in a *codeblock*. A codeblock is a nameless procedure. Codeblocks can be assigned to a memory variable, used in an expression, or passed as a parameter. You can also pass parameters to a codeblock. In this text we will use only simple codeblocks that will contain either command statements or expressions.

Statement Codeblocks. A statement codeblock has the following syntax:

```
{[ |<parameters>| ] ; <statement> [; <statement> ... ]}
```

Notice that each statement must be preceded by a semicolon (`;`) and that the entire codeblock must be delimited with braces (`{}`). If you pass a parameter to a codeblock, it must be delimited with the `"||"` characters. To demonstrate the use of a statement codeblock as an event-handler versus using a procedure, look at the following code. It first closes a form by calling a procedure as the OnClick event-handler of a pushbutton.

```
** Code within a pushbutton control
OnClick CLASS::PUSHBUTTON1_OnClick

** Procedure to close the form
PROCEDURE PUSHBUTTON1_OnClick
     form.CLOSE()
RETURN
```

The preceding code uses a procedure as an event-handler. The following statement in the pushbutton control code uses a codeblock to accomplish the same task:

```
OnClick {;from.CLOSE()}
```

Expression Codeblocks. An expression codeblock will have the following syntax:

```
{[ |<parameters>| ]<expression>}
```

An expression in a codeblock is not preceded by a semicolon. It is especially useful when coding an event-handler that should evaluate to a logical true or false returned. For example, look at the following code segment. It first demonstrates Valid event-handler using a procedure, then uses an expression codeblock to accomplish the same task.

```
** Valid event property code from an entryfield control
Valid CLASS::ENTRYFIELD1_Valid
```

```
** Valid event procedure code

PROCEDURE ENTRYFIELD1_Valid

  IF this.Value <= 10

      RETURN .T.

  ENDIF

RETURN .F.
```

The preceding code uses a procedure as the Valid event-handler. The following statement in the entryfield control code uses an expression codeblock to accomplish the same task:

```
Valid {this.Value <= 10}
```

As you can see, the event-handlers in these examples are much easier to code using codeblocks. However, if an event-handler involves lengthy code or is to be reused, it is better to use a procedure.

REVIEW EXERCISES

The following exercises review the use of procedures and codeblocks in Visual dBASE forms.

PART I: REVIEW QUESTIONS

1. How many values can be designated in the **RETURN** statement of a procedure?
2. How many procedure files can be opened at one time?
3. What command is used to open a procedure file?
4. What three actions are accomplished by the **PROCEDURE** command?
5. When is the **RETURN** statement required in a procedure? Under what circumstances is it not required?
6. What is the difference between a procedure and a user-defined function in Visual dBASE?
7. Define a codeblock.
8. What is the difference between a statement codeblock and an expression codeblock?
9. When would a procedure be preferred over a codeblock?
10. Where can an encrypted password be stored in a Visual dBASE system?

PART II: BUILDING AN `ALLPROPER()` PROCEDURE

The internal function, **PROPER()**, does not allow for all situations that might need to be converted to mixed case. For example, the double "c" in a name such as McCarthy or the double "i" in the film title, *Jaws II*, will not be converted properly.

Specifications. The purpose of this exercise is to build a procedure that will begin to handle all types of strings. Build the procedure according to the following specifications:

- Name the procedure `AllProper`. Add the procedure to your global procedure file, `yproc.prg`.
- The procedure is to convert a name such as "McCarthy" or a film title such as *Jaws II*. Notice that the first "c" in McCarthy is to be lowercase and the second one is to be uppercase. Both occurrences of the letter "i" in the film title should be uppercase.
- The procedure should receive a single parameter that represents the string to be converted.
- Within your procedure, use the internal function, **PROPER()**, to convert the string as much as possible. Additionally, use the **AT()** internal function to locate the double characters and the **STUFF()** function to finalize the conversion each time an additional conversion is necessary.
- The procedure should return the converted string to a calling expression.
- Test the procedure as follows:

```
SET TALK OFF
SET PROCEDURE TO YPROC
? AllProper("mary c. mccarthy")
Mary C. McCarthy
xTitle = "rOCKY ii"
? AllProper(xTitle)
Rocky II
? xTitle
rOCKY ii
```

This will be the beginning of a procedure that will convert any string to mixed case. You can add more situations to your procedure as needed or as directed by your instructor. For example, if a film title such as *Rocky III* needs to be converted, the triple "I"s would need special coding.

PART III: BUILDING A PASSWORD ENTRY FORM (CASE SYSTEM)

In this segment of the Case System, we build a password encryption form. An operator must enter a valid password before entry into the system is allowed. The password is to be an eight-character alphabetic string. The initial password when the system is installed is `"PASSWORD"`. Once into the system, the operator will have the ability to change the password from the Utilities menu.

Specifications. The Video Express system will have an eight-character, all alphabetic, encrypted password stored in a memory variable, `gpass`. That variable will be stored in a memory file, `yglobal.mem`. When access to the system is attempted, the password typed by the operator will be immediately encrypted using the `Encrypt()` procedure developed earlier in this chapter. It will then be compared to the encrypted password stored in `gpass`. To assign the encrypted password to `gpass` and then store `gpass` to the memory file, type the following code into the `Input` pane:

```
SET PROCEDURE TO yproc           && Open procedure file.
gPass = Encrypt("PASSWORD",60)  && Encrypt initial password.
SAVE TO yglobal ALL LIKE g*      && Save to memory file.
```

When the Video Express system is installed, the memory file containing the initial system password will be included. The initial password to the system is `"PASSWORD"`. In the next part of this exercise, you will build a system utility to give the operator the ability to change the initial password.

The password entry form is to appear prior to the Video Express application desktop. If the password is entered correctly, the form will close. The OnClose event of the password entry form will then call the application desktop form, `yvideo.wfm`. If the password entered is incorrect, an Alert dialog will give the operator the option of trying again. The operator will be given three tries to enter a valid password. After the third unsuccessful attempt, the form will close, the Results pane will be cleared, and focus will return to the Command window.

Design the password entry form as follows:

- **Form file name.** Name the form file **ypass.wfm.**
- **Form level properties:**

  The form Title bar should read **VIDEO EXPRESS SYSTEM.**
  Code the Form OnOpen event to cause the following to occur:

  1. Declare the variable `gpass PUBLIC`.
  2. Restore the memory file `yglobal` to memory. Be sure to use the `ADDITIVE` clause.
  3. Open the procedure file `yproc.prg`. Be sure to use the `ADDITIVE` clause.

FIGURE 10.3 PASSWORD ENTRY FORM, `ypass.wfm`

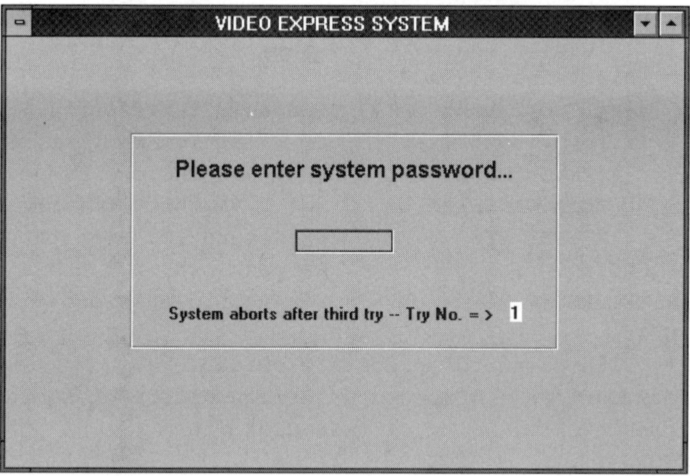

4. Clear the Result page.
5. Turn the `TALK` toggle off.

- **Controls.** The form will contain the following control objects and corresponding property inheritance modifications (see Figure 10.3):

  Rectangle control. Remove any data from the Text property.
  Text controls

  1. **Please enter system password...** prompt message. Use a 10-point Arial font.
  2. **System aborts after third try -- Try No** => message. Use the inherited properties.
  3. Number of tries indicator. Initialize the Text property to a character type value of one (1). Set the background ColorNormal property color to bright white (W+).

  Entry field control

  1. Restrict the data entered to uppercase, alphabetic characters only, right-justified. The size of the field should be restricted to eight characters.
  2. Use a 10-point Courier New font.
  3. The password should not be visible when entered. Therefore set both the normal color and highlighted color to white on white.
  4. Use the following Valid procedure to verify the entered password:

```
Procedure ENTRYFIELD1_Valid
 xProceed = {;DO yvideo.wfm} &&Assign "proceed" codeblock.
 IF ENCRYPT (this.Value, 60) <> gpass .AND. ;
    this.Value <> "APASSKEY"
    ** Invalid password routine.
    this.Value = SPACE (8)
    form.text2.text = STR (VAL(form.text2.text) + 1,1)
    IF form. text2.text = "4"    && Too many tries.
      form.OnClose = = {;CLEAR}  && OnClose event, Clear Result pane.
       form.CLOSE()              && Abort to Command Window.
       RETURN .T.          && Return .T. even though invalid. Accept
    ENDIF                  && password, but abort app.
    RETURN .F.             && Invalid password--try again.
 ENDIF
  **Valid password--proceed with app.
 form.OnClose = xProceed && Assign codeblock memvar to OnClose Event
 form.CLOSE ()          && Close form.
RETURN .T.
**End of procedure
```

Note: In the Valid property of this procedure, we have allowed a passkey password, APASSKEY, in addition to the regular password. This will always allow the programmer access to the system. Check with your data processing manager to ensure that this “back-door” entry technique is acceptable. It may not be within the computer security guidelines of your company or agency.

This Valid procedure tests the entered password against the stored and encrypted password, **gpass**. If password is not valid, the procedure sets the entry field Value property back to blanks to initialize the entry field for the next attempt. It then converts the “number of tries” Text control to numeric, increments the value by one—then converts it back to character type data. When the indicator reaches 4, the form is closed and a logical **.T.** is passed back to the Valid property. The logical true must be returned to satisfy the Valid property even though the password is still incorrect. This will allow the form to close and allow control to return to the Command window. Notice that prior to closing the form, a codeblock to clear the Results pane is assigned to the OnClose property of the form.

If the password is valid, the OnClose event is assigned the memory variable, **xProceed**. This variable was previously assigned the codeblock containing the code to proceed with the execution of the application desktop form, **yvideo.wfm**. You could have assigned this codeblock directly as we did when clearing the Results pane; however, this is an example of using codeblocks previously stored in memory variables.

FIGURE 10.4 INVALID PASSWORD ALERT BOX, `ypass.wfm`

ValidRequired: We want to ensure that the Valid property is executed each time the entry field gets focus—regardless of whether data is entered or not.

ColorHighLight: When the entry field gets focus, this color combination will be in effect. Make both the background and the foreground white (W/W). This way, the entered password will not be visible as it is entered by the operator.

ValidErrorMsg: If the data entered is invalid, display the following message in the Valid Alert box (refer to Figure 10.4):

Invalid Password—Please try again...

- **Order view.** Place the Rectangle object first in the stack, followed by the Text object and the object.

PART IV: BUILDING A PASSWORD MODIFICATION UTILITY (CASE SYSTEM)

The user must have the ability to modify the system password. In the Video Express system, this will be a utility available from the **Utility** menu of the desktop. In this exercise, you will build a password utility and link it to the **Utility** menu.

Specifications

- Prior to building the password modification utility, you will need to code the `Decrypt()` procedure. Add `Decrypt()` to the global procedure file, `yproc.prg`. The only difference between `Encrypt()` and `Decrypt()` is that you will subtract the incremental value, `xPlus`, rather than adding it to each character encrypted. Test `Decrypt()` as follows:

```
SET TALK OFF
SET PROCEDURE TO yproc
xPass = Encrypt("PASSWORD",60)
? Decrypt(xPass,60)
PASSWORD
```

```
? xPass        && xPass string should not change.
î}ÅÅôïÄÇ
SET TALK ON
```

- **Form file name.** Name the form `ychange.wfm`.
- **Form design.** Using the form designer, place controls on the form as shown in Figure 10.5.
- **Form view.** Design the tabbing order of the form so that the two rectangles are on the bottom of the stack (top of list in the Set Control Order dialog) followed by the text controls. The **Change** pushbutton should be next, followed by the single entry field. After the entry field, focus should move to the **Save** pushbutton, then finally to the **Abort** pushbutton.
- **Using the Enabled property.** In the event-driven environment of this form, the operator could inadvertently click the **Save** pushbutton immediately after the form opens and prior to a new password being entered into the entry field—causing an invalid blank password to be accepted. The `Enabled` property of the **Save** pushbutton will prevent this. While the `Enabled` property is set to a logical false, the **Save** pushbutton will be disabled.

FIGURE 10.5 PASSWORD MODIFICATION FORM, `ychange.wfm`

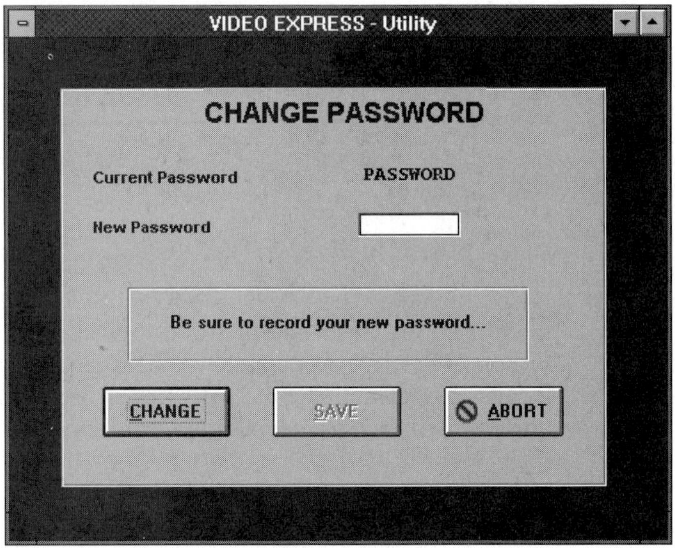

In the OnOpen event-handler of the form, set the `Enabled` property of the **Save** pushbutton to `.F.`, then to `.T.` in the OnLostFocus event-handler of the entry field control. Further, in the OnLostFocus event-handler of the entry field, give focus to the **Save** pushbutton. Use a codeblock to code the OnLostFocus event-handler of the entry field. Notice the visual effect of this in Figure 10.5.

Another problem exists if the operator clicks the entry field without pressing the **Change** pushbutton. To prevent this, set the `Enabled` property of the entry field to `.F.` in the OnOpen event-handler of the form and to `.T.` in the OnClick event-handler of the **Change** pushbutton. In the same handler, you will need to give focus to the entry field after changing the `Enabled` property.

- **Form OnOpen handler considerations.** In addition to the `Enabled` property situations we have mentioned, ensure that the code in the OnOpen handler of the form covers the following items:

  The encrypted password memory variable, `gPass`, from the global memory file, `yglobal.mem`, must be in memory. When the file is opened, the variables are to be added to those already in memory.

  The procedure file containing the Encryption and Decryption procedures must be open.

  In this form, the operator should at no time be able to abort the form by pressing the **Esc** key.

  The current password is to be displayed on the screen (see Figure 10.5). Use the decrypted password as the Text property of a Text control.

  The **Change** pushbutton should be given focus whenever the form opens.

  Pressing <**Enter**> on the entry field should move focus to the next control after data entry.

- **Password entry field considerations.** Consider the following when designing the password entry:

  The new password entry must be eight alphabetic characters, right-justified. Fewer than eight characters is not acceptable. A blank field is also not acceptable.

  The test for valid data is to occur whether or not data is entered by the operator.

  An appropriate message should appear in the Valid Alert box if invalid data is entered.

  When the entry field loses focus, it should enable the **Save** pushbutton and give focus to the **Save** pushbutton. This was previously discussed in the Enabled property discussion and will be your first usage of the `OnLostFocus` event property.

  An appropriate prompt message should appear in the status bar when the entry field gains focus.

- **Pushbutton considerations.** All pushbuttons should have an appropriate prompt message in the status bar as they gain focus. Though some have been mentioned previously, consider the following about each pushbutton:

  The **Change** pushbutton enables the entry field and gives it focus.
  The **Save** pushbutton encrypts the new password and assigns it to the memory variable, `gPass`. It then saves `gPass` to the memory file, **yglobal.mem**. The `SAFETY` toggle should be turned off during this operation. Finally, this pushbutton closes the form.
  The **Abort** pushbutton closes the form without saving the password. An abort bitmap, resource 24, is displayed on the button.
  All three pushbuttons contain an appropriate prompt message in the status bar.

- **Attaching the utility to the desktop menu.** Add the following item to the Video Express desktop **Utility** menu:

  &Password modification

  Attach the password modification form, `ychange.wfm`, as an action to the **Password modification** menu item.

CHAPTER SUMMARY

In this chapter we have discussed an important concept of object-oriented programming: programming reusable procedure modules for use in future systems. We have also discussed parameter passing and codeblocks. The following topics were included:

- **Parameter passing.** In Visual dBASE, we have the ability to pass parameter values to procedures. We can also build one or more procedure files to contain reusable modules to use in other systems.
- **User-defined functions.** Visual dBASE does not make a distinction between procedures and user-defined functions. The developers of the product recommend using procedures exclusively in systems as is done in the Forms Designer.
- **Password encryption/decryption.** The use of password protection is important to many systems. Encryption and decryption is an example of the use of procedures, parameter passing, and the development of reusable modules.
- **Using codeblocks.** A codeblock is a nameless procedure. They are used primarily to code procedures that contain limited statements and will not be reused. Codeblocks can contain either expressions or commands.

  The following new commands were discussed:

- `DO..WITH`
- `PARAMETERS`
- `PROCEDURE`
- `CLOSE PROCEDURE`
- `FUNCTION`
- `SET DECIMALS TO`
- `SAVE TO`
- `RESTORE FROM`

Several functions were introduced:

- `LEN()`
- `SUBSTR(()`
- `ASC()`
- `STUFF()`
- `VAL()`
- `LOWER()`
- `PROPER()`

Five new properties were discussed:

- ValidRequired
- ColorHighLight
- OnChange
- OnLostFocus
- Enabled

In the next chapter, we will discuss the concept of working with multidimensional databases. By creating multiple table views, the programmer reduces the amount of redundant data in a system and avoids the corresponding inconsistent data.

CHAPTER ELEVEN

TOPICS

New Commands and Functions

Concepts

- Multiple table system design
- Table setup for hands-on discussion
- Work areas
- Using the set relation command
- Use of Visual dBASE views
- Child table skip and selection
- Physically joining tables
- Using the Query Designer
- The Query Designer as a two-way tool

Review Exercises

Chapter Summary

Multiple Table Views

11

CHAPTER OBJECTIVES

Visual dBASE allows 225 tables to be open simultaneously. Relationships can be set between tables, linking them together and allowing simultaneous pointer movement between the tables. This multiple table processing capability reduces the need for redundant data in tables and the corresponding inconsistent data that results.

Table relationships can be defined using Visual dBASE code, either from the Command window or from within a program. They can also be developed using the Query Designer. This important two-way design tool is introduced in this chapter.

After studying this chapter, you should be able to design and program multiple table systems either by using source code directly or by means of the Query Designer.

NEW COMMANDS AND FUNCTIONS

COMMAND
```
USE [<database tablename>] [IN <work area number> ]
    [[INDEX <.ndx or .mdx table list> ]
    [ORDER [TAG] <.ndx tablename> / <.mdx tag>
    [OF <.mdx filename> ]] [ALIAS <alias> ]
```

`USE` has been introduced in an earlier chapter. We now add clauses associated with multiple table processing. `USE` opens a table and, if desired, orders it by opening an `.ndx` or `.mdx` file. It will also assign an alias name and a work area number.

COMMAND
```
SELECT <work area name/alias>
```

Used to choose a work area—by number (1-225), by alpha character (A-J), or by alias name.

COMMAND
```
SET RELATION TO
SET RELATION TO <expN>/<expC> INTO <alias>
```

Used to link two tables on a key expression. The tables must be opened in separate work areas. The expression may be either character or numeric type.

COMMAND
```
SET FIELDS on/OFF
SET FIELDS TO [<field>] [,<field>]
```

Used to define a group of fields from a single or multiple table system to be accessed by applicable commands.

COMMAND
```
SET FILTER TO <condition>
```

Used to set a filter condition.

COMMAND
```
CREATE VIEW <.vue filename> FROM ENVIRONMENT
```

Used to store the current view into a view (`.vue`) file.

COMMAND
```
CREATE/MODIFY QUERY <filename>
```

Used to enter the Visual dBASE Query Design editor. The `MODIFY` option can also be used to convert an existing view file (`.vue`) to a query file (`.qbe`).

COMMAND `SET SKIP TO [<alias 1> [<,alias 2>]`

Specifies how to advance the record pointer through records of linked tables. Used in a one-to-many relationship to move the pointer to each record in a child table having the same key as the single record in the parent table prior to moving the pointer in the parent file.

FUNCTION `FOUND([<alias>])`

Indicates whether the last command or function used to search an index (**SEEK()**, **SEEK**, **LOCATE**, and so on) finds a match. In a multiple table relation, it is used to filter records in child tables that do not match records in the parent table.

FUNCTION `MOD(<expN1>,<expN2>)`

Returns the remainder of the division of two numbers.

```
CLEAR
. ? MOD(5,2)
     1
. ? MOD(24,6)
     0
```

FUNCTION `SELECT([<alias>])`

Returns the number of an available work area or the work area number associated with a specific alias.

CONCEPTS

MULTIPLE TABLE SYSTEM DESIGN

Database design must precede database programming—just as architectural design must precede building construction. The completed system will draw upon its databases for most informational needs, so the storage required for those databases and the corresponding efficiency of system searches are critical.

Database design is actually only part of the overall systems analysis and design process. Though systems analysis and design are not the subjects of this book, their importance to proper database design cannot be overemphasized. As you review the following systems development process summary, notice the placement of design.

Systems Development Process Summary. The general steps in the design of a database management system are as follows:

- **Application selection:** Determine the scope of the application, its purpose and desired results. Desired results should be written in terms of measurable benefits. For example, "To decrease the time required for the Sales/Inventory processes of the Video Express store by 30%." This gives us the ability to measure the effectiveness of our completed system against a predefined goal.

  Of course, processing time is a tangible benefit, and easy to quantify. We cannot measure intangible benefits as accurately. For example, "increased employee morale" would require more of a qualitative measure and would be less accurate.
- **Examine current system (data gathering):** Review current procedure manuals, conduct interviews, examine existing reports and other data forms. It may be helpful to diagram the movement of data through the current system.
- **Analysis and design:** Analyze the current system, the desired system, constraints, equipment needs, and any other factor affecting the system. Then design the proposed system. The design should be approached in terms of the following:

  1. Output requirements
  2. Input requirements to produce the output
  3. Storage requirements (database design) to produce the output
  4. Process requirements to produce output not contained in storage or received from input
  5. Security and auditing requirements

  Once a proposed design is obtained, it should be documented (system diagrams, database designs, proposed input and output forms, and so on).
- **Design approval:** Present the proposed design to the user for final approval.
- **Programming:** Program the proposed new system.
- **Testing:** Do initial testing (programmer). Do final testing (user).
- **System documentation:** Document (with user involvement) the completed system.
- **Implementation:** Implement the system, initially parallel to the current system and then as a stand-alone system.
- **Evaluation:** Periodically evaluate the system against the benefits first proposed.

Database design begins with output requirements. In a detailed analysis each element of output should be listed and its source determined. The source will be either storage, input, or the result of an internal process.

Those data elements that originate in storage will either be memory variable files or database tables.

This summary stresses the importance of systems analysis and places database design in the overall process. We recommend that the Visual dBASE programmer study the subject fully prior to the development of major systems.

Design to Reduce Data Redundancy. Reducing redundancy is the most fundamental rule of relational database design. The programmer new to Visual dBASE may tend to put everything into one table, creating one large table for the entire system. A better approach is to design a series of tables, linked by key fields, to form a multidimensional relational database. For example, the Video Express system has three entities (categories of data): (1) customers, (2) sales, and (3) films. Note the three structures listed in Figure 11.1.

If preparing a report such as an invoice, the customer master table would be searched on the **cust_no** key. Because `ycustm` is linked to `ysales` by customer number, sales transaction information can be extracted at the same time from `ysales`. Because `ysales` is linked to `yfilm`, information such as title and rating can also be extracted for display on the invoice. We will learn later in the chapter how to link the tables and create simultaneous pointer movement.

The incorrect alternative is to place all elements into one table. For example, if the sales table, `ysales`, and the film table, `yfilm`, were combined into one table, it might appear as in Figure 11.2.

FIGURE 11.1 MULTIDIMENSIONAL RELATIONAL DATABASE

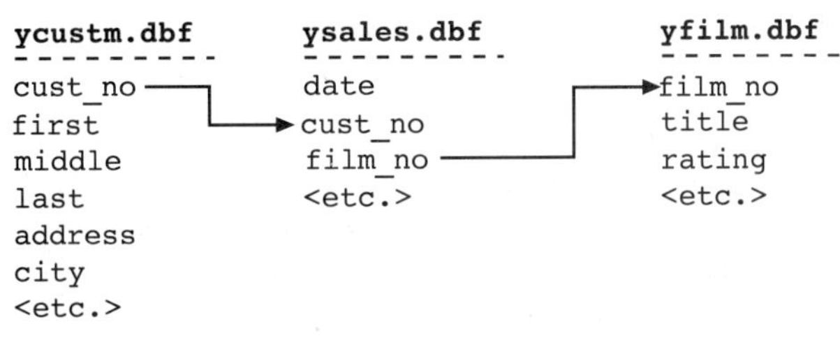

FIGURE 11.2 REDUNDANT DATA EXAMPLE, SALES TABLE

```
date      cust_no  title                  rating      cost
---------------------------------------------------------------
10/10/89 0010      Jane Fonda Workout     G            2.95
10/10/89 0013      Winnie the Pooh        K            1.50
10/11/89 0075      Jane Fonda Workout     G            2.95
10/12/89 0045      Jane Fonda Workout     G            2.95
<etc.>
```

Notice the redundancy this creates. The film title ("Jane Fonda Workout"), rating (G), and cost ($2.95) must be repeated for each sale. However, if separate tables are maintained, the film title and cost need be coded only once (in **yfilm**). This will reduce the amount of storage required in addition to increasing search efficiency. It will also reduce the probability of operator error in redundant typing, thereby reducing the amount of inconsistent information in the database.

Types of Table Relationships. There are several types of relationships to consider when designing relational databases. Those covered here will satisfy most of your design needs.

One-to-One. Though not used often, a one-to-one relationship is important in certain situations. The most common usage in dBASE applications will be to link two tables so that they appear as one (because of the restriction of 255 fields per record). If there is need for a longer record, say 400 fields, the second table can contain a single record comprising fields 256 through 400. When the pointer is moved to the single (one) record in the parent database, a second pointer will automatically move to the single (one) record that will complete the total pseudorecord in the child table.

One-to-Many. In the Video Express system, a single (one) customer in the parent customer master table, **ycustm**, can be related to a group (many) of records associated with that customer in the child sales table, **ysales**. The tables will be linked on customer number. There will be only one unique customer number in the parent table and many with the same customer number in the child table (see Figure 11.3).

FIGURE 11.3 ONE-TO-MANY RELATIONSHIP

```
(ycust.dbf)                            (ysales.dbf)
cust_no  last         <etc.>           date      cust_no       <etc.>
------------------------------         ------------------------------
0010     Jones                         10/10/89  0010
0011     Griesemer                     10/15/89  0010
0013     Ledford -----------+          10/15/89  0010
0014     Taylor             |        +>10/05/89  0013
<etc.>                      +--------+ 10/06/89  0013
                                     +>10/07/89  0013
                                       10/01/89  0014
                                       <etc.>
```

Many-to-One. In a many-to-one relationship, the parent table contains a group of records (many) to be linked to a child table containing a single record (one) that will relate to each record in the parent table. For example, suppose we need a listing of the sales table in the Video Express system. A requirement of the listing is that the last name is to be listed with each record. Rather than relating our customer table into the sales table, we will relate the sales table into the customer table. As each record from the sales table is listed, the single last name for that customer number will be drawn from the customer table. There may be many of a certain customer number in the parent table, but only one such customer number in the child table. Note the relationship and corresponding listing in Figure 11.4.

Table Relation Chains. Tables can be related to form table relation chains. For example, in the Video Express system, the customer master table can be related to the sales table, and the sales table can be related to the film table (Figure 11.5). Don't be concerned at this point about Visual dBASE code that forms the linkage—that will be covered later in this chapter.

FIGURE 11.4 MANY-TO-ONE RELATIONSHIP

```
(ycust.dbf)                            ysales.dbf
cust_no  last          <etc.>          date      cust_no       <etc.>
--------------------------             ---------------------------------

0010     Jones                         10/10/89  0010
0011     Griesemer                     10/15/89  0010
0013     Ledford <-----------+         10/15/89  0010
0014     Taylor              |        [10/05/89  0013
<etc.>                       +--------|10/06/89  0013
                                      [10/07/89  0013
                                       10/01/89  0014
                                       <etc.>

---------------------------------------------------------------------
Partial listing of ysales, related to ycustm, by cust_no.

date      cust_no  last

10/10/89  0010     Jones
10/15/89  0010     Jones
10/15/89  0010     Jones
10/05/89  0013     Ledford
10/06/89  0013     Ledford
10/07/89  0013     Ledford
10/01/89  0014     Taylor
```

Multiple Child Relations. Earlier versions of dBASE allowed only table relation chains. Beginning with dBASE IV and continuing in Visual dBASE, multiple child relations are allowed. You can now relate more than one child table to a parent table. In Figure 11.6, the sales table is related to both the customer master table and the film table.

NOTE: Use of the terms "parent" and "child" in a relational system is not theoretically true. The virtual table created in a relational system by linking individual flat tables doesn't really imply ownership or subordinacy, as in the hierarchical model. (Refer back to Chapter 1, Figure 1.7.) However, to avoid confusion, this text uses parent and child as the terms are used in most dBASE references, including the product reference manuals, instead of terms such as "home" and "source."

FIGURE 11.5 TABLE RELATION CHAIN

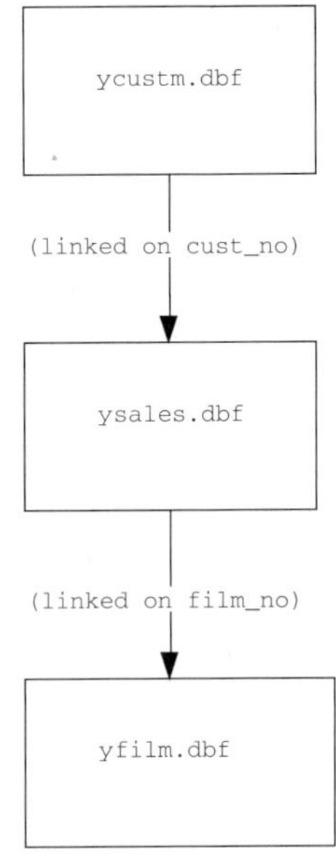

FIGURE 11.6 MULTIPLE CHILD RELATION

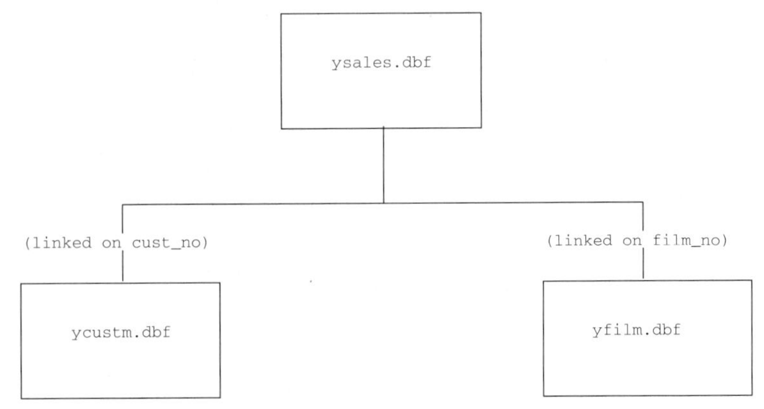

TABLE SETUP FOR HANDS-ON DISCUSSION

The following discussion and examples will assist you in understanding the use of multiple table and array commands. Be sure you have the **ycustm**, **ysales**, and **yfilm** tables on your work disk. To ensure all the multiple index files are current, type the following from the Input pane:

```
CLEAR ALL
SET EXCLUSIVE ON
USE ycustm
SET EXCLUSIVE ON
INDEX ON cust_no TAG cust_no
INDEX ON last TAG last
USE ysales
INDEX ON cust_no TAG cust_no
USE yfilm
INDEX ON film_no TAG film_no
```

WORK AREAS

Visual dBASE allows 225 *work areas*. Thus far, all of our processing has been in work area 1. There are 224 more areas in which we can open additional files and process data. Certain rules govern the use of work areas:

- Work areas are numbered from 1 to 225. The first 10 may also be selected by the letters A through J. Further, a work area can be assigned an alias name. Rather than having to remember the number or letter of a work area, you can reference it by its alias. For example, you might call work area 3 **sales**, if it contains the sales table, **ysales.dbf**. From that point on, you can select the work area by calling it **sales** rather than by remembering that **ysales.dbf** was used in work area 3. The same rules apply to an alias name as to memory or field variable names (for example, a maximum of 10 characters, numbers, or letters; first character must be a letter; no spaces; and the underscore (_) is the only special character allowed).
- You may open the following files in each work area: 1 database table, 1 format file, 1 query file, 1 production **.mdx**, and 10 **.mdx**/**.ndx** files.
- You can open a table in more than one work area by using the **AGAIN** clause of the **USE** command. The files associated with the table will also be opened. For example, if a table is opened in work area 1 and then again in work area 5, the associated **.dbt** and production **.mdx** files will also be opened automatically. If a change is made to those files in one work area, it will be reflected in the other work area as well.
- Each work area has a separate pointer. Moving from one work area to another has no effect on the pointers.

```
CLEAR
SELECT 1
USE ycustm ALIAS customer
SET ORDER TO last
USE ysales ORDER cust_no ALIAS sales IN B
USE yfilm ORDER film_no ALIAS film IN SELECT()
DISPLAY STATUS
```

The `IN` clause opens a table in a work area without having to first select it. This example opens the three named tables in work areas 1, 2, and 3. In work area 1, the order was set with a separate command. In work areas 2 and 3, the order was set in the `USE` command. Either way is acceptable. Work area 2 was assigned using the work area character designator, `B.` Work area 3 was designated using the `SELECT()` function. `DISPLAY STATUS` is a very useful tool here. It displays the complete status of all work areas as a result of the commands executed in the example. For example, it verifies that the currently selected work area is 1. Work areas 2 and 3 were established while 1 was still selected.

To illustrate movement between work areas, type the following:

```
CLEAR
SELECT customer
DISPLAY STRUCTURE
SELECT sales
DISPLAY STRUCTURE
SELECT film
DISPLAY STRUCTURE
SELECT B                 && Select by "B", "2", or the ALIAS.
DISPLAY STRUCTURE
```

The select command is used to move from one work area to another. The numeric, alpha, or alias work area name may be used as a reference. The alias is the preferred method because you do not have to remember the number or letter designating a work area.

USING THE SET RELATION COMMAND

Our discussion continues with examples from the Command window. Work areas 1, 2, and 3 now contain the open tables **ycustm**, **ysales**, and **yfilm** with aliases of **customer**, **sales**, and **film**. Further, **customer** is ordered by last name, **sales** by customer number, and **film** by film number.

FIGURE 11.7 SET RELATION COMMAND EXAMPLE

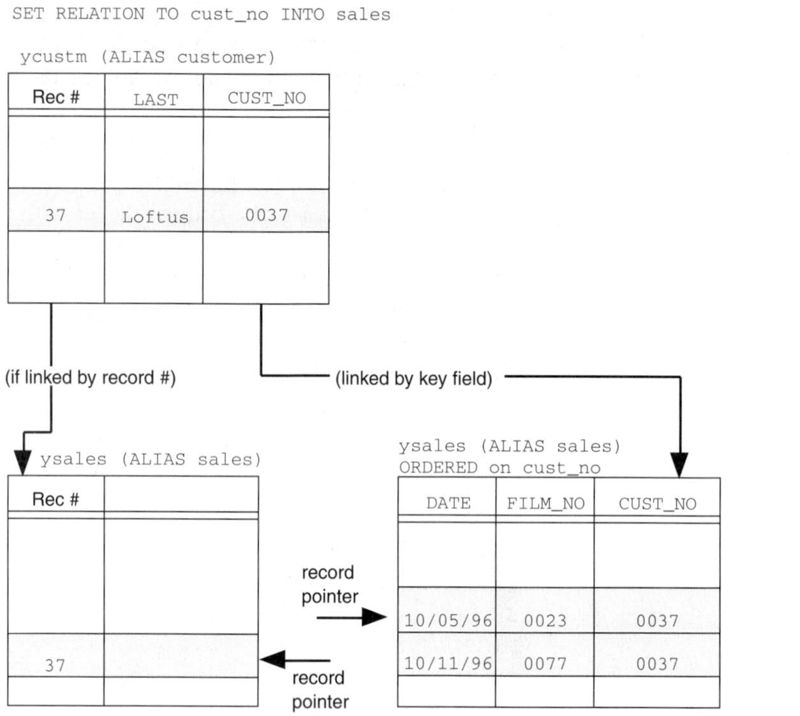

```
CLEAR
SELECT customer
SET RELATION TO cust_no INTO sales
SEEK "Loftus"
DISPLAY cust_no, last
SELECT sales
DISPLAY
```

The **SELECT** command moves control to work area 1, the location of the open customer master table, ordered by last name. The **SET RELATION** command links the customer master table to the sales table in work area two (alias **sales**), establishing a one-to-many relationship (Figure 11.3). The **SEEK** command causes the following to occur (refer to Figure 11.7):

- Moves the pointer in **ycustm** to the last name of "Loftus".
- dBASE locates the **cust_no** field in the "Loftus" last name record (0037).
- Using 0037 as the search key, Visual dBASE automatically initiates another **SEEK** on the child table, **ysales**. The pointer in the sales work area moves to the first occurrence of customer number 0037 in **ysales**.

The first **DISPLAY** command in our example displays the "Loftus" record in **ycustm**, and the second **DISPLAY** command displays the results of the automatic **SEEK** command—the first occurrence of customer number 0037 in **ysales**. This example demonstrates the strength of the **SET RELATION** command. The net effect is that the two tables now appear as a single table. With this relation set, *any* pointer movement in **customer** will produce a corresponding pointer movement in **sales**. For example, type the following:

```
SELECT customer
GO 5            && Or any pointer movement command.
DISPLAY cust_no, last    && Note customer no.
SELECT sales
DISPLAY                  && Note customer no. is the same.
```

The **SET RELATION** command has an option of relating by a numeric expression. For example, type the following from the Command window:

```
SELECT sales
SET ORDER TO            && Set natural order in sales.
SELECT customer
SET RELATION TO RECNO() INTO sales
SEEK "Loftus"
DISPLAY                 && Note record no.
SELECT sales
DISPLAY
SELECT customer         && Note record no.
SET RELATION TO         && Clear relationship.
```

The **SET RELATION TO** command in this example relates the tables by numeric expression, **RECNO()**. The child file is first set to natural order because the link is now by record number rather than an indexed key field. The **SEEK** command will again move the pointer to the "Loftus" record, number 37 in the customer master table, just as in the previous example. However, dBASE will not do the internal **SEEK** on **SALES** as in the previous example. Because it is linked on the numeric expression, **RECNO()**, it will automatically move the pointer to the same record number (37), in the related table, **ysales**. This type of relation is useful when relating two tables containing two parts of the same record. Finally, the **SET RELATION TO** command clears the current relation.

Using the Alias Pointer. In our examples thus far, we have selected a work area to view data. By using the alias pointer (also referred to as the constructed alias symbol), reference to data in any work area can be made from any other work area. The alias pointer symbol is constructed with the hyphen and greater-than symbol, `->`. When a field from another work area is referenced, the syntax is `<ALIAS->fieldname>`.

```
CLEAR
SELECT customer
SET ORDER TO cust_no        && ORDER by customer no. TAG.
SELECT sales
SET RELATION TO cust_no INTO customer, film_no INTO film
DISPLAY ALL cust_no, customer->last, film_no, film->title
```

This example establishes a multiple child relationship (Figure 11.6). It also establishes a many-to-one relationship (Figure 11.4). For each of the many sales records in the parent table, `sales`, a relationship is set to one record in each of the child tables, `customer` and `film`.

Before setting the relationships, the tag was set to customer number in `customer`. Remember, the related table *must* be indexed on the key field specified in the `SET RELATION` command. Then `sales` was selected to establish the relationship. In the `SET RELATION` command, two clauses were used to make it a multiple child relationship. The `DISPLAY` command then uses the alias pointer to refer to fields in the unselected child tables.

The field list can be set with the `SET FIELDS` command as follows:

```
SET FIELDS TO cust_no, customer->last, film_no, film->title
DISPLAY ALL
```

By establishing a fields list, you will enable all commands using the multidimensional relational database model to reference those fields without need for field list coding (for example, `BROWSE`, `EDIT`, `LIST`).

USING VISUAL dBASE VIEWS

A *view* is a specific way of looking at the tables of a system for a certain purpose. A view may contain the following:

- Multiple table relationships
- Field (expression) lists
- Filter conditions
- Sort order

From the Command window, we have developed a multiple table relationship, established a sort order, and defined a field list. To add a filter condition to our current view, enter the following command:

```
SET FILTER TO cust_no > "0020"
DISPLAY ALL
```

The **SET FILTER** command will allow only records meeting the condition specified. This completes the current view of our system. **DISPLAY ALL** needs no other clauses. Any dBASE command executed will *look* at the system databases with this view.

NOTE: You may also use a conditional index tag or the SET KEY command introduced in Chapter 6 to create filter conditions. For example, INDEX ON city TAG citysm FOR City = "San Mateo" would have the same effect as SET FILTER TO city = "San Mateo". Moreover, the index would facilitate faster searches and processing.

A view may either be programmed as separate lines of code or be contained in a separate file that is opened when needed. The files used to store views are (1) the view file (**.vue**) and (2) the query file (**.qbe**). The view file is a carryover from dBASE III PLUS and is still supported in Visual dBASE. A query file is generated by the Query Designer included in Visual dBASE.

Further, a view can be developed from the Command window, as in the preceding sample, then stored in a view file (**.vue**) as follows:

```
** (This example assumes the previous view is still open).
CREATE VIEW yview FROM ENVIRONMENT
CLEAR ALL
DISPLAY STATUS
SET VIEW TO yview
DISPLAY STATUS          && Display current view.
```

Unfortunately, we cannot create a query file from the environment. It is possible, however, to convert a view file (**.vue**) to a query file (**.qbe**) with the following command:

```
MODIFY QUERY <.vue filename>
```

This places the view into the Query Designer. Nevertheless, this will not work properly in Visual dBASE if alias names were used when coding the environmental view.

The advantage of storing the current view in a query (**.qbe**) file is that when called by a program module, it will be compiled, forming a (**.qbo**) file that will execute faster. For maximum efficiency at execution time, the view should be embedded code within a procedure file. The query or view file is a separate file to be opened each time it is executed, which will decrease efficiency. Also, be cautious when building a filter condition with the **SET FILTER** command, or with the Visual dBASE Query Designer. Faster search techniques are better programmed as we discussed in Chapter 6, Efficient Search Techniques.

CHILD TABLE SKIP AND SELECTION

There are several factors to consider when using a one-to-many relationship. First, if there are no records in the child table that match the parent record, they should be suppressed from a display or print. The second situation to consider is pointer movement in the child table. For example, when an invoice is printed, the pointer in the child table should move through *every* record in the child file that matches the linked field of the single parent record.

To demonstrate the code to accomplish this, type the following from the Command window:

```
CLEAR ALL
USE ycustm IN 1
USE ysales ORDER cust_no IN 2
SET RELATION TO cust_no INTO ysales
SET FIELDS TO a->cust_no, a->last, a->first, b->film_no
BROWSE
```

This code uses the letters `a` and `b` as alias names of the work areas. Notice in `BROWSE` that there are parent records without child records to match. For example, record number 2 has no `film_no`. Further, notice that there is only one `film_no` listed for each parent record.

Escape from `BROWSE` and type the following additional commands:

```
SET FILTER TO FOUND("ysales")
BROWSE
```

This example uses the table name as the alias name. `BROWSE` now displays only records that have matching child records. Notice that record number 2 does not display as in the first example. As the pointer moves to each record in the parent table to display in `BROWSE`, the `FOUND()` function filters only those records in the child table that are located by the internal `SEEK` command (caused by the relationship setting).

Escape from `BROWSE` and continue by typing the following:

```
SET SKIP TO ysales
BROWSE
```

In this example, *many* child records matching *one* parent record are displayed. This is caused by the `SET SKIP` command being set in the child table.

PHYSICALLY JOINING TABLES

Visual dBASE has available a `JOIN` command to join tables together physically, forming a *real* rather than a virtual database. The real table is a flat representation of the multidimensional virtual table. Though beyond the scope of an introductory text, it is mentioned here as an alternative to linking flat tables together.

However, joining tables has two drawbacks, which give it the same shortcomings as the **SORT** command. First, it is very slow. It operates by cross-referencing every record in a parent table against every record in a child table to create a third table. The second drawback is that it is disk-space expensive. Every time a new joined table is created to form a physical view of the system, more disk space is used. The advantages of using the virtual views discussed in the last section are apparent.

NOTE: A flat file can be developed from a virtual view of a database without the need for the `JOIN` command. This is accomplished by first creating a virtual view using the `SET RELATION` command, then using the `COPY` command to copy the view to a flat file. Execution will be much faster than with a physical join.

USING THE QUERY DESIGNER

The Query Designer is a two-way tool available to the Visual dBASE programmer to develop database views. The designer generates source code from the information presented to the Designer work surface and stores it in a query file with a **.qbe** extension.

The Query Designer Work Surface. To enter the Query Designer, type the following command from the Command window:

```
CLEAR ALL
USE ycustm                  && Open parent table.
CREATE QUERY yview2
```

The Query Designer requires an open table upon entry. You can either open the table prior to the **CREATE** command, as we have done in this example, or respond to the Open Table Required dialog box. If your query requires multiple tables, the parent should be opened first. Resize/move the Designer window as needed. Refer to Figure 11.8 as we review the various parts of the work surface.

- **Menu system.** As you enter the Designer, the menu items change to query design actions that are specific to query design. We will use various items from this menu system as we build our queries.
- **SpeedBar.** Many of the actions available from the menu system are also available from the Designer SpeedBar. For example, you can move back and forth between design and run using the lightning-bolt run icon and the adjacent design icon. The icons to the right of the **run** and **design** icons allow you to add a table, remove a table, link tables, or unlink tables.
- **View skeleton.** All of the table fields are displayed across the work surface. This visual representation of the fields and related indicators is referred to as the *view skeleton*.

FIGURE 11.8 QUERY DESIGN WORK SURFACE

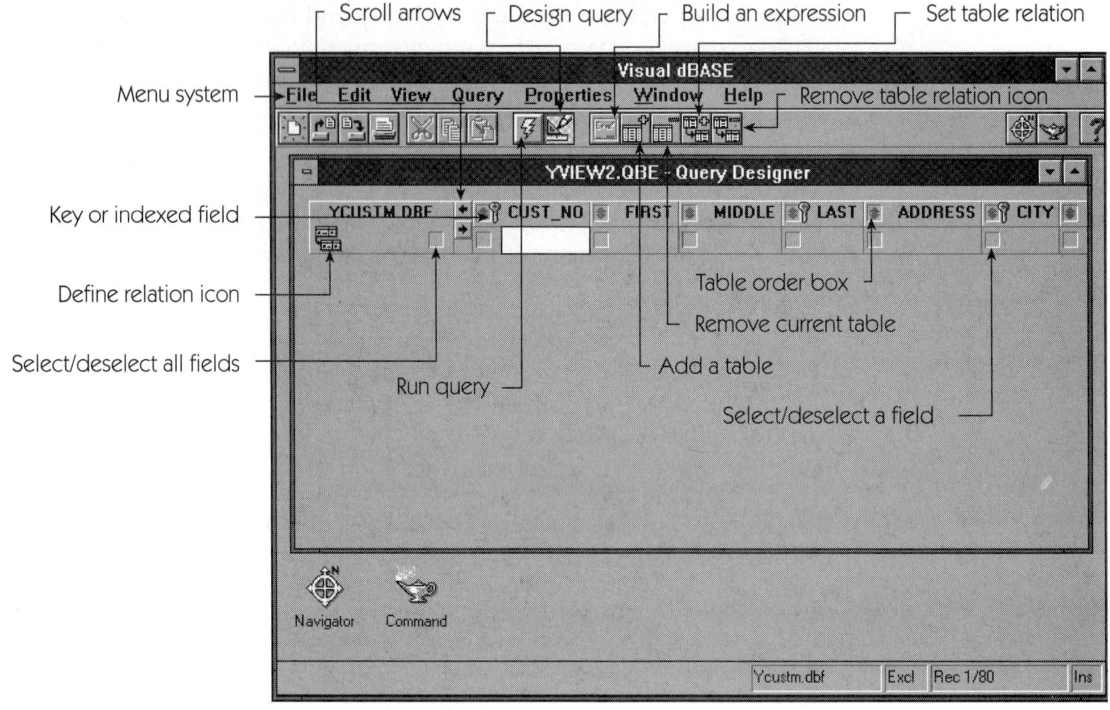

- **Scroll arrows.** Used to navigate the view skeleton. Click to scroll right or left. You can also use **Tab/Shift-Tab** to move one field to the right or left. **F3** and **F4** will move focus back and forth between multiple tables. Press **Ctrl-Home** or **Ctrl-End** to move to the beginning or end of the skeleton.
- **Field select check boxes.** You can either select/deselect all fields or select/deselect individual fields using the field select check boxes.
- **Index or key field indicator.** The **key** icon indicates whether or not there is a tag in the production `.mdx` file on this field.
- **Field order box.** Located to the left of each field name, this drop-down icon menu allows you to select ascending or descending case-sensitive or case-insensitive sorts on that field. As you move the cursor arrow down the menu options, notice the corresponding description of the type of sort in the status bar.

Adding Files to the Designer. The next step in our design will be to add the two child tables to the work surface. Select the tables as follows:

- **ysales.dbf** — Add to the work surface by selecting **Query/ Add Table**. Select the table from the **Open Table Required** dialog box.
- **yfilm.dbf** — Add to the work surface using the **Add Table** icon from the SpeedBar, then select the table from the **Open Table Required** dialog box.

The work surface should now appear as in Figure 11.9. Use **F3** (backward) and **F4** (forward) to move the cursor from one table to another. You can also click on any field in a table to move focus from one table to another.

Setting Table Relations. We will form a chain relation by linking the customer table into the sales table and the sales table into the film table. Proceed as follows:

- **Link ycustm into ysales.** Place the cursor on the parent table, `ycustm.` Select **Query | Set Relation**. This will cause the **Define Relation** dialog box to open. All parent-child relationships are defined from this dialog.

  Parent Table text box. This drop-down list initially contains the names of the tables on the work surface. Select `ycustm.dbf` as the parent table. Once a table is selected, the table list changes to a fields list (see Figure 11.10). From this list, select `cust_no`, which is the field we will link on.

  Child Table text box. This drop-down list initially contains a list of the possible child files from the design work surface. Select `ysales.dbf`. Notice that the drop-down list converts to a list of the index tags contained in the table selected. Select the `cust_no` tag. It may currently be the only tag with `ysales.dbf` (see Figure 11.10).

FIGURE 11.9 QUERY `yview2` WITH THREE TABLES

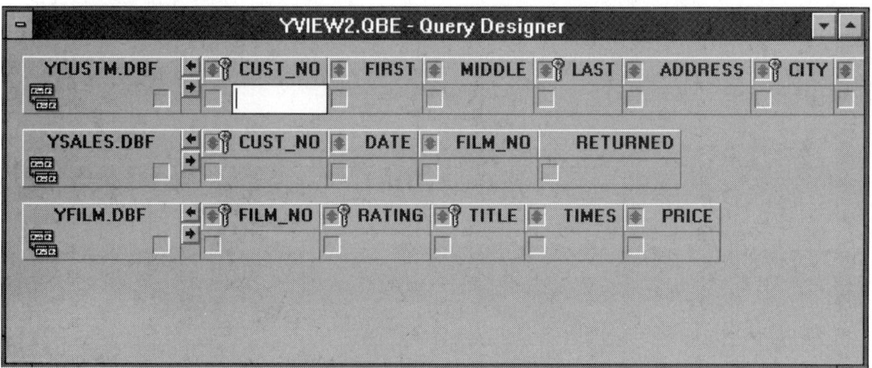

Check box group. The check box group in the center of the **Define Relation** dialog box allows selection of a one-to-many relationship between the parent and child tables. We will retain the checked default setting (see Figure 11.10). From this check box group, you can also check **Every Parent** or **Enforce Integrity**. If **Every Parent** is checked, every parent record is displayed regardless of whether there is a corresponding child record. This might be used in situations where there is no sales activity against a parent record during an accounting period. If **Enforce Integrity** is checked, dBASE safeguards against any action that will interfere with parent-child relations (in dBASE tables only). For example, if an attempt is made to delete a parent record that is linked to child records, an alert box will appear. Further, if a child record is added, it will automatically be given the key value of the current parent record and will make this value read-only. In this query, check only the one-to-many box.

Master Expression text box. As we mentioned earlier, the child file must be indexed on the linked field. If the common linked field already contains a tag, it will appear in the Master Expression text box. This box will contain either the expression that is being used to link the tables or a suggested value if one has not been selected.

This completes the linkage of the parent file, `ycustm.dbf` to the child file, `ysales.dbf`. Press **OK** to return to the Query Design work surface.

- **Link ysales into yfilm.** The next step will be to link `ysales.dbf` to `yfilm.dbf`. Place your cursor anywhere on the `ysales.dbf` skeleton. Select **Query | Set Relation**. In the Define Relation dialog box, select `ysales.dbf` using the Parent Table text box. Select `yfilm.dbf` using the Child Table text box. Link the tables on the `film_no` index tag.

Press the **OK** button to return to the Query Designer work surface. The relationships should appear on the work surface as displayed in Figure 11.11.

FIGURE 11.10 DEFINE RELATION DIALOG BOX

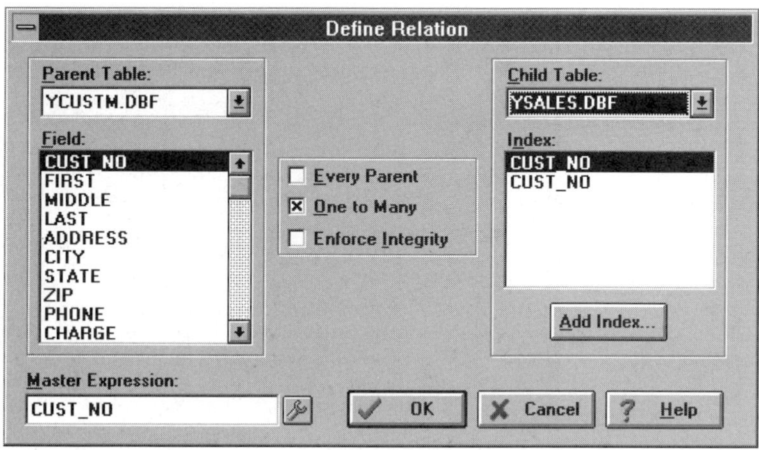

FIGURE 11.11 TABLE RELATIONS AND FIELD LIST, `yview2.qbe`

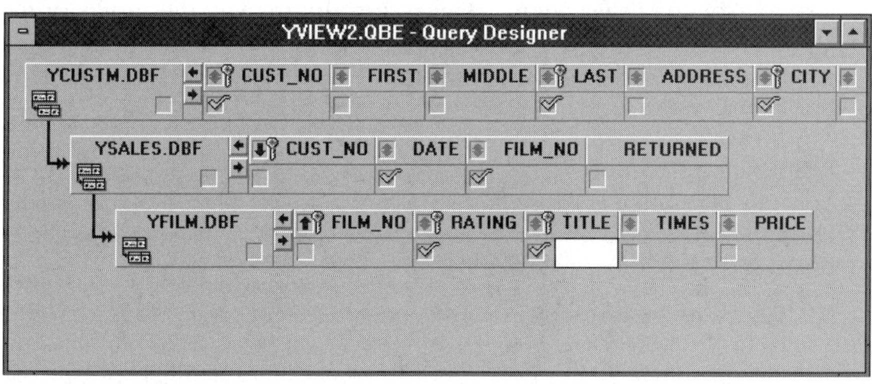

Establishing a Field List. Once the relationships are set, we select the fields to include in the final view. Check the appropriate select/deselect box to select the following fields for this view (see Figure 11.11):

- `ycustm.dbf:  cust_no, last, city`
- `ysales.dbf:  date, film_no`
- `yfilm.dbf:   rating, title`

FIGURE 11.12 QUERY TEST USING BROWSE, `yview2.qbe`

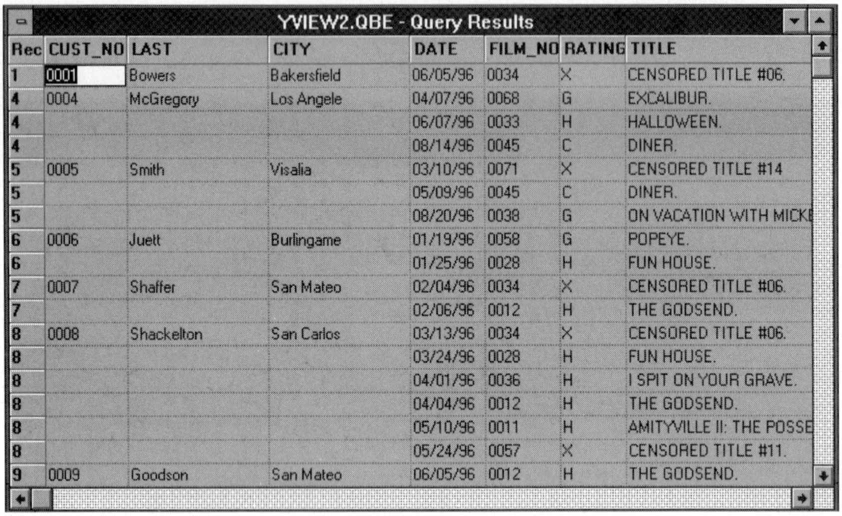

YVIEW2.QBE - Query Results

Rec	CUST_NO	LAST	CITY	DATE	FILM_NO	RATING	TITLE
1	0001	Bowers	Bakersfield	06/05/96	0034	X	CENSORED TITLE #06.
4	0004	McGregory	Los Angele	04/07/96	0068	G	EXCALIBUR.
4				06/07/96	0033	H	HALLOWEEN.
4				08/14/96	0045	C	DINER.
5	0005	Smith	Visalia	03/10/96	0071	X	CENSORED TITLE #14
5				05/09/96	0045	C	DINER.
5				08/20/96	0038	G	ON VACATION WITH MICKE
6	0006	Juett	Burlingame	01/19/96	0058	G	POPEYE.
6				01/25/96	0028	H	FUN HOUSE.
7	0007	Shaffer	San Mateo	02/04/96	0034	X	CENSORED TITLE #06.
7				02/06/96	0012	H	THE GODSEND.
8	0008	Shackelton	San Carlos	03/13/96	0034	X	CENSORED TITLE #06.
8				03/24/96	0028	H	FUN HOUSE.
8				04/01/96	0036	H	I SPIT ON YOUR GRAVE.
8				04/04/96	0012	H	THE GODSEND.
8				05/10/96	0011	H	AMITYVILLE II: THE POSSE
8				05/24/96	0057	X	CENSORED TITLE #11.
9	0009	Goodson	San Mateo	06/05/96	0012	H	THE GODSEND.

Testing the Query During Design. Once a field list is established, periodically test your query. Select **View | Query Results** to view the results of the query in a Browse window (see Figure 11.12). To return to the design work surface, select **View | Query Design**. You can also use **F2 (Data)** and **Shift-F2 (Design)**.

Establishing a Filter Condition. This step isolates certain records in the view. You can filter records by coding an example of the filter condition under the appropriate field and/or by coding the condition using the condition box.

- **Query by example:** We tell the Query Designer how we want the records filtered by coding an example under the field in question. In our query, we want those records with customer numbers less than `0012`. Code the filter example as follows (see Figure 11.13):

  ```
  CUST_NO
  < "0012"
  ```

  This will generate the source code, `SET FILTER TO CUST_NO < "0012"`, in the source code file `yview2.qbe`.
- **Using the condition box:** An *example* of a filter cannot always be used. For example, we need an expression that contains a date function to filter those sales occurring in the month of August. To add

this condition, select **Query | Add condition**, then type the following into the condition text box (see Figure 11.13):

```
MONTH (ysales->date) < 8
```

Records will now be filtered that contain a customer number less than `0012` having films purchased in August.

Establishing a Sort Order. The final segment of our view will cause the parent records to be displayed in city order. To accomplish this, locate and click the **table order** box beside the city field in the table skeleton. Click the **up-arrow sort** icon to sort in ascending order. The message line should read, **"Sort this field in ascending order..."**. The **up-arrow sort** icon should now appear in table sort box beside the last field (see Figure 11.13).

Final Testing and Saving of Query. Proceed with the final test of the query by pressing **F2 (Data)**. The records displayed should be in last order, have customer numbers less than `0012`, and contain only sales that occurred prior to August. Further, there should be no parent records without child counterparts, and all child records associated with the parent that meet the previous conditions should be displayed.

Double-click the **Browse** window control button to save the query. Click the **Yes** button in the **Changes Made - Queries Designer** dialog to complete the operation and return focus to the Command window. Finally, though the query file has been saved, the view is still open. Type `CLEAR ALL` from the Command window to close all tables.

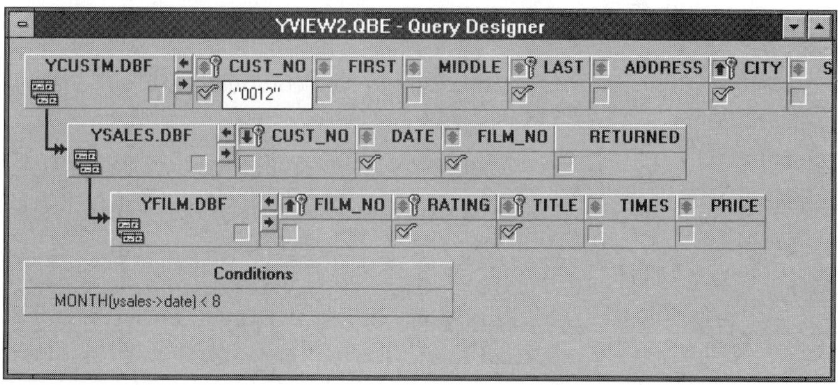

FIGURE 11.13 FINISHED QUERY, `yview2.qbe`

THE QUERY DESIGNER AS A TWO-WAY TOOL

To demonstrate the two-way tool aspects of the Query Designer, type the following from the Command window:

```
MODI COMM yview2.qbe    && Extension must be included.
```

The code displayed here was generated by the Query Designer. Notice its similarity to the code developed earlier in the chapter from the Command window. Our modification will be to the **SET FILTER COMMAND** (approximately line 16). Change the **MONTH()** expression to filter records prior to October rather than August—from <8 to <10. Select **File | Save and close** to return to the Command window.

Test the modification by typing the following:

```
SET VIEW TO yview2
BROWSE                       && Verify December dates only.
```

Verify that only January through September sales records are displayed, then exit Browse. The next step is to verify that the modification has been passed on to the Query Designer. Type the following:

```
MODI VIEW yview2             && Extension not required.
```

Verify that the condition box expression is coded to filter January through September records. Modify the condition box expression to once again filter only records prior to August. Save changes and exit the query designer.

REVIEW EXERCISES

PART I: REVIEW QUESTIONS

1. What is the importance of systems analysis prior to database design?
2. Give an example of a computer system benefit and explain how that benefit could be measured.
3. Name the most important fundamental of relational database design.
4. Define a many-to-one versus a one-to-many relationship.
5. (a) Define a work area. (b) How many work areas are available in Visual dBASE? (c) How many file types can be opened in a work area? (d) Can the same table be opened in more than one work area? (e) What command is used to move from one work area to another?
6. What command is used to link multiple tables?

7. (a) Why is it required to have the child table in a linkage indexed? (b) Is it necessary to have the parent table indexed on the same field as the child table?

8. What symbol is used to reference a field in a work area other than the selected work area?

9. What command is used to capture a view to a file that was developed from the Command window?

10. Name the four characteristics of a view that can be stored in a query file.

PART II: VIEW EXERCISE FROM THE COMMAND WINDOW

Specifications. Using Visual dBASE syntax from the Command window, build a view that will allow the display of the sales table in the browse window.

1. The display is to include the title of each film. A film title is an attribute of the film entity and as such is located in the film table, `yfilm.dbf`.
2. Order the view on customer number.
3. Include the customer number, transaction date, film number, and film title in the field list.
4. Display only those records with transaction dates prior to June (see Figure 11.14).
5. Save the view to a view file, `yview3.vue`.

PART III: VIEW EXERCISE FROM THE QUERY DESIGNER

Specification. Using the Query Designer, build a view of the sales table, `ysales.dbf`, that will include both the customer name and film title of each film.

1. Close all files and release all variables (`CLEAR ALL`).
2. Name the query file `yview4.qbe`.

FIGURE 11.14 CLASS EXERCISE, PART II, `yview3.vue`

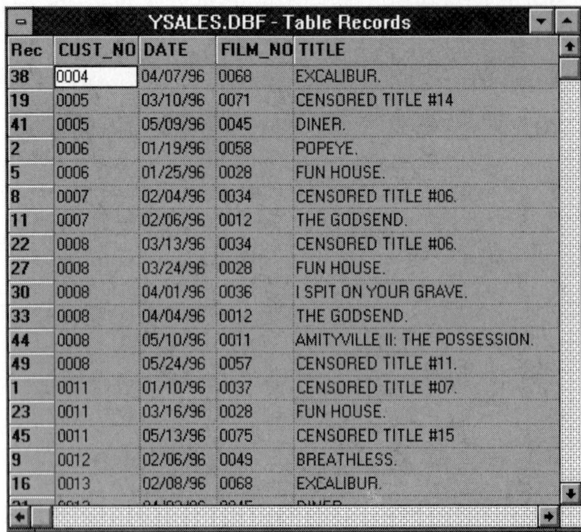

YSALES.DBF - Table Records

Rec	CUST_NO	DATE	FILM_NO	TITLE
38	0004	04/07/96	0068	EXCALIBUR.
19	0005	03/10/96	0071	CENSORED TITLE #14
41	0005	05/09/96	0045	DINER.
2	0006	01/19/96	0058	POPEYE.
5	0006	01/25/96	0028	FUN HOUSE.
8	0007	02/04/96	0034	CENSORED TITLE #06.
11	0007	02/06/96	0012	THE GODSEND.
22	0008	03/13/96	0034	CENSORED TITLE #06.
27	0008	03/24/96	0028	FUN HOUSE.
30	0008	04/01/96	0036	I SPIT ON YOUR GRAVE.
33	0008	04/04/96	0012	THE GODSEND.
44	0008	05/10/96	0011	AMITYVILLE II: THE POSSESSION.
49	0008	05/24/96	0057	CENSORED TITLE #11.
1	0011	01/10/96	0037	CENSORED TITLE #07.
23	0011	03/16/96	0028	FUN HOUSE.
45	0011	05/13/96	0075	CENSORED TITLE #15
9	0012	02/06/96	0049	BREATHLESS.
16	0013	02/08/96	0068	EXCALIBUR.

3. Establish a multiple child relationship that links the sales table, `ysales.dbf`, into both the customer table, `ycustm.dbf`, and the film table, `yfilm.dbf`.
4. Include the customer number, date, last name, and film title in the field list.
5. Restrict the view to those records that contain dates prior to April and film numbers equal to or less than `0050`.
6. Order the view on customer number.
7. Test and save.
8. Using the Program Editor, modify the view to include the film number. Return to the Query Designer to ensure that the modification has been retained at both levels (see Figure 11.15).

FIGURE 11.15 CLASS EXERCISE, PART III, `yview4.qbe`

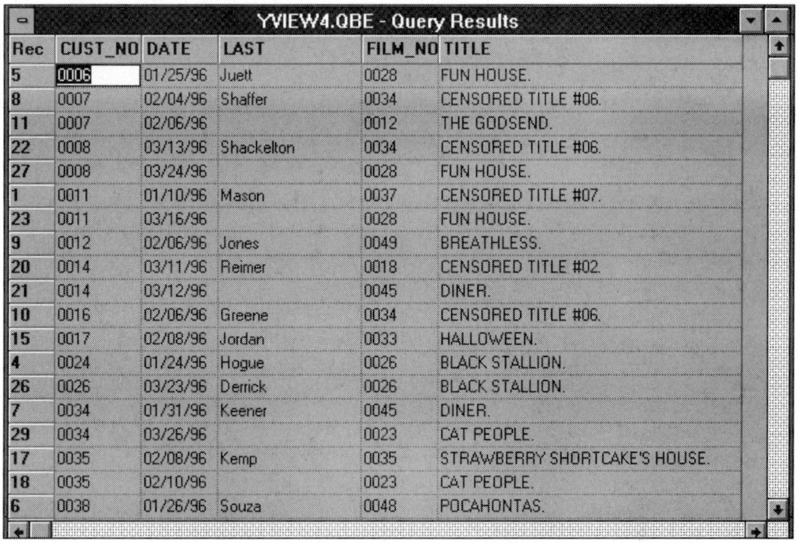

YVIEW4.QBE - Query Results

Rec	CUST_NO	DATE	LAST	FILM_NO	TITLE
5	0006	01/25/96	Juett	0028	FUN HOUSE.
8	0007	02/04/96	Shaffer	0034	CENSORED TITLE #06.
11	0007	02/06/96		0012	THE GODSEND.
22	0008	03/13/96	Shackelton	0034	CENSORED TITLE #06.
27	0008	03/24/96		0028	FUN HOUSE.
1	0011	01/10/96	Mason	0037	CENSORED TITLE #07.
23	0011	03/16/96		0028	FUN HOUSE.
9	0012	02/06/96	Jones	0049	BREATHLESS.
20	0014	03/11/96	Reimer	0018	CENSORED TITLE #02.
21	0014	03/12/96		0045	DINER.
10	0016	02/06/96	Greene	0034	CENSORED TITLE #06.
15	0017	02/08/96	Jordan	0033	HALLOWEEN.
4	0024	01/24/96	Hogue	0026	BLACK STALLION.
26	0026	03/23/96	Derrick	0026	BLACK STALLION.
7	0034	01/31/96	Keener	0045	DINER.
29	0034	03/26/96		0023	CAT PEOPLE.
17	0035	02/08/96	Kemp	0035	STRAWBERRY SHORTCAKE'S HOUSE.
18	0035	02/10/96		0023	CAT PEOPLE.
6	0038	01/26/96	Souza	0048	POCAHONTAS.

CHAPTER SUMMARY

In this chapter, we learned how to build Visual dBASE views of a database. Views were constructed from the Command window and from the Query Designer. The following topics were discussed:

- **Multiple table system design.** Database design is part of the overall systems analysis and design and process. Analysis is a necessary prerequisite to good design. The types of relationships allowed in Visual dBASE are one-to-many, many-to-one, and one-to-one. A many-to-many relationship can also be accomplished. Multiple child relationships are also allowed.
- **Work areas.** Visual dBASE allows 225 work areas. Each work area may contain a database table and all the peripheral files to that table, such as `.fmt`, `.dbt`, `.ndx`, or `.mdx`.

- **Using the set relation command.** The `SET RELATION` command is used to link tables to form a multiple table view of a database.
- **Use of Visual dBASE views.** A view is way of looking at a database for a specific purpose, such as a report or browse windows. A view may contain the table relationships, a field list, sort order, and filter conditions.
- **Physically joining tables.** The `JOIN` command allows the programmer to join tables physically to form a flat file representation of a multiple table view. It is a very slow process and should be used sparingly.
- **Using the Query Designer.** The Query Designer is a two-way tool available to the Visual dBASE programmer to develop database views. This design tool generates source code from the information presented to the designer work surface and stores it in a query file with a `.qbe` extension.

The following new commands were discussed:

- `USE`
- `SELECT`
- `SET RELATION TO`
- `SET FIELDS`
- `SET FILTER`
- `CREATE VIEW FROM ENVIRONMENT`
- `CREATE/MODIFY QUERY`

Three new functions were introduced:

- `MOD( )`
- `SELECT( )`
- `FOUND( )`

In the next chapter we will discuss printing reports from Visual dBASE. We will first use Visual dBASE syntax to develop reports and then introduce the Crystal Reports report generator.

CHAPTER TWELVE

TOPICS

New Commands and Functions

Concepts

Streaming output
Using Crystal Reports

Review Exercises

Chapter Summary

Reporting from Visual dBASE

12

CHAPTER OBJECTIVES

The interface with the user is of paramount importance to the success of a system. The importance of proper programming of the data entry interface has already been discussed. However, the output is one of the primary purposes of the system and in a large way determines its effectiveness.

Visual dBASE offers a variety of nonprogramming methods to produce output. In this chapter we will confine our discussions to programming custom output and to the use of the Crystal Reports report generator. Crystal Reports is a third-party product that has been licensed by Borland to be included in Visual dBASE. It has been retrofitted to work together with Visual dBASE and can be used for a wide variety of reports ranging from simple database table listings to complex reports involving summaries and data grouping. Moreover, it allows the use of graphic pictures, lines, and boxes.

After studying this chapter, the student should understand the output command syntax of Visual dBASE and how to program an efficient custom report model using that syntax. The student should also be able to produce reports using the Crystal Reports report generator. Both types of reports will be attached as menu items to the Case System.

NEW COMMANDS AND FUNCTIONS

Several of the commands introduced in this section will not include examples at this time. They work together with other commands and are part of the overall print concepts of Visual dBASE. These concepts will be discussed and demonstrated later in the chapter, to be followed by the building of an output print model.

COMMAND

```
SET PRINTER TO [[FILE] <>>\filename|?|>filename skeleton]|
    [>device>]
```

Uses a device code that will be recognized by the Windows Print Manager to designate a printer. It is also used to send output to a file. A Windows print document must be opened when printing from Visual dBASE. **SET PRINTER TO <device>** opens a print document for a designated printer.

COMMAND

```
SET PRINTER on/OFF307
```

If toggled on, directs the output of streaming output commands such as **?/??**, **TALK**, **LIST**. If the **CONSOLE** command is also on, data is directed both to the screen and to the printer. The default value of **PRINTER** is **OFF** and **CONSOLE** is **ON**.

COMMAND

```
CLOSE PRINTER
```

Used to close a Windows print document previously opened with the **SET PRINTER TO** command.

EXAMPLE

```
CLEAR
SET PRINTER ON     && Assumes open print document.
? "THIS INFO GOES TO BOTH SCREEN AND PRINTER!!"
SET PRINTER OFF
```

Certain commands have **SET PRINTER ON/SET PRINTER OFF** built in. For example, **LIST lname, address TO PRINTER** toggles the printer on and off automatically. Other examples are **DISPLAY**, **REPORT FORM**, and **TYPE**.

COMMAND

```
?/?? [<expression 1> [PICTURE <expC>>]
    [FUNCTION <function list>] [AT <expN>]
    [STYLE [<fontstyle expN>] | [<fontstyle expC>]]
    [,<expression 2...]
```

This print command was introduced previously, but not all clauses were presented. The **AT** clause allows exact column position of data, and the

STYLE clause allows use of various font numbers or font styles of output presentation. Each expression in the **?/??** expression list can be separately formatted. The following font styles can be used in the **STYLE** clause:

B—Bold
I—Italic
U—Underline
R—Superscript (raised)
L—Subscript (lowered)

EXAMPLE
```
CLEAR
? "This begins in column 5." AT 5
?? "Same ROW, column 40." AT 40
SET PRINTER ON    && Assumes open print document.
? "Begin at column 10--BOLD FACE TYPE." AT 10
     STYLE "B", "NOT BOLD" AT 50
SET PRINTER OFF
```

COMMAND **???**

Sends output directly to the printer. The installed printer driver is bypassed. Primarily used to send control codes to the printer. This command is handy for sending the printer a control code that is not included in the printer driver. If control codes are in the driver, the **?/??** command and the system memory variables are better ways of sending them. System memory variables will be explained later in the chapter.

EXAMPLE
```
??? CHR(27) + "E"   && Send "reset" print code to HP
                    && LaserJet II Printer.
```

The same control code escape sequence, **ESC-E**, can be encoded as follows:

```
??? "{ESC}E"                 && Use control character
                             && specifiers.
or
??? "{27}{69}"               && Use ASCII codes in braces.
```

COMMAND **EJECT**

Causes the printer to eject to top of next page. **SET PRINTER** does not have to be on for **EJECT** to work.

COMMAND **SET MARGIN TO <expN>**

Causes left page offset of printed output to be set to the value of the numeric expression. Does not affect the screen. The default value is 0.

COMMAND **ON PAGE [AT LINE <expN> <command>]**

This is the first Visual dBASE **ON** command to be introduced. **ON** commands allow for the execution of routines when certain events occur during the execution of a program. The event in **ON PAGE** is when a certain line number is reached in the streaming output to the printer. When that line number **<expN>** is reached, the coded **<command>** in the syntax will be executed. Streaming output and usage of this command will be discussed in detail in a separate section of this chapter.

COMMAND `EJECT PAGE`

Either advances the streaming output to the defined page handler or ejects to the top of the next page. This command works in conjunction with the `ON PAGE` command.

COMMAND `PRINTJOB..ENDPRINTJOB`

Structured programming print construct to control a print job.

COMMAND

```
CREATE REPORT |<filename>|
MODIFY REPORT |<filename>|
```

Used to either create a new report from Crystal Reports or to modify an existing report. If a filename is not specified, **CREATE REPORT** opens the Report Designer for design of a new unnamed report.

COMMAND

```
REPORT FORM <filename1> | ? | <filename skeleton1>
    [<scope>] [FOR <condition1>] [WHILE <condition2>]
    [CROSSTAB] [HEADING <expC>]
    [NOEJECT] [PLAIN] [SUMMARY]
    [TO FILE <filename2> | ? | <filename skeleton2>]
    | [TO PRINTER]
```

Generates and displays or prints a report from a specified report file. If the report file was created using Crystal Reports, it will have an **.rpt** extension; if created from DOS dBASE, it will have an **.frm** extension. If no extension is supplied, Visual dBASE will first assume an **.rpt** extension, then look for a **.frm** or **.frg** extension.

FUNCTION `DATE()`

Returns the system date. **DATE()** is in date type format.

EXAMPLE

```
CLEAR
DATE()
? DATE() + 45
? DATE() - 30
```

Note from these examples that you can do date arithmetic with the date function.

FUNCTION `CHOOSEPRINTER (<title expC>)`

Opens the Windows Print Setup dialog for printer selection and options. It also resets appropriate systems memory variables. If the user exits the Print Setup dialog by choosing the **OK** button, `CHOOSEPRINTER()` returns a logical `.T.`; if the user chooses the **Cancel** button, it returns a logical `.F.` The `<title expC>` clause allows passage of a title parameter to the Printer Setup dialog. The following Input pane example assumes you have two Windows printers installed. Execute the commands a second time to select the original printer driver.

```
CLEAR
? _pdriver                             && Current printer.
xValue = CHOOSEPRINTER("My Title") && Open Print Dialog
                                   && change printers.
? xValue, _pdriver      && Display new printer
                        && driver and xValue.
```

FUNCTION `CENTER(<expC|<memo field>[,<length expN> [,<pad expC>\>]])`

Returns a centered character string within a line of specified length. The following example will center a title within a 60-space line.

EXAMPLE

```
? CENTER("REPORT TITLE", 60)
```

CONCEPTS

There are a number of different ways to print from Visual dBASE. We will discuss both the programming of streaming output and the use of Crystal Reports. The advantage of programming streaming output is that the code will be concise and take up less space. The report will also run faster than one using Crystal Reports. The advantage of using Crystal Reports is that no code is written. Once the report is designed within Crystal, it is also executed by Crystal. Further, the report is designed in a full Windows graphical environment.

Visual dBASE allows the selection of a printer driver either programmatically or from within Windows. Programmatically, it can be set using the `_pdriver` systems memory variable. In our Case System chapter exercises, we will use the `CHOOSEPRINTER()` function to give the user the ability to change printers from the Video Express system File menu.

STREAMING OUTPUT

Most Visual dBASE output commands produce *streaming* output. As the name implies, the data moves to the output device in a continuous serial stream. Codes within the data may control the output device. For example, a code within the stream could set a printer to condensed mode. Commands such as `?/??`, `LIST`, `DISPLAY`, `REPORT FORM`, `REPORT LABEL`, `EJECT PAGE`, and `TEXT..ENDTEXT` all produce streaming output.

NOTE: DOS versions of dBASE recommend sending streaming output to the printer and formatted output to the screen. Formatted output allows for the placement of characters at random on the screen. The `@..SAY..GET` command is used to generate DOS formatted screen output. This command remains in Visual dBASE to execute DOS programs through the Results pane but is not used in the Windows environment.

The following is a summary of Visual dBASE streaming output command characteristics:

- Visual dBASE generates and maintains a group of system memory variables to control output (automatic page numbering, page breaks, etc.). They can be used only with streaming output.
- The `ON PAGE AT LINE` command can be used to control headers and footers. This feature is available only when using streaming output.
- The `EJECT PAGE` command is available to automatically supply line feeds until the `ON PAGE` line is reached.
- The `PRINTJOB..ENDPRINTJOB` construct allows automatic page ejects, number of copies printed, and control codes sent to the printer.
- Streaming output can be sent to the screen, the printer, and a file, all at the same time (`SET CONSOLE`, `PRINTER`, and `ALTERNATE ON`). You can `SET DEVICE TO` either `SCREEN`, `PRINTER`, or `FILE` for `FORMATTED` output—but only one at a time.
- The `STYLE` clause is now available in the `?/??` command and not available in the `@..SAY`. This allows coding bold, italic, or other style elements selectively with each expression displayed.
- The `AT` clause in the `?/??` command allows exact column positioning of data within streaming output.

System Memory Variables. System memory variables are initialized and maintained by Visual dBASE to control the appearance of printed output. Each variable begins with the underscore character (_). You'll want to be careful not to precede the names of other memory variables with this character.

We will be using most of the following system memory variables either in chapter exercises or in the student Case System programming problem:

VARIABLE `_alignment = "LEFT"/"CENTER"/"RIGHT"`

Controls alignment of expressions displayed by the **?/??** command. As indicated, the expression can be left- or right-justified or centered.

VARIABLE `_pageno = <expN>`

Determines current page number. Also, can be used to set the page number.

VARIABLE `_pcopies = <expN>`

Determines how many copies will be printed. Works in conjunction with the **PRINTJOB..ENDPRINTJOB** construct. This command is discussed in more detail later in the chapter.

VARIABLE `_pdriver = "<printer driver filename>"`

Used to identify the current printer driver or to activate a new driver. Printer drivers used by Visual dBASE are installed using the Windows Control Panel, and the default driver is specified there. If no default is specified, `_pdriver` will contain a null string (`""`).

EXAMPLE
```
? _pdriver          && Identify current driver.
```

VARIABLE `_peject = "BEFORE"/"AFTER"/"BOTH"/"NONE"`

Used to determine if an eject will occur before and/or after a print job.

VARIABLE `_plength = <expN>`

Establishes the length of the output page. For example, it will contain 66 for an 11-inch page at 6 lines per inch.

VARIABLE `_plineno = <expN>`

Used either to assign a line number or to determine the current line number.

VARIABLE `_ploffset = <expN>`

Used to establish the left page offset. The left margin will begin at this point.

VARIABLE `_pspacing = 1/2/3`

Used to determine line spacing. The options are 1, 2, or 3.

There are system memory variables to control other print functions, such as the number of pages printed, beginning and ending pages of print, control codes sent to the printer, and right and left margins. Though we will not be using them in the Case System or Review Exercises, the remaining system memory variables are listed here for your information.

VARIABLE `_box = <condition>`

If this variable contains a **.T.**, the boxes specified in the **DEFINE BOX** command will be displayed.

VARIABLE `_indent = <expN>`

Specifies the indent of the first line of a new paragraph printed with the **?** command when the **_wrap** variable is **.T.**

VARIABLE `_lmargin = <expN>`

Specifies the left margin when using the **?** command when **_wrap** is **.T.** If **_lmargin** is used, its value is added to the value specified in **_ploffset**.

VARIABLE `_padvance = "FORMFEED"/"linefeeds"`

Determines how printer will advance paper.

VARIABLE `_pbpage = <expN>`

Specifies the beginning page for a **PRINTJOB**.

VARIABLE `_pcolno = <expN>`

Determines starting column of output stream.

VARIABLE `_pecode = <expN>`

Provides the ending control codes for a **PRINTJOB**.

VARIABLE `_pepage = <expN>`

Provides the ending page for a **PRINTJOB**.

VARIABLE `_pform = <expN>`

Contains the name of the current print form file (**.prf**).

VARIABLE `_porientation = <expC>`

Determines whether printing is generated in landscape or portrait mode. The character expression **<expC>** contains either **"PORTRAIT"** or **"LANDSCAPE"**.

VARIABLE `_ppitch = "pica"/"elite"/"condensed"/"DEFAULT"`

Used to set the printer pitch.

VARIABLE `_pquality = <condition>`

Used to select either quality or draft print mode.

VARIABLE `_pscode = <expC>`

Defines starting print codes for a **PRINTJOB**.

VARIABLE `_pwait = <condition>`

Used to determine whether printer will pause after each page.

VARIABLE `_rmargin = <expN>`

Determines the right margin of **?** output when **_wrap** is **.T.**

VARIABLE `_tabs = <expC>`

Defines a character type list of tab stops for output to the screen, printer, or file. Also, sets default stops for the Visual dBASE editor.

VARIABLE `_wrap = <condition>`

If Word Wrap is on, text automatically wraps to the next line when it nears the right margin, and a soft carriage return is inserted at the end of the wrapped line. This variable is used to toggle Word Wrap on or off between margins in the Visual dBASE editors.

Sections of a Visual dBASE Report. Visual dBASE describes a typical report using the following section names—also referred to as *bands* (Figure 12.1):

- Page header — Printed once at the top of each page (for example, page number, date, or column headings).
- Report intro — Printed once at the beginning of each report (for example, report title).
- Detail — This is the body of the report. Usually consists of records from the database.
- Report summary — Usually consists of column totals or related descriptive information.
- Page footer — Printed once at the bottom of each page. Usually contains the page number and other information needed on each page.

FIGURE 12.1 SECTIONS OF A VISUAL dBASE REPORT

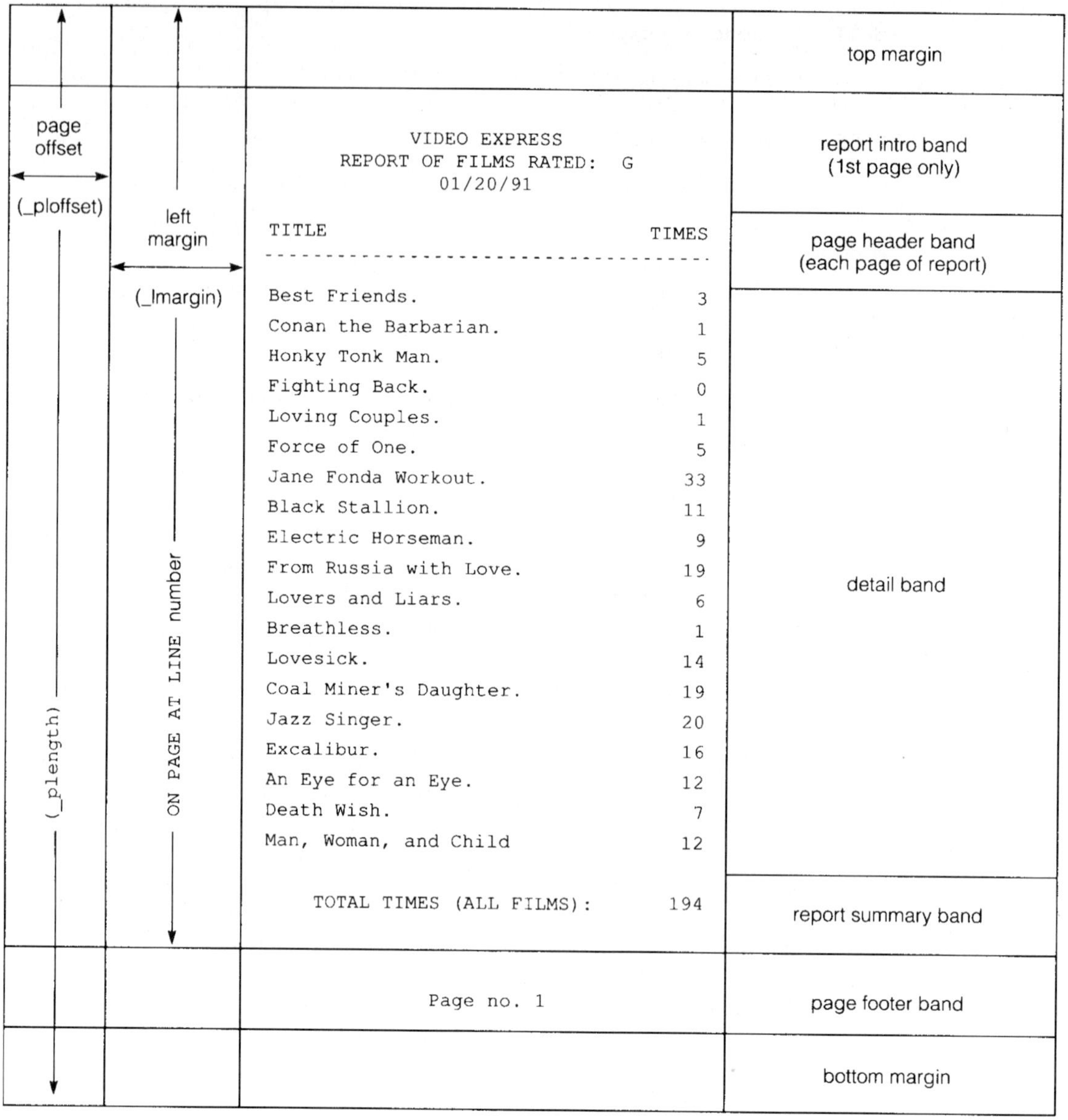
top margin
page offset
(_ploffset)
left margin
(_lmargin)
ON PAGE AT LINE number
(_plength)
VIDEO EXPRESS
REPORT OF FILMS RATED: G
01/20/91
report intro band
(1st page only)
TITLE
TIMES
page header band
(each page of report)
Best Friends. 3
Conan the Barbarian. 1
Honky Tonk Man. 5
Fighting Back. 0
Loving Couples. 1
Force of One. 5
Jane Fonda Workout. 33
Black Stallion. 11
Electric Horseman. 9
From Russia with Love. 19
Lovers and Liars. 6
Breathless. 1
Lovesick. 14
Coal Miner's Daughter. 19
Jazz Singer. 20
Excalibur. 16
An Eye for an Eye. 12
Death Wish. 7
Man, Woman, and Child 12
detail band
TOTAL TIMES (ALL FILMS): 194
report summary band
Page no. 1
page footer band
bottom margin

The `ON PAGE` Command. Visual dBASE has the ability to keep track of page breaks and the printing of headers and footers. To do this, it counts the number of lines printed, including the header, by incrementing the value in the `_plineno` system variable. After a page break, it returns it to its initial value. When `_plineno` reaches a certain value, as determined by the programmer when the report is designed, Visual dBASE gives the programmer the opportunity to print a footer prior to ejecting to the next page. This relieves the programmer of having to keep track of the lines printed with programmed counters and the like. The `ON PAGE` command keeps track of the value in `_plineno` and causes the footer to print and page eject.

As mentioned earlier, in our discussion of new commands, the `ON PAGE` command determines when a page break will occur, and then it executes a specified command. The `<command>` clause can be an individual command or a `DO <program/procedurename>`, which would execute a subprogram or procedure. The individual command or procedure executed is called the *page handler* and usually determines how headers and footers will be presented.

The programmer computes the `AT LINE` number. Visual dBASE then begins counting in `_plineno`, including the lines of the header and title. When it reaches the `AT LINE` number, it triggers the execution of the page handler procedure. As you will see in the following example, once this criteria has been established, the interrupt may occur at any time during the execution of your program. The `AT LINE` expression number is computed using the following formula (see Figure 12.2):

```
<expN> = _plength (page length) - footer lines - bottom margin
```

Notice in Figure 12.2 that the `AT LINE` value includes the page header and title. If `ON PAGE` is executed with no argument, the page handler is canceled.

Streaming Output Print Model. The program segment in Figure 12.2 exemplifies the use of the `ON PAGE` command and system memory variables.

FIGURE 12.2 VISUAL dBASE STREAMING OUTPUT PRINT MODEL

```
* ==> STREAMING OUTPUT PRINT MODEL
USE ycustm
ON PAGE AT LINE 55 DO page_brak

*_pdriver  = "HPPCL5E ,HP LaserJet 4 Plus/4M Plus"  && Set active driver.
_pageno   = 1           && Starting page number.
_pspacing = 1           && Single space report.
_ploffset  = 10         && Left offset to 10.
_plineno  = 1           && Starting line number.
_peject   = "NONE"      && No eject after last page.
SET PRINTER TO LPT1     && Open a Windows print document.
SET PRINTER ON          && Send output to printer.
?
? CENTER ("TOTAL RENT AMOUNT REPORT",60) STYLE "B"    && Header, bold.
? "NAME" + SPACE(46) + "TOTAL RENT"
? REPLICATE ("=",60)    && Double line

SCAN ALL
  ?  last AT 0
  ?? amt_rent FUNCTION "$" AT 53
ENDSCAN

EJECT PAGE
DO footer         && Last page footer.
EJECT

SET PRINTER OFF         && End printed output.
CLOSE PRINTER           && Close print document.
ON PAGE
USE               && Close table.
RETURN
* ==> End of program segment -- ysample.prg

* ==> In-Program Procedures -- ysample.prg
PROCEDURE page_brak
  IF EOF()
     RETURN
  ENDIF
  DO footer
  DO header

RETURN
```

FIGURE 12.2 VISUAL dBASE STREAMING OUTPUT PRINT MODEL (continued)

```
PROCEDURE header
  ?
  ? "NAME" + SPACE(46) + "TOTAL RENT"
  ? REPLICATE ("=",60)
  ?
RETURN

PROCEDURE footer
  ?
  ?
  ? CENTER ("Page No. " + LTRIM(STR(_pageno,3,0)),60)
  EJECT PAGE
RETURN
* ==> End of program segment yprint.prg.
```

Follow the example in Figure 12.2 carefully. It will be the basic model you will want to use when building a streaming output print program. As you look through the example, note the following:

- **ON PAGE AT LINE 55** is coded at the beginning of the program. The **_plength** system variable has a default value of 66 (using a standard 11-inch page with 6 lines per inch spacing). The **AT LINE** number was computed as the page length (**_plength**) minus a footer of 6 lines minus a bottom margin of 5 lines equals 55.
- The appropriate system variables are set to their initial values.
- The first page will contain a page title in addition to column headings. It will be printed as one heading and appear only on the first page. Because the information is printed only once, this routine is not contained in the header procedure. Remember, procedures are routines that will be executed repeatedly.
- **The SCAN..ENDSCAN** will now print the entire database. However, it will take more than one page, so headers and footers will be needed. **ON PAGE** will cause the following to occur during the **SCAN..ENDSCAN** printing:
- The first time the line number reaches 55, the **page_brak** procedure will be executed. The **EOF()** will not have been reached, so the **footer** procedure will be executed. The **EJECT PAGE** in the footer procedure will cause the page eject after the footer print. The first page now has a title header, a set of records listed (detail) and a footer.

- Control now goes back to the **page_brak** procedure, which executes **DO header**. This causes the column headings header to be printed on the second page of the report. Control is then returned to the **SCAN..ENDSCAN** routine.
- Each time line **55** is reached, the same events will occur until the last record is printed. Just after the **ENDSCAN** command, the **EOF()** function will return a **.T.** This will cause **page_brak** to return control to the **EJECT PAGE** command just after the **ENDSCAN**. **EJECT PAGE** will supply line feeds until line **55** is reached. If you omit this command, the last page footer will be printed just after the last line of the report body.
- The last page footer can now be printed.
- Finally, execution of the **ON PAGE** command without an argument will disable the **ON PAGE** function.

The PRINTJOB..ENDPRINTJOB Construct. This construct allows control of continuous print jobs. For example, you may want to give the operator the option of printing only certain pages of a report, ejecting a single page before report printing begins, ejecting a page after printing stops, ejecting a page both before printing begins and after it stops, or allowing more than one copy of each page to be printed. The **PRINTJOB** portion of the construct does the following:

- Sends starting codes assigned to the **_pscode** variable to the printer. For example, you may want an entire report printed in condensed print. An individual line can be controlled by the **STYLE** clause of the **?/??**; however, in this situation the entire job is to be a certain style.
- Sends eject code to printer if **_peject** has been set to **BEFORE** or **BOTH**.
- Sets **_pcolno** to 0.

ENDPRINTJOB will then cause the following at the end of the print job:

- Send ending print codes defined in **_pecode** to the printer. For example, after printing a report in condensed mode, the printer should be set back to its normal style.
- An eject will be sent to the printer if **_peject** has been set to **AFTER** or **BOTH**.
- Causes a loop back to **PRINTJOB** the number of times coded in the **_pcopies** variable.

Use of the **PRINTJOB..ENDPRINTJOB** construct to print three copies of a report is demonstrated in the sample code in Figure 12.3. Similar commands could be added to the streaming print model presented in Figure 12.2.

FIGURE 12.3 PRINTJOB..ENDPRINTJOB EXAMPLE

```
* ==> PRINTJOB..ENDPRINTJOB example, ysample2.prg.

_ploffset   = 10      && Left offset to 10.
_pcopies    = 3       && PRINTJOB to print 3 copies.
_peject     = "NONE"

SET PRINTER TO LPT1 && Open a Windows print document.
SET PRINTER ON      && Send output to printer.

PRINTJOB            && Begin print job.
? "Sample print using PRINTJOB..ENDPRINTJOB"
EJECT               && Eject after each page.
ENDPRINTJOB         && End print job.

SET PRINTER OFF     && Stop sending output to printer.
CLOSE PRINTER       && Close print document.
* ==> End of program ysample2.prg
```

There may be times that you will want use the **REPORT FORM** command to print a Visual dBASE report that was generated using the dBASE DOS report generator. If so, the **PRINTJOB..ENDPRINTJOB** construct is built into the generated code. Notice in the following example that the filename contains an .frm extension.

EXAMPLE

```
_pcopies = 3
_peject = "AFTER"
REPORT FORM yprt.frm TO PRINT
```

USING CRYSTAL REPORTS

Crystal Reports can be opened from within Visual dBASE, and its functions have been integrated into Visual dBASE. However, keep in mind that they are two separate applications and you must use **Alt-Tab** to switch between the two. Also, do not close Visual dBASE while still in Crystal Reports because in some ways, Crystal runs as a child application to Visual dBASE and is still connected to that application.

We will demonstrate the use of Crystal Reports with a listing of the number of rentals taken by each customer listed for a requested city. The Case System program segment containing the report will allow an operator to enter the desired city. The report will also contain a bitmapped graphic in the heading.

Opening the Report Designer. To open the designer, type the following commands from the Input pane:

```
xCity = "Reno"              && City field variable.
CREATE REPORT yreport
```

From the Open Table Required dialog, choose `ycustm.dbf`. `xCity` will be used later in the exercise to receive the desired city from the operator when the report is requested.

There are a number of ways to enter Crystal Reports. Each of the following will take you to the Report Designer by way of the *Report Expert*. From the New Report dialog, you then choose **Designer** to enter the Report Designer.

- **From the Navigator.** Click the **Reports** file icon, then either double-click the **Untitled** icon or right-click **Untitled | New Report**. A faster method is to press **Shift-F2** (**Design**) either from the **Reports** icon or the **Untitled** icon.
- **From the Menu system.** After clicking the **Reports** file icon in the Navigator, select **Navigator | New Report**. You could also select **File | New | Report**.
- **From the Speedbar.** After clicking the **Reports** file icon in the Navigator, click the **Design** icon (the triangle and ruler just to the left of center).

NOTE: We will not be using the Report Expert. It is an excellent tool to design a generic report based on an open view or table. However, our approach is to design each element of a report from the Report Designer. After learning how to use the Report Designer, you may want to explore the Report Expert for generic designs that can be fine-tuned with the Designer itself. If you want to toggle the Report Expert off when entering the Report Designer, select **Properties | Desktop | Application Tab**. Remove the check mark (**x**) from the **Report** checkbox under **Prompt for Experts**.

The following is a general overview of the Report Designer desktop. We will explore each component in more depth later in the chapter (refer to Figure 12.4).

- **Menu system.** Unlike the items of the Form Designer menu system, items of the Report Designer menu remain constant throughout the design process and apply only to the report design process.
- **Speedbar.** As with other segments of Visual dBASE, the Speedbar is used in lieu of a menu item to expedite an action. Refer to Figure 12.5 for the functionality of each icon. Crystal refers to this as the Button Bar.

FIGURE 12.4 CRYSTAL REPORTS DESKTOP

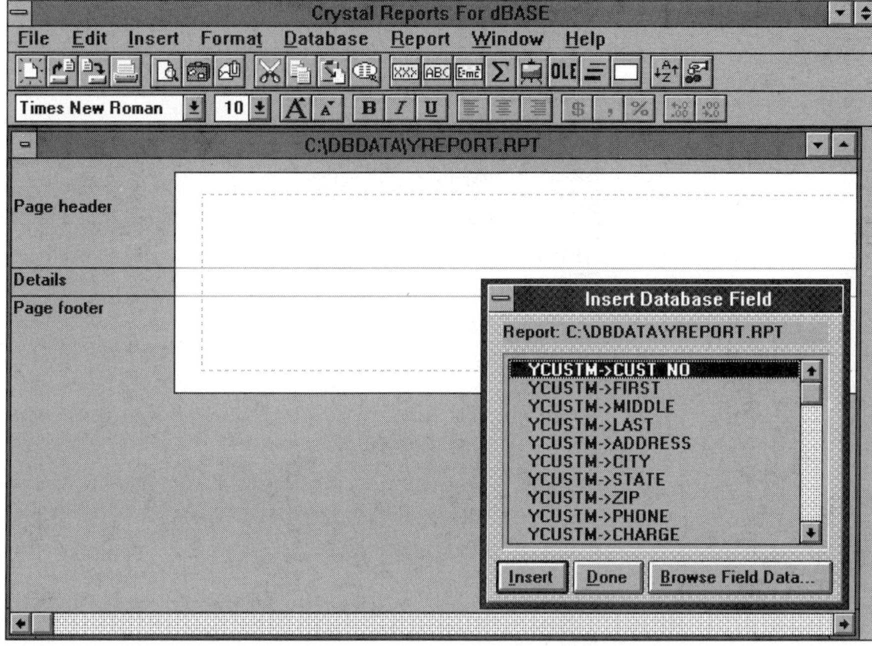

- **Format Bar.** Used to format text with font, font size, bold, italic, or underline styles.
- **Specification window.** You will build your report in this window. It currently contains the Page header, Details, and Page footer bands (referred to as "sections" in Crystal Reports).
- **Insert Database Field dialog.** You will select the fields from the open table or view from this dialog.
- **Status bar.** This area is used to display information such as which table or view is open and the coordinates of items placed in the report.

FIGURE 12.5 CRYSTAL REPORTS SPEEDBAR (BUTTON BAR)

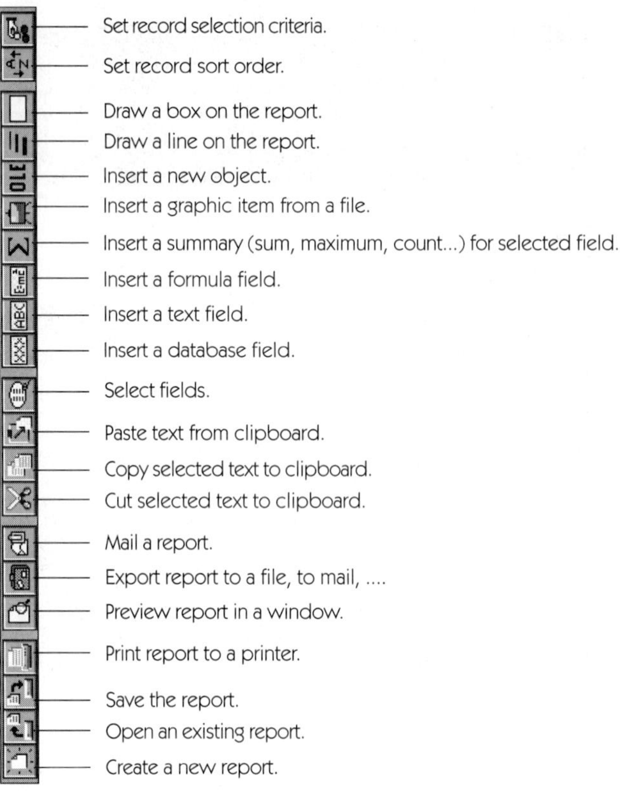

FIGURE 12.6 INSERT FORMULA DIALOG BOX

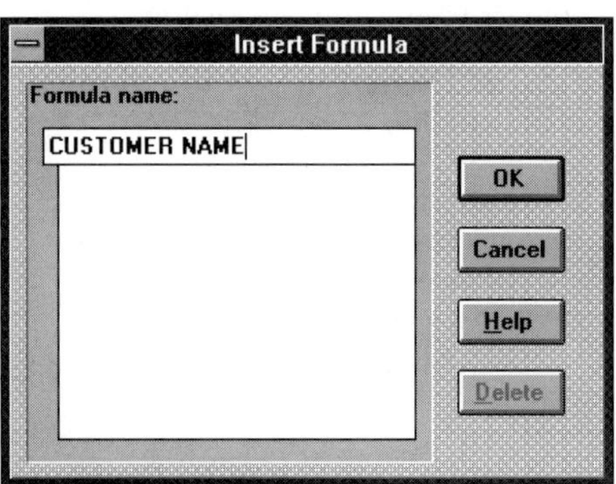

Inserting Fields. Proceed as follows to place field items in the report:

1. The Insert Database Field dialog box should currently be on the screen. It can be opened at any time from the Insert menu, (**Insert | Database field**), or by pressing the **Insert a database field** icon from the Speedbar. From the Insert Database Field dialog, drag the `cust_no` field, to the Details band of the report specification area (see Figure 12.8). Notice that when you begin to drag the field, the cursor becomes a rectangle. The rectangle automatically resizes to the field size as you drag it into the specification area.

2. Drag the `no_rents` field to the report specification area (see Figure 12.8). We won't need the Insert Database Field dialog any more, so remove it from the desktop.

Inserting a Formula Field. Our report will contain the full name of the customer as a character expression. Proceed as follows:

1. Click the **Insert a formula field** icon from the Speedbar (or select **Insert | Formula Field**). This will cause the Insert Formula dialog to appear. Type the formula name, `CUSTOMER NAME` as shown in Figure 12.6. Finally, click the **OK** button.

2. The Expression Builder dialog box should now appear on your screen. We want to include the full name of the customer as the second column on our report. To accomplish this, enter the following expression:

   ```
   RTRIM(YCUSTM->LAST) + ", " + YCUSTM->FIRST
   ```

   Click the **Evaluate** button to ensure the expression was entered properly (see Figure 12.7). If the expression is satisfactory, click the **OK** button.

3. The rectangle cursor should now appear on the Crystal Reports desktop. Move it into position as the second column on the report as shown in Figure 12.8. A left mouse click will finalize the dragging movement.

FIGURE 12.7 EXPRESSION BUILDER DIALOG BOX

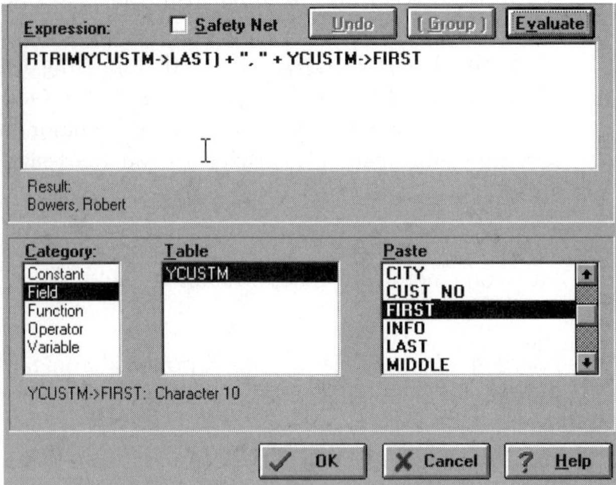

Previewing the Report. Preview the report by clicking the **Preview the report in a window** icon in the Speedbar (or select **File | Print | Window**). You will find another series of Speedbar icons along the bottom of the Preview Window icons. Click the **Magnifying Glass** icon to further magnify the preview, then again to preview the entire page. One final click will bring the preview back to its original size. Finally, click the **CLOSE** button in the preview window speedbar to close the preview.

Inserting a Report Title. Our report will contain a two-line title. The first line will define the report and the second will contain a variable that displays the requested city (see Figure 12.8). Proceed as follows:

1. Click the insertion point cursor in the Header band of the report specification area. Press **<enter>** eight times to open a few lines of blank space to receive the report title and graphic.

   NOTE: To delete a line, press the **delete** key. Once a field has been placed in a section, you can move it by first giving it focus, then pressing the **arrow** keys. The field can also be sized horizontally using standard Windows mouse or arrow-key movements (press **Shift-Right** or **Shift-Left** arrow or click and drag field handles).

2. Click the **Insert a text field** icon or Select **Insert | Text Field**. This will cause the Edit Text Field dialog to appear. Type `NUMBER OF CUSTOMER RENTALS, BY CITY` as shown on the report in Figure 12.8. Click the **Accept** button to complete.

3. Drag the rectangle cursor to a position three lines above the current column header text (`CUST_NO`) to place the title on the report.

4. The second line of the title will be a formula field. Click the **Insert a formula field** icon to access the Insert Formula dialog box. Type `XCITY VALUE` into the dialog to name the formula field and press **OK** to complete this operation and gain access to the Expression Builder dialog. Type the following expression into the Expression Builder dialog, including quotes and spaces:

   ```
   "City = " + XCITY
   ```

   Click the **Evaluate** button to ensure the expression has been entered correctly. Prior to entry into Crystal Reports, we assigned the character string `"Reno"` to `xCity`. This variable must still be active for this expression to evaluate correctly. If it evaluates correctly, click the **OK** button.

5. Drag this completed formula field to the report specification area. Place it on the line just below the first line of the title. Refer to Figure 12.8.

6. Preview the report using the **Preview report in a window** icon. Don't worry about margins or other data formatting at this point.

Inserting a Bit Map. Our report will contain a report header graphic. Borland includes a few bitmap graphic files with the sample problems in Visual dBASE. We will use one of those for our report header graphic. Proceed as follows:

1. Click the **Insert a graphic item from a file** icon (or select **Insert | Graphic**). This will display the Choose Graphic File dialog box. Choose the following file from the `samples` subdirectory (assuming Visual dBASE has been installed in the default directory):

   ```
   C:\VISUALDB\SAMPLES\AIRBRLN2.BMP
   ```

2. Move the AirBorland graphic to the upper left-hand corner of your report using the mouse cursor. Click the mouse to complete the movement. There should be one horizontal space between the graphic and the first line of the report title.

FIGURE 12.8 BASIC REPORT SPECIFICATION, `yreport.rpt`

FIGURE 12.9 INSERT GRAND TOTAL DIALOG BOX

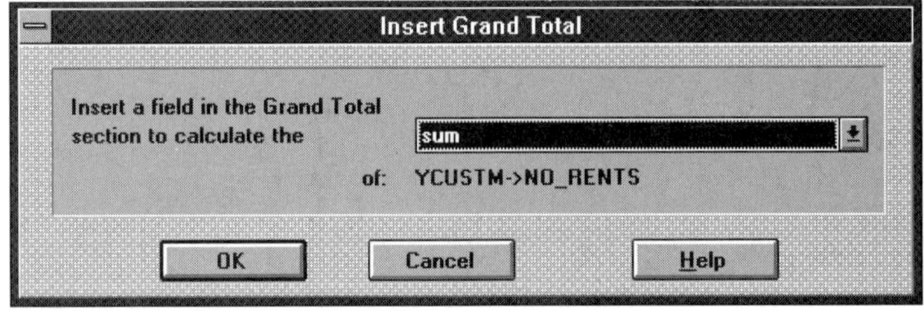

Adding a Summary Band. Our report is to contain a summary of rentals for all customers. To add this item to the report, proceed as follows:

1. Give focus to the `no_rents` field in the Details band of the report specification area. Scroll the report as necessary to bring the field into full view. Select **Insert | Summary Field | Grand Total**.
2. The Insert Grand Total dialog box should now appear on your screen (see Figure 12.9). It allows for many types of summaries. Click the **drop-down list arrow** for a complete list. We will select the default setting **Sum** by clicking the **OK** button.

NOTE: If you need to delete a section from a report, select **Edit | Delete Section**. You also have the ability to hide sections (**Edit | Show/Hide Sections**). This is convenient when designing a busy report. Be sure to show all sections prior to printing.

3. Preview the report to make sure the grand total is presented in the correct location. When this report file is called by your program, the operator will enter the required city for selective printing. Until a specific city is requested, all the records in the table will be displayed by Crystal Reports. For this reason, your summary value may be on the second page of the report during this preview. Use the page scroll arrows at the lower left of the preview window to move forward or back a page.

4. We will want a blank line between the last Detail section item and the grand total summary line. To accomplish this, insert a blank line and then drag the summary field down one line. Finally, add a text field just to the left of the summary field as follows (refer to the final report in Figure 12.18):

   *** **Total Number of Rents:**

Formatting a Report. Crystal Reports gives the designer a number of formatting options to make a report easier to read by the user. Proceed as follows:

1. **Naming the report.** You can supply a title to your report for reference. This title will appear in the title bar of each window containing the report during its design. Click **Format | Report Title** to access the Edit Report Title dialog box. Type `RENTS BY CITY REPORT` as a report title (see Figure 12.10).

FIGURE 12.10 EDIT REPORT TITLE DIALOG BOX

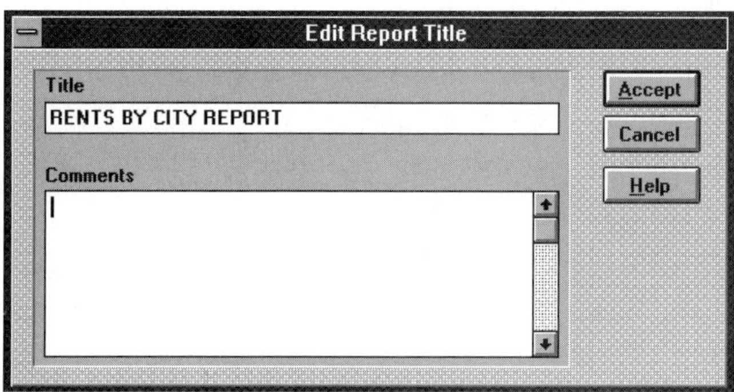

FIGURE 12.11 PRINTER MARGINS DIALOG BOX

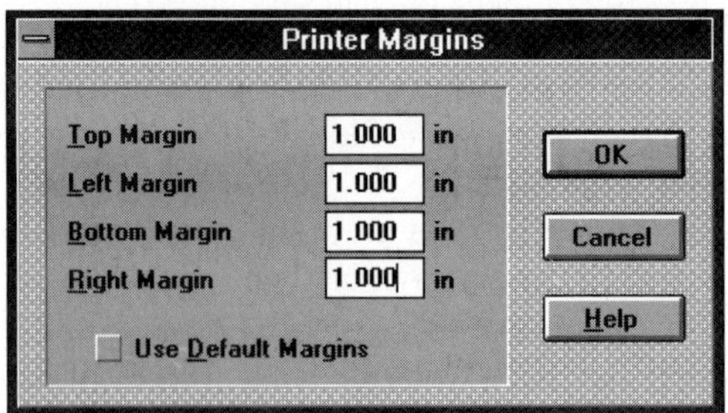

2. **Setting margins.** Select **File | Page Margins**. This will cause the Printer Margins dialog to appear (see Figure 12.11). Set all margins to one inch. Click **OK** to complete.

3. **Adjusting columns.** We want to make the `no_rents` column flush to the right margin of the report. This can be accomplished from the design specification area or from any percentage level of the preview window. To make column adjustments to our report, click the **Preview Report** icon from the speedbar, then click the **Magnifying Glass** icon under the preview window one time.

   Now, click to select, then drag the `NO_RENTS` column heading text field flush to the right margin. Next, click the column data and drag it flush to the right margin. Notice that the entire column of data is highlighted for the dragging operation (see Figure 12.12). Finally, drag the summary field and the adjoining text field descriptor flush to the right margin.

FIGURE 12.12 COLUMN DRAG FROM PREVIEW WINDOW

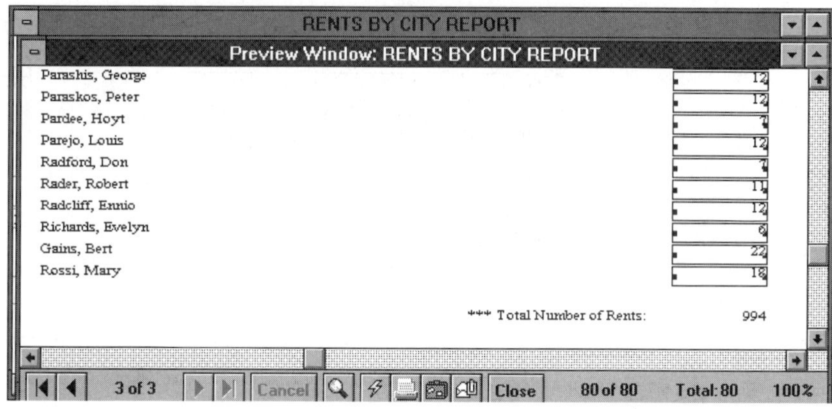

NOTE: The preceding adjustments can also be accomplished from the design specification area rather than from a preview window. The advantage of the preview window is that you can view the entire report during the adjustments. However, you may find the dragging operations easier from the design specification area.

While in the design specification area, to move the cursor across a horizontal line such as the heading line, use the **Tab** key. Use the **Left-arrow** key to return it to the left. Finally, you may find it easier to move the field flush to the right margin using the arrow keys versus using the mouse.

4. **Changing fonts**. Our next exercise will be to change the font of the first line of the report title. If not already there, return to the Report Designer from the preview window. The default font in Crystal Reports is Times New Roman. To change the font, select the first line of the title, then click **Format | Font**. Change the font to a 14 point Arial boldface from the Font dialog box. Refer to Figure 12.13. These font parameters can also be changed from the speedbar.

5. **Centering headings.** We will center all the elements of the heading section of the report. The most accurate method of centering a text element is to adjust the size of the element to the width of the margins, then let Crystal Reports center the text within the element. You can also center text or graphic elements by dragging them with the mouse. Proceed as follows:

FIGURE 12.13 FONT DIALOG BOX

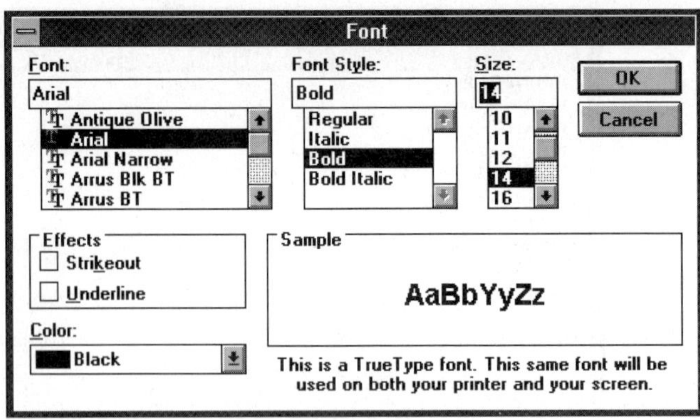

- Adjust the horizontal size of both text lines of the title to make them flush with both margins (see Figure 12.14).
- Rather than centering each line individually, we will select and center both fields in the same operation. Select **Edit | Select Fields.** This will give you a crosshair cursor. Press and hold the left mouse button, then draw a box to select the two text fields. You do not have to select the entire field. Just make sure the box formed covers any segment of both text fields (see Figure 12.15).
- Center the text in the two fields of the title by selecting **Format | Field**. From the **Alignment** drop-down list of the Format String dialog box, click **Centered** then the **OK** button. You can also center text by clicking the center alignment icon in the Format Speedbar (see Figure 12.14).
- Center the AirBorland graphic in the header section by first giving it focus, then dragging it to a centered position between the right and left margin.

6. **Modify column heading text.** We will modify the column heading text to remove the underscore characters. Crystal Reports provides a convenient drop-down menu for this and other formatting modifications. Proceed as follows:

FIGURE 12.14 ADJUSTING TEXT ELEMENTS TO MARGINS

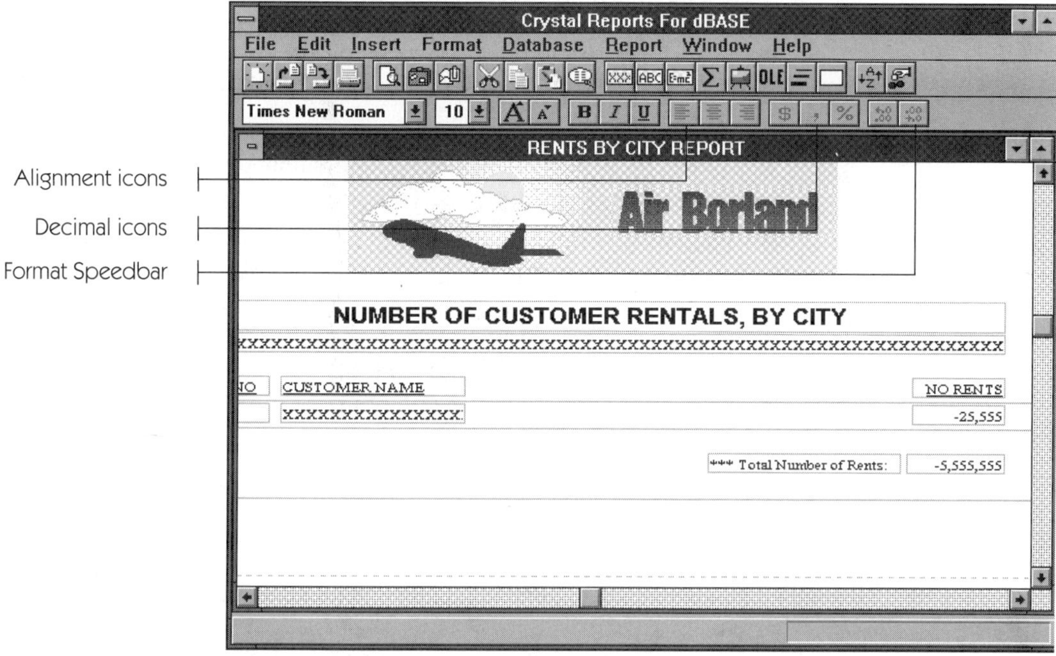

FIGURE 12.15 MULTIPLE FIELD SELECTION

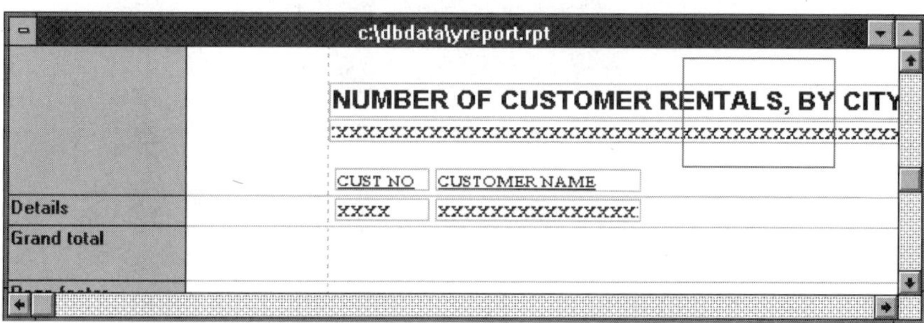

- Give focus to the first column heading text field, `CUST_NO`. Right-click the field to display the **Format Menu** (see Figure 12.16). Select **Edit Text Field** from the menu. Edit the column heading text in the Edit Text dialog to remove the underscore character (`CUST_NO` to `CUST NO`). Click **Accept** to complete.
- Give focus to the third column. Edit the text in the same manner to remove the underscore character (`NO_RENTS` to `NO RENTS`).

7. **Formatting a numeric field.** The `no_rents` field is a whole number and will never be a fraction. However, the summary field for that column is marked to two decimal places. To correct this, proceed as follows:

   - Give focus to the summary field in the Grand Total section of the report. Right-click the field to display the **Format Menu** (see Figure 12.16). Select **Change Format** to display the Format Number dialog box (see Figure 12.17). This could also be accomplished from the menu system with **Format | Field**.
   - Select the whole number one (`1`) from the Decimals list box (see Figure 12.17). Click the **OK** button to close the dialog box.
   - Preview the report to ensure that the format of the grand total field is correct.

FIGURE 12.16 FORMAT MENU

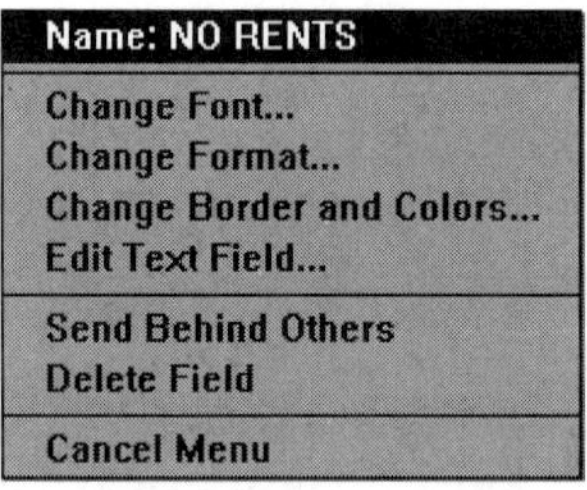

FIGURE 12.17 FORMAT NUMBER DIALOG BOX

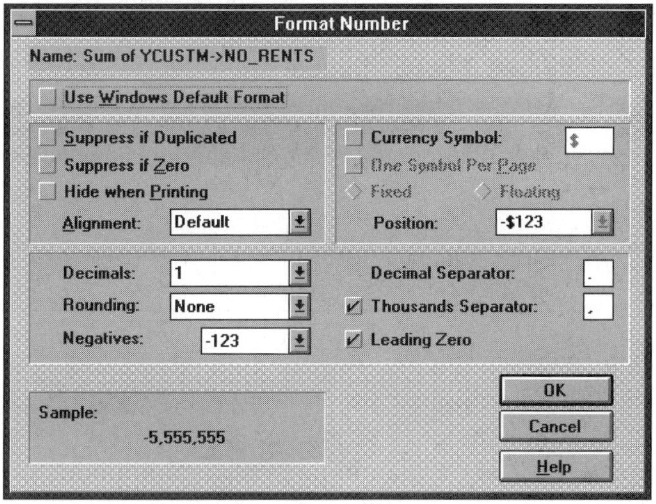

Note: By default, Crystal Reports saves table print data until an update is requested from the Crystal main menu. This can be advantageous at times: for example, when sending a follow-up e-mail about a report printed on an earlier date. Nevertheless, for our tests we want the data to be current with each printing. To change the default setting, select **File | Options** from the Crystal main menu. From the Options dialog that appears, click **General** as a **Category**, then check **Refresh data on every print**.

Final Testing of the Report. Our final test of the report will be from the Command window. Proceed as follows:

1. Select **File | Close | Yes** to save the report. Select **Alt-Tab** to return to Visual dBASE.
2. Type the following command from the Input pane:

```
xCity = "Burlingame"
REPORT FORM yreport FOR city = xCity
```

This should present the report in a window. If everything looks correct, close the print window and proceed to the next step.

3. To test for a different city and send the report to the printer, type the following from the Input pane:

```
xCity = "San Mateo"
REPORT FROM yreport FOR city = xCity TO PRINT
```

Your final printed report should appear as in Figure 12.18.

FIGURE 12.18 FINAL PRINT TEST, `yreport.rpt`

NUMBER OF CUSTOMER RENTALS, BY CITY

City = San Mateo

CUST NO	CUSTOMER NAME	NO RENTS
0007	Shaffer, Mark	7
0009	Goodson, Todd	32
0011	Mason, Al	10
0013	Grey, Dana	4
0014	Reimer, Peter	10
0019	Steele, Karen	4
0021	Wilkenson, Robert	9
0023	Fry, Kenneth	4
0024	Hogue, Janice	10
0025	Dianich, Eva	10
0026	Derrick, Sean	10
0027	Mason, David	10
0028	Hayes, Larry	90
0030	Dube, Jane	10
0032	Grant, Kirby	5
0033	Kehoe, Raymond	9
0034	Keener, Melody	7
0036	Lofgren, Oscar	10
0037	Loftus, Tom	10
0038	Souza, Lawrence	10
0039	Solvak, Ronald	10
0040	Miller, William	1
0041	Martin, Bruce	17
	*** Total Number of Rents	299

This completes our discussion of Crystal Reports. As you can see, there are many other features of the product that are beyond the scope of this text. However, in our chapter exercises, we will program a user interface for the preceding report and add it to the Case System, plus we will explore a few more features of Crystal Reports.

REVIEW EXERCISES

PART I: REVIEW QUESTIONS

1. Define streaming output and differentiate it from formatted output.
2. What is the purpose of a system memory variable?
3. Name the five bands of a Visual dBASE report.
4. What formula is used to compute the `ON PAGE` line number?
5. Name two print functions that are handled automatically by the `PRINTJOB..ENDPRINT` construct.
6. What are two ways to enter Crystal Reports?
7. What is the purpose of the Format bar on the Crystal Reports desktop?
8. Describe how to insert a graphic on a report. How do you center that graphic?
9. Describe the steps involved in placing a grand total summary field on a report.
10. How do you select multiple fields for the purpose of formatting?

PART II: ADDING A PRINTER SETUP MENU ITEM

In this exercise, you will add an item to the **File** menu of the Case System to display the Windows printer setup dialog box. Proceed as follows:

1. Open the menu designer:

   ```
   MODI MENU ymenu
   ```

2. Right-click the **&Printer Setup** item of the **File** menu of the Video Express system and select **Inspector** from the resulting drop-down menu.

3. Using the `CHOOSEPRINTER()` function within a code block, code an **OnClick** event-handler for the **&Printer Setup** menu item.

PART III: FILM TABLE PRINT USING STREAMING OUTPUT

In this exercise, you will build a report to print the film file using the streaming print model. As with all reports, be sure the report is working properly with output to the screen before issuing the printer actuation commands (`SET PRINTER` and `EJECT`). Proceed according to the following specifications:

1. Open the `MODI COMM` editor. Name this program **`yprint`**.
2. Using the streaming output model presented in Figure 12.2, develop a print program to print the entire film table, **`yfilm`**.
3. Format your report as shown in Figure 12.19. The report will be two pages in length. The title, LISTING OF FILM TABLE, is to appear only on the first page. Place the page number centered in the footer.
4. When operational, attach this print program to the File menu of the Case System. We need to add this item to the Print item on that menu. We will add an item for both the film table print and the customer table print. Proceed as follows:
   - Type the following command from the Command window:

     ```
     MODI MENU ymenu
     ```

   - Press **down-arrow** to the &Print item on the &File menu. Press **Tab** to open a new submenu under the Print item. Add the following items (see Figure 12.20). We will be adding actions to all three items in the chapter.

     ```
     &Film Table
     &Customer Table
     &Sales Table
     ```

   - With the cursor on the new `&Film Table` item, right-click to select the Inspector. Select the **Events** tab in the Inspector. Enter the following code block as the OnClick event-handler.

     ```
     {;DO yprint}
     ```

     Select **File | Save and Close** to exit the Menu Designer.

FIGURE 12.19 STREAMING OUTPUT REPORT OF FILM TABLE, `yprint.prg`

```
                         LIST OF FILM TABLE
TITLE                                                   TIMES
-------------------------------------------------------------
BEST FRIENDS.                                               0
CONAN THE BARBARIAN.                                        1
HONKY TONK MAN.                                             5
SPEED.                                                      0
LOVING COUPLES.                                             1
CADDY SHACK.                                                3
DEAD MEN DON'T WEAR PLAID.                                  6
ATTACK OF THE KILLER TOMATOES.                              2
CHEECH & CHONG - NICE DREAMS.                               2
POLTERGEIST.                                                7
AMITYVILLE II: THE POSSESSION.                              7
THE GODSEND.                                                4
CREEPSHOW.                                                  1
ABSENT MINDED PROFESSOR.                                    0
LEGEND OF THE LONE RANGER.                                  3
WINNIE THE POOH.                                            7
CENSORED TITLE #01                                          3
CENSORED TITLE #02                                          2
CENSORED TITLE #03                                          5
FORCE OF ONE.                                               9
JANE FONDA WORKOUT.                                        29
DYNAMITE CHICKEN.                                           5
CAT PEOPLE.                                                 8
CENSORED TITLE #04                                          8
DUMBO.                                                      6
BLACK STALLION.                                            11
ANIMAL HOUSE.                                              13
FUN HOUSE.                                                 15
CENSORED TITLE #05                                          5
ADVENTURE OF CHIP & DALE.                                   6
ELECTRIC HORSEMAN.                                          9
AIRPLANE II.                                                4
HALLOWEEN.                                                 17
CENSORED TITLE #06                                         11
STRAWBERRY SHORTCAKE'S HOUSE.                              20
I SPIT ON YOUR GRAVE.                                       2
CENSORED TITLE #07                                          6
ON VACATION WITH MICKEY MOUSE.                             10
RENAISSANCE MAN.                                           19
BEACH HOUSE.                                                7
PSYCHO II.                                                 10
CENSORED TITLE #08                                         21
```

(continues)

FIGURE 12.19 (continued) STREAMING OUTPUT REPORT OF FILM TABLE, `yprint.prg`

```
SECRET OF N.I.M.H.                                  4
LOVERS AND LIARS.                                   6
DINER.                                              9
WHEN A STRANGER CALLS.                             26
CENSORED TITLE #09                                  8
THE LAST UNICORN.                                   6
BREATHLESS.                                         1
NATIONAL LAMPOON VACATION.                         21
FINAL EXAM.                                        12

                    Page No. 1
```

FIGURE 12.20 ATTACHING `yprint.prg` TO THE MENU SYSTEM

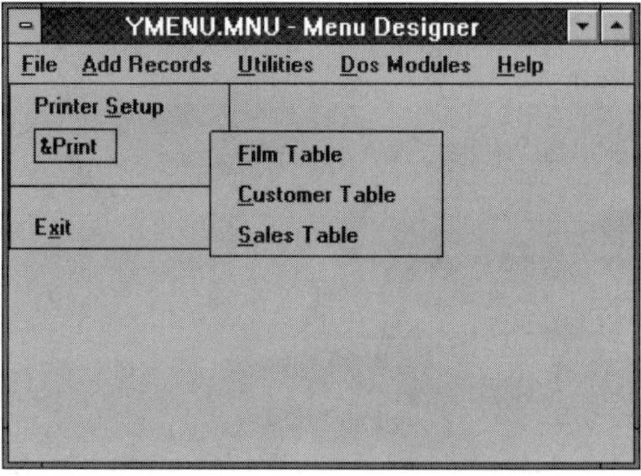

PART IV: INTERFACING THE NUMBER OF RENTALS BY CITY REPORT TO THE CASE SYSTEM MENU

In this exercise, we develop an input form for the Number of Rentals report and connect it to the Case System **File | Print** menu. Proceed as follows:

1. Develop a data entry form to accept a city from the operator. This city will determine which records are printed by Crystal Reports. Name the form `yreport.wfm`. The form should appear as in Figure 12.21. The Print button OnClick event-handler should do the following:

FIGURE 12.21 DATA ENTRY FORM, NUMBER OF RENTS REPORT, `yreport.wfm`

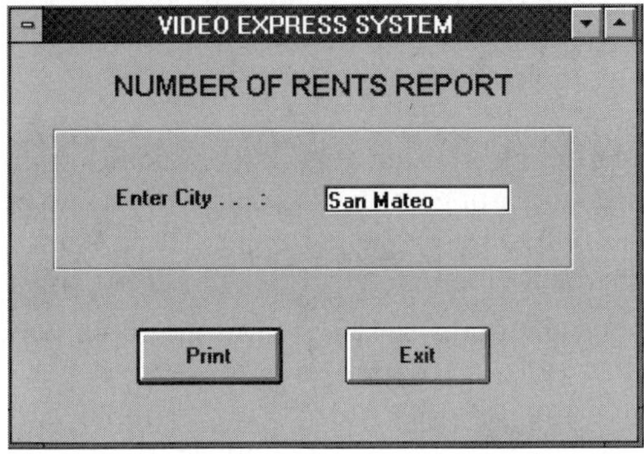

- The formula specification within Crystal Reports prints according to the value assigned to the variable, **`xCity`**. The first command in the handler is to assign the operator entered **`city`** contained in the EntryField value property to the **`xCity`** variable. Be sure to left- and right-trim the value prior to the assignment.
- Use the **`REPORT FORM`** command to print the report, **`yreport.rpt`** as developed in Crystal Reports. The command should read as follows:

```
REPORT FORM yreport FOR city = PROPER(xCity) TO PRINTER
```

  Leave the **`TO PRINTER`** option off until you are sure the handler is working properly.
- Set the tabbing order to Text/Rectangle controls, Entryfield1, Print button, then Exit button. After each print, move focus to the **Exit** pushbutton.
- Disable the Print button until the Entryfield loses focus. This type of operation was used in the password modification exercise in Chapter 10.

2. Attach this form, **`yreport.wfm`** to the **File** menu of the Case System. It will be the action specified by the **Print | Film Customer** item. Test the form by first requesting a report for the city of **`"San Mateo"`**, then for **`"Burlingame"`**. When testing to the screen prior to adding the **`TO PRINT`** clause to the **`REPORT FORM`** command, manually close the print window after each individual test of a **`city`**. If not, Crystal Reports may leave the table view open, thereby causing an error message to occur when a second report is requested.

PART V: PRINTING THE SALES TABLE USING CRYSTAL REPORTS

In this exercise, we will build a report of the Sales History table using Crystal Reports. The report will group the sales by customer number and use a multiple-table view. Proceed as follows:

1. **Create the view.** This report is primarily a listing of the Sales table. However, the listing must also contain the name and price of the film rented and the full name of the customer. These items must come from the film and customer tables respectively. To accomplish this, proceed as follows:
   - Open the query designer from the Input pane using the command, `CREATE QUERY yreport2`.
   - Add `ysales.dbf` as the parent table, then `ycustm.dbf` and `yfilm.dbf` as the child tables.
   - Link `ysales` into `ycustm` on `cust_no` and `ysales` into `yfilm` on `film_no`. This will be a multiple child relationship.
   - Select the following fields:

     ```
     ysales->cust_no      ycustm->last      yfilm->title
     ysales->date                           yfilm->price
     ysales->film_no
     ysales->returned
     ```

   - Sort the parent table on `cust_no`. This is required because we want to group the items on this field.
   - Save and close this query file.

2. **Open Crystal Reports**. Prior to entering Crystal Reports, type `CLEAR ALL` from the Input pane. Open Crystal Reports using the command `CREATE REPORT yreport2` from the Input pane. Select the view file developed above, `yreport2.qbe`, from the Open Table Required dialog box.

3. **Report reference name.** For future reference, name the report SALES HISTORY LISTING. This is not the actual title of the report itself.

4. **Report margins.** Set report margins: top, 0.50; left, 1.00; bottom, 0.50; and right, 0.50.

5. **Report title.** In the header section, insert and center a report title using a 16 point Arial boldface font as follows:

   SALES HISTORY LISTING

FIGURE 12.22 INSERT GROUP SECTION DIALOG BOX

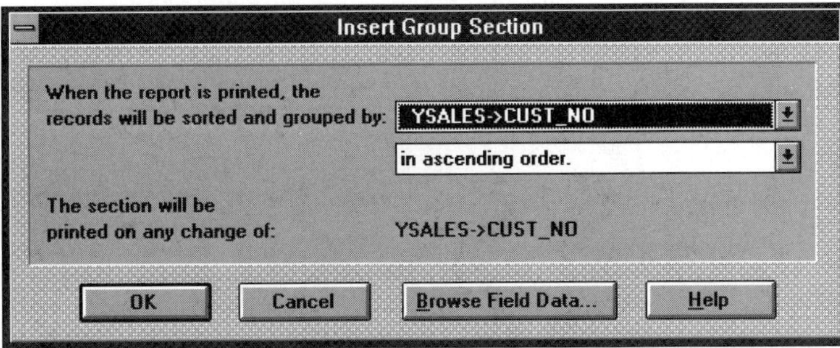

6. **Insert Group Section.** This feature has not been covered as yet in this chapter. Select **Insert | Group Section** to display the Insert Group Section dialog. Our report will be grouped on **cust_no**, so click **OK** to accept the dialog as such (see Figure 12.22).

7. **Insert fields.** Select **Insert | Database Fields** to insert the following fields into the appropriate sections of the report (refer to Figures 12.25A and 12.25B for placement):

   - #1: CUST_NO - A Section

     `ysales->cust_no, ycustm->last`

   - Details Section

     `ysales->date, ysales->film_no, yfilm->title, yfilm->price`

   The film number field column heading, `FILM_NO`, contains an underscore character. **Right-click | Edit Text Field** the column heading text field and edit to remove it.

8. **Insert Subtotal field.** Each group will need to be subtotaled on the price field. To place a Subtotal summary field on your report, give focus to the `yfilm->price` field, then select **Insert | Summary | Subtotal**. This will display the Insert Subtotal dialog box. The default settings in the dialog box should be correct so click the **OK** button to complete the operation (see Figure 12.23). We will **Sum** on Group #1. The Subtotal summary field should now appear in the Group #1 section just under the price field in the Details section. Finally, insert the following text field just to the left of the summary field to describe its content:

   *****Subtotal:**

FIGURE 12.23 INSERT SUBTOTAL DIALOG

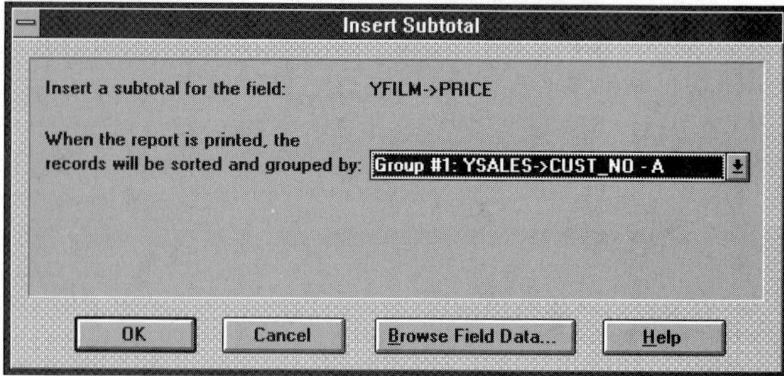

9. **Insert a Grand Total field.** Using the techniques described earlier in the chapter, insert a Grand Total field just under the Subtotal field in the Grand Total section of the report. Drag the field down one line and place the following text field on the same line to describe grand total (see Figure 12.25B):

   ***** Grand total - all customers . . . :**

10. **Column headings.** Insert the following column heading text field over the customer number and name fields:

    CUSTOMER # AND NAME

    Underline the customer number and name column heading (with focus on the heading, click the **Underline** icon in the Format bar).

11. **Formatting.** Using the **Format** menu, format the following fields:
    - **Numeric fields.** Format the price, group total, and grand total fields to place a leading dollar sign in front of each value. First, select **Edit | Select Fields** to select all three fields at the same time. Select **Format | Fields** to access the Format Number dialog box. Check Currency Symbol in the upper-right corner of the dialog, then click **OK**.
    - **Date field.** We will format the date field to include leading zeros. Place the date field in focus, then select **Format | Field** to display the Format Date dialog box. Drop down the list boxes at the bottom of the dialog to select month and day leading zeros (see Figure 12.24). Click **OK** to complete.

- **Subtotal and Grand Total text fields.** Select **Format | Field | Alignment = Right** to right-justify the two descriptor text fields to the left of the associated numeric fields.

12. **Insert Page Number.** Select **Insert | Special Field | Page Number** to display the rectangle cursor. Drag the cursor to place the page number at the bottom of the Page footer section of the report, then center it (see Figure 12.25A).

FIGURE 12.24 FORMAT DATE DIALOG BOX

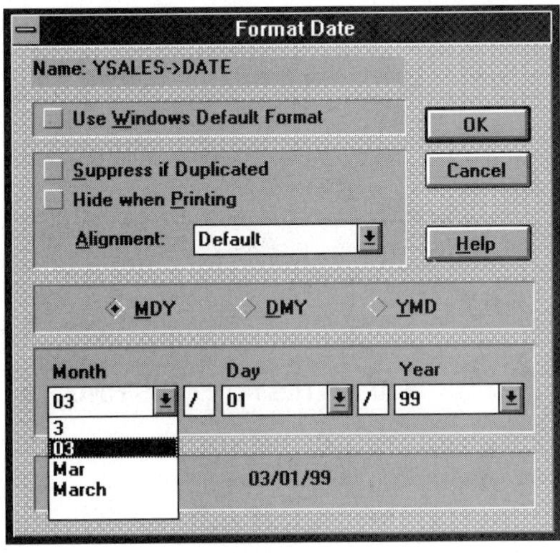

FIGURE 12.25A SALES HISTORY FINAL REPORT SPECIFICATION, `yreport2` (left)

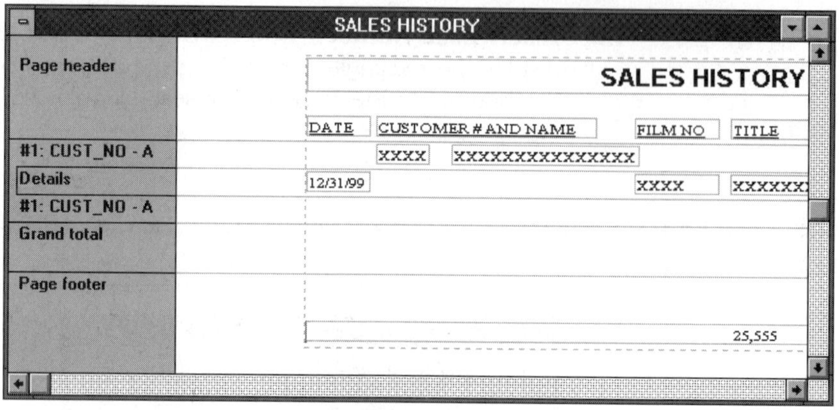

SALES HISTORY					
Page header					SALES HISTORY
	DATE	CUSTOMER # AND NAME		FILM NO	TITLE
#1: CUST_NO - A		XXXX	XXXXXXXXXXXXXXX		
Details	12/31/99			XXXX	XXXXXXX
#1: CUST_NO - A					
Grand total					
Page footer					25,555

FIGURE 12.25B SALES HISTORY FINAL REPORT SPECIFICATION, `yreport2` (right)

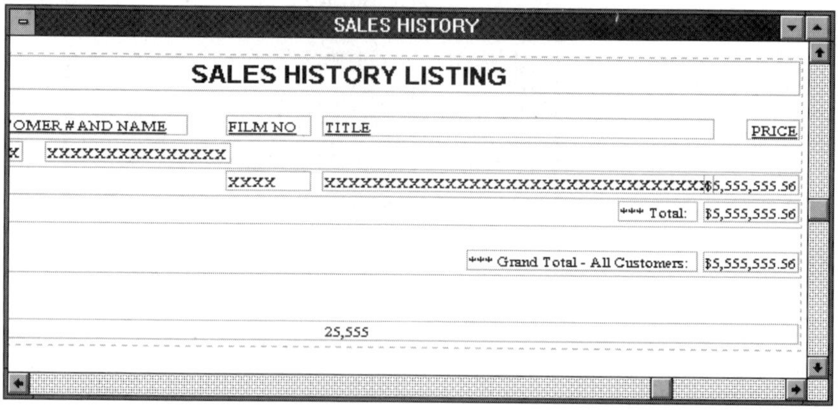

SALES HISTORY				
SALES HISTORY LISTING				
OMER # AND NAME	FILM NO	TITLE		PRICE
X XXXXXXXXXXXXXXX				
	XXXX	XXXXXXXXXXXXXXXXXXXXXXXXXXXXXXXXXX		$5,555,555.56
			*** Total:	$5,555,555.56
			*** Grand Total - All Customers:	$5,555,555.56
		25,555		

13. **Save and test.** This completes the report specification. Save the specification and Exit Crystal Reports. From the Input pane of the Command window, type the following command to test the report design:

```
REPORT FORM yreport2 FOR cust_no > "0001" .AND.
                         cust_no < "0012" TO PRINT
```

This command restricts the test report to a single page (see Figure 12.26). Omit the `TO PRINT` option until the report is functioning properly.

FIGURE 12.26 SALES HISTORY REPORT FINAL TEST, yreport2

SALES HISTORY LISTING

DATE	CUSTOMER # AND NAME		FILM #	TITLE		PRICE
	0004	McGregory				
04/07/96			0068	EXCALIBUR.		$3.95
06/07/96			0033	HALLOWEEN.		$3.95
08/14/96			0045	DINER.		$3.95
					*** Subtotal:	$11.85
	0005	Smith				
03/10/96			0071	CENSORED TITLE #14		$4.95
05/09/96			0045	DINER.		$3.95
08/20/96			0038	ON VACATION WITH MICKEY MOUSE.		$3.95
					*** Subtotal:	$12.85
	0006	Juett				
01/19/96			0058	POPEYE.		$3.95
01/25/96			0028	FUN HOUSE.		$3.95
					*** Subtotal:	$7.90
	0007	Shaffer				
02/04/96			0034	CENSORED TITLE #06.		$4.95
02/06/96			0012	THE GODSEND.		$3.95
					*** Subtotal:	$8.90
	0008	Shackleton				
03/13/96			0034	CENSORED TITLE #06.		$4.95
03/24/96			0028	FUN HOUSE.		$3.95
04/01/96			0036	I SPIT ON YOUR GRAVE.		$3.95
04/04/96			0012	THE GODSEND.		$3.95
05/10/96			0011	AMITYVILLE II: THE POSSESSION.		$3.95
05/24/96			0057	CENSORED TITLE #11.		$4.95
					*** Subtotal:	$25.70
	0009	Goodson				
06/05/96			0012	THE GODSEND.		$3.95
07/10/96			0034	CENSORED TITLE #06.		$4.95
					*** Subtotal:	$8.90
	0010	Jackson				
07/18/96			0027	ANIMAL HOUSE.		$3.95
07/24/96			0028	FUN HOUSE.		$3.95
08/01/96			0048	POCAHONTAS.		$3.95
08/08/96			0017	CENSORED TITLE #01.		$4.95
09/10/96			0034	CENSORED TITLE #06.		$4.95
10/14/96			0010	POLTERGEIST.		$3.95
10/14/96			0023	CAT PEOPLE.		$3.95
12/24/96			0020	FORCE OF ONE.		$3.95
12/25/96			0031	ELECTRIC HORSEMAN.		$3.95
					*** Subtotal:	$37.55
	0011	Mason				
01/10/96			0037	CENSORED TITLE #07.		$4.95
03/16/96			0028	FUN HOUSE.		$3.95
05/13/96			0075	CENSORED TITLE #15		$4.95
07/13/96			0071	CENSORED TITLE #14		$4.95
08/09/96			0066	MOTHER'S DAY.		$3.95
					*** Subtotal:	$22.75
					*** Grand Total - All Customers:	$136.40

14. **Attach to Case System menu**. From the Case System **File | Print | Sales Table** menu item, we will print the entire file. Proceed as follows:

- Type `MODI MENU ymenu` into the Input pane to modify the current menu system to add an action to the Sales Table submenu.
- Using a code block, attach the following command to the OnClick property of the Sales Table menu item:

```
REPORT FORM yreport2 TO PRINT
```

15. **Final test.** Run the Video Express Case System. From the **File | Print** menu, run all three table report print items (Customer table, Film table, and Sales table).

CHAPTER SUMMARY

In this chapter we discussed printing and programming of print modules from Visual dBASE.

- **Streaming output.** As the name implies, printing is directed serially in stream to the output device. Control codes are embedded in the output stream. Some programmers prefer this type of output from Visual dBASE because the code is tighter and the resulting report will run faster than one generated from the report generator. However, the print program must be hard coded.
- **Systems memory variables.** Used to control certain print operations in Visual dBASE. These variables are initialized and maintained automatically when coding streaming output. Reports generated using the report generator in DOS versions of dBASE also use system memory variables.
- **Using Crystal Reports.** Crystal Reports is a third-party product that has been licensed by Borland to be included in Visual dBASE. It has been retrofitted to work together with Visual dBASE and can be used for a wide variety of reports ranging from simple database table listings to complex reports involving summaries and data grouping. Moreover, it allows the use of graphic pictures, lines, and boxes.

The following commands were introduced:

- `SET PRINTER`
- `CLOSE PRINTER`
- `?/??`
- `???`
- `EJECT`
- `SET MARGIN`
- `ON PAGE AT LINE`
- `EJECT PAGE`
- `PRINTJOB..ENDPRINTJOB`
- `CREATE/MODIFY REPORT`
- `REPORT FORM`

Also discussed were three new functions:

- `DATE()`
- `CHOOSEPRINTER()`
- `CENTER()`

In the next chapter we discuss editing in Visual dBASE and the use of the Browse object.

CHAPTER THIRTEEN

TOPICS

New Commands, Functions, and Properties

Concepts

Components of a custom editor
The deletion operation in Visual dBASE
Using Browse from the Command window
Using the Browse Control Object

Review Exercises

Chapter Summary

Editing in Visual dBASE

13

CHAPTER OBJECTIVES

One of the primary objectives of this text is to build a Case System containing those modules essential to most programmed systems. A custom editor is an important part of that system. In an earlier chapter, we discussed adding information to the tables of an application database. We designed an efficient interactive screen to ensure the integrity of all data entered. Now we must also give the operator the ability to change or delete information currently stored in the database. Most of the rules governing effective input screens also apply to editor screens.

Visual dBASE offers a number of different methods to edit application tables. You can use full screen editors provided by the `BROWSE` or `EDIT` command, or develop a completely custom editor through program code. In earlier versions of dBASE, custom programming was necessary to provide fully functional and buffered editing capability. Fortunately, the Browse object now allows the programmer to add a very comprehensive editing tool to each application.

In this chapter, we will first examine the commands associated with editing and demonstrate their use. We will then explore the Browse object and learn how to develop an application editor form that utilizes it.

After studying this chapter, you should understand all of the editing options available in Visual dBASE and be able to program a Browse object into an application form. Several Browse forms will be developed for the student Case System.

NEW COMMANDS, FUNCTIONS, AND PROPERTIES

COMMAND

```
DELETE [<scope>][FOR/WHILE <condition>]
```

Marks records for deletion. Unless otherwise specified in the command, only the current record is marked. Records marked remain in the table. The marking character is an asterisk in first position of record. All commands associated with the **DELETE** operation will be discussed in more detail later in the chapter.

COMMAND

```
SET DELETED ON/OFF
```

When set to **ON**, records marked for deletion are ignored by other Visual dBASE commands. The default setting is **ON**. **INDEX** and **REINDEX** are not affected by this command.

COMMAND

```
RECALL [<scope>][FOR/WHILE <condition>]
```

Reinstates records marked for deletion. Will not reinstate records removed by **PACK** or **ZAP**. The **SET DELETED** toggle must be **OFF** to **RECALL**.

COMMAND

```
PACK
```

Removes record marked for deletion from the table. All open index files will be automatically reindexed. Directory information about the status of the table may not be correct until the table is closed. Disk space for the removed records is reclaimed after the table is closed.

COMMAND

```
ZAP
```

Removes *all* records from the active table. All open index files will be automatically reindexed. Also, space devoted to each record is removed from disk and returned to the operating system. Though this command will not be used in the student Case System, it is an important command to be aware of—both for its usefulness and for its potential adverse impact on the tables of a database.

COMMAND

```
BROWSE [<scope>] [FOR <condition 1>] [WHILE <condition 2>]
  [COLOR [<standard text>]
    [, [<enhanced text>]
    [, [<perimeter color>]
    [, [<background color>]]]]]
  [FIELDS <field 1> [<field option list 1>] |
      <calculated field 1>=<exp 1>
    [<calculated field option list 1>]
```

```
[, <field 2> [<field option list 2>] |
   <calculated field 2>=<exp 2>
[<calculated field option list 2>] ...]]
[FORMAT]
[FREEZE <field 3>]
[KEY <exp 3>[, <exp 4>] [EXCLUDE]]
[LOCK <expN 2>]
[NOAPPEND]
[NODELETE]
[NOEDIT | NOMODIFY]
[NOFOLLOW]
[NOINIT]
[NOORGANIZE]
[NORMAL]
[NOTOGGLE]
[NOWAIT]
[TITLE <expC 1>]
[WIDTH <expN 3>]
[WINDOW <window name>]
```

FUNCTION `DELETED()`

Used in logical expressions to note whether record has been marked for deletion. The **SET DELETED** toggle must be **OFF**.

EXAMPLE

```
SET DELETED OFF
LIST FOR DELETED()
COPY TO backup FOR DELETED()
```

This function will be demonstrated in more detail later in the chapter.

FUNCTION

```
MSGBOX (<message expC>,
   [<title expC>,[<box type expN>]])
```

Opens a dialog box that contains a message and pushbuttons. It returns a numeric value dependent upon the pushbutton pressed. The following numeric values for `<box type expN>` will present the corresponding pushbuttons:

0	**OK**
1	**OK, Cancel**
2	**Abort, Retry, Ignore**
3	**Yes, No, Cancel**
4	**Yes, No**
5	**Retry, Cancel**

To specify a dialog box with an icon, add one of the following numbers to the `<box type expN>` number:

16	Red **!**
32	Green **?**
48	Yellow **!**
64	Blue **i**

When the operator presses one of the `MSGBOX()` pushbuttons, the dialog will disappear and one of the following numbers will be returned indicating which pushbutton was pressed. For example, if `<boxtype expN>` is coded as 1, an **OK** and a **Cancel** button will be inserted in the dialog. If the user then presses the **Cancel** button when responding to the dialog, `MSGBOX()` will return a 2 to the expression.

OK	1
Cancel	2
Abort	3
Retry	4
Ignore	5
Yes	6
No	7

EXAMPLE

```
xValue = MSGBOX("Hello World")
xOK = MSGBOX("Press OK","Video Express Alert",1)
xCancel = MSGBOX("Press Cancel","Video Express Alert",1)
xIconYes=MSGBOX("Press Yes","Video Express Alert",67)
? xvalue, xOK, xCancel, xIconYes
```

PROPERTY `ShowRecNo`

Determines if the Browse object's record number column is displayed.

Property of class: `BROWSE`, `EDIT`

PROPERTY `Alias`

Names the table accessed by the Browse object.

Property of class: `BROWSE`, `EDIT`

PROPERTY `Fields`

Names the fields to be displayed in the Browse object and the options to be applied to those fields.

Property of class: `BROWSE`, `EDIT`

PROPERTY `CUATab`

Determines whether the **Tab** key moves through the form tabbing order or across a Browse or Edit object. If set to the default of `.T.`, it will move through the form tabbing order.

Property of class: `BROWSE`, `EDIT`

PROPERTY `Toggle`

Determines whether the user can toggle between display modes.

Property of class: `BROWSE`

PROPERTY `Mode`

Determines the format of a Browse object. The default value is 0, or Browse layout. Form layout is 1 and Column layout is 2.

Property of class: `BROWSE`

CONCEPTS

COMPONENTS OF A CUSTOM EDITOR

Prior to programming our student Case System editor, we will need to discuss the components of a custom editor and the function of each. A custom editor should contain the following capabilities:

- **Operator-oriented screen design.** The screen for an editor should be well thought out. It must be easy to use and allow the operator uncomplicated access to the various functions of the editor. As with all custom screen design, the operator should be involved in the design if possible.
- **Data validation.** The key feature of a custom editor is its ability to allow validity tests on the changes made to the table by the operator. Fortunately, each field in a Visual dBASE table can be validated as needed as the operator performs changes or deletions.
- **Searching and scrolling.** Usually, a number of edits will be made in an editing session. If the second edit is close to the first in the table, the operator should be able to scroll easily to the next location rather than go through the search routine again. A good editor will enable the operator to search for a given record and scroll forward or backward as necessary.
- **Record deletion.** One editing option will be deletion of a record. How the program handles marking, packing, and reindexing (terms we discuss in this chapter) is very important. Records are usually

marked during an editing session, but not removed—and the corresponding indexes updated—until after the session.

- **Effective message system.** The editor must keep the operator constantly informed of what is happening and what to do next. This includes the dynamic messages concerned with data validity, prompts, and edit keystrokes. An operator should seldom need to look at a procedure manual or call the programmer if the system has self-explanatory screens with an effective message system.

Of course, editing needs will vary somewhat with each system. However, the editor we will develop for the student Case System will serve as a model on which you can build, adding features unique to the systems you develop in the future.

THE DELETION OPERATION IN VISUAL dBASE

An important function of an editor is the delete operation. Visual dBASE has a series of commands to handle the various aspects of deletion, and an understanding of how they are used will be necessary before programming the editor. Enter the following example from the Input pane:

```
CLEAR
SET DELETED OFF
SET EXCLUSIVE ON
USE ycustm
GOTO 2
DELETE
DISPLAY ALL        && Cancel by pressing ESC.
```

The `SET DELETED` toggle is first turned `OFF` from its default setting of `ON`. The `DELETE` command in this example *marks* the record at the current pointer position (record 2) for deletion. Note the deletion mark (*) when the records are displayed. It will stay with the record until removed. Also note that the record is not physically removed from the table and that it appears in the display. We can also reference it with all other Visual dBASE commands. To keep it in the table, but remove it from command reference, the `SET DELETED` toggle must be turned on. Continue by typing the following from the Input pane:

```
CLEAR
SET DELETED ON
DISPLAY ALL
```

Now record 2 is not displayed. Note the record numbers (1, 3, 4, and so on). The record is still physically in the table, but is not referenced by any Visual dBASE command except `INDEX` and `REINDEX`. This is very convenient. Even though a record is deleted, it is still kept for future reference. An example is a deletion listing. If you want to physically remove the record, the `PACK` command is used. Enter the following:

```
CLEAR
SET DELETED OFF
PACK
DISPLAY ALL
```

SET DELETED may be either **ON** or **OFF** to execute **PACK**. Note the display does not contain the deleted record, and the record number has been reused. This is because the record has been physically removed, and all the records below record 2 have been renumbered. This is a good reason for not remembering records for future reference by record number.

The drawback of keeping records marked for deletion in the table is that performance begins to get sluggish. For this reason, it is a good idea to physically remove them on a regular schedule. However, they should first be copied to another table for future reference. To do this, use the **DELETED()** function. Type the following:

```
CLEAR
SET DELETED OFF
USE ycustm
DELETE FOR city =  "San Mateo"
DISPLAY ALL city           && Cancel by pressing ESC.
COPY TO yback FOR DELETED()
USE yback
DISPLAY ALL
```

After ensuring **SET DELETED** is **OFF**, the **DELETE FOR** option of the command marks all records from **San Mateo** for deletion. This is verified with the **DISPLAY ALL** command. The **DELETED()** function will return a logical **.T.** when a record contains a deletion mark (*). To remove the deletion marks, use the **RECALL** command. Type the following:

```
CLEAR
USE ycustm
RECALL ALL
DISPLAY ALL
SET DELETED ON       && Return toggle to default setting.
```

Normally, you would now **PACK** the table to physically remove the **San Mateo** records. However, we want to keep them in the table for our future examples, so we removed the deletion marks. This was accomplished with the **RECALL ALL** command.

USING BROWSE FROM THE COMMAND WINDOW

We will initially explore the use of the Browse editing operation from the Command window. Most of the capabilities of the `BROWSE` command are also available from the Browse Form control. Our programmed module for the Case System will utilize the latter.

Components of the BROWSE Command. Proceed as follows to examine the `BROWSE` command:

```
CLOSE ALL
USE YCUSTM
GOTO 15
BROWSE REST
```

This sequence of commands demonstrates the `BROWSE` command in its simplest form. All fields and all records are displayed (see Figure 13.1). The `<scope>` of `REST` causes the display to begin with record 15. A **PgUp** will display prior records. Use the scroll bars to move to sections of the table that are not displayed in the window. Cursor movements are similar to the display or design of a table structure and the layout windows for appending records as used in Chapter 3. For example, the usage of **PgUp/PgDn** and **Tab/Shift-Tab** are the same. When we use the Browse control in a form, usage of the **Tab** key will be discussed in more detail. Close Browse by double-clicking the **Control Menu Box**.

FIGURE 13.1 GENERAL BROWSE WINDOW

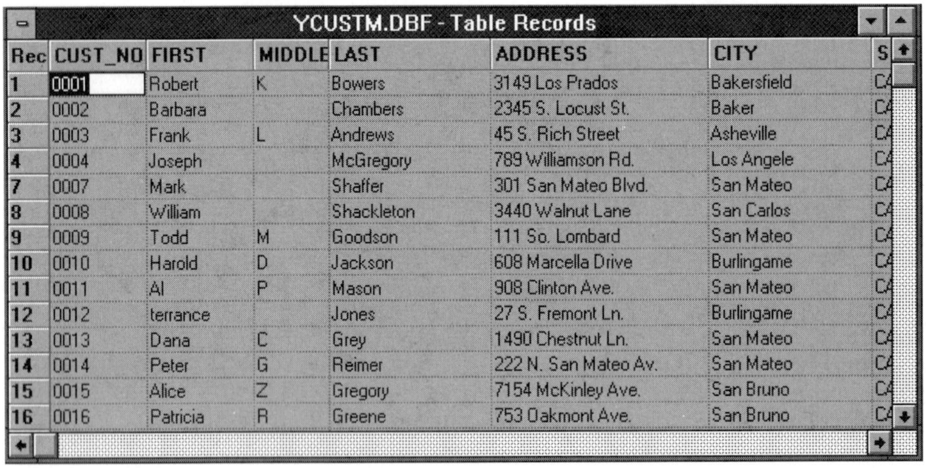

YCUSTM.DBF - Table Records

Rec	CUST_NO	FIRST	MIDDLE	LAST	ADDRESS	CITY	S
1	0001	Robert	K	Bowers	3149 Los Prados	Bakersfield	CA
2	0002	Barbara		Chambers	2345 S. Locust St.	Baker	CA
3	0003	Frank	L	Andrews	45 S. Rich Street	Asheville	CA
4	0004	Joseph		McGregory	789 Williamson Rd.	Los Angele	CA
7	0007	Mark		Shaffer	301 San Mateo Blvd.	San Mateo	CA
8	0008	William		Shackleton	3440 Walnut Lane	San Carlos	CA
9	0009	Todd	M	Goodson	111 So. Lombard	San Mateo	CA
10	0010	Harold	D	Jackson	608 Marcella Drive	Burlingame	CA
11	0011	Al	P	Mason	908 Clinton Ave.	San Mateo	CA
12	0012	terrance		Jones	27 S. Fremont Ln.	Burlingame	CA
13	0013	Dana	C	Grey	1490 Chestnut Ln.	San Mateo	CA
14	0014	Peter	G	Reimer	222 N. San Mateo Av.	San Mateo	CA
15	0015	Alice	Z	Gregory	7154 McKinley Ave.	San Bruno	CA
16	0016	Patricia	R	Greene	753 Oakmont Ave.	San Bruno	CA

Type the following sequence of commands to view a few more of the options available in BROWSE.

```
SET ORDER TO city
GO TOP
BROWSE REST COLOR W+/GB FIELDS CUST_NO\R,
   NAME=TRIM(LAST)+", "+FIRST \R, CITY, AMT_RENT KEY "Reno"
NOORGANIZE TITLE "MY BROWSE WINDOW"
```

The first command sets a new master index of `city`. This causes the table to be ordered on city and allows the `KEY "Reno"` clause of the command to begin the display on the first Reno record (see Figure 13.2). In addition, we coded the following clauses:

- **COLOR.** Modifies the standard display.
- **FIELDS.** Sets the fields list. Also, establishes a calculated field, NAME, to display the full name of the customer. The \R option after the CUST_NO field and the name calculated field causes those fields to be Read Only.
- **NOORGANIZE.** Disables the ability of the user to access the indexing features of the menu system.
- **TITLE.** Gives a title to the BROWSE window.

FIGURE 13.2 BROWSE WINDOW WITH OPTIONS

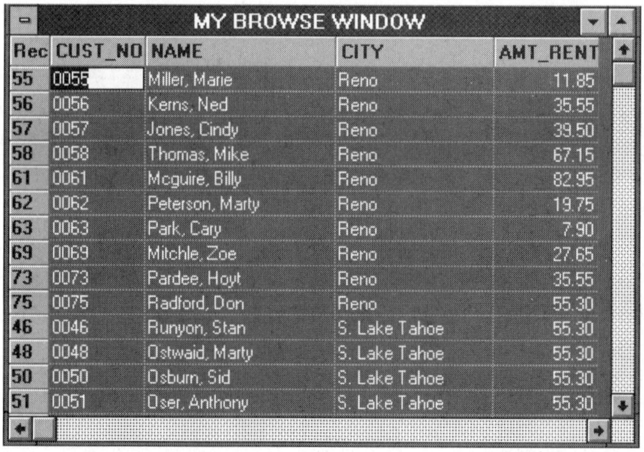

MY BROWSE WINDOW

Rec	CUST_NO	NAME	CITY	AMT_RENT
55	0055	Miller, Marie	Reno	11.85
56	0056	Kerns, Ned	Reno	35.55
57	0057	Jones, Cindy	Reno	39.50
58	0058	Thomas, Mike	Reno	67.15
61	0061	Mcguire, Billy	Reno	82.95
62	0062	Peterson, Marty	Reno	19.75
63	0063	Park, Cary	Reno	7.90
69	0069	Mitchle, Zoe	Reno	27.65
73	0073	Pardee, Hoyt	Reno	35.55
75	0075	Radford, Don	Reno	55.30
46	0046	Runyon, Stan	S. Lake Tahoe	55.30
48	0048	Ostwaid, Marty	S. Lake Tahoe	55.30
50	0050	Osburn, Sid	S. Lake Tahoe	55.30
51	0051	Oser, Anthony	S. Lake Tahoe	55.30

Finally, press **F2** to move to the Form layout and then again to move to the Column layout of the `BROWSE` window. Again, this is similar to the `APPEND` command layouts presented in Chapter 3, Figure 3.5.

Pointer Movement in BROWSE. The operator can move the record pointer by selecting **Table | Go to Record (Ctrl-G)**. This will cause the Go to Record dialog to appear (see Figure 13.3). Other record number pointer movements can be selected from the Table menu such as **Next**, **Previous**, **Top**, and **Bottom Record**. Close the Browse window.

Searching in BROWSE. We will begin our record search by opening the customer table with no master index tag in place.

```
USE ycustm
SET ORDER TO
```

To locate a record by specific information, select **Table | Find Records (Ctrl-F)**. This will cause the Find Records dialog box to appear (see Figure 13.4). For example, enter the following items in the dialog:

Find What:	**Mason**
Located in Field:	**LAST**
Search Rules:	**Standard**
Advanced Button:	Click to expand the dialog box.
Scope:	**All**
For:	**CITY = "San Mateo"**

Press **Find**, then **Close** to exit the dialog.

FIGURE 13.3 GOTO RECORD DIALOG BOX

The preceding will cause a sequential search of the table and move the pointer to the first occurrence of a record that meets the entered condition. Give focus to the Command window to view the actual command (**LOCATE FOR**) developed and executed by the Find Records dialog. To find the next occurrence of a record meeting the same condition, either reenter the Find Records dialog or type the **CONTINUE** command from the Command window. As mentioned in an earlier chapter, this is not a very efficient search technique, but it may do when the user is managing a small table.

FIGURE 13.4 FIND RECORDS DIALOG BOX

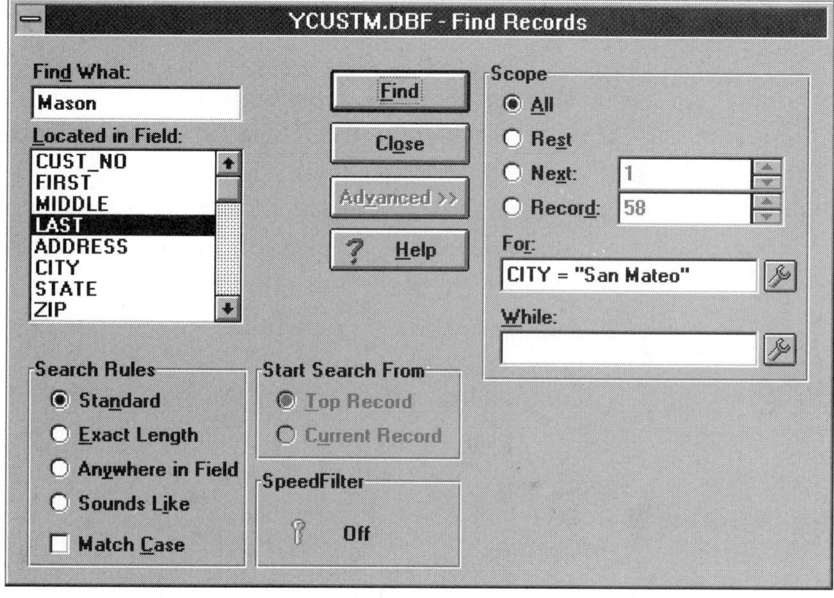

USING THE BROWSE CONTROL OBJECT

Most of the **BROWSE** command options mentioned in this chapter are available when using the Browse object in a form. We build a form now containing a Browse object. It will be added to the Case System as an editor for the film table. Proceed as follows:

1. Open the Form Designer from the Command window as follows:

```
CLOSE ALL
CREATE FORM yedit
```

2. Set the following form level properties using the Inspector. The View property opens the proper Table and the OnClose event will close it. Finally, we want to ensure that the default setting for **SET DELETED** is maintained as the form opens.

Text:	Table Edit	
View:	YFILM.DBF	
OnOPen():	{;SET DELETED ON}	&& Ensure default setting.
OnClose():	{;USE}	&& Close view.

3. From the Controls palette, select the Browse object and drag it to the new form. Using the properties Inspector, set the following properties for the new Browse control, `form.Browse1`:

- Data Linkage Properties

  Alias: `YFILM`
  Fields: `TITLE`, `PRICE`, `RATING`, `TIMES`

  Click the Fields **Tool** icon to access the Choose Fields dialog. Select the fields from the dialog in the order shown above (see Figure 13.5). From this dialog we also set the options for each field. For example, place the cursor on the `TITLE` field and click **Properties** in the lower left of the Choose Fields dialog. This displays the Field Properties dialog box. To ensure all edits to the `TITLE` field will be upper case, code a `@!` template in the Options section of the dialog (see Figure 13.6).

FIGURE 13.5 CHOOSE FIELDS DIALOG BOX

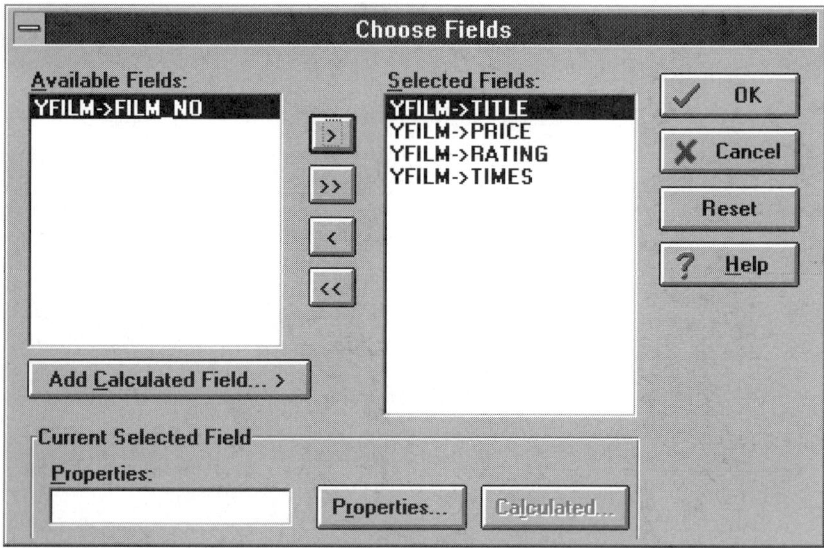

Additionally, ensure upper case when modifying the `RATING` field by coding a ! template symbol in the Options section of the dialog. Also, restrict modified ratings to `G`, `C`, `H`, or `X` by coding the following Expression and Error Message in the Valid section of the dialog (click the **Tool** icon to access the Expression Builder if so desired):

```
YFILM->RATING $ "GCHX"
Rating must be either G, C, H, or X ...
```

- Visual Properties

  ColorNormal: GB+
  ShowRecNo: `.F.`

FIGURE 13.6 FIELD PROPERTIES DIALOG BOX

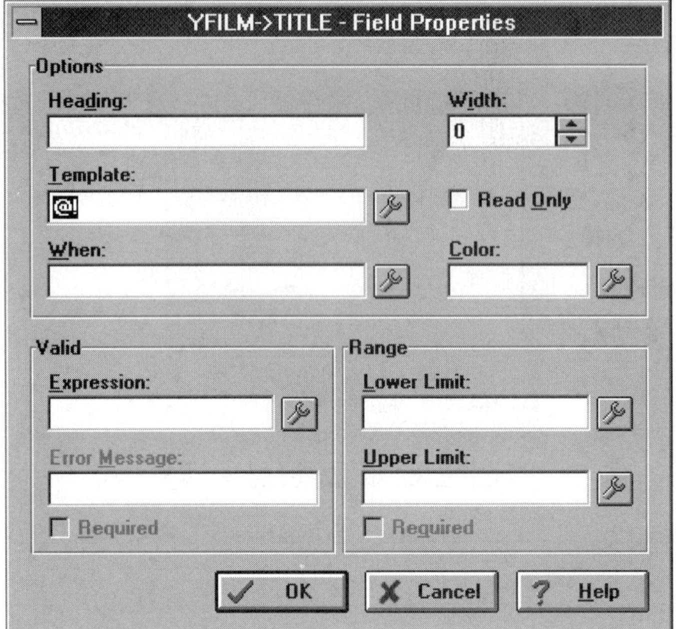

4. Add a title to the form by dragging a Text object from the Controls palette (see Figure 13.8). Set the following properties:

   Text: FILM TABLE EDITOR
   Position Properties
   Alignment: Center
   Font Properties
   FontBold: `.T.`
   FontName: Arial
   FontSize: 14

5. The `film_no` field will not be edited. Rather than including this field in the Browse control, we will display it as a single Text control and place it over the Browse object (see Figure 13.8). Proceed as follows:

   - Drag a Text control from the Controls palette and place it between the form title and the Browse object (see Figure 13.8). For now, center it roughly under the form title.

- Using the Inspector, change the following properties:

  FontSize: 10
  Alignment: Center Left

- The Text property of the Text control is currently **Text2** by default. Each time the Browse control is given focus and each time the cursor is moved within the Control, we want the Text property to be the `film_no` of the current record. Both are event properties of the Browse object. From the Inspector of the Browse object, select the **Events Tab**, then click the **OnOpen** event. Add the following code block as both the OnOpen and OnNavigate event-handlers:

```
{; form. Text2.text = yfilm->film_no}
```

6. Next we will add a Text control to describe the `film_no`. Drag a Text control from the Controls palette and place in on the form just to the left of the `film_no` Text control. Center it together with the `film_no` text field under the form title (see Figure 13.8). Change the properties of the new control as follows:

   Text: FILM NUMBER
   Alignment: Center Right
   FontSize: 10

7. The final controls to be added to our form will be Next, Previous, and Close pushbuttons. Rather than building these buttons from scratch using the Pushbutton Control, we will use *Custom Controls*. A custom control is a user-interface object with customized appearance and behavior such as an entry field or pushbutton. Visual dBASE allows the programmer to build custom controls, then add them to the Custom Controls Tab section of the Controls palette. This makes form building much easier. The programmer can build an object such as a specialized pushbutton for usage in other forms with only slight property revision in the new form.

   A number of custom controls are included with Visual dBASE and are contained in files in the `C:\VISUALDB\SAMPLES` subdirectory. The `BUTTONS.CC` custom control file that we will use is installed by default, whereas the other included custom control files must be installed if needed (select **FILE | SET UP CUSTOM CONTROLS** from within the Form Designer). Though building new custom controls is beyond the scope of this text, we will demonstrate the usage of existing custom controls within this Browse object form.

From the Controls palette select the **Custom Tab**. Click and drag the **Next**, **Previous**, and **Close** custom controls into position on the form as shown in Figure 13.8. Give focus to the Close button and open the properties Inspector. Click both the **Properties Tab** and the **Events Tab**. Notice that properties and events are already in place. If we desired, we could modify any of these for use in our form. We will use all three custom control objects as they are.

8. Click the **Order View** icon to set the tabbing order of the form. The order should be as shown in Figure 13.7. The **Tab** key should move from one object in the order to the next. This causes a bit of problem because the **Tab/Shift-Tab** can also be used to move back and forth across the Browse window. To cause the **Tab** key to move through the tabbing order of the form, leave the `CUATab` property set to its default setting of `.T.`.

FIGURE 13.7 ORDER VIEW OF BROWSE OBJECT, `yedit.wfm`

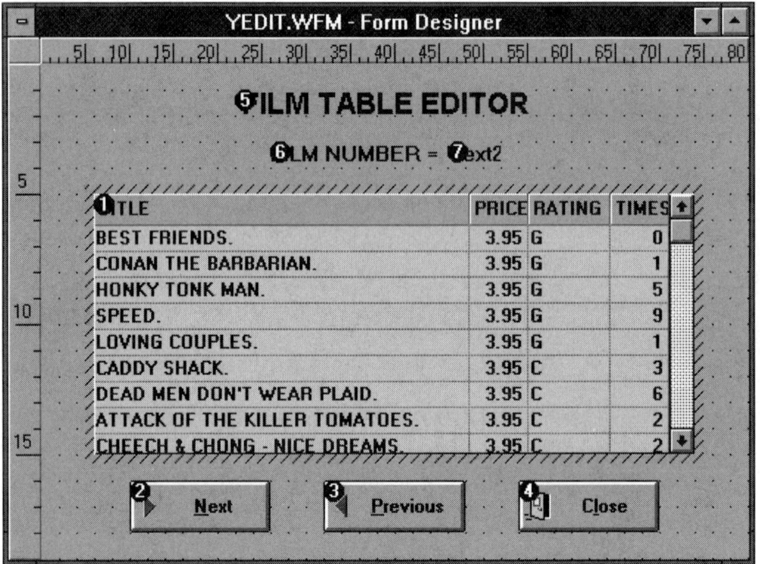

9. Select **View | Form** to view and test the final form. The form should appear as in Figure 13.8. Once displayed on the screen, perform the following tests

- **Tabbing order.** Move the **Tab** key through the tabbing order of the form.
- **Pointer movement and search.** Select **Form | Go to Record Number** to move the pointer to record 12. Select **Form | Find Records** to locate the title THE LION KING. Remember, with `EXACT` set to `OFF`, you can enter a shorter string such as THE LIO. Finally, find the POCAHONTAS film by searching for the `film_no` of 0048.
- **Film number display.** Using the mouse, then the **Up/Down-Arrow** keys, move through the table to ensure that the proper `film_no` is displayed over the Browse object and changes appropriately as the record highlight moves.
- **Next and Previous buttons.** Press both buttons to ensure the pointer moves ahead and back in the table. Also, the proper `film_no` should be displayed as the pointer moves.
- **Data validation.** Try modifying a `rating` to a letter other than `G`, `C`, `H`, or `X`.
- **Marking records for deletion.** Move the highlight to film number `0002`. Select **Form | Delete Current Record (Ctrl–U)**. The record should disappear from the Browse object. However, it is only marked for deletion. With `SET DELETED ON` by default, it is no longer displayed, though it remains in the table. We will `RECALL` it later.

NOTE: If the `DELETED` toggle is set to `OFF` prior to entry into the Browse object, the record will remain displayed together with the deletion mark. An additional column will be supplied for this purpose. The record can then be recalled from the Browse object by selecting **Form | Recall Current Record**.

- **Toggle between layouts.** Press **F2** to move between the Browse, Form, and Columnar display layouts. This is controlled by the Toggle and Mode properties of the Browse object. The default of Toggle is `.T.`, so toggling is allowed in our form. The default of Mode is `0`, so the initial layout in our form is the Browse layout.
- **Closing the form.** Click the **Close** button to close the form. This should take you to the Command window.

FIGURE 13.8 COMPLETED FILM EDITOR FORM, `yedit.wfm`

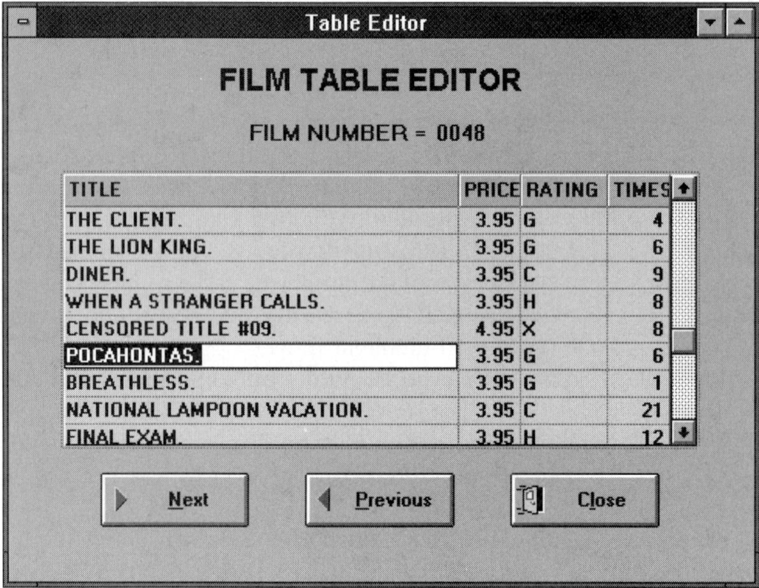

10. Attach the editor form, `yedit.wfm` to the Case System menu as follows:

- Type the following command from the Command window:

```
MODI MENU ymenu
```

- Tab to the **&Utilities** menu. Press **Down-Arrow** to add the following items. We will be using the Pack and Recall items later in the chapter.

&Table Editors
Pac&k all Tables
&Recall all Table Records

- With the cursor on the new item, **&Table Editors**, press **Tab** to create a new submenu containing the following items (Figure 13.9):

&Customer
&Film

- With the cursor on the new **&Film** item, right click to select the Inspector. Enter the following code block as the OnClick event-handler (see Figure 13.9).

```
{;DO yedit.wfm}
```

FIGURE 13.9 ATTACHING yedit.wfm TO THE MENU SYSTEM

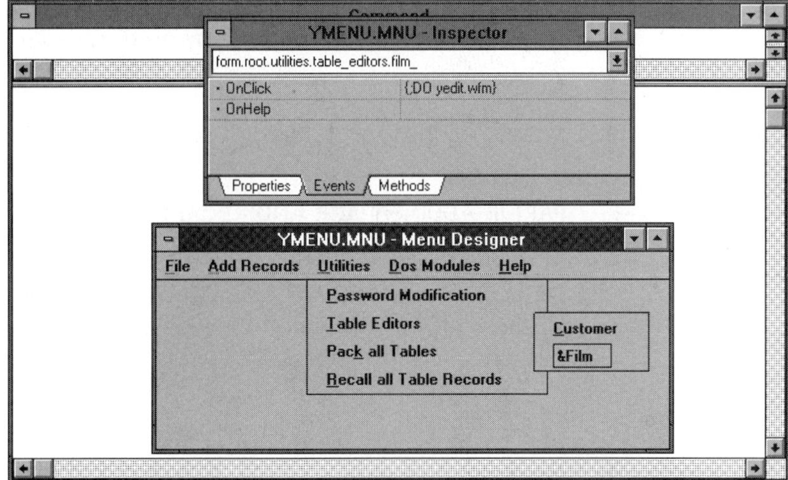

This completes the concepts discussion. In the following exercises, you will build a Browse object editor for the Customer table similar to the one just created for the Film table. To recall the records marked for deletion in the preceding exercise, type the following from the Command window:

```
USE yfilm
RECALL ALL
```

REVIEW EXERCISES

PART I: REVIEW QUESTIONS

1. Name three components of a custom editor.
2. Does the `DELETE` command physically remove a record from a table?
3. What is the function of the `SET DELETED` command?
4. What is returned by the `DELETED()` function and how is it used?
5. What command is used to remove a deletion mark?

6. Name the option in the `BROWSE` command that denies access to the management of indexes.

7. What is the function of the `NAME` option in the `BROWSE` command?

8. Name the Browse object property used to control the use of the **Tab** key.

9. Define a Custom control.

10. What speedbar icon is used to set the tabbing order on a form?

PART II: ADDING PACK AND RECALL OPTIONS TO THE CASE SYSTEM MENU

In this exercise, you will attach an action to the **&Pack all Tables** menu item and the **&Recall all Table Records** item of the Utilities menu to pack all the tables in the Video Express database to remove all records previously marked for deletion.

Specifications

1. Modify the menu file, **`ymenu.mnu`**, to attach the `PACK` procedure.

2. Create a procedure within the menu file as the OnClick handler of the **&Pack all Tables** menu item. Create the procedure according to the following pseudocode:

   - Present a `MSGBOX()` dialog containing the following message (see Figure 13.10):

     OK to pack database tables? ...

     Title the dialog as follows:

     Video Express Alert

     The dialog is to contain an **OK** button and a **Cancel** button.
   - If the operator clicks the **OK** button, perform the following—otherwise, return to the main menu.
   - Place the following message in the status bar to let the operator know what is occurring.

     ```
     STAND BY -- PACKING DATABASE TABLES ...
     ```
   - Set the exclusive toggle on.
   - Close all tables.
   - Open the customer table.
   - Pack the customer table.
   - Follow the same procedure for each table.

FIGURE 13.10 MSGBOX() FUNCTION

- Close all tables.
- Remove the status bar message
- Using the `MSGBOX()` function present a message dialog box to the screen to indicate that the process is complete. The dialog will not have a title, but will present the following message together with an **OK** button:

  `PACKING OPERATION COMPLETE ...`

3. Finally, create another procedure within the menu file as the OnClick handler of the **&Recall all Table Records** menu item. After you change the dialog and status bar messages, the process will be exactly the same as the Pack routine. The only addition will be to `SET DELETED OFF` when recalling records containing deletion marks and back `ON` when the procedure is complete. Use the following messages within your procedure:

- Initial `MSGBOX()` dialog: `OK to recall table records ? ...`
- Status bar message: `STAND BY -- RECALLING ALL TABLE RECORDS ...`
- Final `MSGBOX()` dialog: `RECALLING OPERATION COMPLETE ...`

4. Test both procedures by executing the Video Express Case System. Select **Utilities | Pack all** Tables from the main menu, then **Utilities | Recall all Table Records.**

PART III: CREATE A BROWSE OBJECT EDITOR FOR THE CUSTOMER TABLE

The objective of this exercise is to build a Browse object editor for the customer table. You will create the form to have the same basic features as the film table editor and modify it to include the features listed in the specifications that follow.

Specifications

1. Name the form file **`yedit2.wfm.`**
2. Build the form using the customer table, **`ycustm.dbf.`** Restrict the fields within the Browse object to those displayed in Figure 13.11.
3. Move the Text, Browse, Rectangle, and custom control Pushbutton controls to the form as shown in Figure 13.11. Notice the Rectangle control is to be placed around the **Customer#:** text fields.
4. As in the film table editor, each movement of the highlight cursor in the customer table editor is to cause a corresponding change in the customer number display. Remember also to display the customer number each time the Browse object is given focus.
5. Place an additional Pushbutton control on the form to toggle between the Browse layout mode and the Edit layout mode. The Pushbutton OnClick event-handler is to cause the following to occur:
   - Toggle the Toggle property to **`.T.`**.
   - If the Pushbutton Text property currently reads `GO BROWSE`, do the following:

     Toggle the Browse object from Columnar mode to Browse mode.
     Expand the size of the Browse object as shown in Figure 13.11.
     Change the Pushbutton Text property to read `GO EDIT`.
   - If the Pushbutton Text property currently reads `GO EDIT`, do the following:

     Toggle the Browse object from Browse mode to Columnar mode.
     Shrink the size of the Browse object as shown in Figure 13.12.
     Change the Pushbutton Text property to read `GO BROWSE`.
   - Toggle the Toggle property to **`.F.`**
   - Give focus back to Browse object.

FIGURE 13.11 CUSTOMER TABLE EDITOR `yedit2.wfm` (BROWSE MODE)

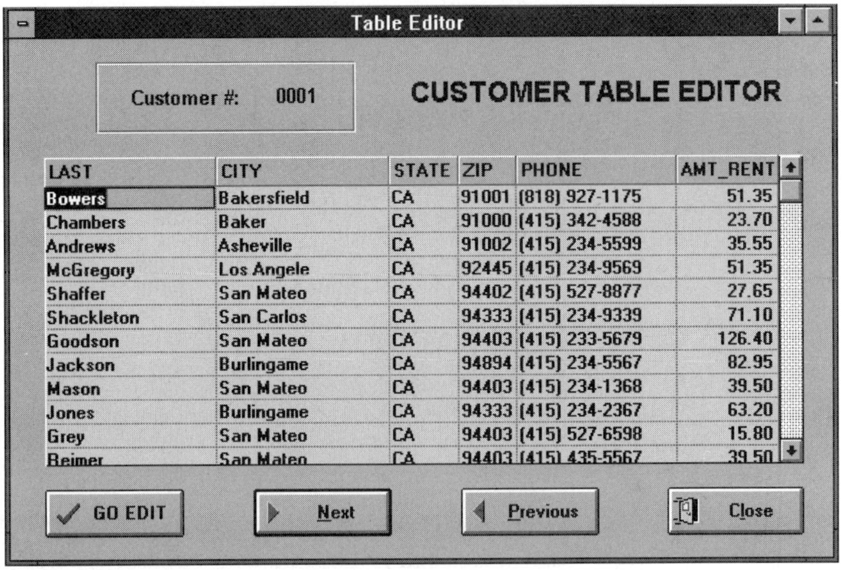

Table Editor

Customer #: 0001

CUSTOMER TABLE EDITOR

LAST	CITY	STATE	ZIP	PHONE	AMT_RENT
Bowers	Bakersfield	CA	91001	(818) 927-1175	51.35
Chambers	Baker	CA	91000	(415) 342-4588	23.70
Andrews	Asheville	CA	91002	(415) 234-5599	35.55
McGregory	Los Angele	CA	92445	(415) 234-9569	51.35
Shaffer	San Mateo	CA	94402	(415) 527-8877	27.65
Shackleton	San Carlos	CA	94333	(415) 234-9339	71.10
Goodson	San Mateo	CA	94403	(415) 233-5679	126.40
Jackson	Burlingame	CA	94894	(415) 234-5567	82.95
Mason	San Mateo	CA	94403	(415) 234-1368	39.50
Jones	Burlingame	CA	94333	(415) 234-2367	63.20
Grey	San Mateo	CA	94403	(415) 527-6598	15.80
Beimer	San Mateo	CA	94403	(415) 435-5567	39.50

GO EDIT | Next | Previous | Close

6. Perform the following data validation:

State: Restrict to uppercase
Zip code: Restrict to all numeric
Phone field template: `(999) 999-9999`
Phone field Valid property: Restrict area codes to either `916`, `415`, `818`, or `702`
Phone field invalid data message: Present a message to describe a data entry error (see Figure 13.13).

FIGURE 13.12 CUSTOMER TABLE EDITOR `yedit2.wfm` (COLUMNAR MODE)

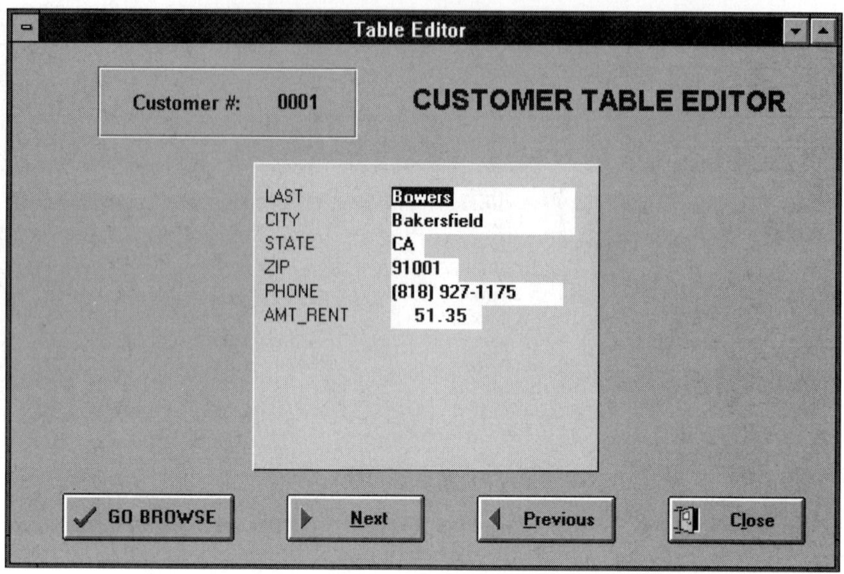

FIGURE 13.13 VALID MESSAGE DIALOG `yedit2.wfm`

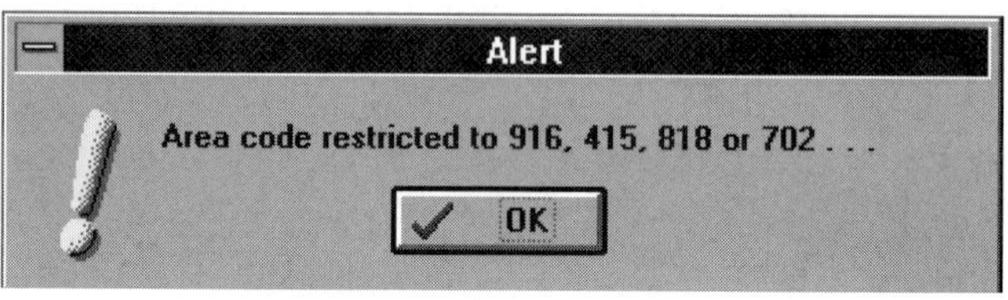

7. Set the tabbing order of the form in the following order:

   Rectangle
   All text
   Browse
   `GO EDIT`, `GO BROWSE` Pushbutton
   Next Pushbutton
   Previous Pushbutton
   Close Pushbutton

8. The deletion function is to be handled as in the film table editor. If the operator marks a record for deletion, that record should disappear from the Browse object display. Records can then be packed or recalled from the **Utilities** menu.
9. When the editor form is closed, close the customer table.
10. Attach the completed customer editor form to the **Table Editors | Customer** item of the main menu of the Case System.
11. Test all elements of the editor.

CHAPTER SUMMARY

In this chapter, we discussed the building of a custom editor using the Browse object of Visual dBASE.

- **Components of a custom editor.** The main features of a custom editor are an operator-oriented screen design, sufficient data validation, scrolling capability, record selection capability, and an effective messaging system.
- **The Deletion operation in Visual dBASE.** In Visual dBASE, records are marked with an asterisk character when a deletion command is executed. The record remains in the table until removed physically with the `PACK` command. Records that have been marked for deletion can be hidden from all table displays using the `SET DELETED` command.
- **Using Browse from the Command window.** For those using Visual dBASE from the Command window or Navigator, a very nice `BROWSE` command editor is available. It contains all the preceding components that apply to an effective editor.
- **Using the Browse control object.** Most of the features of the `BROWSE` command are available when using the Browse control as part of the design of a customer editor within an application.

New Commands

- DELETE
- SET DELETED
- RECALL
- PACK
- ZAP
- BROWSE

New Functions

- DELETED()
- MSGBOX()

New Properties

- ShowRecNo
- Alias
- Fields
- CUATab
- Toggle
- Mode

Visual dBASE Syntax of Commands

APPENDIX A

Commands appearing here are those related to Visual dBASE. Most commands specifically related to dBASE IV have been omitted. Visual dBASE syntax includes additional commands that are still in the language to maintain upward compatibility from dBASE IV.

```
!<DOS command>
```

Runs a DOS command or program from the Command window.

```
?/?? [<expression1>> [PICTURE <expC>]
    [FUNCTION <FUNCTION LIST>][AT <expN>]
       [STYLE <font number>]]
    [,<expression2> ...] [,]
```

? displays an expression list on the next line. ?? Displays an expression list on the current line.

```
???    <expC>
```

Sends character string to printer, bypassing installed printer driver.

```
APPEND [BLANK]/[NOORGANIZE]
```

Adds records to the end of a database table.

```
APPEND FROM <filename>/? [[TYPE] <file type>]
     [FOR <condition>] [REINDEX] [POSITION] [REINDEX]
```

Copies records from an existing (dBASE or non-dBASE) file to the end of the current table.

```
APPEND FROM ARRAY <array name>
     [FOR <condition>] [REINDEX]
```

Adds records to a database table from information in an array.

```
APPEND MEMO <memo field name> FROM <filename> [OVERWRITE]
```

Imports a file into a named memo field.

```
AVERAGE [<expN list>] [<scope>] [FOR <condition>]
     [WHILE <condition>] [TO <memvar list>/TO ARRAY
     <array name>]
```

Computes the arithmetic mean of numeric expressions.

```
BLANK [FIELDS <field list>/LIKE <skeleton>/EXCEPT
<skeleton>]
     [REINDEX][<scope>][FOR/WHILE <condition>]
```

Fills fields and records with blanks

```
BROWSE [NOINIT][NOFOLLOW][NOAPPEND][NOMENU][NOORGANIZE]
     [NOEDIT]
     [NODELETE][NOCLEAR][COMPRESS][FORMAT][LOCK <expN>]
     [WIDTH <expN> ][FREEZE <field name> ]
     [WINDOW <window name>]
```

```
[FIELDS <field name1> [/R] [/COLUMN WIDTH>]
   /<calculated field name 1> = <expression 1>
[,<field name 2> [/R] [/<column width >]
   /<calculated field name 2> = <expression 2]...]
```

A full-screen, menu-assisted command for editing and appending records in database tables and views.

```
BUILD <filename list> | FROM <response filename>
    [ICON <icon filename>]
    [SPLASH <bitmap format filename>]
    [TO <executable filename>]
```

Links object code files (such as `.pro` *and* `.wfo`*) and resources into a Windows executable file (*`.exe`*) if the optional Visual dBASE Compiler is installed.*

```
CALCULATE [scope] <option list>
    [FOR <condition>] [WHILE <condition>]
    [TO <memvar list> /TO ARRAY <array name>]
```

where `<option list>` *can be any one of the following functions:*

```
AVG( <expN>)
CNT()
MAX(<exp>)
MIN(<exp>)
NPV(<rate>,<flows>,<initial>)
STD(<expN>)
SUM(<expN>)
VAR(<expN>)
```

Computes financial and statistical functions.

```
CANCEL
```

Aborts program execution and returns to dot prompt.

```
CD [<path>]
```

Changes the current default drive or directory.

```
CHANGE [NOINIT][NOFOLLOW][NOAPPEND][NOMENU][NOORGANIZE]
    [NOEDIT]
    [NODELETE] [NOCLEAR] [<record number>] [FIELDS <field
    list>]
    [<scope>] [FOR <condition>] [WHILE <condition>]
```

Identical to `EDIT`*.*

```
CLASS <class name>[(<parameters>)]
       [OF <superclass name>[(<parameters>)]
          [CUSTOM]
          [FROM <filename>]]
      [PROTECT <propertyList>]
      <constructor code>
      <member functions>
ENDCLASS
```

Declares a custom class and specifies the member variables and functions for that class.

```
CLEAR
   [ALL/FIELDS/GETS/MEMORY/MENUS/POPUPS/SCREENS/TYPEAHEAD/
   WINDOWS]
```

Erases the screen, repositions the cursor to the lower left corner of the screen, and releases all pending **`GET`***s.*

Various forms of the **`CLEAR`** *command also close database tables, field lists, windows, popups, and menus; release memory variables; and empty the type-ahead buffer.*

```
CLEAR AUTOMEM
```

Initializes automem variables with empty values for the current table.

```
CLOSE ALL/ALTERNATE/DATABASES/FORMAT/INDEX/PRINTER/
      PROCEDURE/FORMS/TABLES]
```

Closes specified types of files.

```
COMPILE <filename> | <filename skeleton>
      [AUTO][LOG <filename>][TO <response filename>]
```

Compiles program files (`.prg`*,* `.wfm`*, etc.), creating object code files (*`.pro`*,* `.wfo`*, etc.).*

```
CONTINUE
```

Positions the record pointer to the next record meeting the condition specified in the most recent **`LOCATE`** *command.*

```
CONVERT [TO <expN>]
```

Adds to the database table's structure a field that stores information required for a multiuser lock detection.

```
COPY BINARY <fieldname> TO <filename> [ADDITIVE]
```

Copies a specified binary field to a file.

```
COPY FILE <filename> TO <filename>
```

Creates a duplicate of any closed file.

```
COPY INDEXES <.ndx file list> [TO <.mdx filename>]
```

Converts a list of index (`.ndx`) files into file tags in a single `.mdx` (multiple index) file.

```
COPY MEMO <memo field name> TO <filename> [ADDITIVE]
```

Copies information from a single memo field to a text file.

```
COPY STRUCTURE TO <filename>
    [FIELDS <Field List>] [[WITH] PRODUCTION]
```

Duplicates the structure of the file in use to new database.

```
COPY TABLE  <source table name> TO <target tablename>
    [[TYPE] [PARADOX|dBASE]]
```

Copies a specified table.

```
COPY TAG <tag name> [OF .mdx filename] TO <.ndx filename>
```

Converts multiple index (`.mdx`) tags into index (`.ndx`) files.

```
COPY TO <filename>
    [[TYPE] <file type>]/[[WITH] PRODUCTION][FIELDS
    <field list>]
    [<scope>] [FOR <condition>]
    [WHILE <condition>]
```

Duplicates all or part of the current table, creating a new table file.

```
COPY TO <filename> STRUCTURE EXTENDED
```

Creates a new database table, the records of which contain the structure of the current file. Structure contains new index option.

```
COPY TO ARRAY <array name> [FIELDS <fields list>]
    [<scope>] [FOR <condition>] [WHILE <condition>]
```

Fills an existing array with the contents of one or more records from the current table.

```
COUNT [TO <memvar>] [<scope>] [FOR <condition>]
    [WHILE <condition>]
```

Tallies the number of records in the current table that meet specified conditions.

```
CREATE [<filename> | ? | <filename skeleton>]
     [EXPERT [PROMPT]]
     [[TYPE] PARADOX | dBASE]
```

Opens the Table Designer.

```
CREATE APPLICATION/FORM [<filename> |?| <filename
skeleton>]
```

Opens the Form Designer.

```
CREATE/MODIFY CATALOG [<filename> |?| <filename skeleton>]
```

Creates a catalog file.

```
CREATE/MODIFY COMMAND/FILE [<filename> |?|
     <filename skeleton>]
     [WINDOW <window name>]
```

Allows editing of an existing program file, or opens an empty editing window.

```
CREATE/MODIFY FORM/SCREEN [<filename> |?| <filename
skeleton>]
     [EXPERT[PROMPT]]
```

Opens the Form Designer.

```
CREATE <filename>|? [[TYPE] PARADOX|dBASE]
     FROM <filename2> |?| <filename skeleton>
     [[TYPE] PARADOX|dBASE]
```

Creates a table with the structure defined by using the ***COPY TO...STRUCTURE EXTENDED*** *or* ***CREATE...STRUCTURE EXTENDED*** *commands.*

```
CREATE POPUP [<filename>|?|<filename skeleton>]
```

Opens the Menu Designer to create or modify a pop-up menu file.

```
CREATE <tablename>|? STRUCTURE EXTENDED
     [[TYPE] PARADOX|dBASE]
```

Creates a new database table that can be used to design the structure of a new table.

```
CREATE/MODIFY LABEL [<filename>|?|<filename skeleton>]
     [EXPERT[PROMPT]]
```

Opens the Report Designer. Labels are generated from Crystal Reports.

```
CREATE/MODIFY MENU [<filename> |?| <filename skeleton>]
```

Opens the Menu Designer.

```
CREATE/MODIFY QUERY <filename>/?
      or
CREATE/MODIFY VIEW <filename>/?
```

Opens the Query Designer.

```
CREATE/MODIFY REPORT [CROSSTAB][<filename>|?|
        <filename skeleton>][EXPERT[PROMPT]]
```

Opens Crystal Reports creates or modifies report form (`.frm`*) files using fields specified in current database or in related database tables.*

```
CREATE SESSION
```

Creates a new session and immediately selects it. Subsequent commands that are session-based apply to the new session.

```
CREATE VIEW <.vue filename> FROM ENVIRONMENT
```

Builds a view (`.vue`*) file compatible with dBASE III PLUS.*

```
DEBUG <filename>/<procedure name> [WITH <parameter list>]
```

Starts the Visual dBASE program debugger.

```
DEFINE <class name> <object name>
      [OF <container object>]
      [FROM <row,col> TO <row,col>>|<AT <row,col>]
      [PROPERTY <stock property list>]
      [CUSTOM <CUSTOM PROPERTY LIST>]
      [WITH <parameter list>]
```

Creates an object from a class.

```
DELETE [<scope>] [FOR<condition>] [WHILE <condition>]
```

Marks records in the current table for deletion.

```
DELETE FILE [<filename> |?| <filename skeleton>]
```

Used to delete an individual file. See also ***ERASE.***

```
DELETE TABLE [<filename> |?| <filename skeleton>]
      [[TYPE] PARADOX|dBASE]
```

Used to delete a specific table.

```
DELETE TAG <tag name 1> [OF <.mdx filename>]/
      <.ndx filename 1>
      [,<tag name 2> [OF <.mdx filename>]/
      <.ndx filename 2>...]
```

Deletes the specified tags from a multiple index (`.mdx`) file or closes index (`.ndx`) files depending on specified filename.

```
DIRECTORY/DIR [[ON] <drive>:][[LIKE] [<path>] <skeleton>
```

Displays directory information similar to the **DOS DIR** *command.*

```
DISPLAY [<Scope>] [FIELDS <exp list>]
     [FOR/WHILE <exp>] [OFF]
```

Displays records and fields from the current table.
Other display commands:
LIST/DISPLAY COVERAGE *or* FILES *or* MEMORY *or* STATUS *or* STRUCTURE
See the **LIST** *command for full syntax of these commands*

```
DO <program filename>/<procedure name>
     [WITH <parameter list>]
```

Executes a dBASE command file or procedure and may pass parameters to the named program.

```
DO CASE
   CASE<condition>
     <commands>
   [CASE <condition>
     <commands>]
   .
   .
   [OTHERWISE
     <commands>]
ENDCASE
```

A programming structure that selects only one course of action from a mutually exclusive set of alternatives.

```
DO WHILE <expL>
   <commands>
   [LOOP]
   [EXIT]
ENDDO
```

A programming structure that allows command statements between **DO WHILE** *and its associated* **ENDDO** *to be repeated while the specified condition is true.* **LOOP** *returns control to the beginning of a* **DO WHILE...ENDDO** *program structure.* **EXIT** *transfers control from within a* **DO WHILE...ENDDO. LOOP** *to the command immediately following the* **ENDDO**.

```
DO
    <commands>
    [LOOP]
    [EXIT]
UNTIL <expL>
```

Executes the statements between the `DO` *and* `UNTIL` *as long as the condition is false or until an* `EXIT` *is encountered.*

```
DOS
```

Interrupts Visual dBASE and displays the DOS prompt.

```
EDIT
    [<starting record expN>|<bookmark>] [<scope>]
    [FOR <condition1>] [WHILE<condition2]
    [COLOR[<standard text>][,[<enhanced text>][,<border>]
    [COLUMNAR] [COMPRESS]
    [FIELDS <field1>[<field option list 1]|
        <calculated field1> = <exp1> [<calculated field
        option list1>]
        [<field2> [<field option list 2>]|
        <calculated field2> = <exp2>
        [<calculated field option list2>]...]]
    [FORMAT]
    [FREEZE <field3] [KEY exp3> [,<exp4>]] [LOCK <expN>]
    [NOAPPEND][NODELETE][NOEDIT/MODIFY][NOFOLLOW][NOINIT]
    [NORMAL][NOTOGGLE][NOWAIT][TITLE <expC1>]
    [WIDTH <expN>][WINDOW <window name>]
```

A full-screen command to change the contents of a record in the current table or view.

```
EJECT
```

Sends a form feed to the printer to cause page eject.

```
EJECT PAGE
```

Advances the streaming output either to the defined `ON PAGE` *handler on the current page, or to the beginning of the next page.*

```
ERASE [<filename> |?| <filename skeleton>]
```

or

```
DELETE FILE [<filename> |?| <filename skeleton>]
```

Removes a closed file from the disk directory.

```
EXTERN [CDECL] <return type> <function name>
    ([<parameter type list>]) [<path>] <filename>
```

Declares a prototype for a non-dBASE function contained in a Dynamic Link Library (DLL) file.

```
FIND <literal key>
```

Searches an indexed database table for the first index key matching the specified character string or number.

```
FLUSH
```

Writes data buffers to disk and releases unallocated memory.

```
FOR <memvar> = <start expN> TO <end expN> [STEP <step
expN>]
    <statements>
    [LOOP]
    [EXIT}
NEXT
```

Executes the statements between **FOR** *and* **NEXT** *the number of times indicated by the* **FOR** *statement.*

```
FUNCTION <UDF name>
    [PARAMETERS]
    <other commands>
    RETURN <expression>
```

Identifies a user-defined function. **PROCEDURE** *is recommended in Visual dBASE.*

```
GENERATE [expN]
```

Adds a requested number of random records to the current table.

```
GO/GOTO BOTTOM/TOP [IN <alias>]
```

or

```
GO/GOTO [RECORD] <record number> [IN <alias>]
```

or

```
<record number>
```

Moves the pointer to a specific record in the current table according to the record's position.

```
HELP [<help topic>]
```

A menu-driven command providing information about dBASE IV.

```
IF <condition expL1>
    <statements>
[ELSEIF <condition expL2>
    <statements>
[ELSEIF <condition expL3>
    <statements>...]]
[ELSE
    <statements>]
ENDIF
```

Processes statements by evaluating one or more conditions and executing the statements following the first condition that evaluates to true.

```
IMPORT FROM <filename> ? [[TYPE] WB1|
```

Copies a file from a foreign format into Visual dBASE.

```
INDEX ON <key expression> TO <.ndx filename>/
      TAG <tag name> [OF <.mdx filename>] [UNIQUE]
      [DESCENDING]
```

Creates an index file in which records from a database table are in the ASCII order of the specified key fields.

```
INPUT [<prompt>] TO <memvar>
```

Allows the entry of an expression into a memory variable.

```
INSERT [BEFORE][NOORGANIZE][BLANK]
```

Puts a record into a specified position in a database table.

```
INSERT AUTOMEM [BEFORE]
```

See STORE AUTOMEM

```
JOIN WITH <alias> TO <filename> FOR  <Condition>
      [FIELDS <field list>] [[TYPE] [PARADOX|dBASE]]
```

Combines specified records and fields from two database tables to create a new database table.

```
KEYBOARD <expC> [CLEAR]
```

Enters a series of characters into the type-ahead buffer.

```
LABEL FORM [<filename1 |?| <filename skeleton1>]
     [<scope>] [FOR <condition1>] [WHILE <condition2>]
     [SAMPLE]
     [TO FILE [<filename2 |?| <filename skeleton2>|
     TO PRINTER]
```

Uses a specified Crystal Reports label form file (.RPL) designed with ***CREATE/MODIFY LABEL*** *to print, display, or write labels to a file on disk.*

```
LIST/DISPLAY [[FIELDS] <expression list>] [OFF]
     [<scope>] [FOR <condition>] [WHILE <condition>]
     [TO PRINTER/TO FILE <filename>]
```

Lists the contents of a database table in a columnar list.

```
LIST COVERAGE
     [<filename> |?| <filename skeleton>]
     [ALL] [SUMMARY]
     [TO FILE [<filename> |?| <filename skeleton>]|[TO
     PRINTER]
```

Displays contents of a coverage file (.COV) in the results pane of the Command window.

```
LIST/DISPLAY FILES [LIKE <skeleton>]
     [TO PRINTER/TO FILE <filename>] [ON <drive>]
```

Displays directory information similar to that displayed by the **DOS DIR** *command.*

```
LIST/DISPLAY MEMORY [TO PRINTER/TO FILE <filename>]
```

Provides information on how Visual dBASE is allocating your computer's memory.

```
LIST/DISPLAY STATUS [TO PRINTER/TO FILE <filename>]
```

Provides information about the current Visual dBASE session.

```
LIST/DISPLAY STRUCTURE [IN <alias>]
     [TO PRINTER/TO FILE <filename>]
```

Displays the data dictionary of the specified database table.

```
LOAD DLL [<path>] <DLL filename>
```

Initiates a DLL file.

```
LOCAL <memvar list>
```

Declares memory variables that are visible only in the subroutine where they are declared.

```
LOCATE [FOR] <condition> [<scope>] [WHILE <condition>]
```

Sequentially searches the current table for a record that matches a specified condition.

```
LOGOUT
```

Logs out the current user and sets up a new log-in dialog.

```
MD|MKDIR <directory>
```

Creates a new DOS directory.

```
MODIFY APPLICATION or FILE or FORM or LABEL or MENU or
 QUERY/VIEW or REPORT or SCREEN or STRUCTURE
```

These commands are synonymous with the corresponding **CREATE** *commands. See the* **CREATE** *command for the proper syntax and usage of these commands.*

```
MODIFY COMMAND/FILE <filename> [WINDOW <window name>]
```

Full-screen text editor used to create or edit dBASE programs, format files, or any standard ASCII text file.

```
NOTE/* <text> and [<command>] && <text>
```

Indicate comment lines in a program (`.prg`) file.

```
OPEN DATABASE <database name>
     [AUTOEXTERN] [LOGIN <username>/<password>]
     [WITH <option string>]
```

Establishes a connection to a database server or a database defined for specific directory location.

```
OPEN FORM <formname1>[ON <object name1>]
   [,<formname2> [ON <object name2]...]
```

Opens forms as modeless windows.

```
ON PAGE [AT LINE <expN> <command>]
```

Triggers an action when the streaming output reaches a particular line on the current page during a printing process.

```
PACK
```

Permanently removes database records marked for deletion.

```
PARAMETERS <parameter list>
```

Specifies memory variables that use information passed from a calling program by the **DO..WITH** *command.*

```
PLAY SOUND FILENAME [<filename>|?|<filename skeleton>]
     BINARY <binary>
```

Plays a sound stored in a `.Wav` *file or binary field.*

```
PRINTJOB
   <commands>
ENDPRINTJOB
```

Structured programming commands that control a print job.

```
PRIVATE ALL [LIKE/EXCEPT <Skeleton>]
```

or

```
PRIVATE <memvar list>
```

Declares memory variables that you can use in the program where they are declared and in all subroutines the program calls.

```
PROCEDURE <procedure name> [(parameter list>)]
     [<statements>]
     [RETURN [<return exp]]
```

Defines a procedure in a program file and optionally declares memory variables to represent parameters passed to the procedure.

```
PROTECT
```

Creates and maintains security on a dBASE system.

```
PUBLIC <memvar list>|ARRAY <array name1>"["<expN list1>"]"
     [,<array name2>"["<expN list2>"]"...]
```

Defines specified memory variables and array elements as global, allowing use in any dBASE program or subprogram.

```
QUIT [WITH <expN>]
```

Closes all files, releases all memory variables, and returns control to the operating system. With **<expN>** *returns an integer upon termination.*

```
RECALL  [<scope>] [FOR <condition>] [WHILE <condition>
```

Reinstates records that are marked for deletion in the current table.

```
REDEFINE <class name> <object name>
     [OF <container object>]
     [FROM <row, col> TO <row, col> > | <AT <row, col>]
     [PROPERTY <stock property list>]
     [CUSTOM <custom property list>]
     [WITH <parameter list>]
```

Changes an object definition in memory.

```
REFRESH [,<alias>]
```

Updates the current or specified work area data buffers to reflect the latest changes to data.

```
REINDEX
```

Rebuilds active `.mdx` *and* `.ndx` *files in the current work area.*

```
RELEASE <memvar list>
RELEASE ALL [LIKE/EXCEPT <skeleton>]
```

Deletes memory variables freeing memory for other use.

```
RELEASE AUTOMEM
```

Clears all stored automem variables from memory.

```
RELEASE DLL <DLL filename list>
```

Deactivates DLL files.

```
RELEASE OBJECT <container reference>.<object reference>
```

Removes object definitions from memory.

```
RENAME <filename1>|?|<filename skeleton1>
     TO <filename>2|?|<filename skeleton2>
```

Changes the name of a file.

```
RENAME TABLE <old table name1>|?|<filename skeleton1>
     TO <new table name>2|?|<filename skeleton2>
     [[TYPE] PARADOX|dBASE]
```

Changes the name of a table.

```
REPLACE <field> WITH <exp> [ADDITIVE] [,<field> WITH <exp>
     [ADDITIVE]] [<scope>] [FOR <condition>]
     [WHILE <condition>][REINDEX]
```

Changes the contents of specified fields in the current table.

```
REPLACE AUTOMEM
```

Transfers the contents of specified fields in the current table with data from specified expressions.

```
REPLACE BINARY <binary field name>
     FROM <filename> |?| <filename skeleton>
     [TYPE <binary type user number>]
```

Replaces the contents of a binary field with the contents of another binary file.

```
REPLACE FROM ARRAY <array name> [FIELDS <field list>]
    [<scope>]
    [FOR <condition>] [WHILE <condition>] [REINDEX]
```

Replaces fields in a database table with data from an array.

```
REPLACE MEMO <memo field> WITH ARRAY <array name>
```

Replaces the text of a memo field with the contents of an array.

```
REPLACE MEMO <memo field> FROM <filename>|?|
    <filename skeleton> [ADDITIVE]
```

Inserts a text file in a memo field.

```
REPLACE OLE <OLE field name>
    FROM <filename>|?|<filename skeleton> [LINK]
```

Inserts an OLE document into an OLE field.

```
REPORT FORM <filename 1>|?|<filename skeleton 1>
    [VIEW <filename 2> |?| <filename skeleton 2>]
    [<scope>] [FOR <condition 1>] [WHILE <condition 2>]
    [CROSSTAB][HEADING <expC>][NOEJECT][PLAIN][SUMMARY]
    [TO FILE <filename 3>|?|<filename skeleton 3>] |
    [TO PRINTER]
```

Generates and displays or prints a report, using the report format stored in a specified report file and information derived from records in the current table or specified view.

```
RESTORE FROM <filename> [ADDITIVE]
```

Retrieves and activates memory variables and arrays from a memory file, overwriting unless **`ADDITIVE`** *is used.*

```
RESTORE IMAGE FROM
    <filename>|?|<filename skeleton>|BINARY <binary
    field> [TIMEOUT <expN>] [TO PRINTER]
    [[TYPE] PCX | TIF[F] | ICO | WMF | EPS]
```

Displays an image stored in a file or a binary field.

```
RESUME
```

Resumes execution of a temporarily suspended program.

```
RETRY
```

Reexecutes a command sequence that caused an error.

RETURN [<expression> /TO MASTER/TO <procedure name>]

Used to restore control to calling programs, procedure, UDF, or to the Command window.

RUN/! <DOS command>

Executes a specified DOS command, or DOS program from within Visual dBASE.

SAVE TO <filename> [ALL LIKE/EXCEPT <skeleton>]

Stores all or part of the current set of memory variables and array elements to a disk file.

SCAN [<scope>] [FOR <condition>] [WHILE <condition>]
    [<commands>]
    [LOOP]
    [EXIT]
ENDSCAN

Automatically selects records from a database table, and applies processing commands to those records.

SEEK <expC> list | <expN list>

Rapidly searches for the first record in an indexed database table with a key that matches a specified expression.

SELECT <work area name/alias>

Chooses a work area in which to open a database table, or specifies a work area where a database table is already open.

SET

Displays a dialog box for viewing and changing the values of many SET *commands. The changed values are stored in the* dBASEWIN.INI *file.*

SET ALTERNATE on|OFF
SET ALTERNATE TO [<filename> [ADDITIVE]]

Records all output other than that of full-screen commands to a named text file.

SET AUTOSAVE on|OFF

Saves each record to disk as each editing change is made.

SET BELL ON|off
SET BELL TO [<frequency>, <duration>]

Controls the audible tone that alerts you to the end of a field or to an invalid entry by turning the bell on or off, or resetting its frequency or duration.

SET BLOCKSIZE TO <expN>

Changes the default block size of memo fields and multiple index (`.mdx`) files.

SET CARRY on|OFF

Copies data from a prior record to a new record when using **APPEND** *or* ***INSERT***.

SET CARRY TO [<field list> [ADDITIVE]]

Copies the specified fields from the previous record to the new record when using ***APPEND***, ***BROWSE***, *or* ***INSERT***.

SET CATALOG on|OFF
SET CATALOG TO [<filename>/?]

Used to create or open a catalog file. When a catalog is open and ***SET CATALOG*** *is ON, new files that you use or create are added to the catalog.*

SET CENTURY on|OFF

Allows the input and display of century prefixes in the year portion of dates.

SET CONFIRM on|OFF

Determines cursor movement at the end of an entry field.

SET CONSOLE ON|off

Turns the screen display on and off from within a program.

SET COVERAGE on|OFF

Determines whether dBASE creates/updates a coverage file (.COV).

SET CUAENTER ON|off

Determines whether `<enter>` *works in Windows mode or dBASE DOS mode.*

SET CURRENCY TO [<expC>]

Changes the symbol used for currency.

SET CURRENCY LEFT/right

Designates whether the currency symbol appears to the left or right of the currency amount.

SET DATABASE TO [<database name>]

Sets the default database from which tables are accessed.

```
SET DATE [TO] AMERICAN
     |ANSI|BRITISH|FRENCH|GERMAN|ITALIAN|JAPAN|USA
     |MDY|DMY|YMD
```

Determines the format for date displays.

```
SET DATE TO <expC>
```

Sets the system date.

```
SET DBTYPE TO [PARADOX|dBASE]
```

Sets the default table type to either Paradox or dBASE.

```
SET DECIMALS TO <expN>
```

Determines the number of decimal places Visual dBASE displays for the result of numeric functions and calculations.

```
SET DEFAULT TO <drive> [:]
```

Selects the drive where all operations take place and all files are stored.

```
SET DELETED ON|off
```

Determines whether records that are marked for deletion are included or ignored by other Visual dBASE commands.

```
SET DESIGN ON|off
```

Determines whether **CREATE** *and* **MODIFY** *commands can be executed.*

```
SET DEVELOPMENT ON|off
```

Determines whether Visual dBASE automatically compiles a program, procedure, or format file when you change the file and then execute it or open it for execution.

```
SET DIRECTORY TO [[<drive:>] [<path>]]
```

Specifies the operating system working drive and directory from within Visual dBASE.

```
SET DISPLAY TO MONO/COLOR/EGA25/EGA43/MONO43/VGA25/
    VGA43/VGA50
```

Selects between a monochrome and color monitor, and sets the screen display mode to monochrome, color, EGA, or VGA.

```
SET EDITOR TO [<expC>]
```

Specifies the text editor to use when creating and editing programs and text files.

```
SET ENCRYPTION ON|off
```

Establishes whether a newly created dBASE table is encrypted if **PROTECT** *is used.*

```
SET ERROR TO [<preceding expC> [, <following expC>]]
```

Specifies one character expression to precede error messages and another one to follow them.

```
SET ESCAPE ON|off
```

Specifies whether pressing **Esc** *interrupts program execution.*

```
SET EXACT on|OFF
```

Determines whether a comparison between two character strings requires the strings to be the same length.

```
SET EXCLUSIVE on|OFF
```

A network command; when ON, files cannot be shared by other users on the network.

```
SET FIELDS on|OFF
```

When ON, only fields designated with **SET FIELDS TO** *can be accessed or displayed.*

```
SET FIELDS TO [<field list> | ALL [LIKE <skeleton 1>]
    [EXCEPT <skeleton 2>]]
```

Defines a field list.

```
SET FILTER TO [FILE <filename>/?] [<condition>]
```

Limits access to only those records of a table that meet a specified condition.

```
SET FORMAT TO <format filename>
```

Opens a format file for data entry.

```
SET FULLPATH on|OFF
```

Specifies whether functions that return file names return the full path with the file name.

```
SET FUNCTION <expN>/<expC>/<key label> TO <expC>
```

Programs a function key with a character string of up to 238 characters for each function key.

```
SET HEADING on|OFF
```

Field names display or do not display above the fields in **LIST** *or* **DISPLAY**, **SUM** *or* **AVERAGE** *results.*

```
SET HELP ON|off
```

Determines whether the user will be prompted for help when an error is encountered.

```
SET IBLOCK TO <expN>
```

Allows changing the default size of the indexing block that dBASE allocates to new index data (`.mdx`*) files.*

```
SET INDEX TO [?/<filename list> [ORDER [TAG]
    <.ndx filename>/<.mdx tagname> [OF <.mdx filename>]]]
```

Opens the specified index files, both index (`.ndx`*) and multiple index (*`.mdx`*). Also, may specify the controlling index or tag for an active table.*

```
SET KEY TO [<exp:match>/RANGE <exp:low>,<exp:high>/
    <exp:low [,]/,<exp:high>] [IN <alias>][EXCLUDE]
```

Allows the display of only those records of a table whose ordering index key meets a specified range of conditions.

```
SET KEY <expN> | <expC> TO
    [<program name> | <procedure name>]
```

Assigns a program or a procedure to a specified key or key combination.

```
SET LDCHECK ON|off
```

Enables or disables language driver ID checking.

```
SET LDCONVERT ON|off
```

Determines whether data read from and written to character and memo fields is transliterated when the table character set does not match the global language driver.

```
SET LIBRARY TO [<filename>|?|<filename skeleton>]
```

Points to a library of general procedures that any Visual dBASE application can access.

```
SET LOCK ON|off
```

Determines whether automatic lock is activated in multi-user systems to prevent a record from being updated by more than one user at the same time.

```
SET MARGIN TO [<expN>]
```

Adjusts printer offset for left margin for all printed output.

```
SET MARK TO <expC>
```

Alters delimiter between month, day, and year in date display.

`SET MBLOCK TO <expN>`

Allows changing the default size of the block that dBASE allocates to new memo field files (.DBT).

`SET MEMOWIDTH TO [<expN>]`

Adjusts width of memo field output.

`SET MESSAGE TO [<expC>]`

Displays a user-defined character string in the status bar. Use of the StatusMessage property is the preferred method.

`SET MOUSE ON|off`

Enables or disables the mouse cursor, if one is installed.

`SET NEAR on|OFF`

Positions the pointer to the record immediately following the potential location of the sought-after key in the open file.

```
SET ORDER TO
SET ORDER TO [<expN>]
SET ORDER TO [TAG]
    <filename> / <.mdx tagname> [OF <.mdx filename>]
    [NOSAVE]
```

Sets up any open index file or tag as the master index, or removes control from all open index files or `.mdx` *tags.*

`SET PATH TO [<path list>]`

Specifies a path for file search.

`SET PCOL TO <expN>`

Sets the printing column position of a printer, which is the value of `PCOL()`.

`SET POINT TO [<expC>]`

Changes the character used for decimal point.

`SET PRECISION TO [<expN>]`

Sets the number of decimal places used internally in all fixed-point math operations; `<expN>` *is an integer between 10 and 20.*

`SET PRINTER on|OFF`

Controls whether dBASE also directs streaming output that appears in the Command window to the device or file specified by `SET PRINTER TO`.

```
SET PRINTER TO
```

Specifies a file to receive streaming output, or uses a device code recognized by the Windows Print Manager to designate a printer.

```
SET PROCEDURE TO [<procedure filename>]
```

Opens a named procedure file.

```
SET PROW TO <expN>
```

Sets the printing row position of a printer, which is the value of `PROW()`.

```
SET REFRESH TO <expN>
```

Specifies the time interval between file checks, to determine if a record has changed in a table.

```
SET RELATION TO [<key exp list 1> | <expN 1>
     INTO <child table alias 1>
     [CONSTRAIN]
     [INTEGRITY
        [CASCADE | RESTRICTED] ]
     [, <key exp list 2> | <expN 2>
        INTO <child table alias 2>]
        [CONSTRAIN]
        [INTEGRITY
           [CASCADE | RESTRICTED] ] ... ][ADDITIVE]
```

Links two or more open tables according to a key expression that is common to all related files.

```
SET REPROCESS TO <expN>
```

Sets the number of times Visual dBASE tries a network file or record lock command before producing an error message.

```
SET SAFETY ON|off
```

Sets the level of protection against a file being overwritten.

```
SET SEPARATOR TO [<expC>]
```

Changes the comma used for the numeric separator, which is the U.S. convention, to a specified character.

```
SET SKIP TO [<alias> [, <alias>]...]
```

Supports multiple detail record handling in tables linked with the `SET RELATION` *command. It allows access to all records in the linked files matching a particular key.*

SET SPACE ON|off

Lets the ? and ?? commands print a space between expressions.

SET STATUS ON|off

Determines whether the status bar displays at the bottom of the screen.

SET TALK ON|off

Determines whether a response to certain Visual dBASE commands is displayed.

SET TIME TO <expC>

Resets the system time.

SET TITLE ON|off

Turns the catalog file title prompt on and off.

SET TOPIC TO <[<expC>]

Determines initial Help topic displayed.

SET TYPEAHEAD TO <expN>

Specifies the size of the type-ahead buffer.

SET UNIQUE on|OFF

Determines whether first or all record(s) with identical keys appear in index file.

SET VIEW TO <query filename>/?

Specifies the query file (.QBE) previously created to set the current view.

SET WP TO [<expC>]

Determines which text editor to use during memo field edits.

SHOW OBJECT <form name>.<object name>

Updates the appearance of an object to reflect the most recent property settings.

SKIP [<expN>] [IN <alias>]

Moves the record pointer forward or backward in a database table.

SLEEP <seconds expN> |
    UNTIL <time expC> [,<date expC>]

Pauses a program for a specified interval or until a specified time.

```
SORT TO <filename> ON <field1> [/A] [/D]
     [,<field2> [/A] [/C] [/D]...] [ASCENDING]/
     [DESCENDING]
     [<scope>] [FOR <condition>] [WHILE <condition>]
```

Creates a new database table in which the records of the current table are positioned in the ASCII order of the specified key fields.

```
STORE <expression> TO  <memvar list>/<array element list>
```

or

```
      <memvar>/<array element> = <expression>
```

Creates and initializes memory variables and initializes array elements previously created with the **DECLARE** *command.*

```
STORE AUTOMEM
```

Stores the contents of all the current record's fields to a set of memory variables.

```
STORE MEMO <memo field> TO ARRAY <array name>
```

Stores the text of a memo field to an array-type memory variable.

```
SUM [<expN list>] [TO <memvar list>/TO ARRAY <array name>]
     [<scope>] [FOR <condition>] [WHILE <condition>]
```

Totals numeric expressions to memory variables or arrays.

```
SUSPEND
```

A debugging tool that interrupts program execution, allowing entry of commands at the dot prompt.

```
TOTAL ON <key field> TO <filename> [FIELDS <field list>]
     [<scope>] [FOR <condition>] [WHILE <condition>]
     [[TYPE] [PARADOX|dBASE]]
```

Sums the numeric fields of the current table and creates a second database table to hold the results.

```
TYPE <filename> [TO PRINTER/TO FILE <filename>] [NUMBER]
```

Displays the contents of an ASCII text file.

```
UNLOCK [ALL/IN <alias>]
```

A network command to release record and file locks.

```
UPDATE ON <key field> FROM <alias>
     REPLACE <field name 1> WITH <expression 1>
     [,<field name 2> WITH <expression 2>...]
     [RANDOM] [REINDEX]
```

Uses data from another database table to replace fields in the current database table making the changes by matching records in the two files based on a key field.

```
USE [<filename 1> |?| <filename skeleton 1>
     [ [TYPE] PARADOX|dBASE][IN <alias>]
     [INDEX <index name list> |
       <? list> | <index name skeleton list>]
     [ORDER [TAG] <.ndx filename> |
       <tag name> [OF <.mdx filename>] ]
     [AGAIN][ALIAS <alias name>][AUTOMEM][EXCLUSIVE|
     SHARED][NOSAVE][NOUPDATE]]
```

Opens an existing database table and associated `.dbt` *file; may also open* `.mdx` *and* `.ndx` *index files.*

```
WAIT [<prompt>] [TO <memvar>]
```

Causes all processing to pause until any key is pressed.

```
ZAP
```

Removes all records from the current table.

Visual dBASE Functions

APPENDIX B

Functions appearing here are those related to Visual dBASE. Most of the functions specifically related to dBASE IV have been omitted. Visual dBASE syntax includes additional functions that are still in the language to maintain upward compatibility from dBASE IV.

```
& <Character Variable)
```

Macro substitution.

```
ABS(<expN>)
```

Returns absolute value.

```
ACCESS()
```

Returns the access level of the current user, as assigned with the **PROTECT** *command.*

```
ACOPY(<source array name>, <target array name>
      [, <starting element expN> [, <elements expN>
      [, <target element expN>]]])
```

Copies elements from one declared array to another and returns the number of elements copied.

```
ACOS(<expN>)
```

Returns the angle size in radians for cosine value.

```
ADEL(<array name>, <position expN> [, <row/column expN>])
```

Deletes an element from a one-dimensional array, or deletes a row or column of elements from a two-dimensional array. Returns 1 if successful, an error if unsuccessful.

```
ADIR(<array name>
    [, <filename skeleton expC> [,
    <file attribute list expC>]])
```

Stores to a declared array five characteristics of specified files: name, size, date stamp, time stamp, and attribute(s). Returns the number of files whose characteristics are stored.

```
AELEMENT(<array name>, <subscript1 expN>
      [, <subscript2 expN>])
```

Returns the number of a specified element in a one- or two-dimensional array.

```
AFIELDS(<array name>)
```

Stores the current table's structural information to a declared array and returns the number of fields whose characteristics are stored.

```
AFILL(<array name>, <exp>
    [, <start expN> [, <count expN>]])
```

Inserts a specified value into one or more locations in a declared array, and returns the number of elements inserted.

```
AGROW (<array name>, <expN>)
```

Adds an element, row, or column to an array and returns a numeric value representing the number of added elements.

```
AINS(<array name>, <position expN> [, <row/column expN>])
```

Inserts an element with the value `.F.` *into a one-dimensional array, or inserts a row or column of elements with the value* `.F.` *into a two-dimensional array. Returns 1 if successful, an error if unsuccessful.*

```
ALEN(<array name> [, <expN>])
```

Returns the number of elements, rows, or columns of an array.

```
ALIAS([<expN>])
```

Returns alias name assigned to a specified work area.

```
ANSI(<expC>)
```

Returns a character string that is the American National Standards Institute (ANSI) value of a specified Original Equipment Manufacturer (OEM) character expression.

```
ARESIZE(<array name>, <new rows expN>
    [,<new cols expN> [, <retain values expN>]])
```

Increases or decreases the size of an array according to the specified dimensions and returns a numeric value representing the number of elements in the modified array.

```
ASC(<expC>)
```

Character to ASCII Code conversion.

```
ASCAN(<array name>, <exp>
    [, <starting element expN> [, <elements expN>]])
```

Searches an array for an expression. Returns the number of the first element that matches the expression if the search is successful, or 0 if the search is unsuccessful.

```
ASIN(<expN>)
```

Returns angle in radians for any given sine value.

```
ASORT(<array name>
    [, <starting element expN> [,<elements to sort expN>
    [, <sort order expN>]]])
```

Sorts the elements in a one-dimensional array or the rows in a two-dimensional array, returning 1 if successful or an error if unsuccessful.

ASUBSCRIPT(<array name>, <element expN>, <row/column expN>)

Returns the row number or the column number of a specified element in an array.

AT(<expC>,<expC>/[,<expN>]

or

AT(<expC>,<memo field name> [,<expN>])

Returns starting position of a substring within a second character string.

ATAN(<expN>)

Returns angle in radians for given tangent value.

ATN2(expN1>,<expN2>)

Returns the angle in radians when cosine and sine of the angle are specified.

BEGINTRANS([<database name expC>] [,<isolation level expN>])

Starts a transaction and returns **.T.** *if the transaction started successfully.*

BINTYPE(),BITAND(),BITLSHIFT(),BITOR(),BITRSHIFT(), BITSET(),BITXOR()

Functions used to examine and manipulate data at the bit level.

BOF([<alias>]))

Beginning of File.

BOOKMARK([<alias>])

Returns a bookmark for the current record. Bookmarks are used in place of record number for tables that do not support record pointers (for example, Paradox and SQL tables).

CATALOG()

Returns the name of the active catalog file.

CDOW(<expD>)

Returns character day of week.

CEILING(<expN>)

Returns the smallest integer >= the specified number.

`CENTER(<expC> | <memo field> [, <length expN> [, <pad expC> ]])`

Returns a character string that contains a string centered in a line of specified length.

`CERROR()`

Returns the number of the last compiler error message.

`CHANGE([<alias>])`

Determines if a record has been changed.

`CHARSET( [<alias>] )`

Returns the name of the character set the current table or a specified table is using. If no table is open and you issue **`CHARSET()`** *without an argument, it returns the global character set in use.*

`CHOOSEPRINTER(<title expC>)`

Opens the Print Setup dialog box for choosing a printer or specifying print options, and resets the appropriate system memory variables for the printer or print options you specify. Returns true (`.T.`) if you exit the dialog box by choosing OK, and false (`.F.`) if you choose Cancel.

`CHR(<expN>)`

Converts numeric expression to character type.

`CMONTH(<expD>)`

Returns name of month from a date expression.

`COL()`

Current screen column position.

`COMMIT( [<database name expC>] )`

Ends a transaction initiated by **`BEGINTRANS()`** *and writes to the open files any changes made during the transaction. Returns* **`.T.`** *if the data was committed successfully.*

`COMPLETED()`

Determines whether a transaction has been completed.

`COS(<expN>)`

Returns the cosine value for any angle in radians.

`CTOD(<expC)/{expC}`

Converts character to date.

`DATABASE()`

Returns the name of the current database from which tables are accessed.

`DATE()`

Returns system date.

`DAY(<expD>)`

Returns day of month.

`DBF([<alias>])`

Returns name of table in `USE`.

`DBERROR()`

Returns the number of the last Borland Database Engine (BDE) error.

`DBMESSAGE()`

Returns the error message of the last Borland Database Engine (BDE) error.

`DELETED([<alias>])`

Identifies records marked for deletion.

`DESCENDING([[<.mdx filename,>] <expN> [,<alias>]])`

Returns a true (`.T.`*) if the specified* `.mdx` *index tag was created with the* `DESCENDING` *key word.*

`DIFFERENCE(<expC>,<expC)`

Determines difference between two literal strings.

`DISKSPACE()`

Returns number of free bytes on default disk drive.

`DMY(<expD>)`

Converts a date to a day/month/year format.

`DOW(<expD>)`

Returns day of the week as a number.

`DTOC(<expD>)`

Converts a date expression to a character string.

`DTOR(<expN>)`

Converts degrees to radians.

`DTOS(<expD>)`

Converts a date expression to a character string.

`ELAPSED(<stop time expC>, <start time expC>)`

Returns the number of seconds elapsed between two specified times.

`EMPTY(<exp>)`

Returns `.T.` *if a specified expression or field is 0 or blank,* `.F.` *if it contains any other value.*

`EOF([<alias>])`

Indicates end of file.

`ERROR()`

Returns number of error causing `ON ERROR` *condition.*

`EXP(<expN>)`

Exponential (e *to the* X).

`FACCESSDATE(<filename expC>)`

Returns the last date a file was opened under Windows 95.

`FCLOSE(<expN>)`

Closes a low-level file previously opened with the `FCREATE()` *or* `FOPEN()` *function.*

`FCREATE(<filename expC>[, <access expC>] )`

Creates and opens a specified file. Returns the file handle number of the file if successful or −1 if unsuccessful.

`FCREATEDATE(<filename expC>)`

Returns the date a file was created under Windows 95.

`FCREATETIME(<filename expC>)`

Returns the time a file was created under Windows 95.

`FDATE(<expC>)`

Returns, from the operating system, the date that the specified file was last modified.

`FDECIMAL(<field number expN> [, <alias>] )`

Returns the number of decimal places in a specified field of a table.

FEOF(<expN>)

Tests whether the file pointer is at the end of a low-level file.

FERROR()

Returns the operating system error status number for a low-level file operation.

FFLUSH(<expN>)

Writes the contents of the system buffer for a specified low-level file to disk.

FGETS(<expN1> [,<expN2>] [,<expC>])

*Reads and returns a string of characters from a low-level file opened with the **FCREATE()** or **FOPEN()** function.*

FIELD(<expN>[,<alias>])

Returns field name of the file structure field number of the selected database.

FILE(<expC>)

Returns .T. *if specified file exists.*

FKLABEL(<expN>)

Returns name of function key as character string.

FKMAX()

Returns number of programmable function keys on keyboard.

FLDCOUNT([<alias>])

Returns the number of fields in the specified table.

FLDLIST(<expN>)

Returns the nth *field or expression of a* ***SET FIELDS TO*** *list.*

FLOAT(<expN>)

Converts numeric-type data to float-type data.

FLOCK([alias])

A network function to lock database files.

FLOOR(<expN>)

Returns the largest integer <= the specified number.

FNAMEMAX([<expC>])

Returns the maximum allowable file-name length on a given drive or volume.

`FOPEN(<expC1> [,<expC2>])`

Opens an existing file and returns a file handle number.

`FOR([[<.mdx filename>,] <expN> [,<alias>]])`

Returns the **FOR** *condition used to create an* **.mdx** *file index tag.*

`FOUND([<alias>])`

Returns **.T.** *if previous record search was successful.*

`FPUTS(<expN1>,<expC1> [,<expN2>] [,<expC2>])`

Writes a character string and end-of-line indicator to the file at the current pointer position; returns the number of bytes written to the file.

`FREAD(<expN1>,<expN2>)`

Reads and returns a string of characters, including any end-of-line indicators, from a file opened with the **FCREATE()** *or* **FOPEN()** *function.*

`FSEEK(<expN1>,<expN2> [,<expN3>])`

Moves the file pointer to a specified location within a file opened by **FCREATE()** *or* **FOPEN()**.

`FSHORTNAME(<filename expC>)`

Returns the short name (i.e., the DOS-compatible name) of a file created under Windows 95.

`FSIZE(<expC>)`

Returns an integer for the size, in bytes, of the specified file as reported by the operating system.

`FTIME(<expC>)`

Returns, from the operating system, the time that the specified file was last modified.

`FUNIQUE(<expC>)`

Creates a unique file name.

`FV(<payment>,<rate>,<periods>)`

Returns the future value of equal regular deposits made in equal intervals yielding fixed interest.

`FWRITE(<expN1>,<expC1> [,<expN2>])`

Writes a specified character string to a file opened with **FCREATE()** *or* **FOPEN()**. *It also returns the number of bytes written to the file.*

```
GETCOLOR([<title expC>])
```

Calls a dialog box in which you can define a custom color or select a color from the color palette. Returns a character string containing the red, green, and blue values for the color selected.

```
GETDIRECTORY([<directory expC>])
```

Displays a dialog box from which you can select a directory for use with subsequent commands.

```
GETENV(<expC>)
```

Returns contents of operating system's environmental variables.

```
GETEXPR([<expression expC> [, <title expC> [,
     <data type expC>]]])
```

Displays a dialog box in which you can create or edit an expression, and returns the expression you specify.

```
GETFILE([<filename skeleton expC>
     [, <title expC>
     [, <filetype expL>
     [, <change filetype expL>]]]] )
```

Displays a dialog box from which the user can choose or enter an existing file name, and returns the file name. Returns an empty string if the user exits the dialog box by any method except by double-clicking on a file name or choosing OK.

```
GETFONT( [<title expC>] )
```

Calls a dialog box in which you select a character font. Returns a string containing the font name, point size, font style (if you choose a style other than Regular), and family.

```
HOME()
```

Returns the path from which the current Visual dBASE session was invoked.

```
HTOI(<expC>)
```

Returns the decimal-number equivalent of a specified hexadecimal number.

```
ID()
```

Returns the name of the current user on a Local Area Network.

```
IIF(<condition>,<exp1>,<exp2>)
```

Immediate ***IF..*** *shortcut to the* ***IF...ENDIF*** *programming construct.*

`INKEY ([<seconds expN>] [, <mouse expC>])`

Returns an integer representing the most recent key pressed. Can also be used to wait for a keystroke and return its value.

`INSPECT(<object reference>)`

Opens the Inspector, a window that lists object properties and lets you change their settings.

`INT(<expN>)`

Returns integer of number.

`ISALPHA(<expC>|<memo field>)`

Returns `.T.` *if specified character string begins with an alpha character.*

`ISBLANK(<exp>)`

Tests whether the specified expression is blank.

`ISLOWER(<expC>)`

Returns `.T.` *if specified expression begins with lower case.*

`ISMOUSE()`

Returns a logical true (`.T.`*) or false (*`.F.`*) that indicates whether or not a mouse driver has been installed.*

`ISTABLE(<table name>)`

Tests for the existence of a table in a specified database and returns `.T.` *if the table exists or* `.F.` *if it does not.*

`ISUPPER(<expC>|<memo field>)`

Returns `.T.` *if specified expression begins with upper case.*

`ITOH(<expN 1>[, <expN 2>]`

Returns the hexadecimal equivalent of a specified decimal number as a character string.

`KEY([[<.mdx filename>,]<expN>[,<alias>]])`

Returns the key expression for the specified index file.

`KEYMATCH(<exp [,<index number> [,<exp work area>]])`

Returns a logical true (`.T.`*) or false (*`.F.`*) that indicates whether or not a specified expression is found in a specified index.*

LDRIVER([<alias>])

Returns the name of the language driver the current table or a specified table is using. If no table is open and you issue **LDRIVER()** *without an argument, it returns the global language driver in use.*

LEFT(<expC>/<memofield name>,<expN>)

Returns specified number of leftmost characters.

LEN(<expC>/<memofield name>)

Returns the number of characters specified.

LENNUM(<expN>)

Returns the display length of a specified number, including leading spaces.

LIKE (<pattern>,<expC>)

Returns **.T.** *if wildcard string matches compared value.*

LINENO()

Returns line number of the next command to be executed.

LISTCOUNT(<form reference>.<list box reference>)

Returns the number of prompts in a list box.

LISTSELECTED(<form reference>.<list box reference>
[, expN])

Returns a list box prompt.

LKSYS(n)

Returns date, time, or user i.d. pertaining to a locked record or file.

LOCK([<expC list>,<alias>]/[<alias>])

Locks one or more database records, same as **RLOCK()**.

LOG(<expN>)

Returns log to base e.

LOG10(<expN>)

Returns log to base 10.

LOOKUP(<return field>,<look-for exp>,<look-in field>)

Searches a field and returns **.T.** *if a specified value is found.*

LOWER(<expC>)

Converts upper to lowercase.

`LTRIM(<expC>)`

Removes leading blanks from character expression.

`LUPDATE([<alias>])`

Returns date of last table update.

`MAX(<expN1>/<expD1>,<expN2>/<expD2>)`

Returns the larger of the two numeric, date, or character expressions.

`MDX(<expN>[,<alias>])`

Returns the filename for the `.mdx` *file specified by the index order number.*

`MDY(<expD>)`

Converts date format to (char) month, day, year.

`MEMLINES(<memo field name>)`

Returns number of lines contained in a memo field.

`MEMORY([expN])`

Returns the amount of memory in kilobytes that is available in or allocated to various memory regions.

`MESSAGE()`

Returns error message character string.

`MIN(<expN1>/<expD1>,<expN2>/<expD2>)`

Returns the smaller value of two numeric, date, or character expressions.

`MLINE(<memo field name>,<expN>)`

Extracts a specified line of text from a memo field in the current record.

`MOD(<expN1>,<expN2>)`

Returns remainder of division.

`MONTH(<expD>)`

Returns number of month from a date expression.

`NDX(<expN>[,<alias>])`

Returns name of active `.ndx` *file.*

`NETWORK()`

Returns `.T.` *if Visual dBASE is running on a network.*

`NEXTKEY([<expN>])`

Returns the decimal value associated with a key or key combination held in the keyboard type-ahead buffer; does not remove the keystroke from the buffer.

`OEM(<expC>)`

Returns a character string that is the Original Equipment Manufacturer (OEM) value of a specified American National Standards Institute (ANSI) character expression.

`ORDER([<alias>])`

Returns the name of the primary order index file or `.mdx` *tag.*

`OS()`

Returns name of current operating system.

`PAYMENT(<principal>,<rate>,<periods>)`

Returns the payment required to amortize a loan with constant interest over equal intervals.

`PCOL()`

Returns the current column position on the printer (relative to `_poffset`*), and helps keep track of printer column positions within programs.*

`PCOUNT()`

Returns the number of parameters passed to a procedure or user-defined function.

`PI()`

Returns π (the irrational number 3.14159).

`PRINTSTATUS()`

Returns (`.T.`*) if the printer is ready to accept output.*

`PROGRAM([<expN>])`

Returns the name of the program or procedure that was executing when an error occurred.

`PROPER(<expC> | <memo field>)`

Converts a character string to proper-noun format and returns the resulting string.

`PROW()`

Returns the printer row position.

PV(<payment>,<rate>,<periods>)

Returns present value of equal payments at a constant interest rate over regular payment periods.

RANDOM([<expN>])

Generates random number.

RAT(<expC>,<expC>/[,<expN>])
or
RAT(<expC>,<memo field name> [,<expN>])

Returns starting position of a substring within a second character string. Search begins from the last character of the string or memo field.

READMODAL(<object reference> [, <expL>])

Opens a form as a modal window and returns the name of the object that has input focus when the user submits the form.

RECCOUNT([<alias>])

Returns number of records in selected table.

RECNO([<alias>])

Returns current record number of specified file.

RECSIZE([<alias>])

Returns record size in the current or specified table.

RELATION(<expN> [,<alias>])

Returns the key expression defined with the ***SET RELATION*** *command for the current or specified work area.*

REPLICATE(<expC>|<memo field>,<expN>)

Repeats character expression.

RESOURCE(<resource id>, <DLL filename expC>)

Returns a character string from a DLL file.

RIGHT(<expC>/<memo field name>,<expN>)

Returns specified number of characters from a string or memo field beginning at right.

RLOCK(<[expC list>,<alias>]/[<alias>])

Locks multiple records.

`ROLLBACK([<database name expC>])`

Returns **`.T.`** *if last* **`ROLLBACK`** *command was successful.*

`ROUND(<expN1>,<expN2>)`

Rounds numbers to specified number of decimal places.

`RTOD(<expN>)`

Converts radians to degrees.

`RTRIM(<expC>)or TRIM(<expC>)`

Removes trailing blanks.

`RUN([<expL1>,] <DOS command expC> [,expL2>])`

Returns a completion code after executing an operating system command or program from within Visual dBASE.

`SECONDS()`

Returns the number of seconds that have elapsed on your computer's system clock since 12 a.m. (midnight).

`SEEK(<exp>[,<alias>])`

Returns **`.T.`** *if index search value is located.*

`SELECT([<alias>])`

Returns the work area number of the specified alias. If no alias is specified, returns the number of highest unused work area.

`SET(<expC>)`

Returns the status of the **`SET TO`** *and* **`SET ON`** *commands.*

`SIGN(<expN>)`

Returns a number that represents mathematical sign of a numeric expression.

`SIN(<expN>)`

Returns the sine of an angle in radians.

`SOUNDEX(<expC>)`

Returns a sound-alike code to provide phonetic match.

`SPACE(<expN>)`

Generates blank spaces.

`SQLERROR()`

Returns the number of the last server error.

`SQLEXEC(<SQL statement expC> [,<Answer table expC>] )`

Executes an SQL statement in the current database or on specified dBASE or Paradox tables.

`SQLMESSAGE()`

Returns the latest server error message.

`SQRT(<expN>)`

Returns square root.

`STR(<expN>[,<length>][,<decimal>])`

Converts a number to a character string.

`STUFF(<expC1>,<expN1>,<expN2>,<expC2>)`

Inserts or replaces a portion of a character string with another character string.

`SUBSTR(<expC>/<memo field name>,<starting position> [,<number of characters>])`

Extracts a specified number of characters from a character string.

`TAG([<.mdx filename>,]<expN>[,<alias>])`

Returns the `TAG` *name in a specified* `.mdx` *file.*

`TAGCOUNT([<.mdx filename> [,<alias>]])`

Returns the number of active indexes in the specified work area.

`TAGNO([order name> [,<.mdx filename> [,<alias>]]])`

Returns the index number for the specified index.

`TAN(<expN>)`

Returns the trigonometric tangent of an angle.

`TARGET(<expN> [,<alias>] )`

Returns the name of a table linked to the current or specified work area.

`TIME([<exp>])`

Returns system time.

`TRANSFORM(<exp>,<expC>)`

Allows `PICTURE` *formatting without* `@..SAY` *command.*

`TRIM(<expC>)`

Removes trailing blanks. It has the same function as `RTRIM()`.

TYPE(<expC>)

Returns data type of current field or variable.

UNIQUE([[<expC>,] <expN> [,<alias>]])

Returns a true (`.T.`) if the specified index was created with the `UNIQUE` *keyword or with* ***SET UNIQUE ON***.

UPPER(<expC>|<memo field>)

Lower to uppercase conversion.

USER()

Returns the log-in name of a network user.

VAL(<expC>)

Character data to number data conversion.

VALIDDRIVE(<drive expC>)

Returns `.T.` *if the specified drive exists and can be read. Returns* `.F.` *if the specified drive does not exist or cannot be read.*

VERSION()

Determines dBASE version number.

WINDOW()

Returns the version number of Visual dBASE that is currently executing.

WORKAREA()

Returns the number of the current work area.

YEAR(<expD>)

Returns the four-digit numeric value of the year from a date expression.

Using the Visual dBASE Debugger

APPENDIX

C

Testing and *debugging* are very important steps in the programming cycle. Testing is conducted to determine if there are any errors (bugs) in the program. The objective of this appendix is to examine briefly the strategies of testing and debugging and the tools Visual dBASE provides to assist in the process, including the Visual dBASE Debugger.

STRATEGIES OF TESTING AND DEBUGGING

Most initial drafts of programs will contain errors. However, if the program development plan includes a strategy to reduce their existence, and a logical method of eliminating those that do slip through, the associated costs—and frustration—will be minimized.

MODULAR PROGRAMMING ADVANTAGE

A major advantage of object-oriented programming is that its modular design lessens the time spent on debugging. By independently testing modules, smaller units of the system can be undertaken at one time. Once tested, modules of a system are reusable in other systems without need for further testing.

STRAIGHTFORWARD PROGRAMMING

When programming the methods of a system, use simple, straightforward code whenever possible. Ingeniously tricky routines can come back to haunt you at testing time. Unless such routines result in appreciable time and space advantages at execution time, they should be avoided.

DOCUMENTATION

Maintain a good documentation book while programming. This will help you during the testing process and will ensure continuity if another programmer needs to take over your program at any time. You will find that all the documentation practices set forth in Chapter 4 (indenting, comments, and so on) will lessen the testing effort. If a module is somewhat complex, a diagram of the logic is very helpful.

DESK CHECKING CODE

A review of code at your desk prior to testing on the computer can be invaluable. However, don't carry this idea too far. Desk checking is good for finding general bugs in syntax and logic—but after a certain point, the computer can uncover them faster than you can.

COMPILER SYNTAX CHECKS

Visual dBASE tests for syntax errors in coding when the program is compiled. Because of this feature, most misspellings and other syntax errors will not have to be tracked down when execution testing begins.

BREAKPOINT TESTING

An important technique in testing is to place breakpoints within a module to isolate errors. This will either cause program execution to stop while testing of elements such as memory variable content takes place, or simply display those elements as program execution continues.

Though not used primarily for debugging, the **WAIT** command is an excellent tool to break down larger modules into logical segments when testing. It is also useful in isolating an error. The **WAIT** prompt clause in the command can be used to identify its location in the program. For example, note the following code segment:

```
* == > Program segment
<program commands>
DISPLAY MEMORY
WAIT "1"
<program commands>
DISPLAY STATUS
WAIT "2"
<program commands>
WAIT "3"
<program commands>
* == > End of program segment
```

By temporarily inserting the **WAIT** commands, you can isolate a program bug quickly. Notice that **DISPLAY MEMORY** is coded prior to the second **WAIT** breakpoint and **DISPLAY STATUS** prior to the third. A display of one or more variables or the status of the system can be very helpful to the tester.

DEBUGGING COMMANDS

The following commands are included in Visual dBASE to assist in the testing and debugging process:

COMMAND **SET TALK ON/off**

Usually **TALK** is toggled off during execution of a program. However, if the results of all expression evaluations are needed for testing, it can be toggled on. Expression evaluations are displayed in the Results pane.

COMMAND `SET ALTERNATE TO [<filename> [ADDITIVE]]`
`SET ALTERNATE on/OFF`

This two-part command allows program segments being tested to be recorded to a file for later printing or review. `SET ALTERNATE TO <filename>` opens a file to store your program trace segment. `SET ALTERNATE ON/OFF` temporarily embedded in a program toggles transmission of program trace code to the file. The `ADDITIVE` clause begins each transmission from the end of the file rather than overwriting a previous transmission. The file data is ASCII text and can be reviewed in `MODIFY COMMAND` or any ASCII text word processor.

COMMAND `SUSPEND`

When temporarily embedded in a program, this command will pause execution and return control to the Command window. The programmer can then display stored data elements as they exist at the time of the suspension.

COMMAND `RESUME`

This command will continue execution of a program from the point that it was suspended.

Suspend is also one of the options of the Visual dBASE Program Interrupted dialog box (see Figure C.1). It will be displayed whenever a program error occurs. For example, the dialog in Figure C.1 was generated by placing a `WAIT` command on line 18 of the program, `ypartc.prg`, then pressing **Esc** during the `WAIT` command execution. If the operator selects **Suspend** from this dialog, control returns to the Command window just as if the `SUSPEND` command were embedded in a program. While in a suspended mode, various data elements such as the content of a memory variable or table pointer position can be displayed. Typing `RESUME` from the Command window will return control to the program. You must type `CANCEL` from the Command window this point if you want to close the program file—perhaps for reentry into `MODIFY COMMAND`. If **Ignore** is selected, the error is ignored and control continues within the program. Selecting the **Cancel** button will close the program file, release all memory variables initialized in the module, and return control to the Command window. Selecting **Fix** suspends the program and gives control to the Program Editor, and selecting **Debug** opens the Visual dBASE Debugger. The **Edit** option also opens and gives control to the Program Editor; however, the program is not maintained in a suspended mode.

FIGURE C.1 PROGRAM INTERRUPTED DIALOG BOX

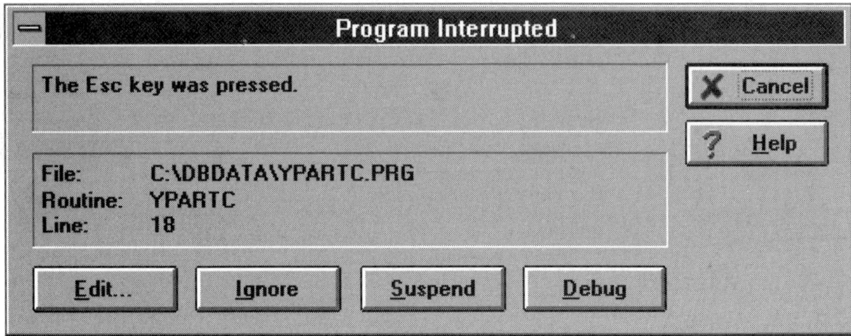

THE VISUAL dBASE DEBUGGER UTILITY

Included within Visual dBASE is an excellent debugging utility that incorporates many of the capabilities discussed in the individual debugging commands we have just noted. The Debugger can be used to control program execution; to watch and inspect the values of variables, fields, arrays, objects, and expressions; to view subroutine program calls and see when they are called; and to stop program execution at any point. We will use the program `ypartc.prg`, developed in Chapter 4, to demonstrate the use of the Debugger.

OPENING THE DEBUGGER

To open the Debugger utility, type the following command from the Input pane:

```
DEBUG ypartc
```

If no extension is included, a program file (`.prg`) is assumed. If no file name is provided, the Open Source File dialog will appear for file selection. Your screen should now appear as in Figure C.2. Finally, you can run the Debugger from within dBASE, or you can run it as a separate application from Windows using its own application icon.

FIGURE C.2 VISUAL dBASE DEBUGGER, OPENING SCREEN

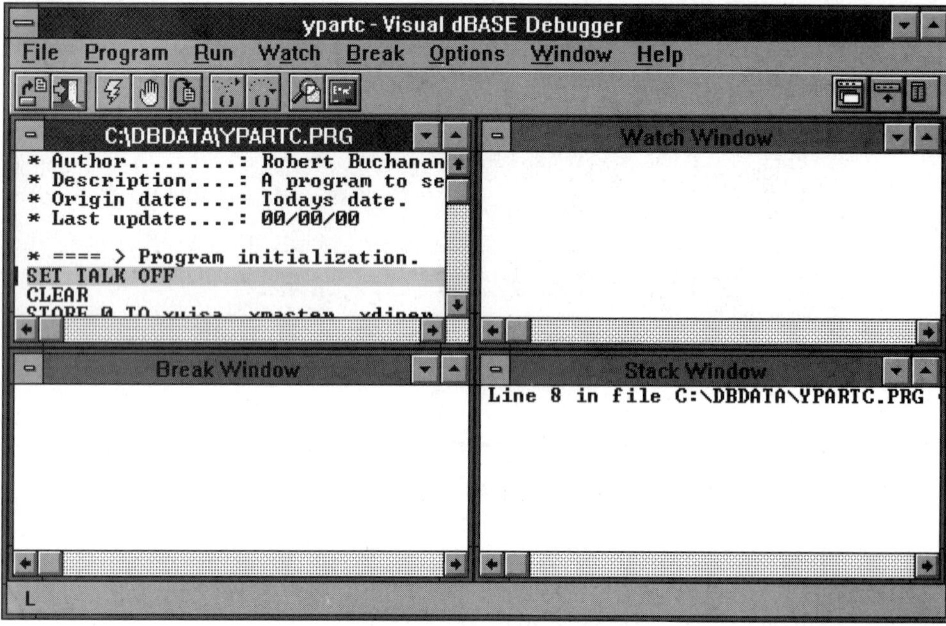

The Debugger Work Surface. Before moving ahead with the example, notice the four main windows of the Debugger, the menu system, and the speedbar.

- **Module window:** The program code being debugged is displayed here. The current command is highlighted.
- **Watch window:** This window literally allows the operator to watch expressions of the program as they develop and change. Expressions are coded in this window as watchpoints. The evaluated values of the expressions will appear in the Watch window as the program executes. This is much less cumbersome than having to code watch-points directly into the program code and then remove them after a test session.
- **Break window:** Desired breakpoints are encoded in this window in the form of expressions. For example, `xsum = 2` would cause the program to pause execution when the value in `xsum` is equal to 2.

- **Stack window:** Displays the names of modules called by the program you are debugging. This includes calls to other modules, procedures, and UDFs. It also displays the line number of the highlight at any time during the execution of a program.
- **Menu system:** Used to open files, print, execute a program, and develop watchpoints and breakpoints.
- **Speedbar:** Used as a shortcut to most of the items contained in the menu system.

USING THE DEBUGGER

In this exercise, we will demonstrate the use of the Debugger using the program file `ypartc.prg`, developed in Chapter 4. We will enter a breakpoint and also watch the values accumulate in several memory variables prior to reaching that breakpoint. We will also slow down the execution of the program to an animation speed to better observe the process.

Entering Breakpoints. As mentioned earlier, breakpoints constitute an important element of a debugging session. In this exercise, we will place a breakpoint on the command line just after the `ENDDO` statement. Proceed as follows:

1. The Debugger should be open at this point with the file `ypartc.prg` visible in the module window. If not, open it as instructed earlier.
2. Place the blinking cursor on the `?` command just after the `ENDDO` command line (approximately line 35). Move the mouse pointer to the far left of the command line. When the pointer turns into a hand, left-click the mouse. This should cause the entire command line to turn red. If you select the wrong line, a second click will remove the red notation. When the line turns red, a breakpoint referencing the number of the line noted in red should appear in the Break window.
3. Run the program by selecting **Run | Run**, or by clicking the **Run a program at full speed** icon from the speedbar. The program should run at full speed and stop on the breakpoint line. Finally, give focus to the Command window and note that the headings have been printed from `ypartc.prg`. Return focus to the Debugger and click the **Run** icon again to complete execution of the program execution.

Another type of breakpoint is based on a predefined condition. For example, we may want to break the program when the value in `xSum` reaches `10`. Proceed as follows:

1. Reload the program `ypartc.prg` by selecting **Run | Reset** or by clicking the **Reload the program from disk** icon. This will initialize the session.

2. Select **Break | Add** to display the Add Breakpoint dialog.

3. Code the expression, `xSum = 10`, into the Location text box (see Figure C.3). Whenever this expression evaluates to `.T.`, the program break would occur.

4. Code the command, `? xSum, xDiner, xMaster, xOther`, into the Action text box (see Figure C.3). This command will execute when the break occurs.

5. Click the **Global** check box and the **Expr TRUE** radio button (see Figure C.3). A global breakpoint affects all program files and is not linked to a specific line of code. Click the **OK** button to save the dialog contents.

6. Select the **Run** icon to execute the program. When it stops at the breakpoint, give focus to the Command window to verify the content of the memory variables listed in the Action text box.

7. Return focus to the Debugger and continue to press the **Run** icon until the program completes its execution. You will need to click the button several times because the Debugger will continue to stop after each command until `xSum` becomes greater than 10.

FIGURE C.3 ADD BREAKPOINT DIALOG BOX

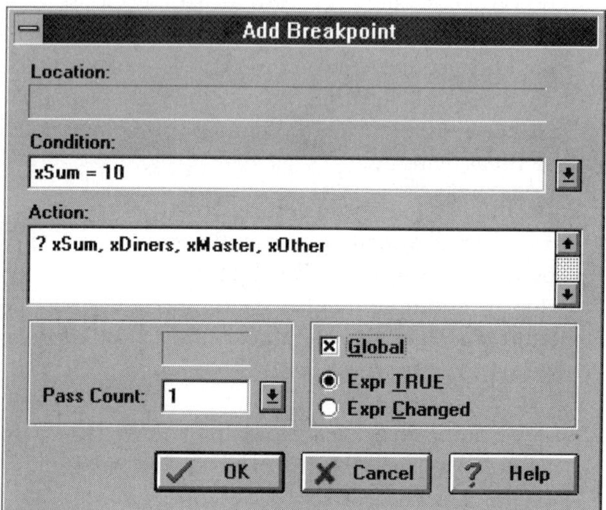

Entering Watchpoints. As the program in the Debugger executes, we will "watch" the results develop in the credit-card summary variables. We will also watch the variable containing the sum of all types of credit charges down to a specified breakpoint. Proceed as follows:

1. Select **Run | Reset** and then **Break | Remove All** to reload the program file and to delete the breakpoint set in the preceding exercise.
2. Place the cursor on the last **?** command in the program (approximately line 48). Specify this line as a breakpoint with a left mouse click when the pointer becomes a hand. The line should now be red.
3. Select **Watch | Add** to display the Add Watchpoint dialog. This could also be accomplished with a right mouse click from within the Watch window, then selecting **Add** from the speed menu.
4. Type `xVisa` into the Add Watchpoint dialog combo box, then select **OK**. Open the dialog again and type each of the following as variables to watch (see Figure C.4). After all variables are entered, the Debugger window should appear as in Figure C.5).

```
xMaster
xDiner
xOther
xSum
```

FIGURE C.4 ADD WATCHPOINT DIALOG BOX

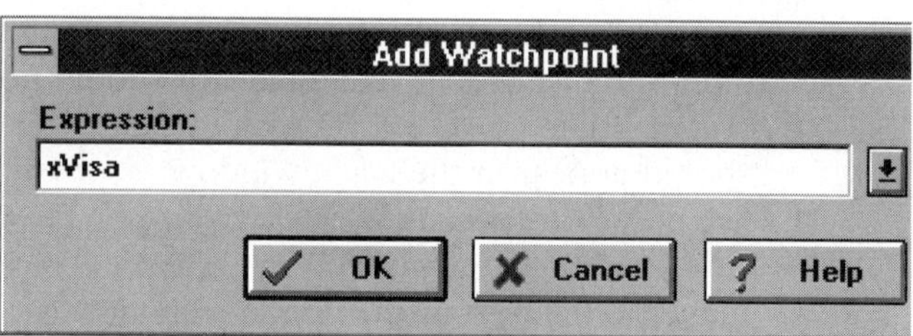

FIGURE C.5 FINAL DEBUGGER WINDOW

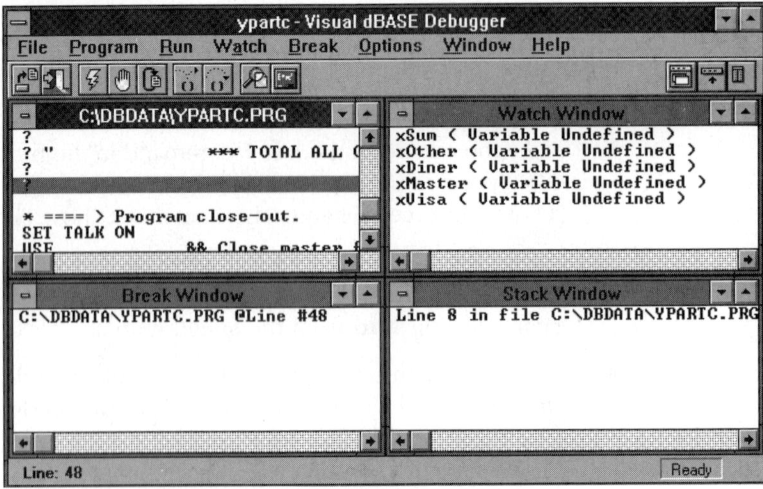

Executing the Program with Watchpoints. There are several ways to execute the program in the Debugger. We can execute it one instruction at a time, execute it at a reduced speed, or we can let it run at full speed until it reaches our first breakpoint. Let's examine each of these alternatives.

1. **Stepping through the program.**
   - To ensure that the highlight cursor appears at the beginning of the program, select **Run | Reset** or click the **Reload the program from disk** icon in the speedbar. The highlight should now be on the `SET TALK` command in the Module window and the associated line number should appear in the Stack window.
   - Select **Run | Trace Into** or click once on the **Execute a single source line e of instruction** icon in the speedbar. Notice that the highlight moves to the next instruction. Also notice that the line number changes in the Stack window. The Stack window will continually keep you posted as to where you are in the program or within a call from a program.
   - Continue clicking the same icon until the highlight is on the first occurrence of the `SKIP` command. The memory variables `xMaster` and `xSum` should now be assigned and contain a value of 1 (see the Watch window).

2. **Running at reduced speed.** In this segment, we will execute the program at a reduced rate of speed. The Debugger allows us to adjust that speed. Proceed as follows:

   - Select **Options | Animate Speed** to display the Set Animate Speed dialog box. Set the speed to approximately 50 percent of full speed, then click the **OK** button (see Figure C.6).
   - Select **Run | Animate** to begin execution of the program at the reduced rate of speed. Observe the cursor movement through the loop several times, then select **Run | Stop** to halt execution. As the program halts, note the changes in the watchpoint variables in the Watch window.

3. **Running the program at full speed.** Finally, we will run the program at full speed down to the breakpoint set earlier. Proceed as follows:

   - Select **Run | Run** or click the **Run program at full speed** speedbar icon to begin full speed execution.
   - The cursor should now be located on the breakpoint **?** command line. Again, observe the watchpoint variables. They should now contain their maximum values.
   - Finally, select **Run | Run** again or click the **Run program at full speed** speedbar icon to continue full speed program execution. The program should now run down to the breakpoint line. The Watch window should contain the maximum values for each memory variable. Press the **Run** icon again to run the program to its conclusion. To exit the Debugger, double-click the **Debugger window control button**.

FIGURE C.6 SET ANIMATION SPEED DIALOG BOX

CONCLUSIONS

The importance of the debugging portion of the programming cycle cannot be overemphasized. The discussion in this appendix has introduced the various commands available and introduced you to the Visual dBASE Debugger utility. It is suggested that you explore all the alternatives presented to arrive at the right combination for your debugging sessions. For small modules with fewer errors, individual commands might be the most productive, whereas you could improve your efficiency in larger systems by using the Debugger utility.

ASCII Character Table

APPENDIX

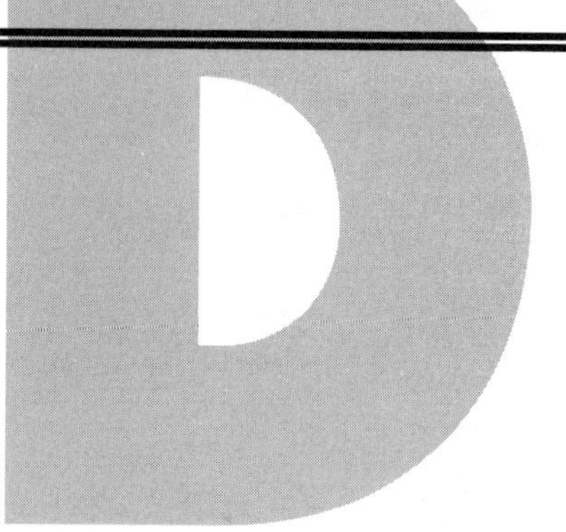

This appendix is to be used for reference. It should be especially useful in Chapter 10 when developing the password encrytion and decryption procedures.

Binary	Hex	Decimal	Character	Code	Symbol	Description
00000000	00	0		^@	NUL	Null
00000001	01	1	☺	^A	SOH	Start of heading
00000010	02	2	☻	^B	STX	Start of text
00000011	03	3	♥	^C	ETX	End of text
00000100	04	4	♦	^D	EOT	End of transmission
00000101	05	5	♣	^E	ENQ	Enquiry
00000110	06	6	♠	^F	ACK	Acknowledge
00000111	07	7	•	^G	BEL	Bell
00001000	08	8	◘	^H	BS	Backspace
00001001	09	9	○	^I	SH	Horizontal tabulation
00001010	0A	10	◙	^J	LF	Line feed
00001011	0B	11	♂	^K	VT	Vertical tabulation
00001100	0C	12	♀	^L	FF	Form feed
00001101	0D	13	♪	^M	CR	Carriage return
00001110	0E	14	♫	^N	SO	Shift out
00001111	0F	15	☼	^O	SI	Shift in
00010000	10	16	►	^P	DLE	Data link escape
00010001	11	17	◄	^Q	DC1	Device control 1
00010010	12	18	↕	^R	DC2	Device control 2
00010011	13	19	‼	^S	DC3	Device control 3

Binary	Hex	Decimal	Character	Code	Symbol	Description
00010100	14	20	¶	^T	DC4	Device control 4
00010101	15	21	§	^U	NAK	Negative acknowledge
00010110	16	22	▬	^V	SYN	Synchronous idle
00010111	17	23	↨	^W	ETB	End of transmission block
00011000	18	24	↑	^X	CAN	Cancel
00011001	19	25	↓	^Y	EM	End of medium
00011010	1A	26	→	^Z	SUB	Substitute
00011011	1B	27	←	^[	ESC	Escape*
00011100	1C	28	∟	^\	FS	File separator
00011101	1D	29	↔	^]	GS	Group separator
00011110	1E	30	▲	^^	RS	Record separator
00011111	1F	31	▼	^_	US	Unit separator
00100000	20	32				
00100001	21	33	!			
00100010	22	34	"			
00100011	23	35	#			
00100100	24	36	$			
00100101	25	37	%			
00100110	26	38	&			
00100111	27	39	'			

*Escape cannot be trapped.

Binary	Hex	Decimal	Character	Binary	Hex	Decimal	Character
00101000	28	40	(	00101110	2E	46	.
00101001	29	41	)	00101111	2F	47	/
00101010	2A	42	*	00110000	30	48	0
00101011	2B	43	+	00110001	31	49	1
00101100	2C	44	,	00110010	32	50	2
00101101	2D	45	-	00110011	33	51	3

Binary	Hex	Decimal	Character
00110100	34	52	4
00110101	35	53	5
00110110	36	54	6
00110111	37	55	7
00111000	38	56	8
00111001	39	57	9
00111010	3A	58	:
00111011	3B	59	;
00111100	3C	60	<
00111101	3D	61	=
00111110	3E	62	>
00111111	3F	63	?
01000000	40	64	@
01000001	41	65	A
01000010	42	66	B
01000011	43	67	C
01000100	44	68	D
01000101	45	69	E
01000110	46	70	F
01000111	47	71	G
01001000	48	72	H
01001001	49	73	I
01001010	4A	74	J
01001011	4B	75	K
01001100	4C	76	L
01001101	4D	77	M
01001110	4E	78	N
01001111	4F	79	O
01010000	50	80	P
01010001	51	81	Q
01010010	52	82	R
01010011	53	83	S
01010100	54	84	T
01010101	55	85	U
01010110	56	86	V
01010111	57	87	W
01011000	58	88	X
01011001	59	89	Y
01011010	5A	90	Z
01011011	5B	91	[
01011100	5C	92	\
01011101	5D	93	]
01011110	5E	94	^
01011111	5F	95	–
01100000	60	96	\´
01100001	61	97	a
01100010	62	98	b
01100011	63	99	c
01100100	64	100	d
01100101	65	101	e
01100110	66	102	f
01100111	67	103	g
01101000	68	104	h
01101001	69	105	i
01101010	6A	106	j
01101011	6B	107	k
01101100	6C	108	l
01101101	6D	109	m
01101110	6E	110	n
01101111	6F	111	o
01110000	70	112	p
01110001	71	113	q

Binary	Hex	Decimal	Character
01110010	72	114	r
01110011	73	115	s
01110100	74	116	t
01110101	75	117	u
01110110	76	118	v
01110111	77	119	w
01111000	78	120	x
01111001	79	121	y
01111010	7A	122	z
01111011	7B	123	{
01111100	7C	124	|
01111101	7D	125	}
01111110	7E	126	~
01111111	7F	127	⌂
10000000	80	128	Ç
10000001	81	129	ü
10000010	82	130	é
10000011	83	131	â
10000100	84	132	ä
10000101	85	133	à
10000110	86	134	å
10000111	87	135	ç
10001000	88	136	ê
10001001	89	137	ë
10001010	8A	138	è
10001011	8B	139	ï
10001100	8C	140	î
10001101	8D	141	ì
10001110	8E	142	Ä
10001111	8F	143	Å
10010000	90	144	É
10010001	91	145	æ
10010010	92	146	Æ
10010011	93	147	ô
10010100	94	148	ö
10010101	95	149	ò
10010110	96	150	û
10010111	97	151	ù
10011000	98	152	ÿ
10011001	99	153	Ö
10011010	9A	154	Ü
10011011	9B	155	¢
10011100	9C	156	£
10011101	9D	157	¥
10011110	9E	158	₧
10011111	9F	159	ƒ
10100000	A0	160	á
10100001	A1	161	í
10100010	A2	162	ó
10100011	A3	163	ú
10100100	A4	164	ñ
10100101	A5	165	Ñ
10100110	A6	166	ª
10100111	A7	167	º
10101000	A8	168	¿
10101001	A9	169	⌐
10101010	AA	170	¬
10101011	AB	171	½
10101100	AC	172	¼
10101101	AD	173	¡
10101110	AE	174	«
10101111	AF	175	»

Binary	Hex	Decimal	Character
10110000	B0	176	░
10110001	B1	177	▒
10110010	B2	178	▓
10110011	B3	179	│
10110100	B4	180	┤
10110101	B5	181	╡
10110110	B6	182	╢
10110111	B7	183	╖
10111000	B8	184	╕
10111001	B9	185	╣
10111010	BA	186	║
10111011	BB	187	╗
10111100	BC	188	╝
10111101	BD	189	╜
10111110	BE	190	╛
10111111	BF	191	┐
11000000	C0	192	└
11000001	C1	193	┴
11000010	C2	194	┬
11000011	C3	195	├
11000100	C4	196	─
11000101	C5	197	┼
11000110	C6	198	╞
11000111	C7	199	╟
11001000	C8	200	╚
11001001	C9	201	╔
11001010	CA	202	╩
11001011	CB	203	╦
11001100	CC	204	╠
11001101	CD	205	═
11001110	CE	206	╬
11001111	CF	207	╧
11010000	D0	208	╨
11010001	D1	209	╤
11010010	D2	210	╥
11010011	D3	211	╙
11010100	D4	212	╘
11010101	D5	213	╒
11010110	D6	214	╓
11010111	D7	215	╫
11011000	D8	216	╪
11011001	D9	217	┘
11011010	DA	218	┌
11011011	DB	219	█
11011100	DC	220	▄
11011101	DD	221	▌
11011110	DE	222	▐
11011111	DF	223	▀
11100000	E0	224	α
11100001	E1	225	β
11100010	E2	226	Γ
11100011	E3	227	π
11100100	E4	228	Σ
11100101	E5	229	σ
11100110	E6	230	µ
11100111	E7	231	τ
11101000	E8	232	Φ
11101001	E9	233	Θ
11101010	EA	234	Ω
11101011	EB	235	δ
11101100	EC	236	∞
11101101	ED	237	φ

Binary	Hex	Decimal	Character
11101110	EE	238	ε
11101111	EF	239	∩
11110000	F0	240	≡
11110001	F1	241	±
11110010	F2	242	≥
11110011	F3	243	≤
11110100	F4	244	⌠
11110101	F5	245	⌡
11110110	F6	246	÷
11110111	F7	247	≈
11111000	F8	248	°
11111001	F9	249	∙
11111010	FA	250	·
11111011	FB	251	√
11111100	FC	252	^{n}
11111101	FD	253	^{2}
11111110	FE	254	■
11111111	FF	255	

Index

D

E

F

G